BTOOOM!

JUNYA INOUE

07

THE COMPLETE CONQUER GUIDE

HIMIKO

GENDER: Female
AGE: 15
BLOOD TYPE: B
JOB: High school student
HOME: Tokyo
BIM TYPE: Timer

After Sakamoto defeated his first enemy player, Yoshiaki Imagawa, he ran across this mysterious high school girl. She harbors a deep resentment against men, but after surviving some battles thanks to Sakamoto, she begins to trust him and joins up with his team.

KIYOSHI TAIRA

GENDER: Male
AGE: 51
BLOOD TYPE: A
JOB: Real estate business manager
HOME: Osaka
BIM TYPE: Homing

Taira is a player Sakamoto came across while in pursuit of Himiko. He's a friendly man from the Kansai region who teams up with Sakamoto in hopes of getting off the island without resorting to murder. He is seriously injured by Miyamoto.

RYOUTA SAKAMOTO

GENDER: Male
AGE: 22
BLOOD TYPE: B
JOB: Unemployed
HOME: Tokyo
BIM TYPE: Timer

After spending every day cooped up in his home playing online, he suddenly wakes up to find that he's been taken to a mysterious deserted island and is being made to kill people just like in "BTOOOM!", the online third-person shooter he's really into.

IN ORDER TO ESCAPE WITH THEIR LIVES, THE THREE THEN START PUTTING THEIR HEADS TOGETHER TO UNRAVEL THE MYSTERIES OF THE ISLAND AND TO FLESH OUT THE CONSPIRACY THEORY ABOUT TYRANNOS JAPAN, THE DEVELOPER BEHIND "BTOOOM!", WHICH THEY BELIEVE HAS SOMETHING TO DO WITH THIS GAME OF DEATH. SOON SAKAMOTO AND HIMIKO COME ACROSS MASAHITO DATE, A DOCTOR. HAVING TREATED TAIRA'S WOUNDS, DATE WINS THE TRUST OF THE PAIR, BUT IN TRUTH, HE IS A REPEAT PLAYER OF THE GAME WHO SURVIVED SIX MONTHS EARLIER AND RETURNED HOME. SAKAMOTO AND HIMIKO ARE ALSO CONFRONTED BY THE MYSTERIOUS NOBUTAKA ODA, WITH HIS EXCEPTIONAL AGILITY AND CUNNING, AND HIDEMI KINOSHITA, WHO ISN'T AFRAID TO CHARGE INTO BATTLE. AND THEY'RE NOT ALONE! THE FAMILIAR FACE OF JUNIOR HIGH STUDENT KOUSUKE KIRA APPEARS ONCE MORE...! DEADLY "BTOOOM!" TAKES AN EXTREME TURN WITHIN THE DEPTHS OF THE ISLAND!

BTOOOM! 07

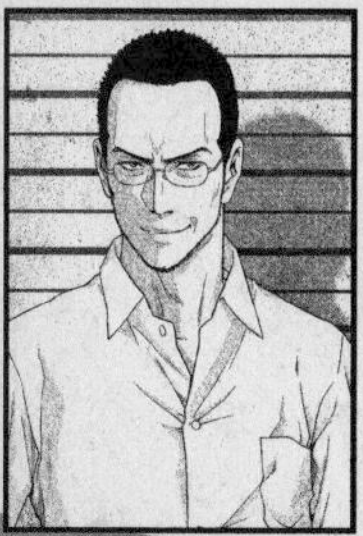

MASAHITO DATE

GENDER: Male
AGE: 40
BLOOD TYPE: AB
JOB: Doctor
HOME: Chiba
BIM TYPE: Remote Control

A survivor from an earlier game who collected all eight chips. He has a merciless, cruel personality and is particularly good at winning people over only to throw them under the bus. He's being made to play "BTOOOM!" over again.

SHIKI MURASAKI

GENDER: Female
AGE: 39
BLOOD TYPE: O
JOB: Nurse
HOME: Chiba
BIM TYPE: NO DATA

A mysterious woman Sakamoto and Himiko encountered while in the abandoned building. Since her left hand with the embed-ded chip has been severed, she doesn't appear on any radar. She's a player from the previous run of the game and was betrayed by her former colleague, Date.

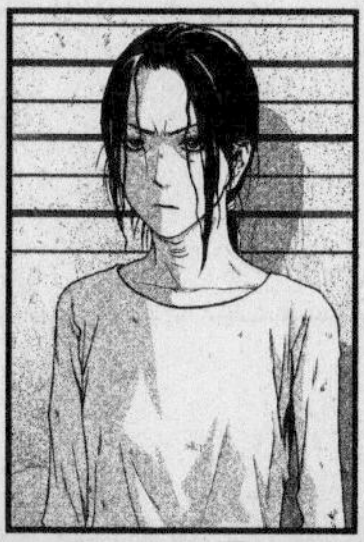

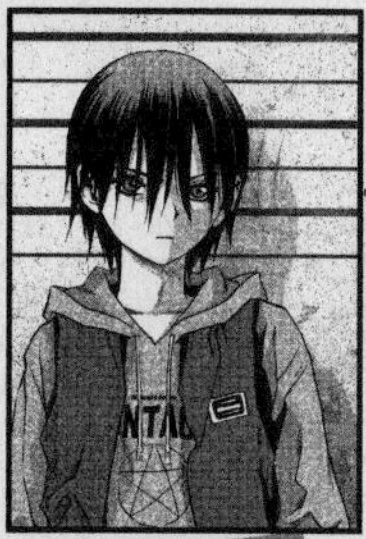

KOUSUKE KIRA

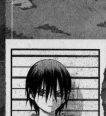

GENDER: Male
AGE: 14
BLOOD TYPE: AB
JOB: Junior high student
HOME: Tokyo
BIM TYPE: Implosion

A student with a dark, brutal, murderous past, he has always been a big fan of "BTOOOM!". But now that it's come to life, he enjoys this game of "kill or be killed" even more, deep down. His dream is to defeat "SAKA-MOTO," the top world ranker in "BTOOOM!".

NOBUTAKA ODA

GENDER: Male
AGE: 22
BLOOD TYPE: AB
JOB: Restaurant manager
HOME: Tokyo
BIM TYPE: Homing

A super-high-level player who has the ability to carry out elaborate plans with his superior athleticism. His all-or-nothing operations involve carefully laid traps to defeat his foes. He knows Saka-moto's past.

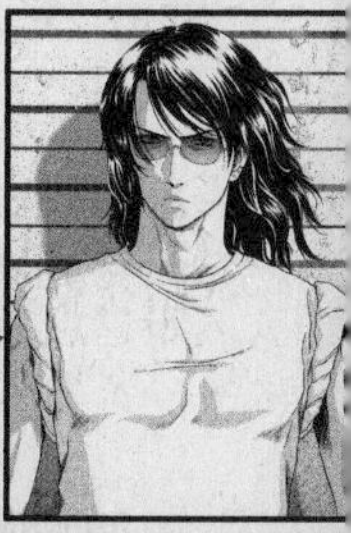

Story

OUR MAIN CHARACTER, RYOUTA SAKAMOTO, IS A TYPICAL NEET ("NOT IN EDUCATION, EMPLOYMENT, OR TRAINING") ONLINE GAMER. THEN ONE DAY, HE'S SUDDENLY KIDNAPPED BY MYSTERIOUS MEN IN BLACK AND TAKEN TO A DESERTED ISLAND. THERE, HE'S FORCED TO USE EXPLOSIVES CALLED BIMS IN A DEATH MATCH AGAINST PEOPLE LIKE HIM WHO HAVE ALSO BEEN BROUGHT TO THE ISLAND. IN FACT, THE WHOLE EXPERIENCE IS VIRTUALLY IDENTICAL TO THE GAME PLAY OF THE ONLINE THIRD-PERSON SHOOTER CALLED "BTOOOM!" THAT SAKAMOTO IS CURRENTLY INTO AND WITHIN WHICH HE RANKS AMONG THE WORLD'S BEST. IN THE GAME, PLAYERS USE A VARIETY OF EXPLOSIVES—INCLUDING TIMER, CRACKER, AND REMOTE TYPES—TO OBLITERATE THEIR OPPONENTS WITHOUT MERCY. NOW SAKAMOTO IS BEING FORCED TO PLAY THIS GAME IN REAL LIFE. WHILE FIGHTING TO STAY ALIVE, HE MEETS AND TEAMS UP WITH KIYOSHI TAIRA AND HIMIKO.

CONTENTS

CHAPTER 42 • OLD FRIEND 007

CHAPTER 43 • TRUE NATURE 053

CHAPTER 44 • PROVIDENCE 101

CHAPTER 45 • TWO SACRIFICES 147

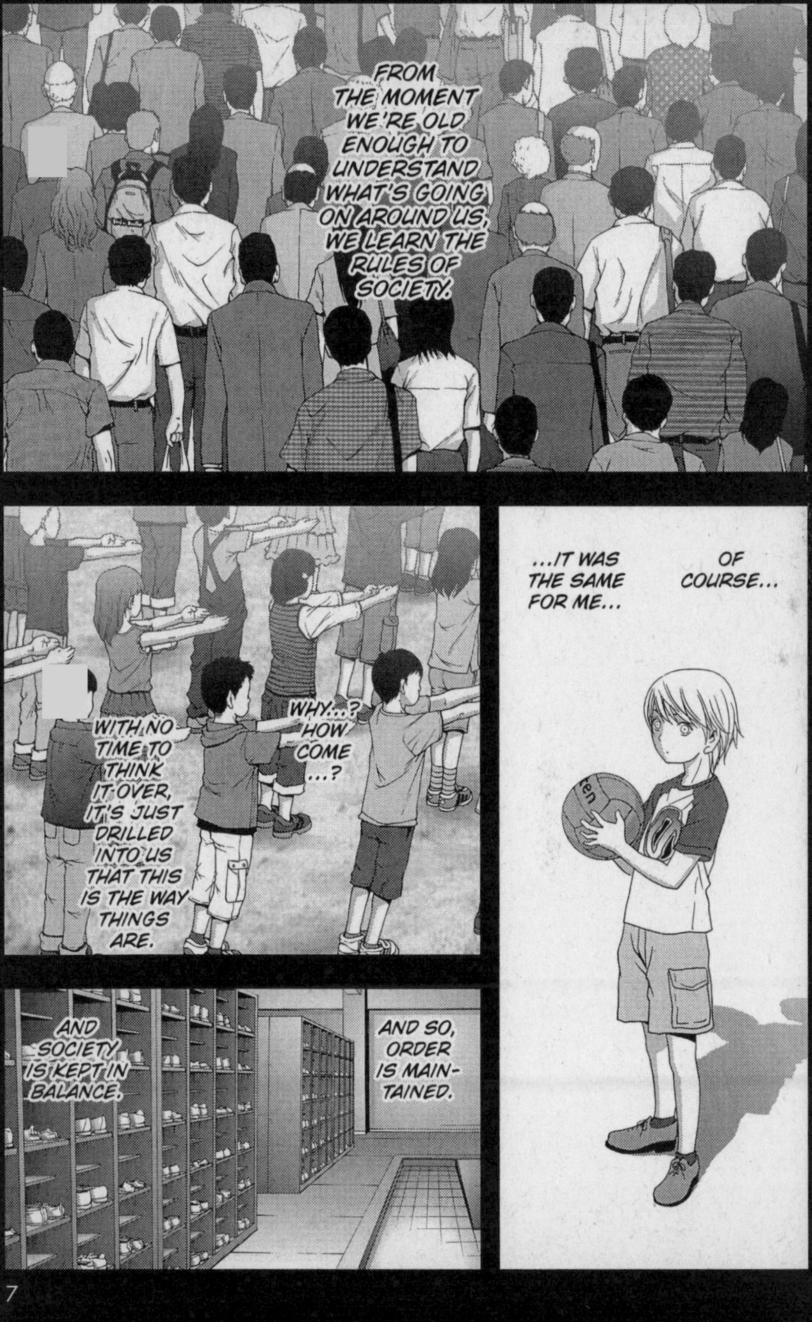
FROM THE MOMENT WE'RE OLD ENOUGH TO UNDERSTAND WHAT'S GOING ON AROUND US, WE LEARN THE RULES OF SOCIETY.
OF COURSE...
...IT WAS THE SAME FOR ME...
WHY...? HOW COME ...?
WITH NO TIME TO THINK IT OVER, IT'S JUST DRILLED INTO US THAT THIS IS THE WAY THINGS ARE.
AND SO, ORDER IS MAIN-TAINED.
AND SOCIETY IS KEPT IN BALANCE.

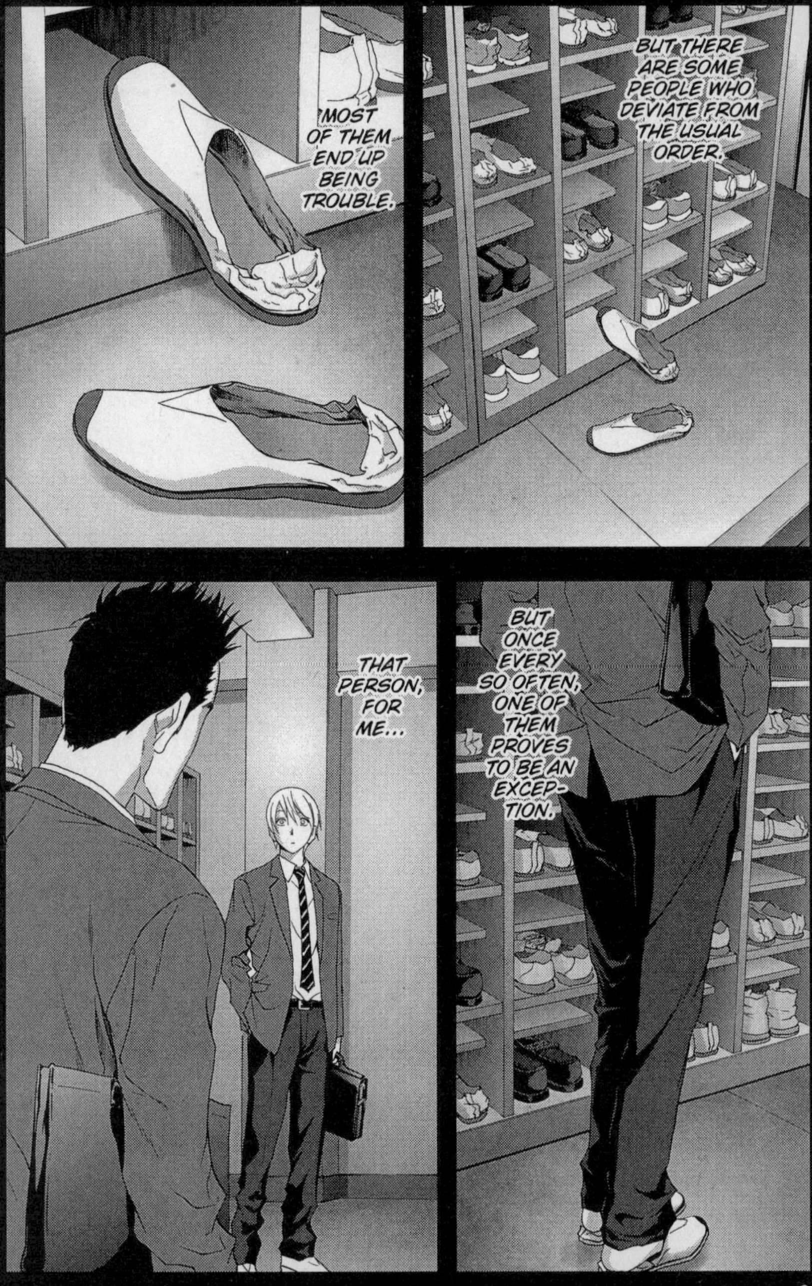
BUT THERE ARE SOME PEOPLE WHO DEVIATE FROM THE USUAL ORDER.
MOST OF THEM END UP BEING TROUBLE.
BUT ONCE EVERY SO OFTEN, ONE OF THEM PROVES TO BE AN EXCEP-TION.
THAT PERSON, FOR ME...

42 OLD FRIEND

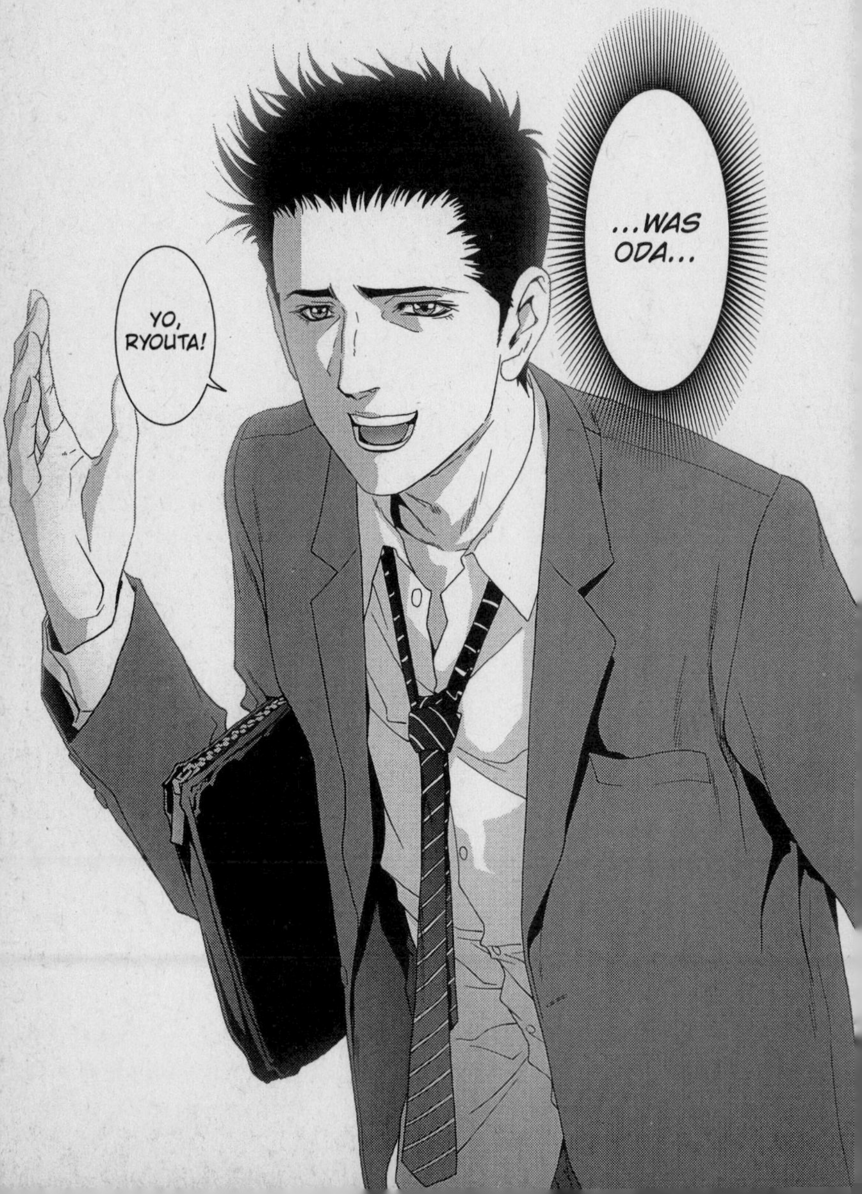
...WAS ODA...
YO, RYOUTA!

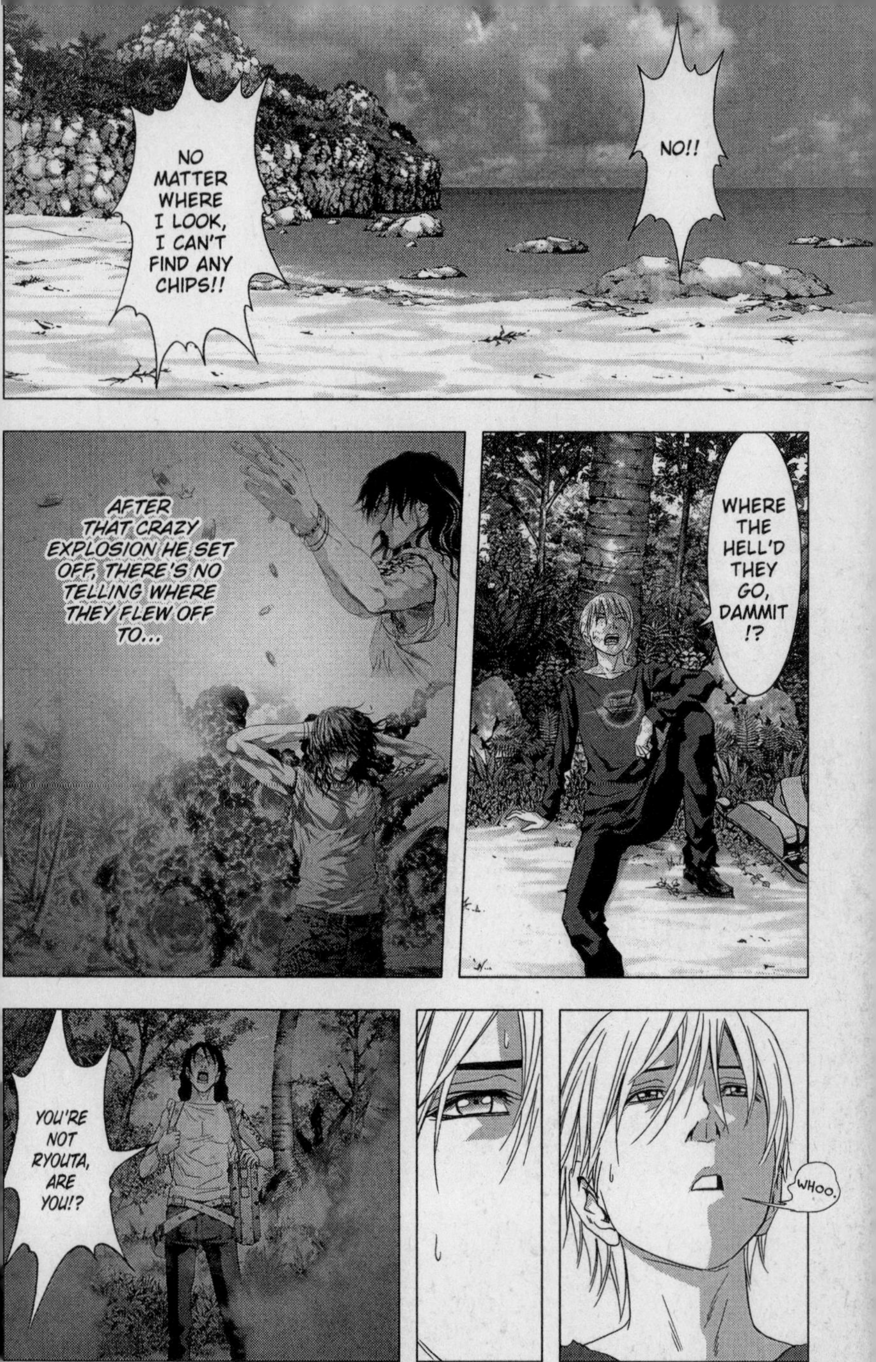
NO!!
NO MATTER WHERE I LOOK, I CAN'T FIND ANY CHIPS!!
WHERE THE HELL'D THEY GO, DAMMIT!?
AFTER THAT CRAZY EXPLOSION HE SET OFF, THERE'S NO TELLING WHERE THEY FLEW OFF TO...
WHOO.
YOU'RE NOT RYOUTA, ARE YOU!?

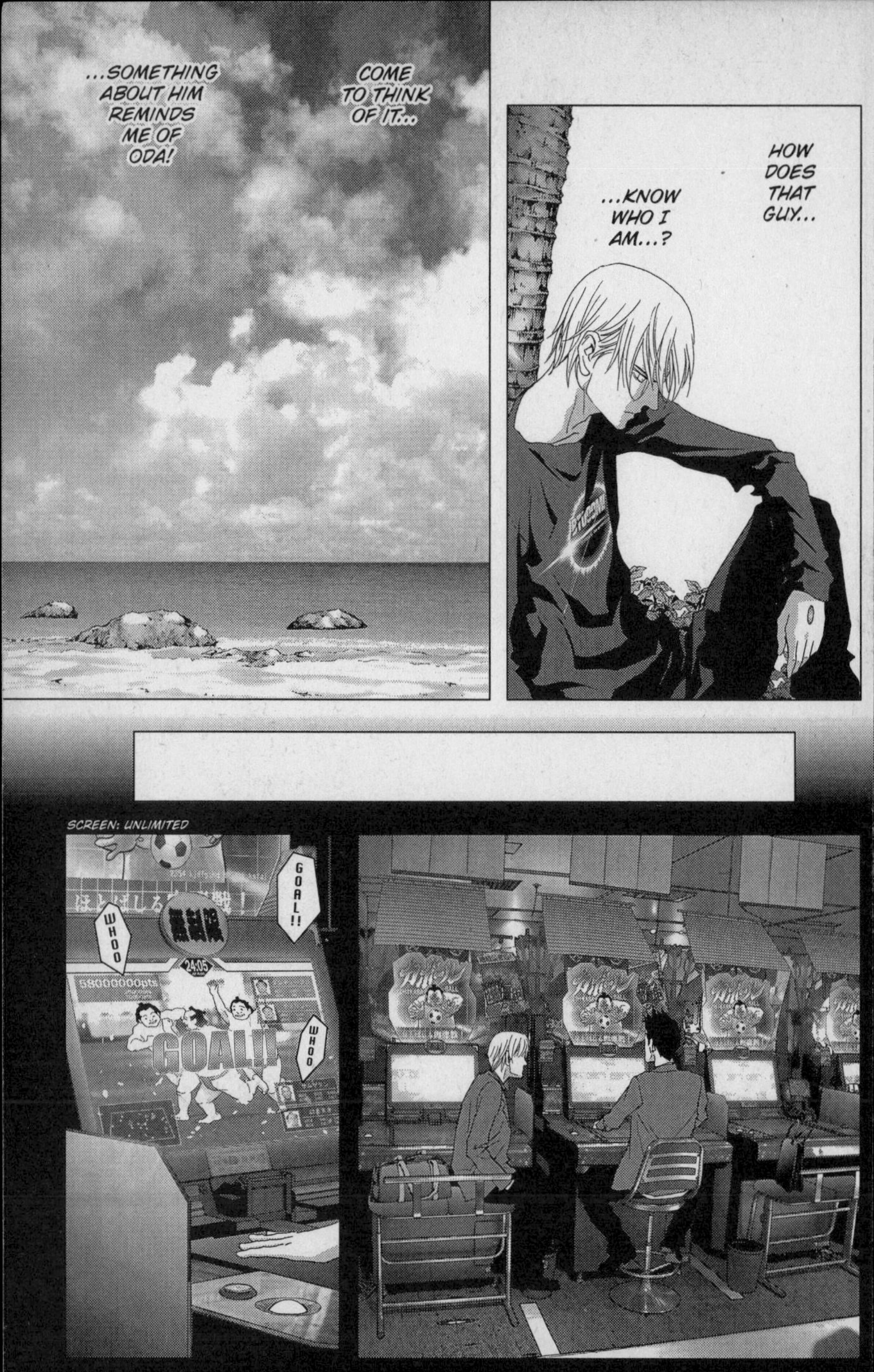
HOW DOES THAT GUY...
...KNOW WHO I AM...?
COME TO THINK OF IT...
...SOMETHING ABOUT HIM REMINDS ME OF ODA!
SCREEN: UNLIMITED
GOAL!!
WHOO
WHOO
GOAL!!
58000000pts
24:05

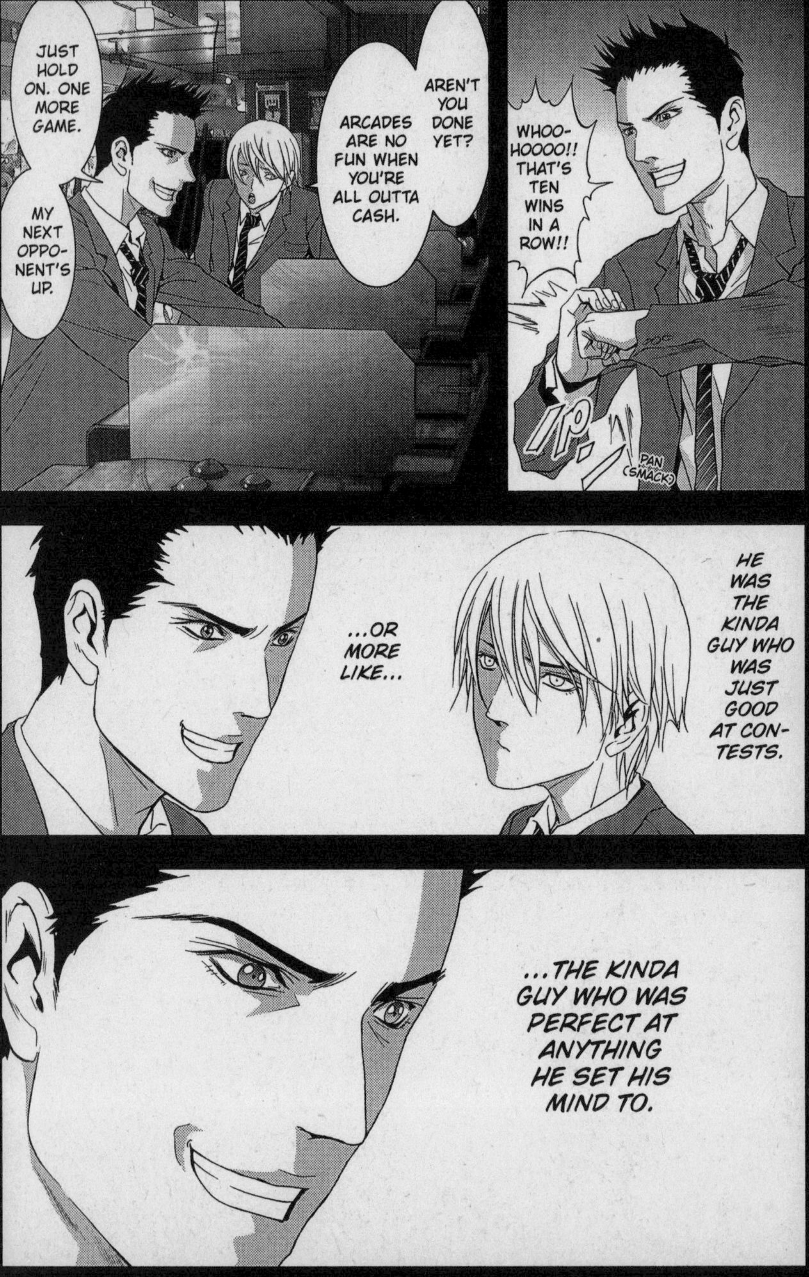
WHOO-HOOOO!! THAT'S TEN WINS IN A ROW!!
PAN (SMACK)
AREN'T YOU DONE YET?
ARCADES ARE NO FUN WHEN YOU'RE ALL OUTTA CASH.
JUST HOLD ON. ONE MORE GAME.
MY NEXT OPPO-NENT'S UP.
HE WAS THE KINDA GUY WHO WAS JUST GOOD AT CON-TESTS.
...OR MORE LIKE...
...THE KINDA GUY WHO WAS PERFECT AT ANYTHING HE SET HIS MIND TO.

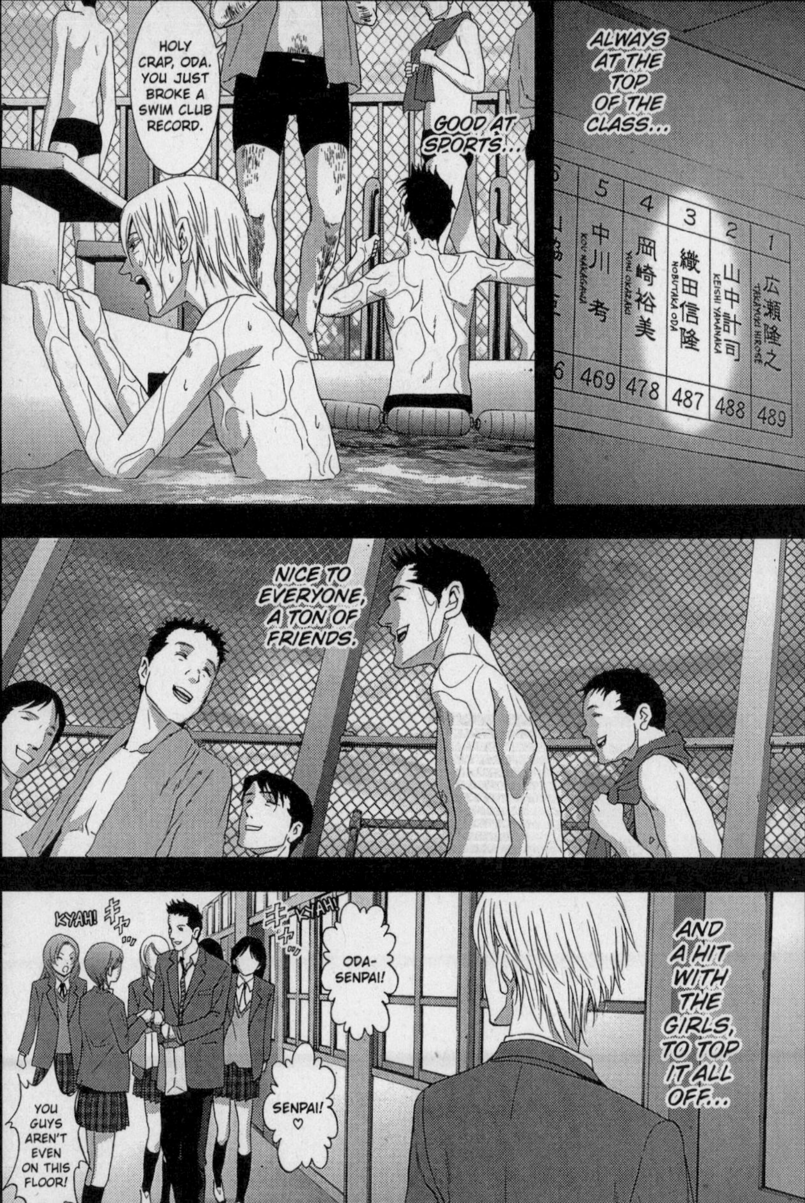
ALWAYS AT THE TOP OF THE CLASS...
1 広瀬隆之 TAKAYUKI HIROSE 489
2 山中計司 KEISHI YAMANAKA 488
3 織田信隆 NOBUTAKA ODA 487
4 岡崎裕美 YUMI OKAZAKI 478
5 中川考 KOU NAKAGAWA 469
GOOD AT SPORTS...
HOLY CRAP, ODA. YOU JUST BROKE A SWIM CLUB RECORD.
NICE TO EVERYONE, A TON OF FRIENDS.
AND A HIT WITH THE GIRLS, TO TOP IT ALL OFF...
キャッ KYAH!
ODA-SENPAI!
SENPAI! ♡
KYAH! キャッ
YOU GUYS AREN'T EVEN ON THIS FLOOR!

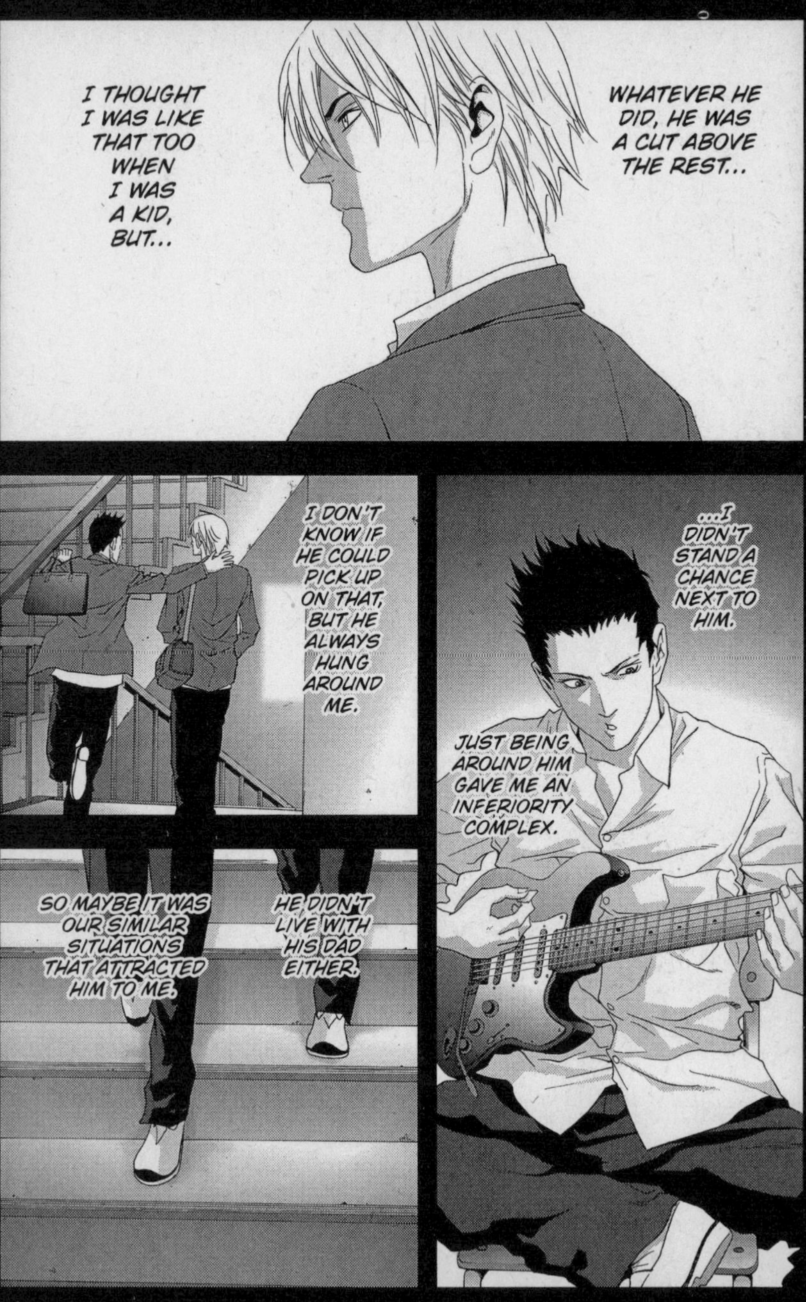
WHATEVER HE DID, HE WAS A CUT ABOVE THE REST...
I THOUGHT I WAS LIKE THAT TOO WHEN I WAS A KID, BUT...
...I DIDN'T STAND A CHANCE NEXT TO HIM.
JUST BEING AROUND HIM GAVE ME AN INFERIORITY COMPLEX.
I DON'T KNOW IF HE COULD PICK UP ON THAT, BUT HE ALWAYS HUNG AROUND ME.
HE DIDN'T LIVE WITH HIS DAD EITHER.
SO MAYBE IT WAS OUR SIMILAR SITUATIONS THAT ATTRACTED HIM TO ME.

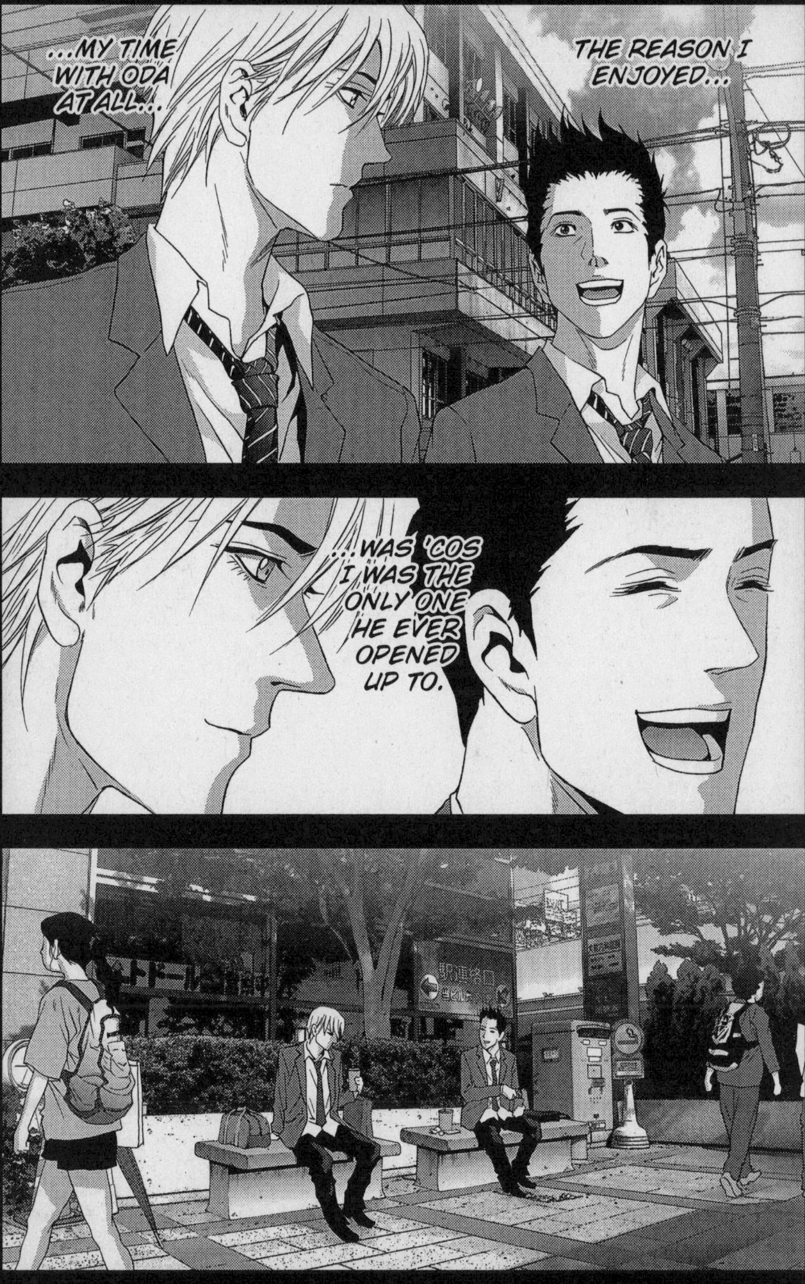
THE REASON I ENJOYED...
...MY TIME WITH ODA AT ALL...
...WAS 'COS I WAS THE ONLY ONE HE EVER OPENED UP TO.

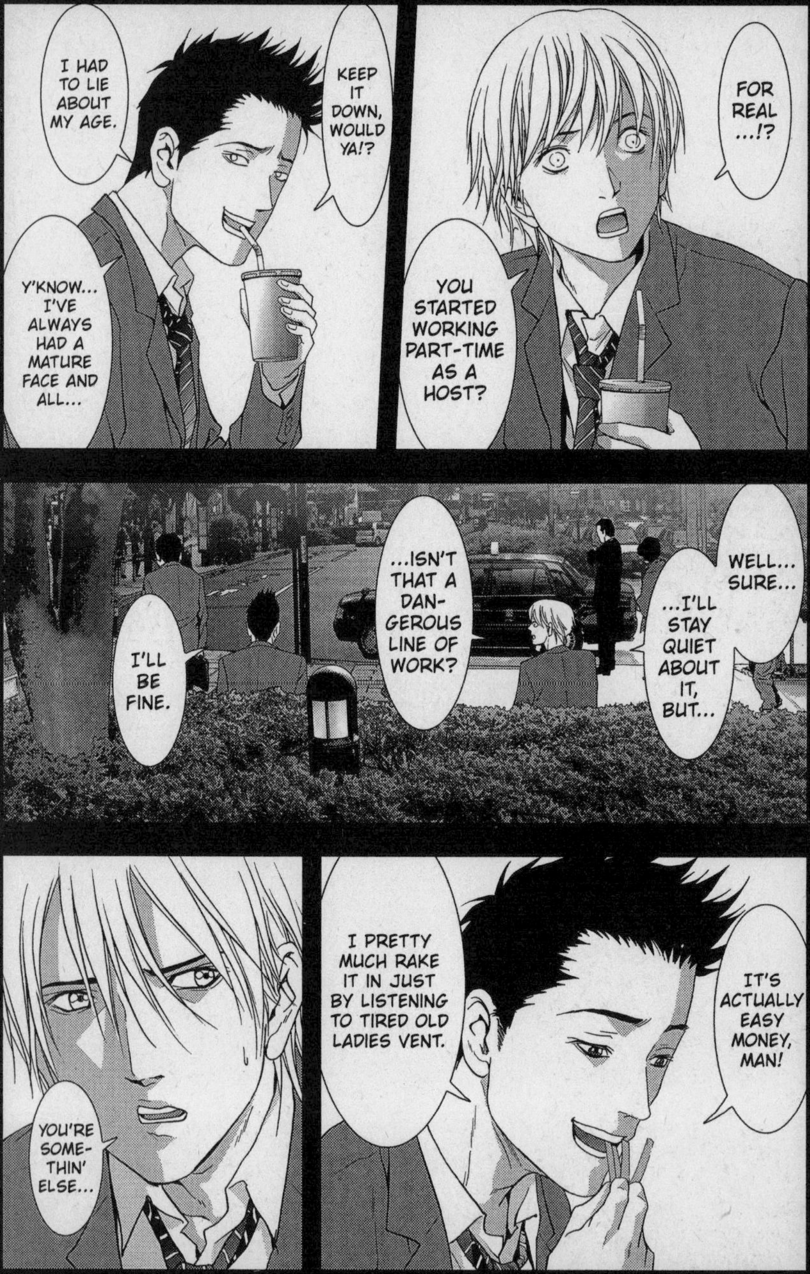
FOR REAL ...!?
YOU STARTED WORKING PART-TIME AS A HOST?
KEEP IT DOWN, WOULD YA!?
I HAD TO LIE ABOUT MY AGE.
Y'KNOW... I'VE ALWAYS HAD A MATURE FACE AND ALL...
WELL... SURE...
...I'LL STAY QUIET ABOUT IT, BUT...
...ISN'T THAT A DAN-GEROUS LINE OF WORK?
I'LL BE FINE.
IT'S ACTUALLY EASY MONEY, MAN!
I PRETTY MUCH RAKE IT IN JUST BY LISTENING TO TIRED OLD LADIES VENT.
YOU'RE SOME-THIN' ELSE...

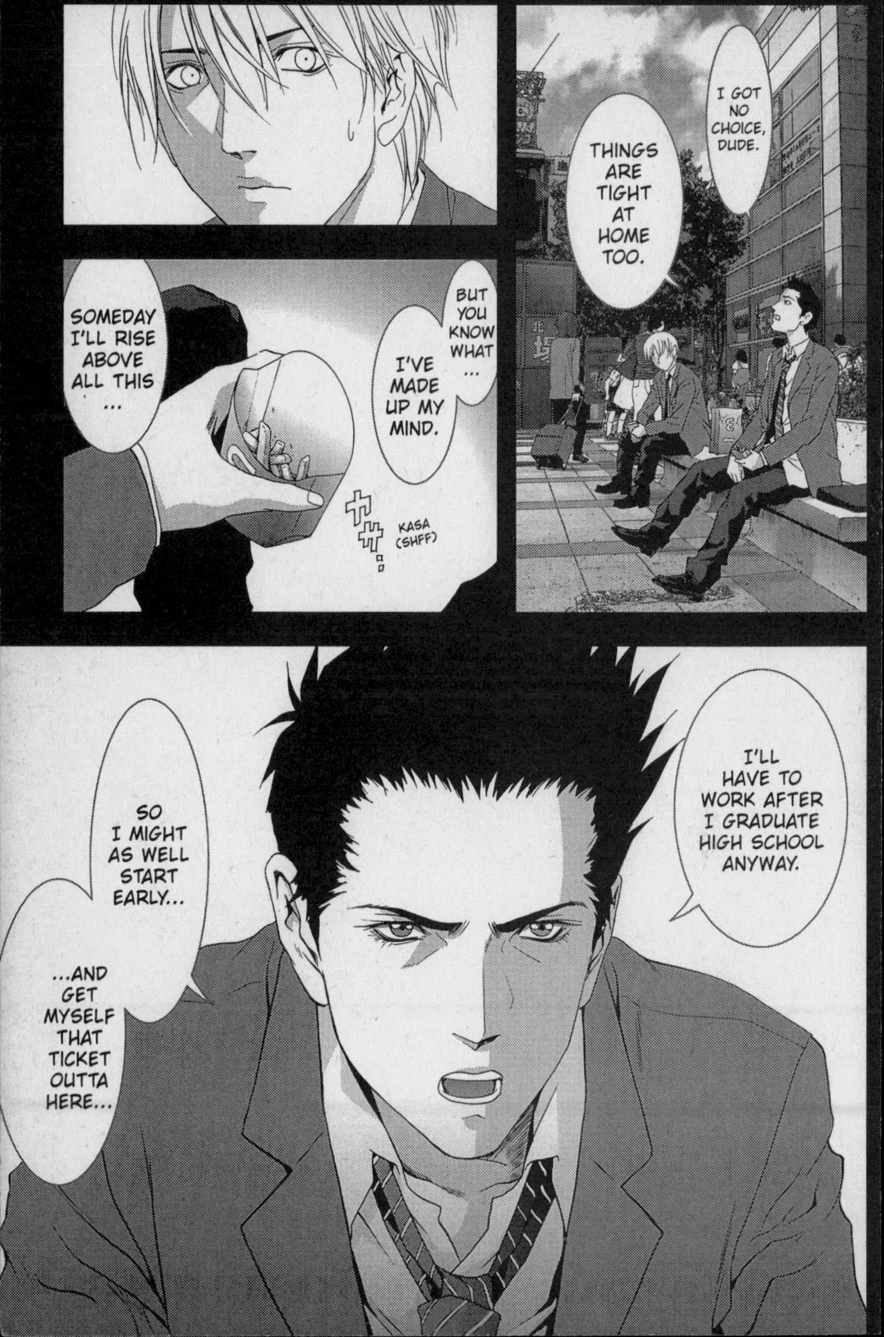
I GOT NO CHOICE, DUDE.
THINGS ARE TIGHT AT HOME TOO.
BUT YOU KNOW WHAT...
I'VE MADE UP MY MIND.
SOMEDAY I'LL RISE ABOVE ALL THIS...
KASA (SHFF)
I'LL HAVE TO WORK AFTER I GRADUATE HIGH SCHOOL ANYWAY.
SO I MIGHT AS WELL START EARLY...
...AND GET MYSELF THAT TICKET OUTTA HERE...

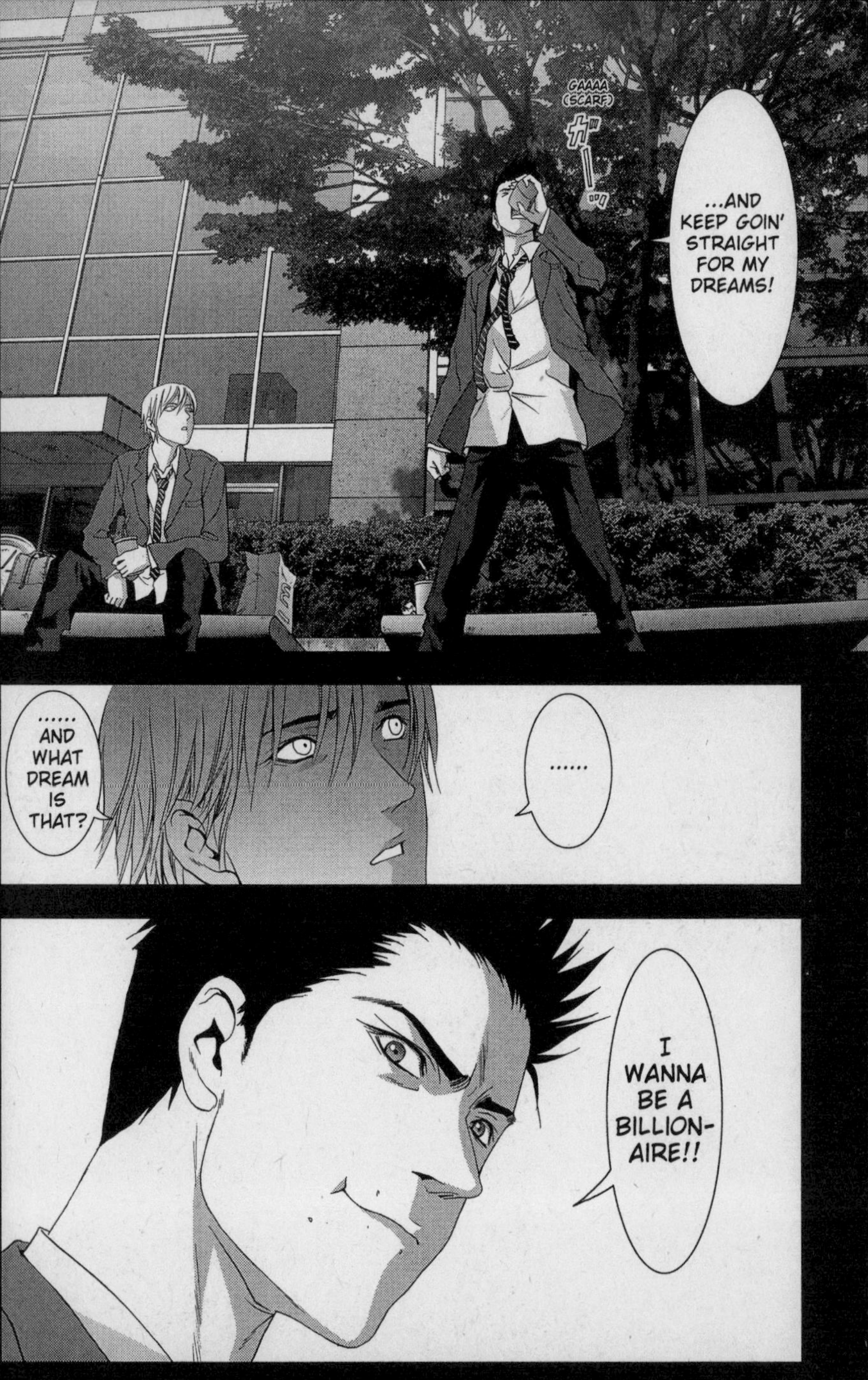
...AND KEEP GOIN' STRAIGHT FOR MY DREAMS!
GAAAA (SCARF)
......
...... AND WHAT DREAM IS THAT?
I WANNA BE A BILLION-AIRE!!

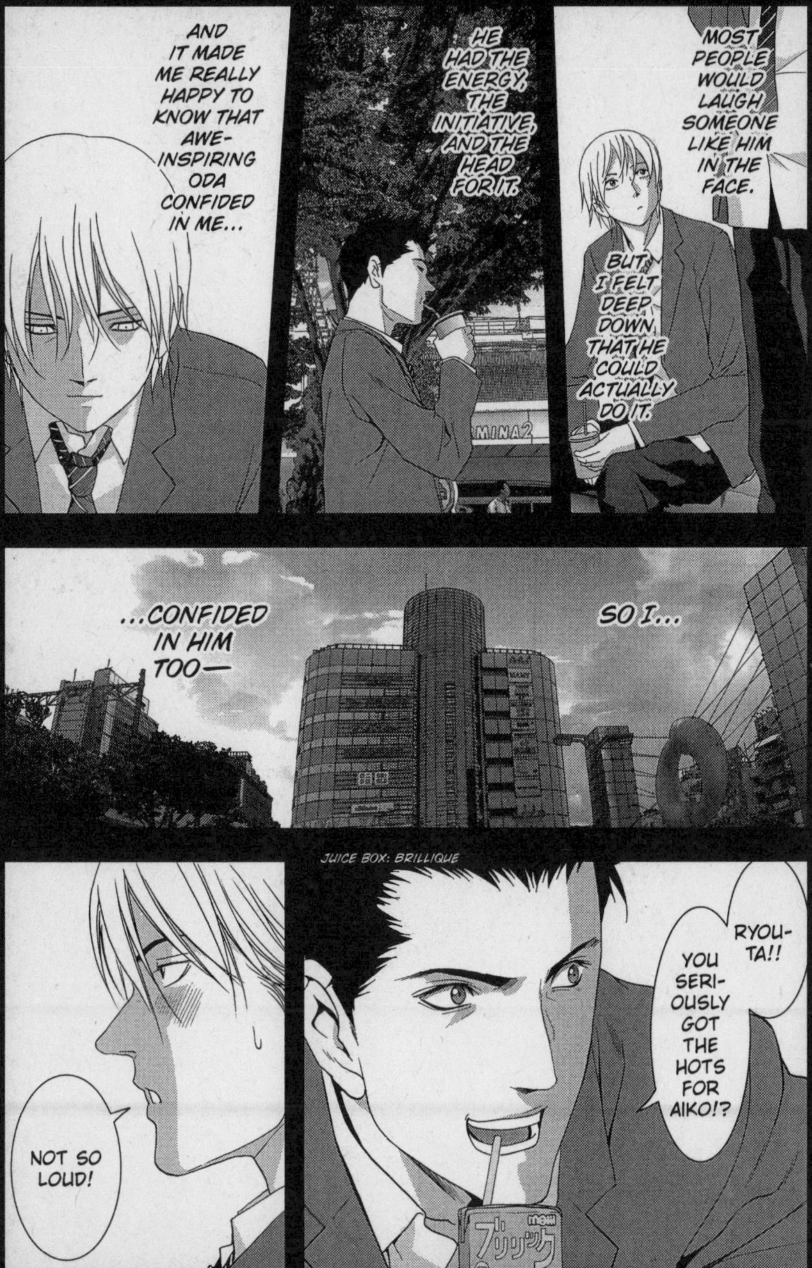

MOST PEOPLE WOULD LAUGH SOMEONE LIKE HIM IN THE FACE.
BUT I FELT DEEP DOWN THAT HE COULD ACTUALLY DO IT.
HE HAD THE ENERGY, THE INITIATIVE, AND THE HEAD FOR IT.
AND IT MADE ME REALLY HAPPY TO KNOW THAT AWE-INSPIRING ODA CONFIDED IN ME...
MINA2
SO I...
...CONFIDED IN HIM TOO—
JUICE BOX: BRILLIQUE
RYOU-TA!!
YOU SERI-OUSLY GOT THE HOTS FOR AIKO!?
NOT SO LOUD!

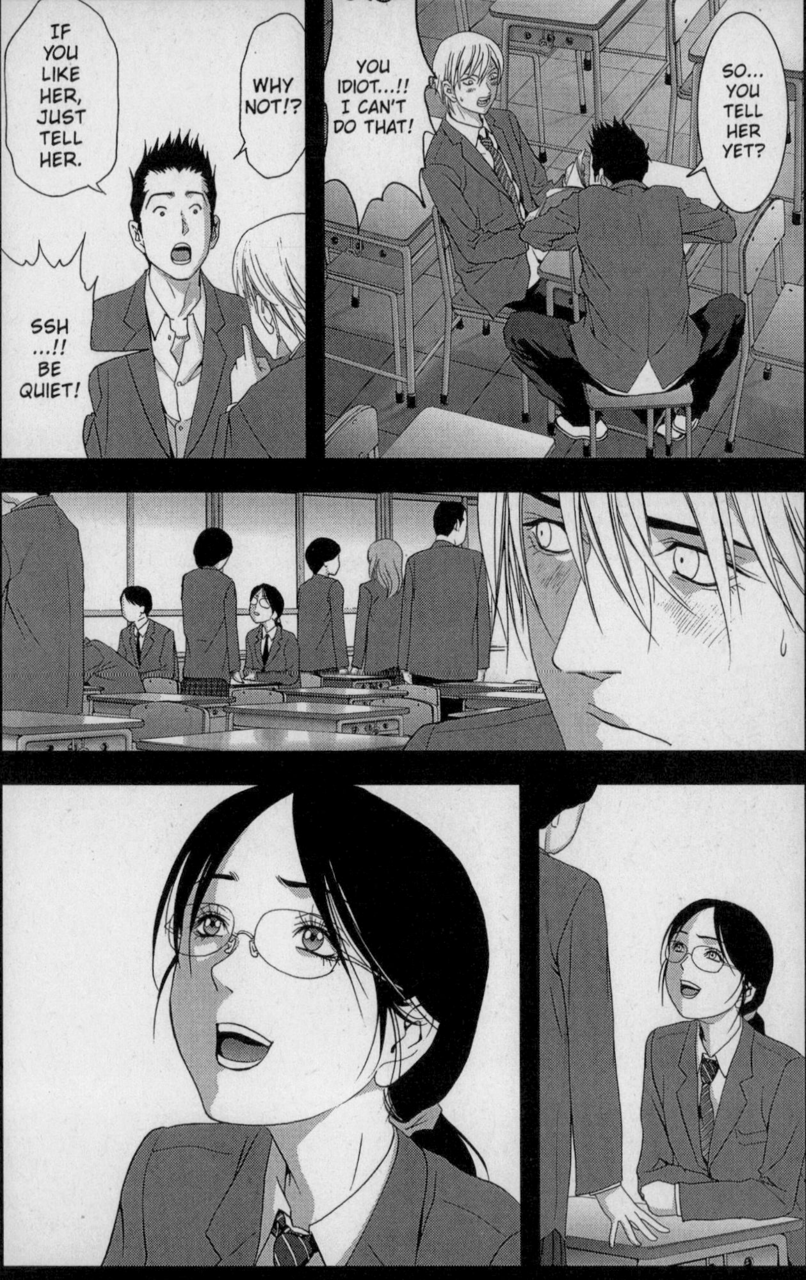
SO... YOU TELL HER YET?
YOU IDIOT...!! I CAN'T DO THAT!
WHY NOT!?
IF YOU LIKE HER, JUST TELL HER.
SSH ...!! BE QUIET!

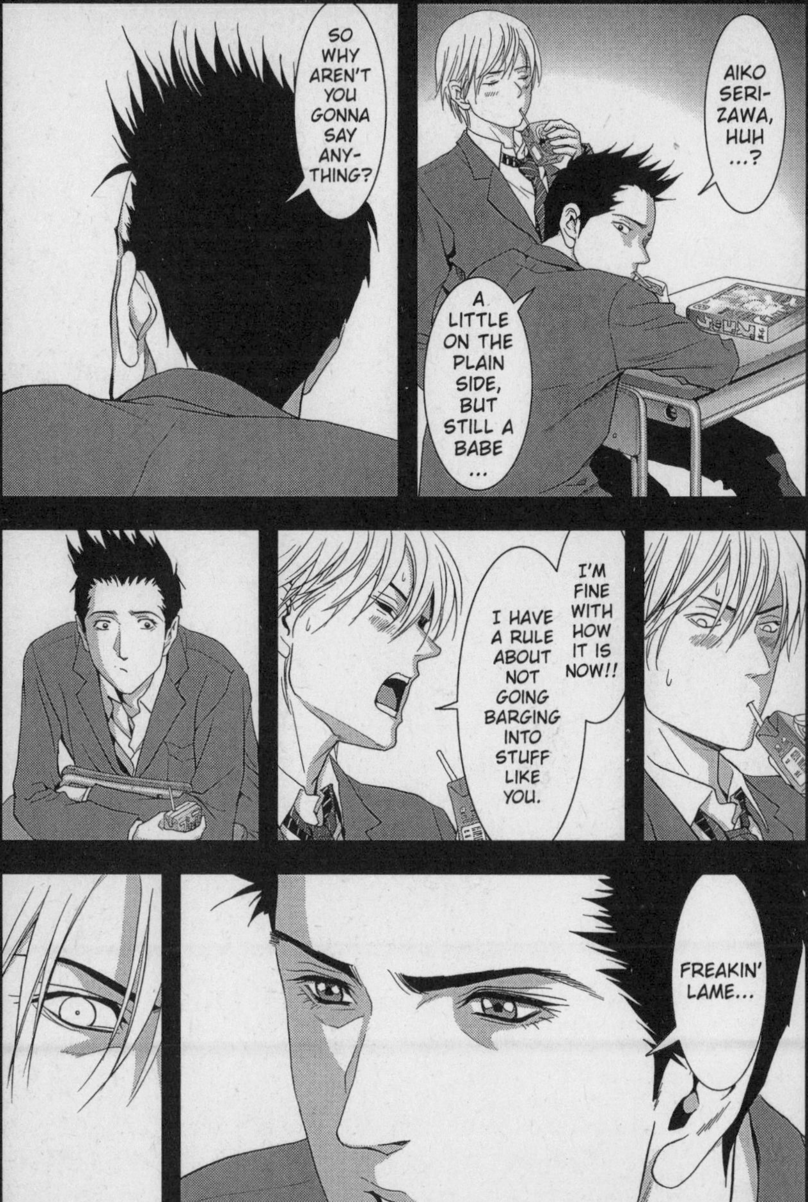
AIKO SERIZAWA, HUH ...?
A LITTLE ON THE PLAIN SIDE, BUT STILL A BABE ...
SO WHY AREN'T YOU GONNA SAY ANYTHING?
I'M FINE WITH HOW IT IS NOW!!
I HAVE A RULE ABOUT NOT GOING BARGING INTO STUFF LIKE YOU.
FREAKIN' LAME...

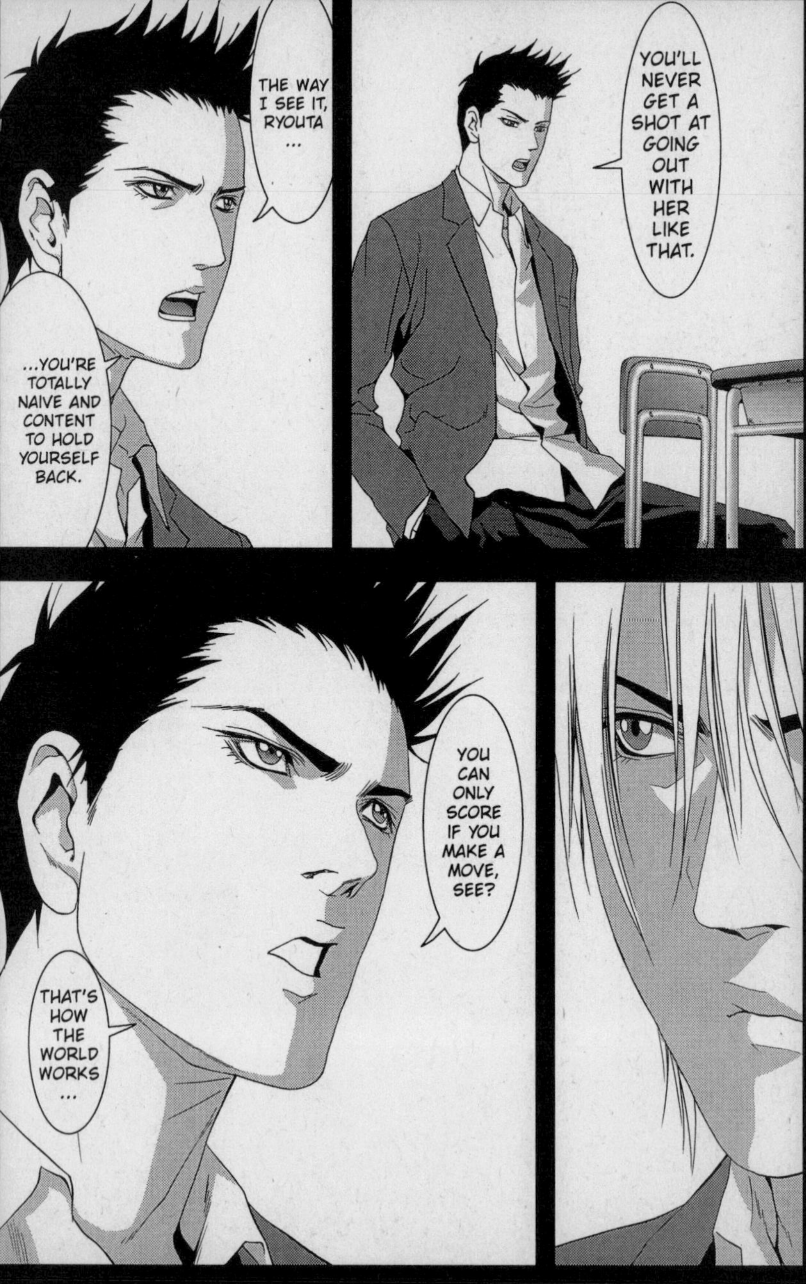
THE WAY I SEE IT, RYOUTA ...
...YOU'RE TOTALLY NAIVE AND CONTENT TO HOLD YOURSELF BACK.
YOU'LL NEVER GET A SHOT AT GOING OUT WITH HER LIKE THAT.
YOU CAN ONLY SCORE IF YOU MAKE A MOVE, SEE?
THAT'S HOW THE WORLD WORKS ...

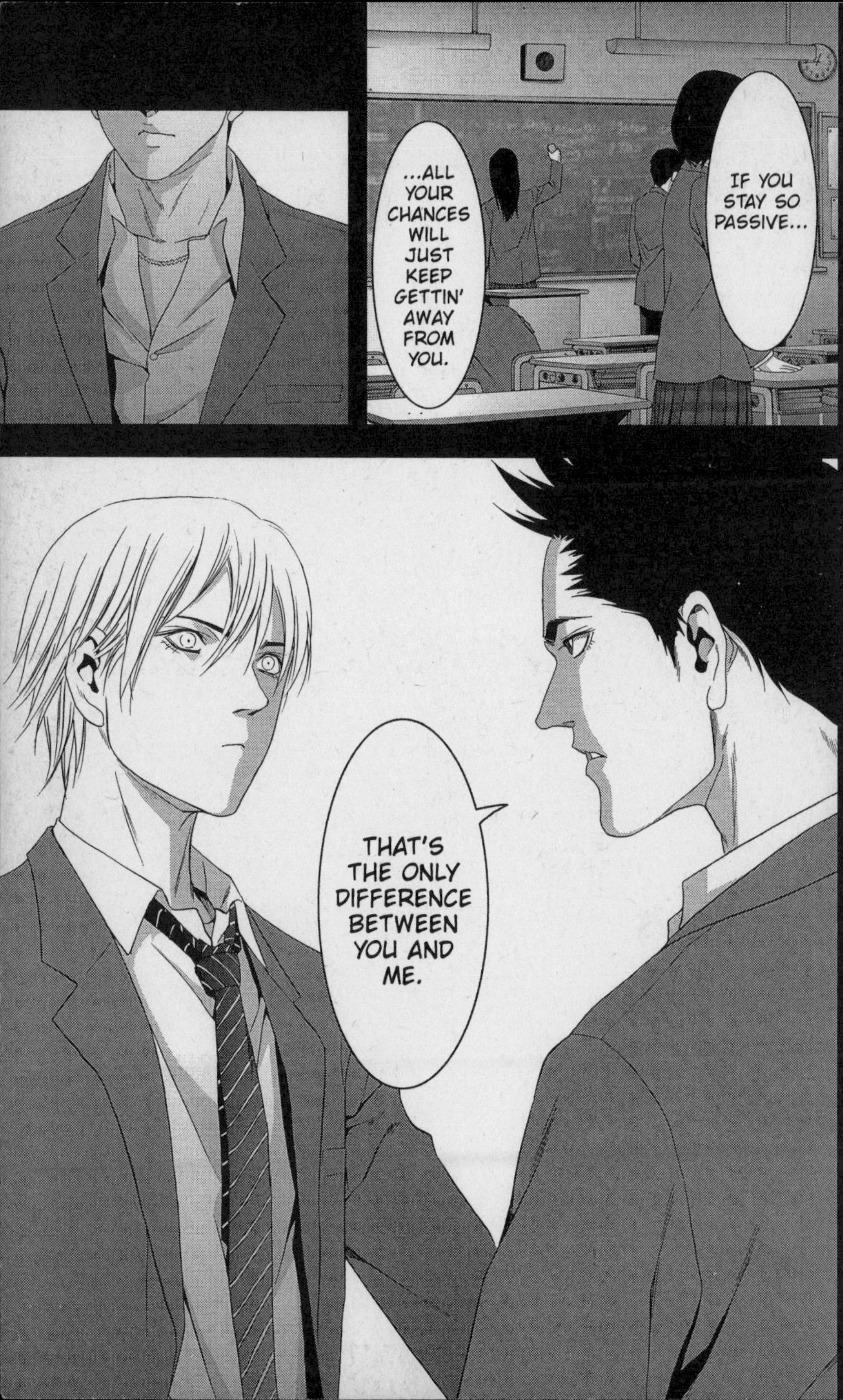
IF YOU STAY SO PASSIVE...
...ALL YOUR CHANCES WILL JUST KEEP GETTIN' AWAY FROM YOU.
THAT'S THE ONLY DIFFERENCE BETWEEN YOU AND ME.

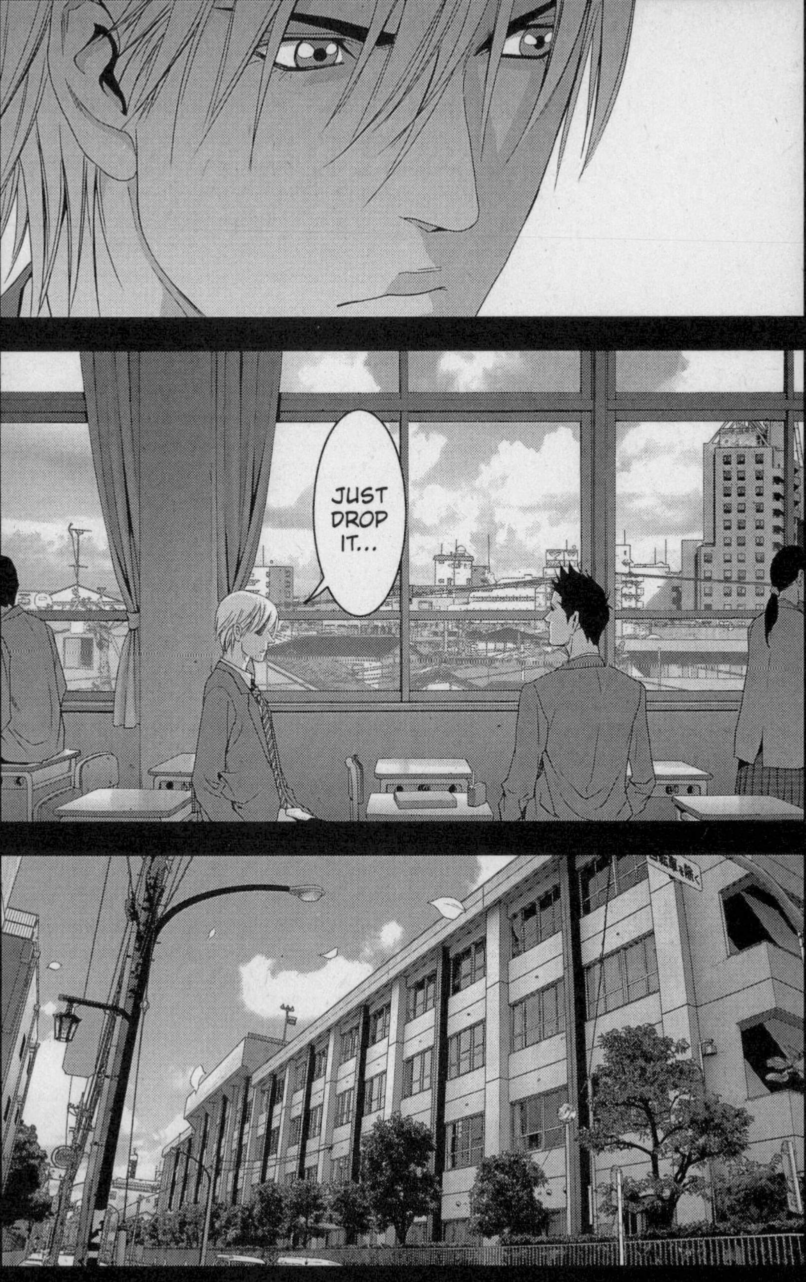
JUST DROP IT...

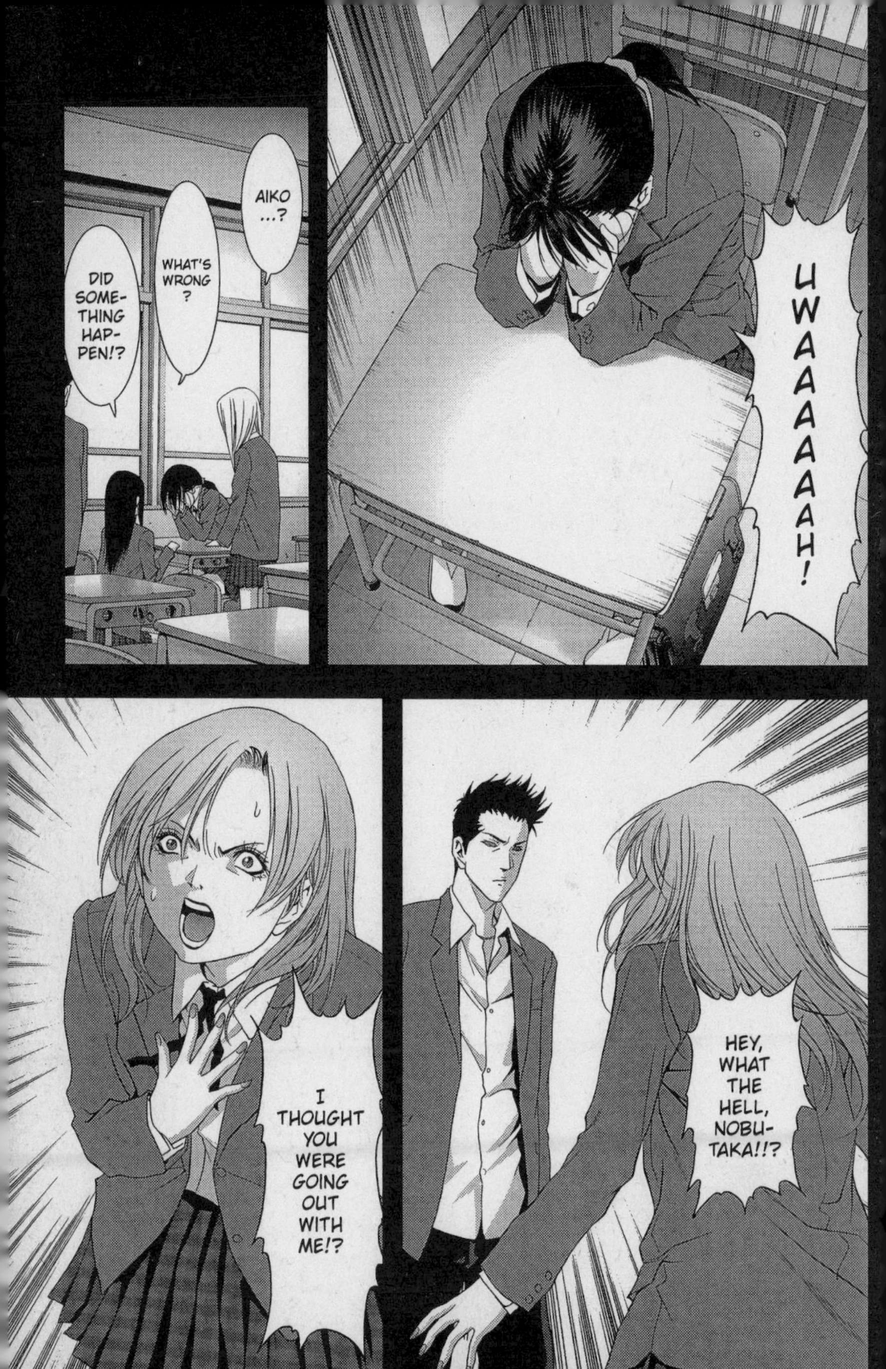
UWAAAAAAAAH!
AIKO ...?
WHAT'S WRONG?
DID SOMETHING HAPPEN!?
HEY, WHAT THE HELL, NOBUTAKA!!?
I THOUGHT YOU WERE GOING OUT WITH ME!?

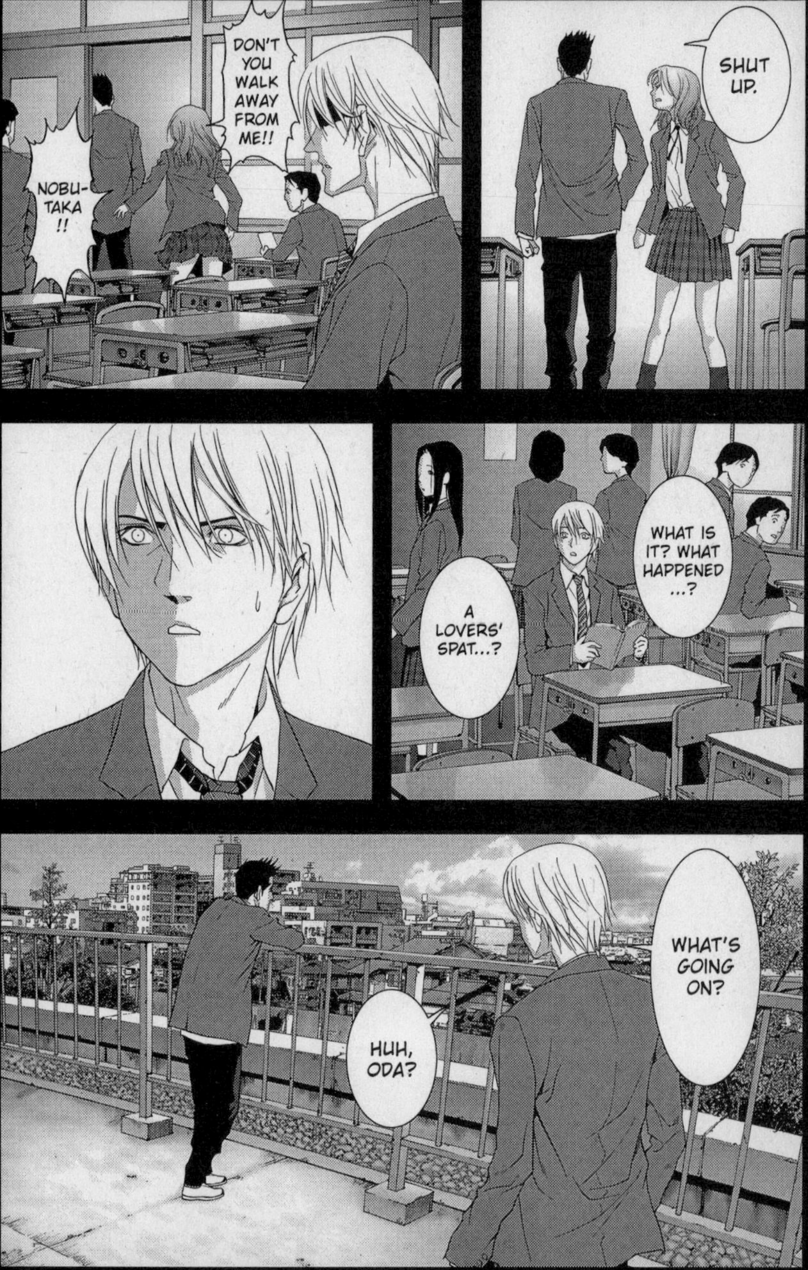
SHUT UP.
DON'T YOU WALK AWAY FROM ME!!
NOBU-TAKA !!
WHAT IS IT? WHAT HAPPENED ...?
A LOVERS' SPAT...?
WHAT'S GOING ON?
HUH, ODA?

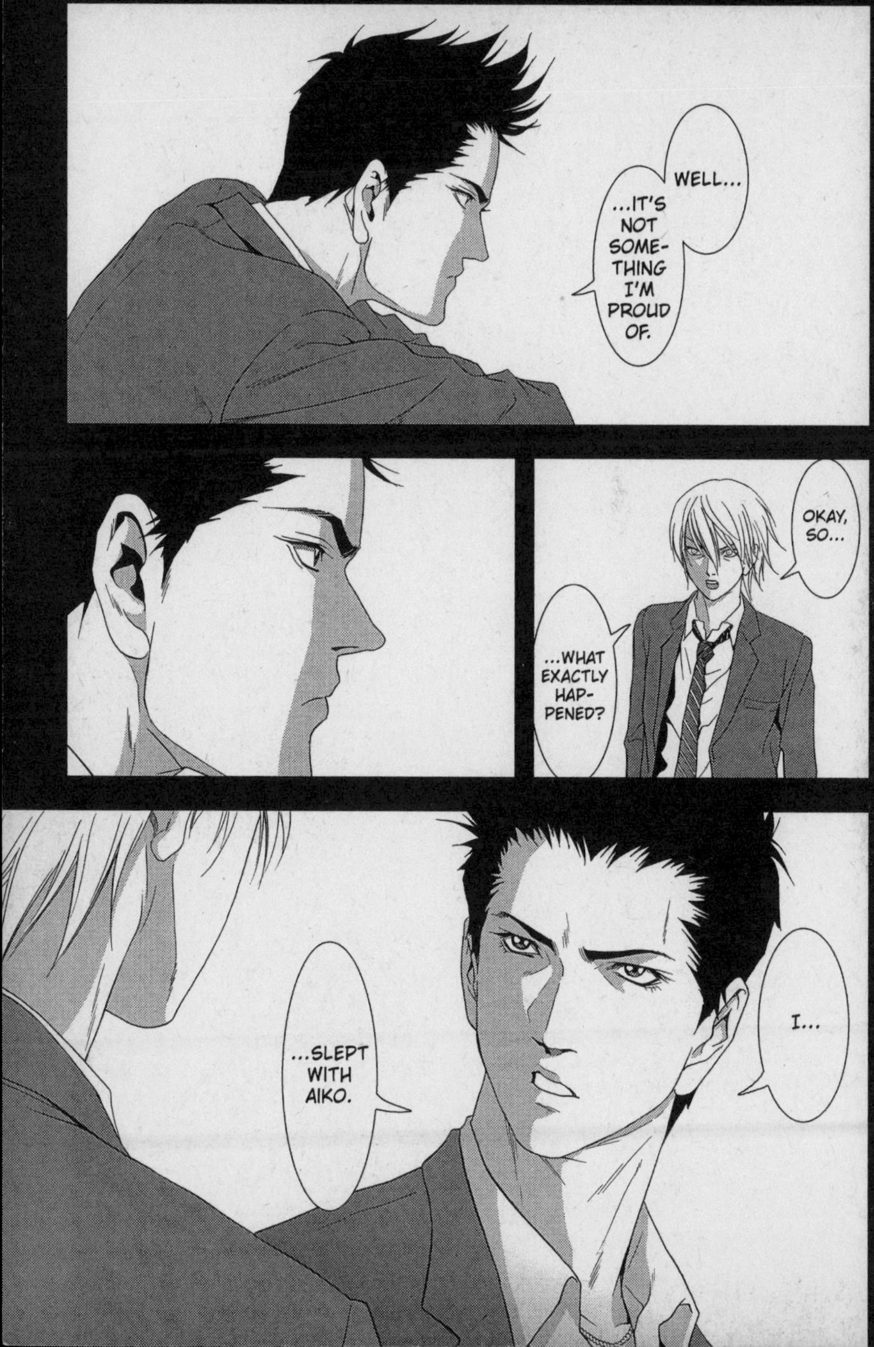
WELL...
...IT'S NOT SOME-THING I'M PROUD OF.
OKAY, SO...
...WHAT EXACTLY HAP-PENED?
I...
...SLEPT WITH AIKO.

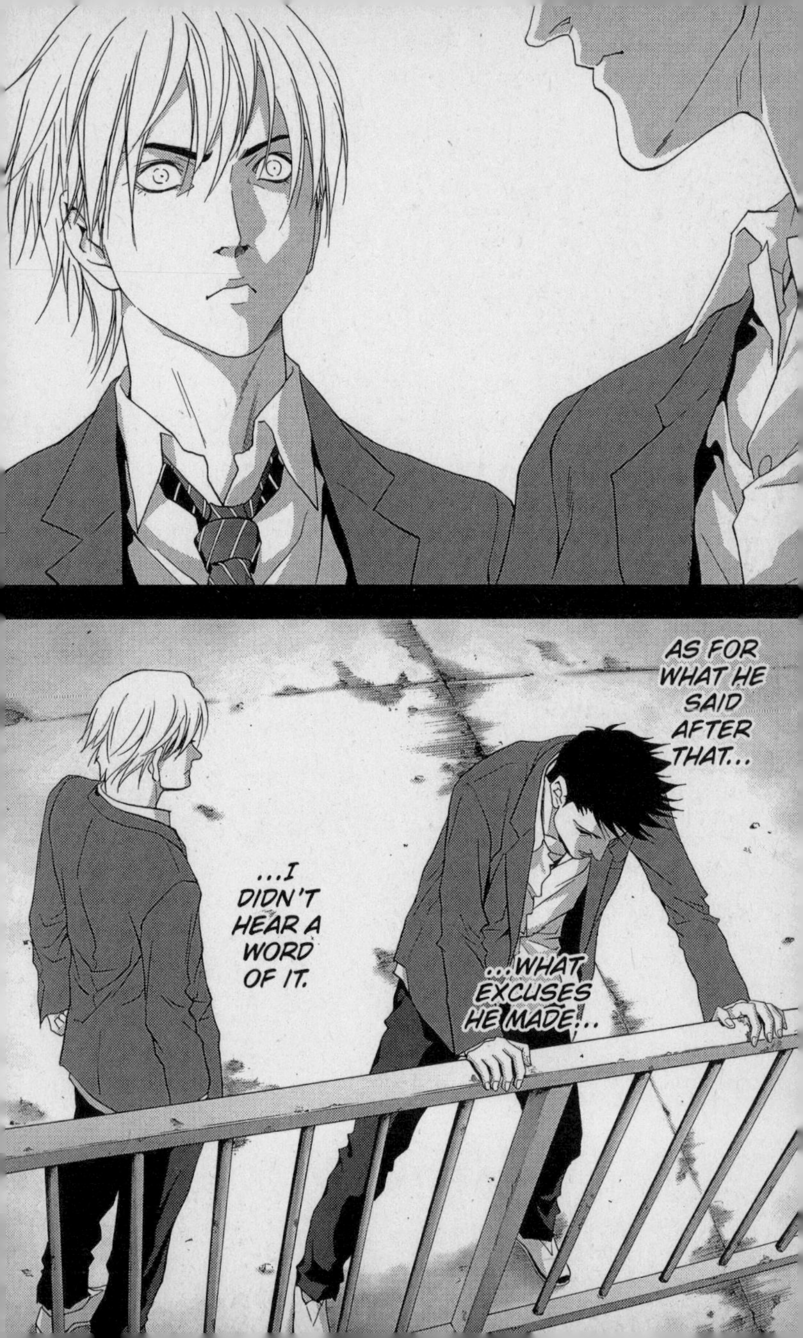
AS FOR WHAT HE SAID AFTER THAT...
...WHAT EXCUSES HE MADE...
...I DIDN'T HEAR A WORD OF IT.

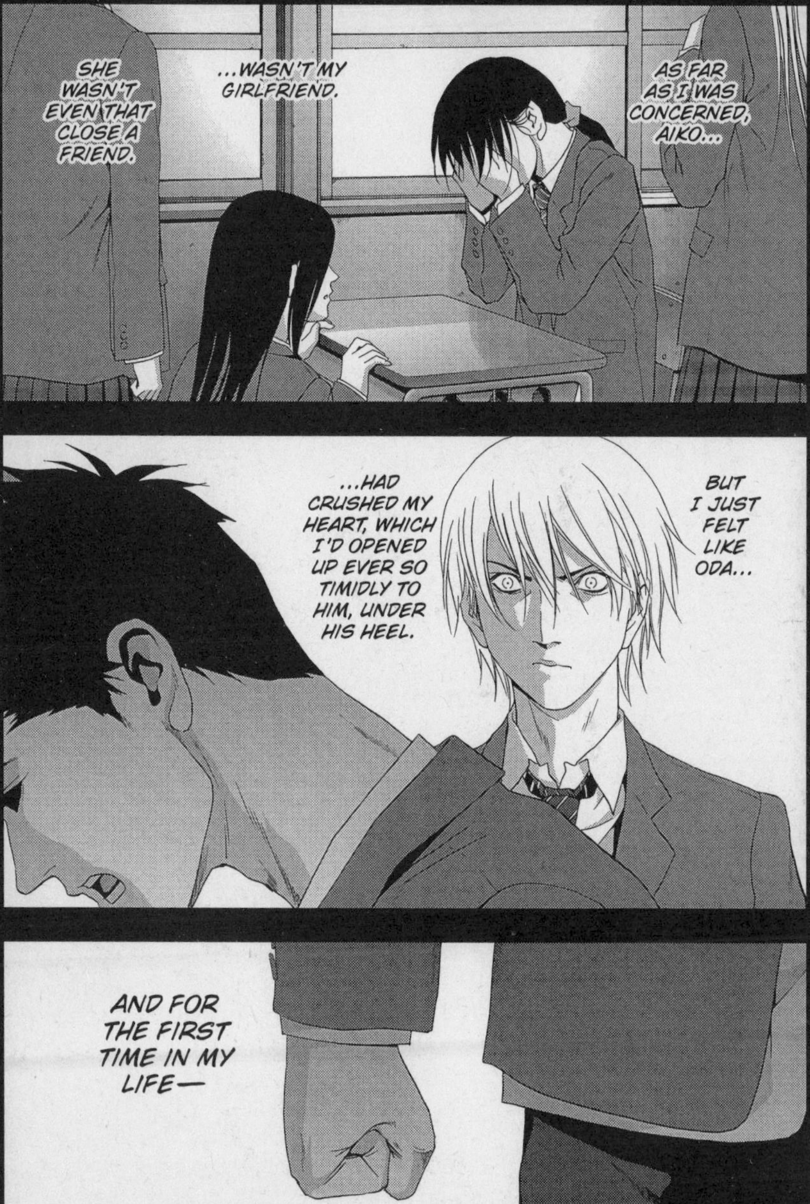
AS FAR AS I WAS CONCERNED, AIKO...
...WASN'T MY GIRLFRIEND.
SHE WASN'T EVEN THAT CLOSE A FRIEND.
BUT I JUST FELT LIKE ODA...
...HAD CRUSHED MY HEART, WHICH I'D OPENED UP EVER SO TIMIDLY TO HIM, UNDER HIS HEEL.
AND FOR THE FIRST TIME IN MY LIFE—

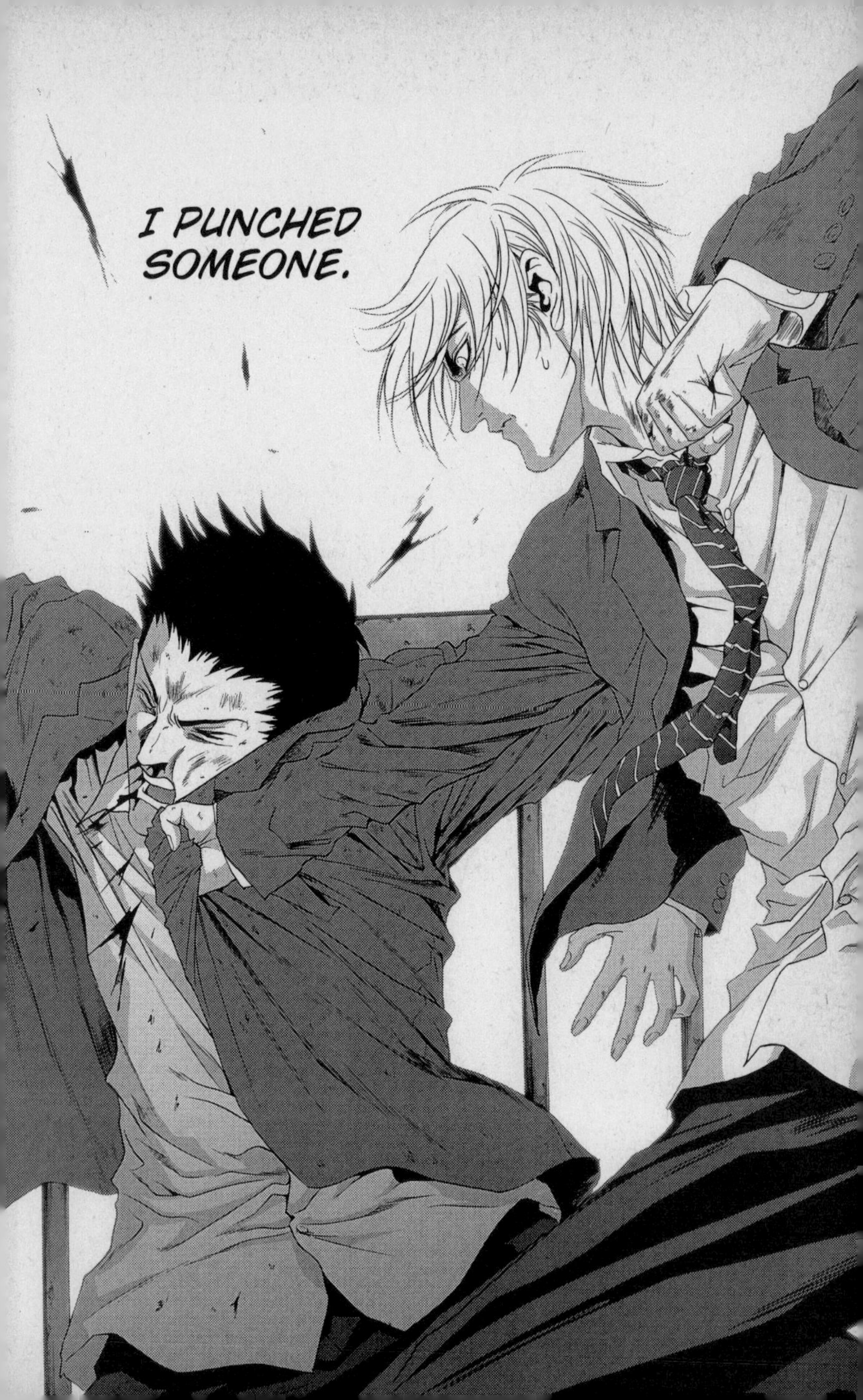
I PUNCHED SOMEONE.

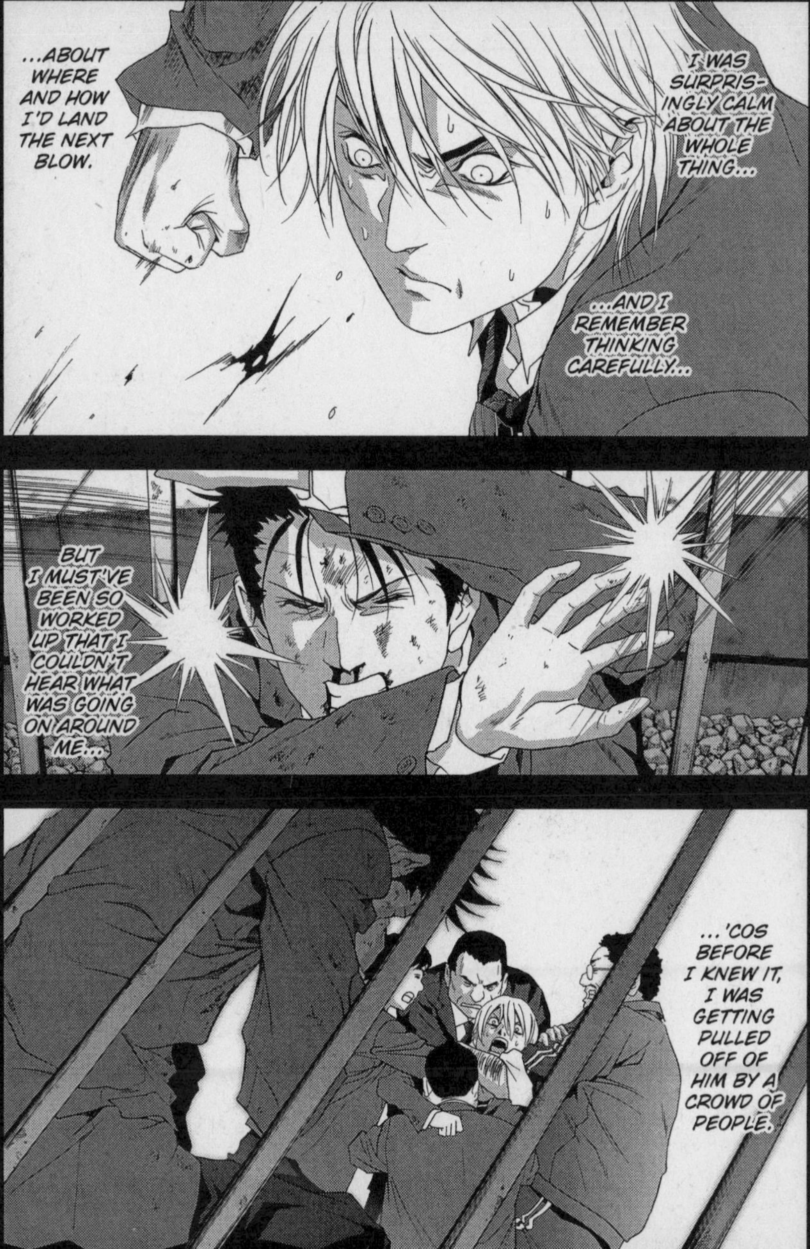
I WAS SURPRISINGLY CALM ABOUT THE WHOLE THING...
...AND I REMEMBER THINKING CAREFULLY...
...ABOUT WHERE AND HOW I'D LAND THE NEXT BLOW.
BUT I MUST'VE BEEN SO WORKED UP THAT I COULDN'T HEAR WHAT WAS GOING ON AROUND ME...
...'COS BEFORE I KNEW IT, I WAS GETTING PULLED OFF OF HIM BY A CROWD OF PEOPLE.

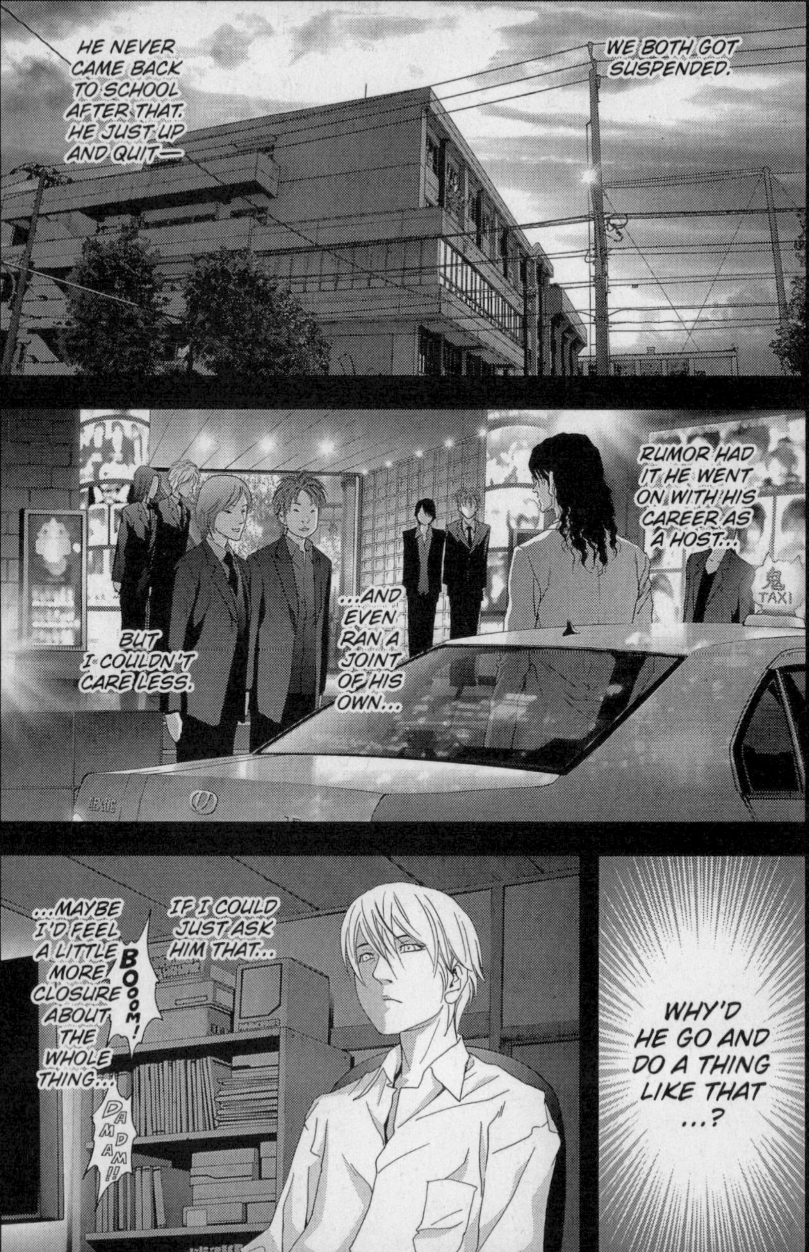
WE BOTH GOT SUSPENDED.
HE NEVER CAME BACK TO SCHOOL AFTER THAT. HE JUST UP AND QUIT—
RUMOR HAD IT HE WENT ON WITH HIS CAREER AS A HOST...
TAXI
...AND EVEN RAN A JOINT OF HIS OWN...
BUT I COULDN'T CARE LESS.
WHY'D HE GO AND DO A THING LIKE THAT ...?
IF I COULD JUST ASK HIM THAT...
...MAYBE I'D FEEL A LITTLE MORE CLOSURE ABOUT THE WHOLE THING...
BOOOOM!
DADAMM!!

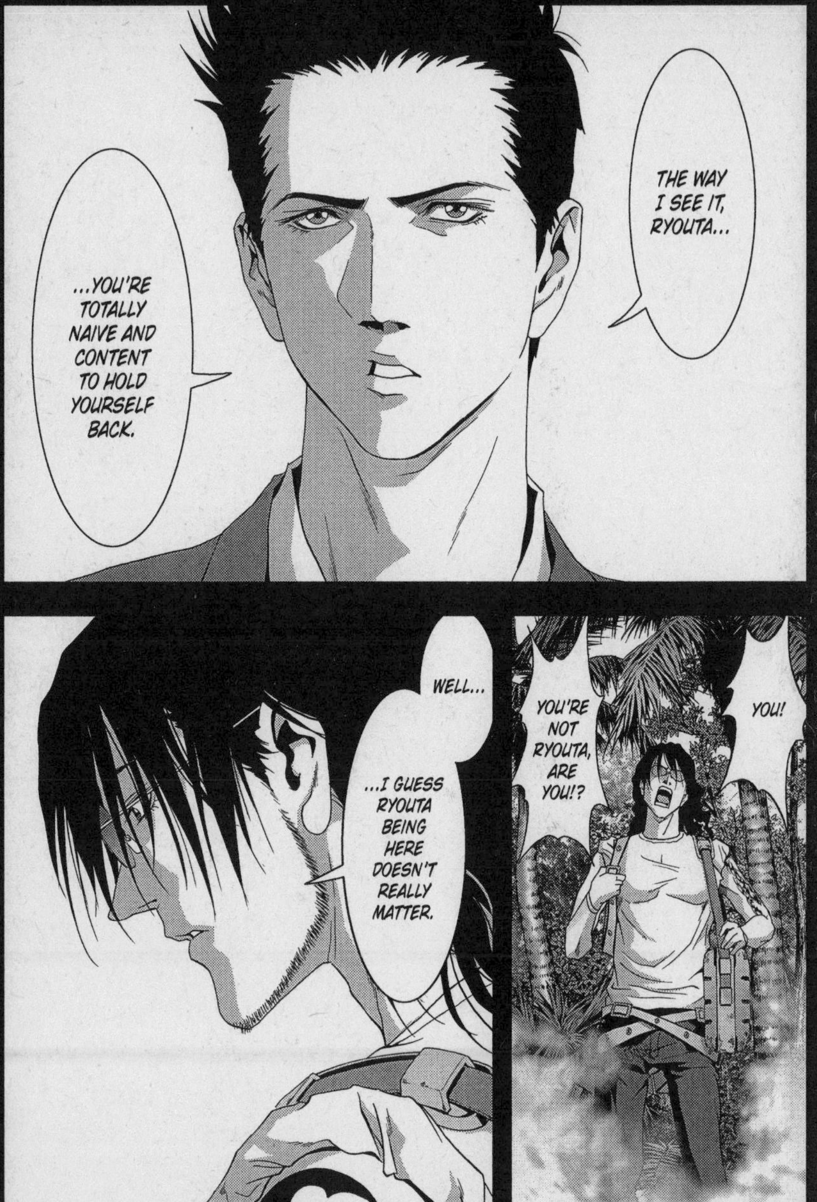
THE WAY I SEE IT, RYOUTA...
...YOU'RE TOTALLY NAIVE AND CONTENT TO HOLD YOURSELF BACK.
YOU!
YOU'RE NOT RYOUTA, ARE YOU!?
WELL...
...I GUESS RYOUTA BEING HERE DOESN'T REALLY MATTER.

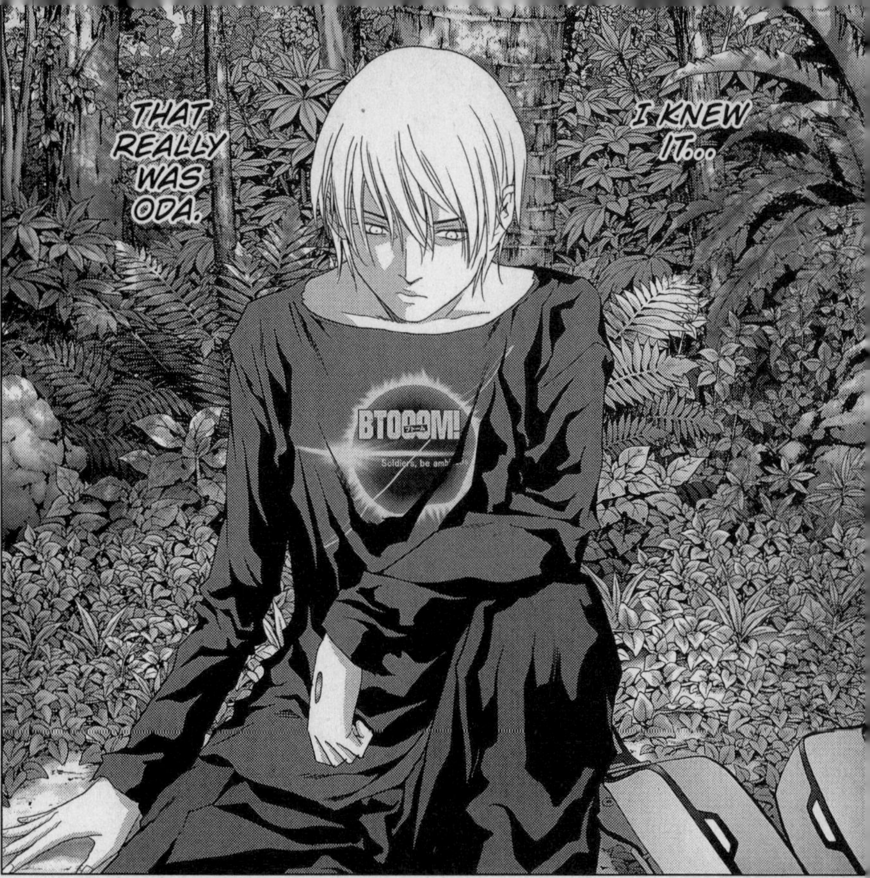
I KNEW IT...
THAT REALLY WAS ODA.
BTOOOM!

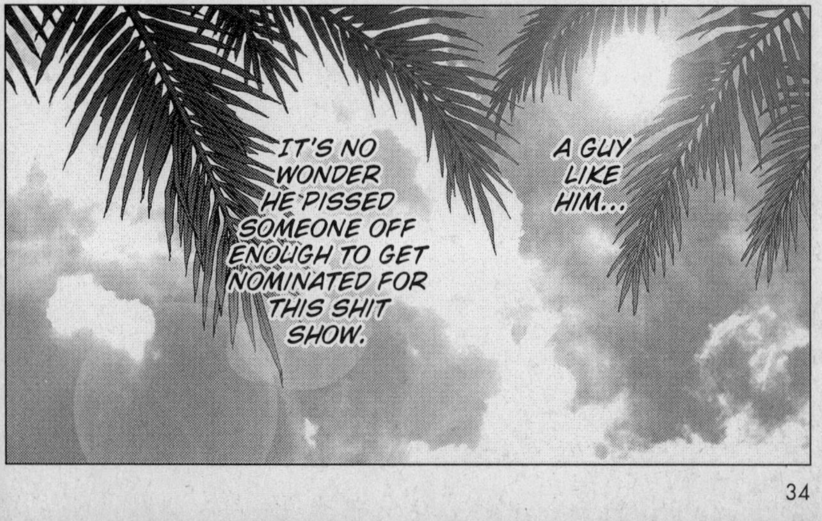
A GUY LIKE HIM...
IT'S NO WONDER HE PISSED SOMEONE OFF ENOUGH TO GET NOMINATED FOR THIS SHIT SHOW.

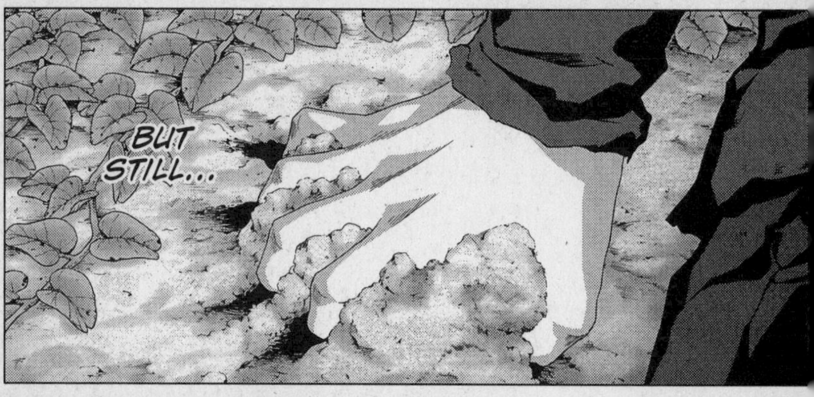
BUT STILL...
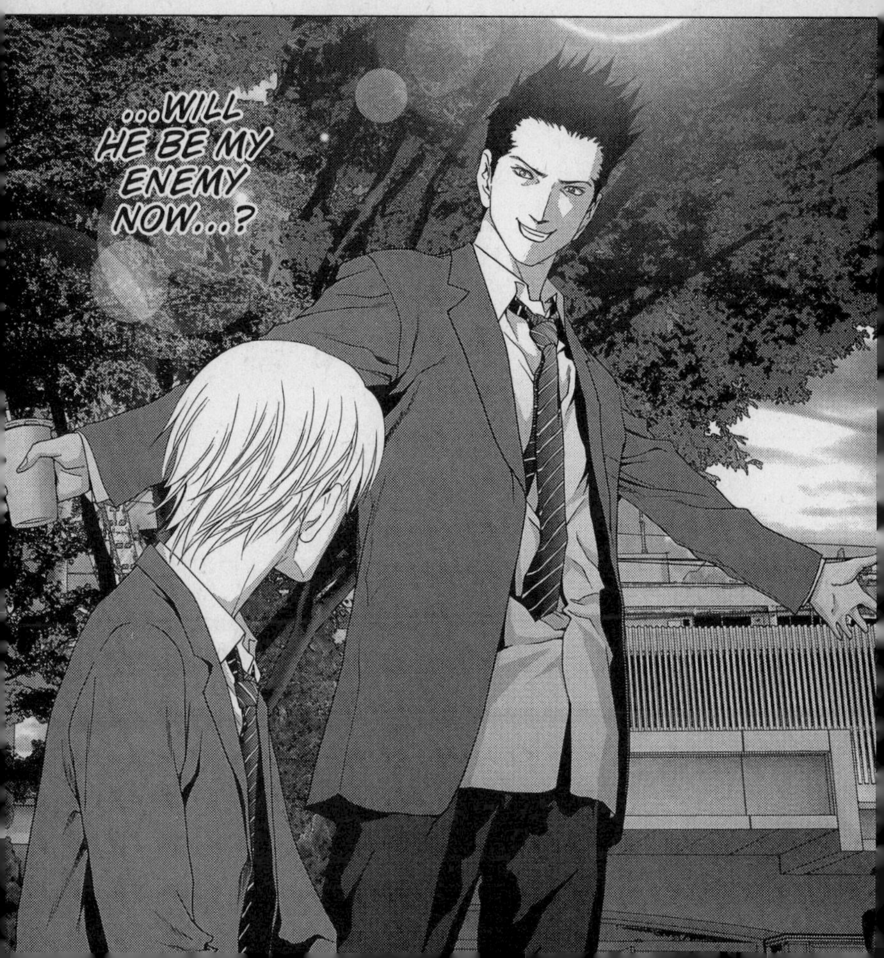
...WILL HE BE MY ENEMY NOW...?

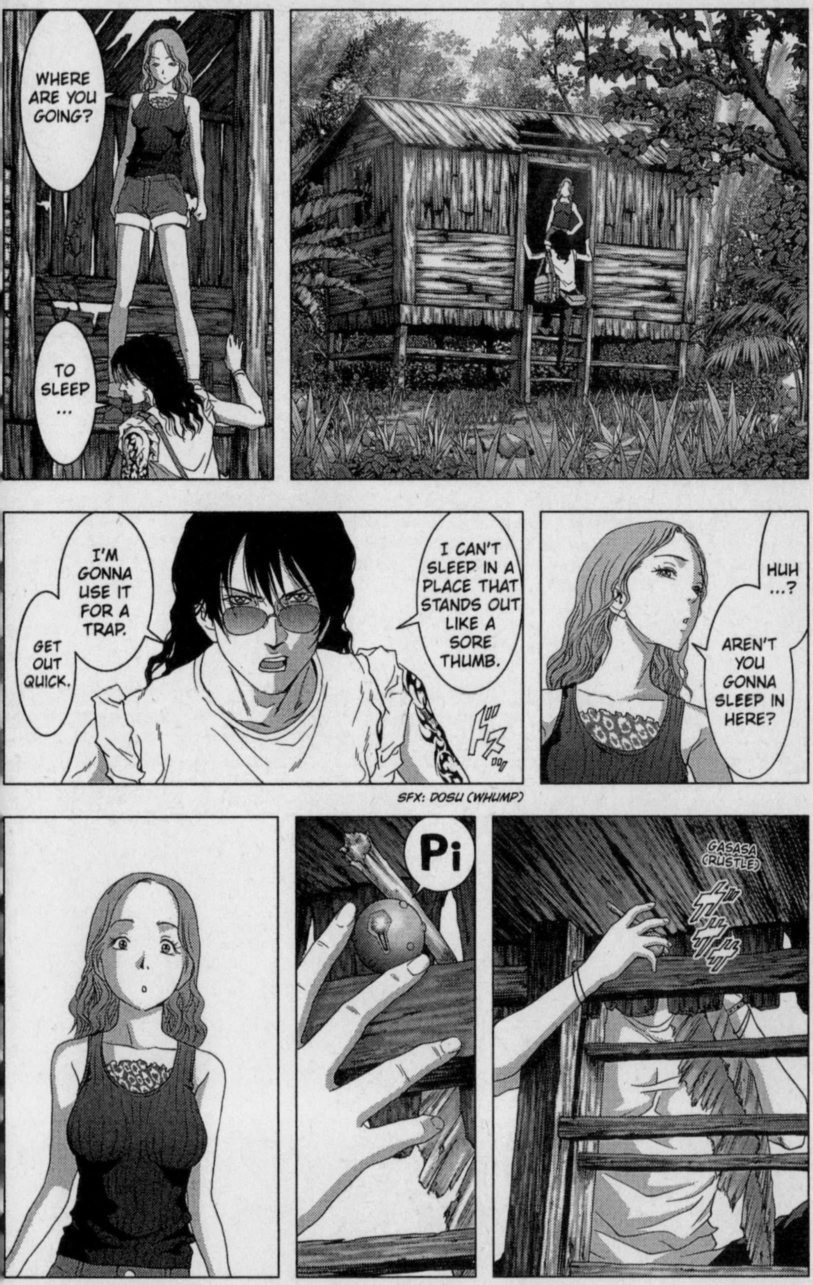
WHERE ARE YOU GOING?
TO SLEEP ...
HUH ...?
AREN'T YOU GONNA SLEEP IN HERE?
I CAN'T SLEEP IN A PLACE THAT STANDS OUT LIKE A SORE THUMB.
I'M GONNA USE IT FOR A TRAP.
GET OUT QUICK.
SFX: DOSU (WHUMP)
GASASA (RUSTLE)
Pi

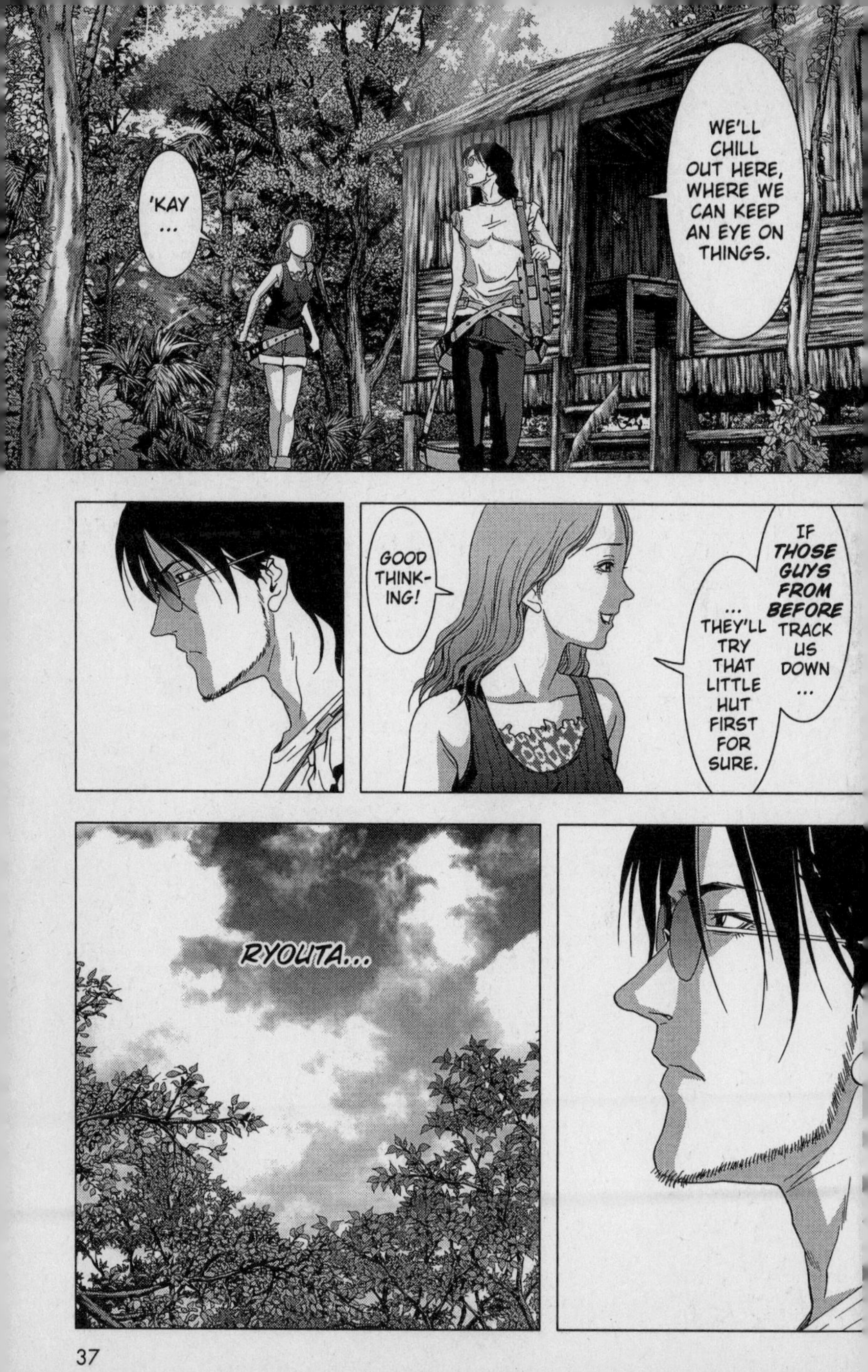
WE'LL CHILL OUT HERE, WHERE WE CAN KEEP AN EYE ON THINGS.
'KAY...
IF THOSE GUYS FROM BEFORE TRACK US DOWN...
...THEY'LL TRY THAT LITTLE HUT FIRST FOR SURE.
GOOD THINKING!
RYOUTA...

ZAAAA
(SSSHH)

ZAAAA
(SSSHH)

?

PIKOOOON
(PAAAAANG)

Soldiers, be ambitious.

GABA
(JUMP)

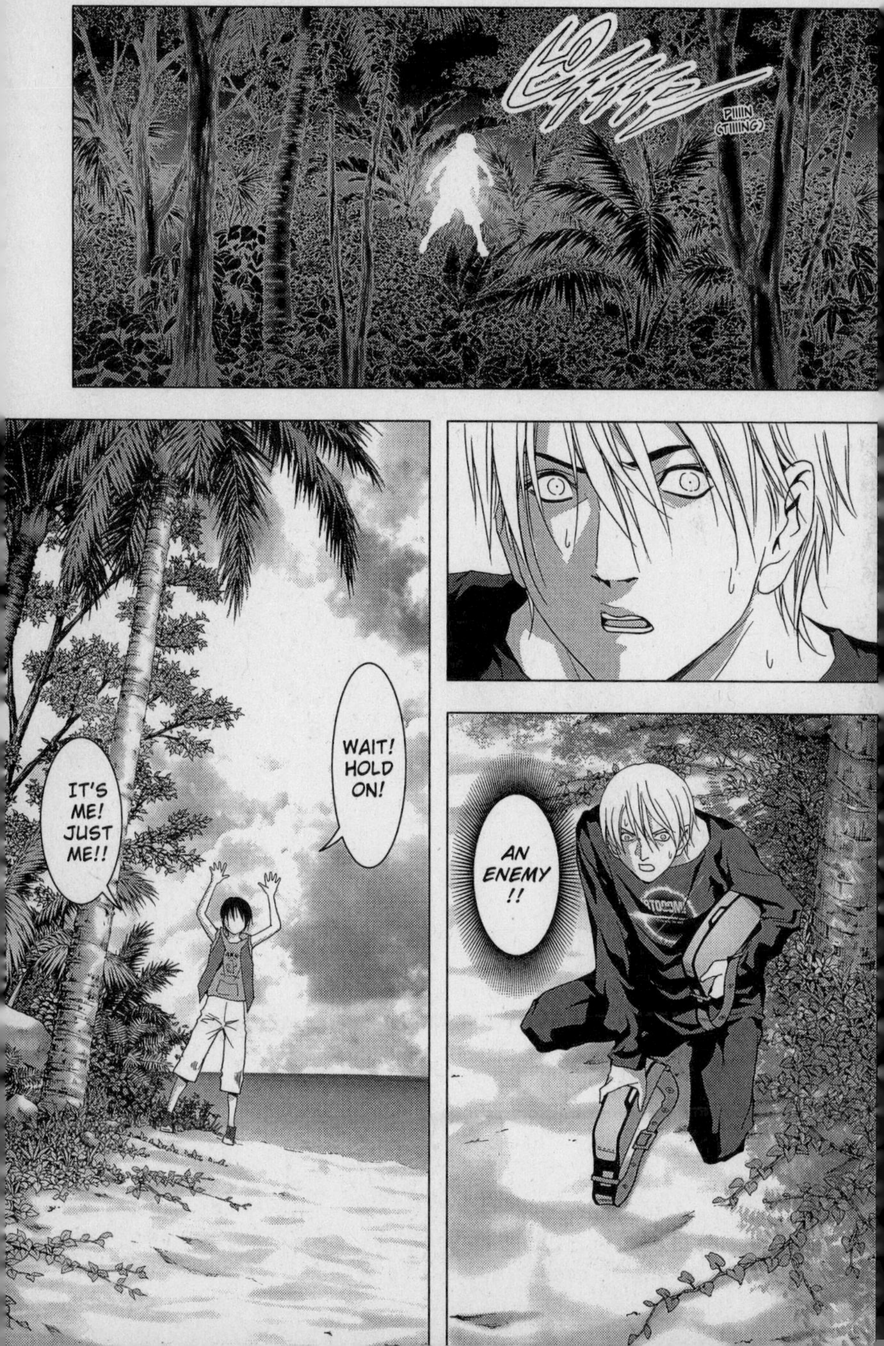
PIIIN (TIIIING)
AN ENEMY !!
WAIT! HOLD ON!
IT'S ME! JUST ME!!

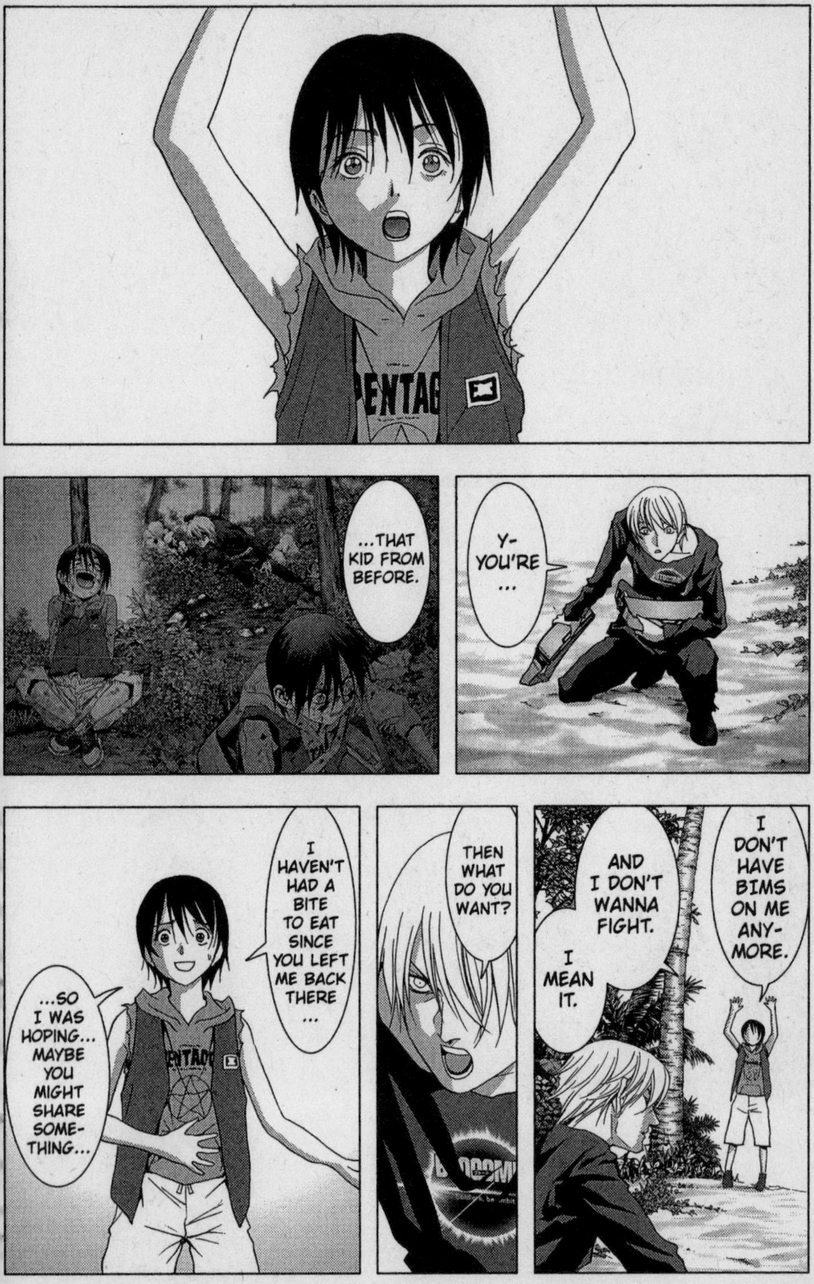
Y- YOU'RE ...
...THAT KID FROM BEFORE.
I DON'T HAVE BIMS ON ME ANYMORE.
AND I DON'T WANNA FIGHT.
I MEAN IT.
THEN WHAT DO YOU WANT?
I HAVEN'T HAD A BITE TO EAT SINCE YOU LEFT ME BACK THERE ...
...SO I WAS HOPING... MAYBE YOU MIGHT SHARE SOMETHING...

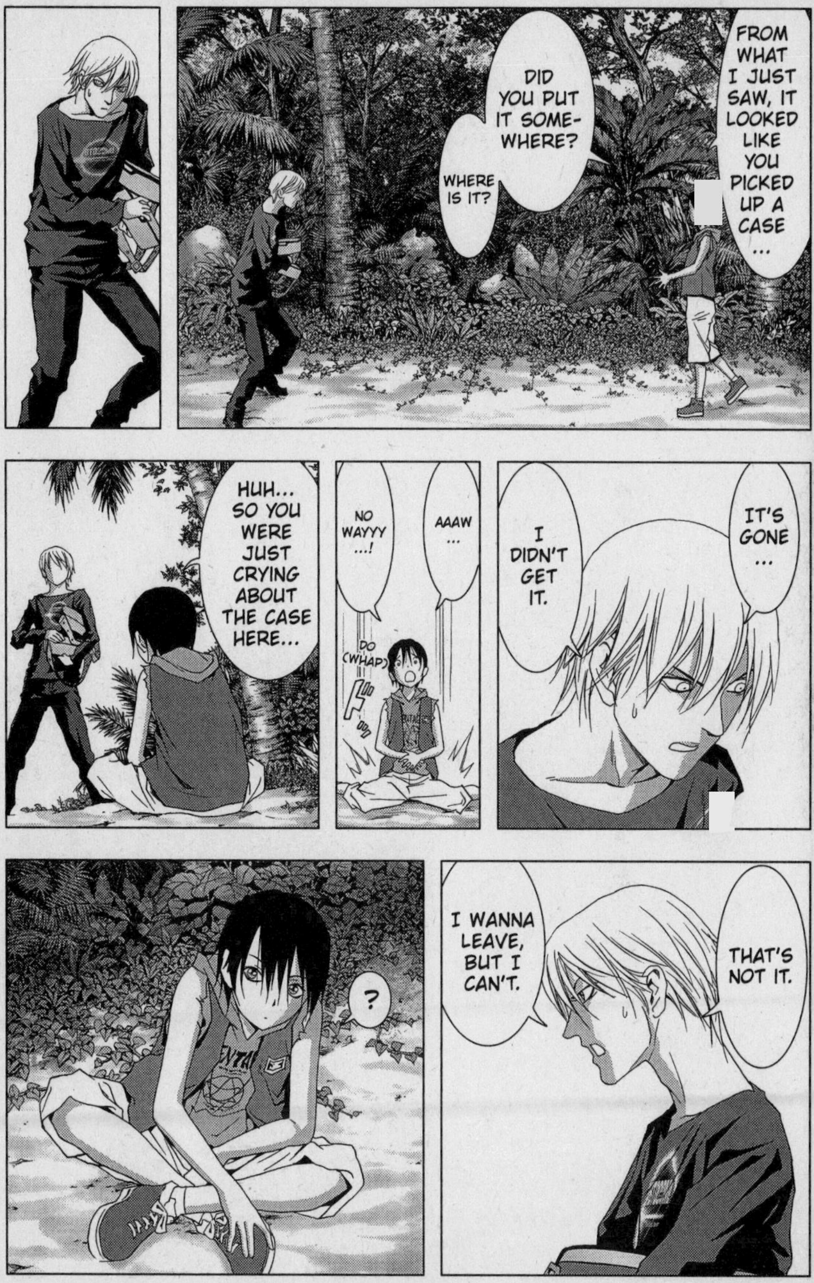
FROM WHAT I JUST SAW, IT LOOKED LIKE YOU PICKED UP A CASE...
DID YOU PUT IT SOME-WHERE?
WHERE IS IT?
IT'S GONE...
I DIDN'T GET IT.
AAAW...
NO WAYYY...!
DO (WHAP)
HUH... SO YOU WERE JUST CRYING ABOUT THE CASE HERE...
THAT'S NOT IT.
I WANNA LEAVE, BUT I CAN'T.
?

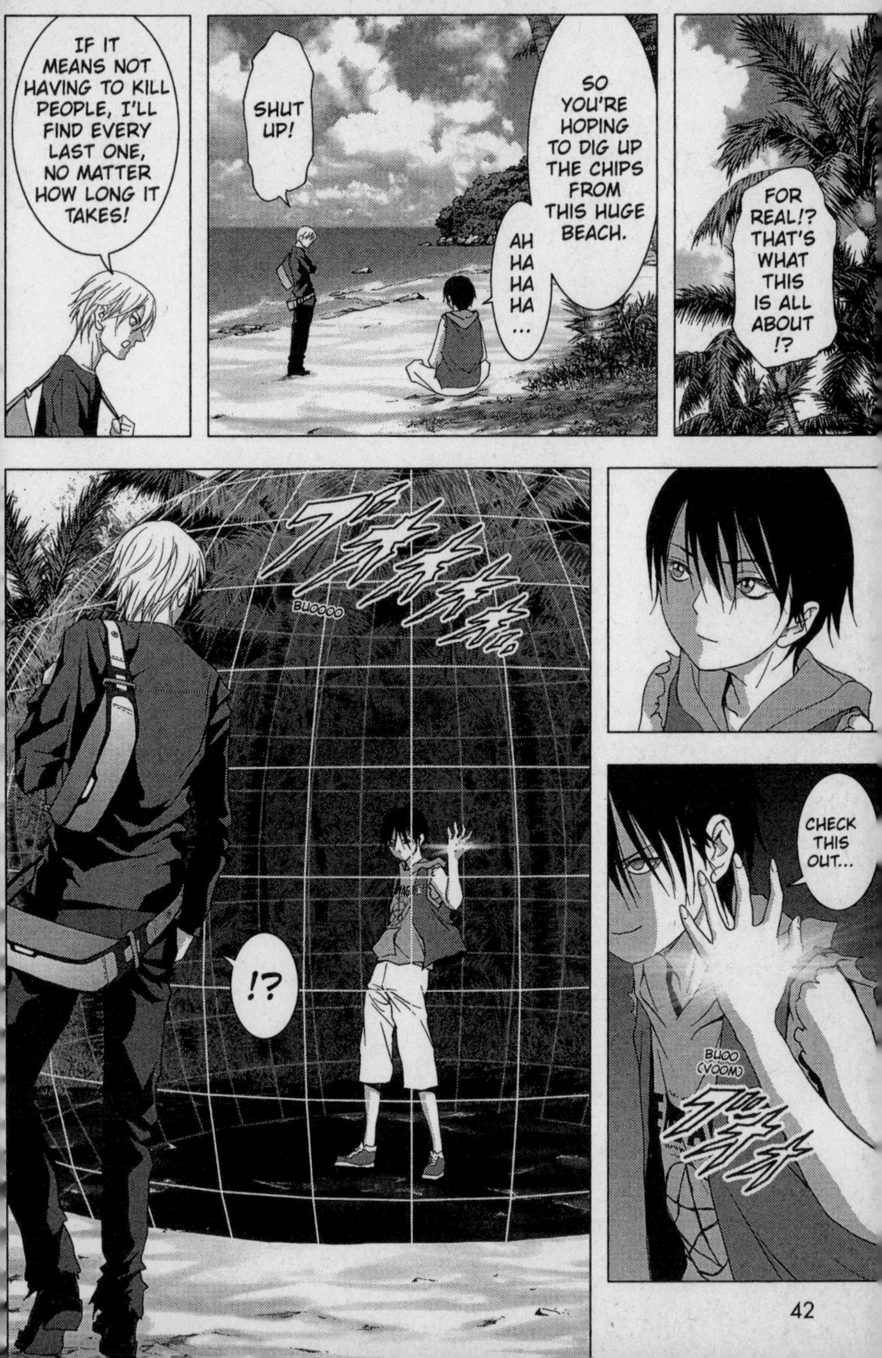
FOR REAL!? THAT'S WHAT THIS IS ALL ABOUT!?
SO YOU'RE HOPING TO DIG UP THE CHIPS FROM THIS HUGE BEACH.
AH HA HA HA...
SHUT UP!
IF IT MEANS NOT HAVING TO KILL PEOPLE, I'LL FIND EVERY LAST ONE, NO MATTER HOW LONG IT TAKES!
CHECK THIS OUT...
BUOO (VOOM)
BUOOOO
!?

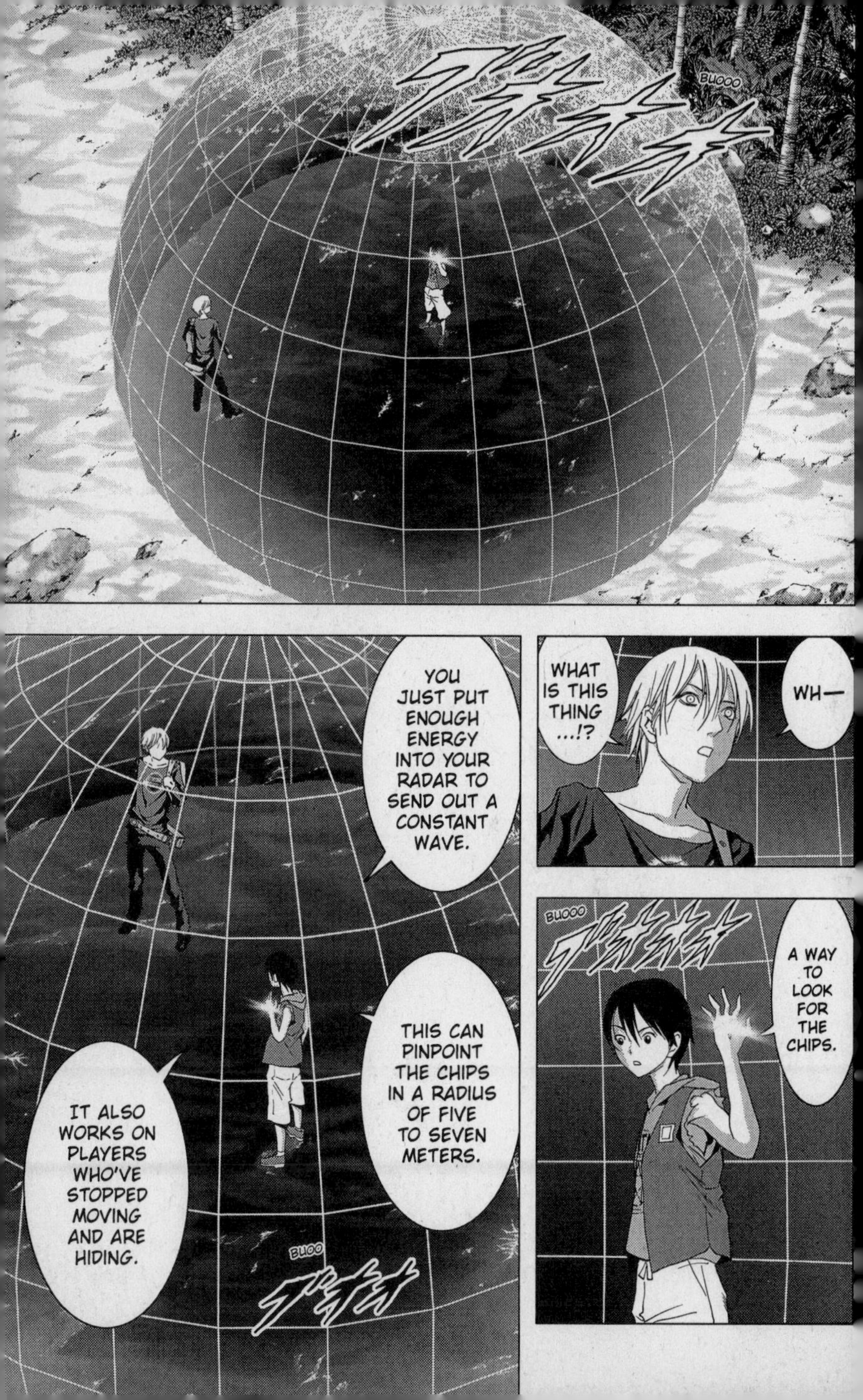
BUOOO
WH—
WHAT IS THIS THING ...!?
BUOOO
A WAY TO LOOK FOR THE CHIPS.
YOU JUST PUT ENOUGH ENERGY INTO YOUR RADAR TO SEND OUT A CONSTANT WAVE.
THIS CAN PINPOINT THE CHIPS IN A RADIUS OF FIVE TO SEVEN METERS.
IT ALSO WORKS ON PLAYERS WHO'VE STOPPED MOVING AND ARE HIDING.
BUOO

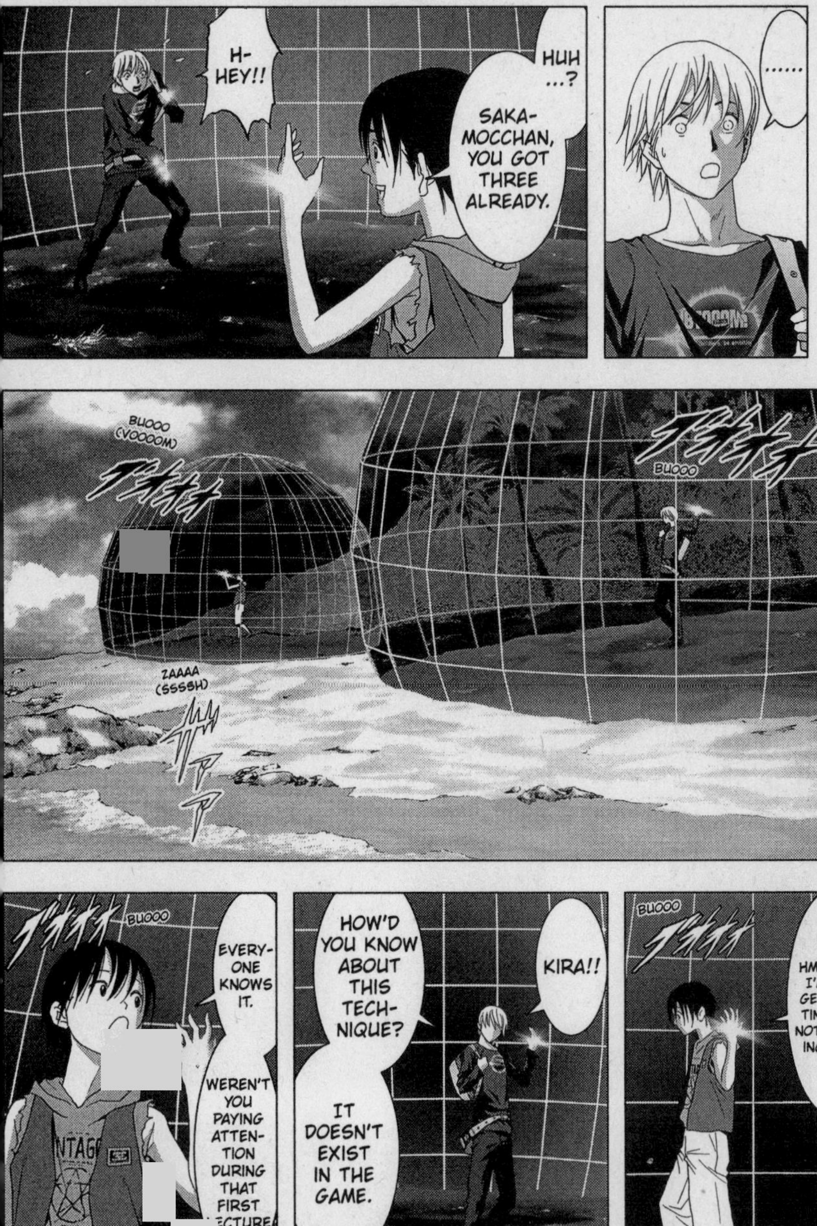
......
HUH ...?
SAKA-MOCCHAN, YOU GOT THREE ALREADY.
H- HEY!!
BUOOO
BUOOO (VOOOOM)
ZAAAA (SSSSH)
BUOOO
HMM, I'M GET-TING NOTH-ING.
KIRA!!
HOW'D YOU KNOW ABOUT THIS TECH-NIQUE?
IT DOESN'T EXIST IN THE GAME.
BUOOO
EVERY-ONE KNOWS IT.
WEREN'T YOU PAYING ATTEN-TION DURING THAT FIRST LECTURE?

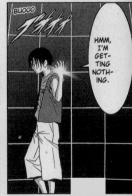

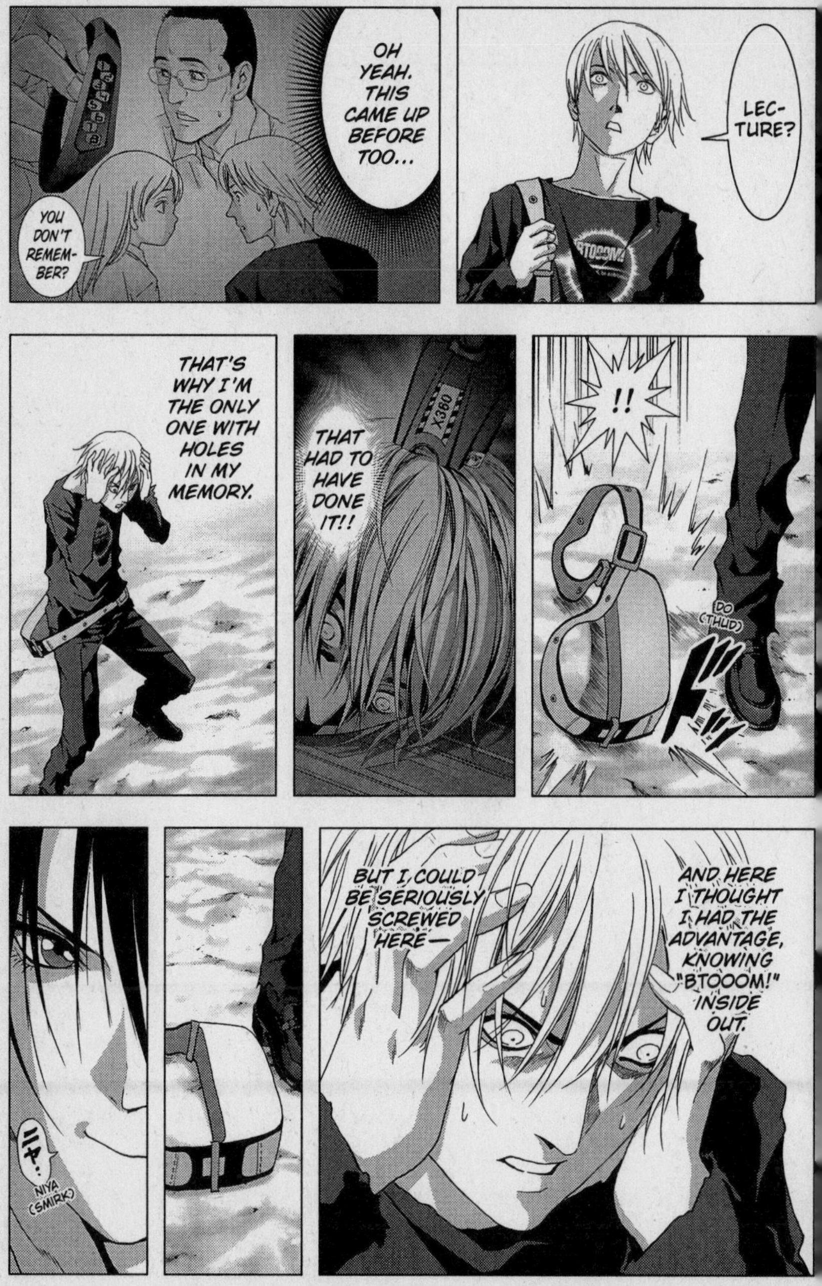
LEC-TURE?
OH YEAH. THIS CAME UP BEFORE TOO...
YOU DON'T REMEM-BER?
!!
DO (THUD)
THAT HAD TO HAVE DONE IT!!
THAT'S WHY I'M THE ONLY ONE WITH HOLES IN MY MEMORY.
AND HERE I THOUGHT I HAD THE ADVANTAGE, KNOWING "BTOOOM!" INSIDE OUT.
BUT I COULD BE SERIOUSLY SCREWED HERE—
ニヤ…
NIYA (SMIRK)

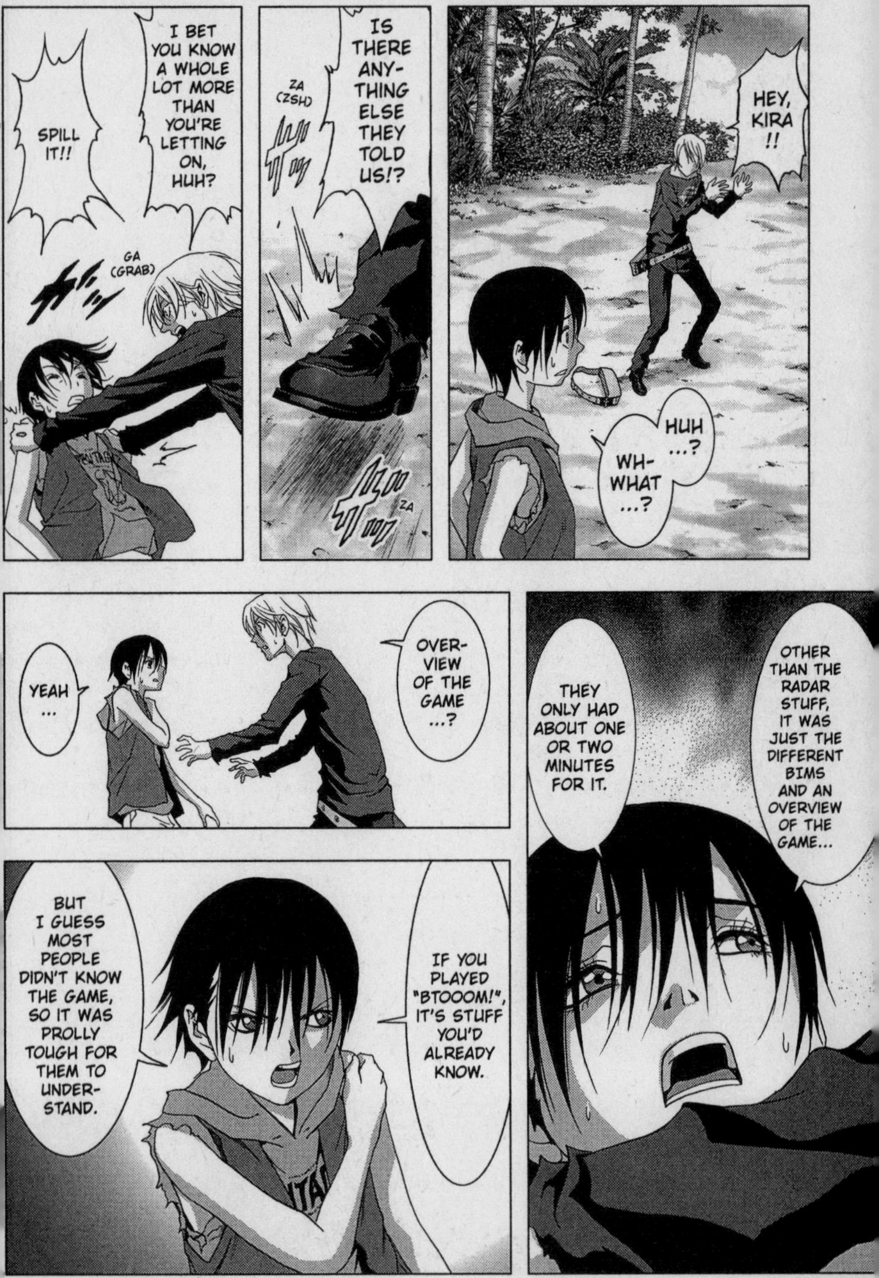
HEY, KIRA!!
HUH...?
WH-WHAT...?
IS THERE ANYTHING ELSE THEY TOLD US!?
ZA (ZSH)
ZA
I BET YOU KNOW A WHOLE LOT MORE THAN YOU'RE LETTING ON, HUH?
SPILL IT!!
GA (GRAB)
OTHER THAN THE RADAR STUFF, IT WAS JUST THE DIFFERENT BIMS AND AN OVERVIEW OF THE GAME...
THEY ONLY HAD ABOUT ONE OR TWO MINUTES FOR IT.
OVERVIEW OF THE GAME...?
YEAH...
IF YOU PLAYED "BTOOOM!", IT'S STUFF YOU'D ALREADY KNOW.
BUT I GUESS MOST PEOPLE DIDN'T KNOW THE GAME, SO IT WAS PROLLY TOUGH FOR THEM TO UNDERSTAND.

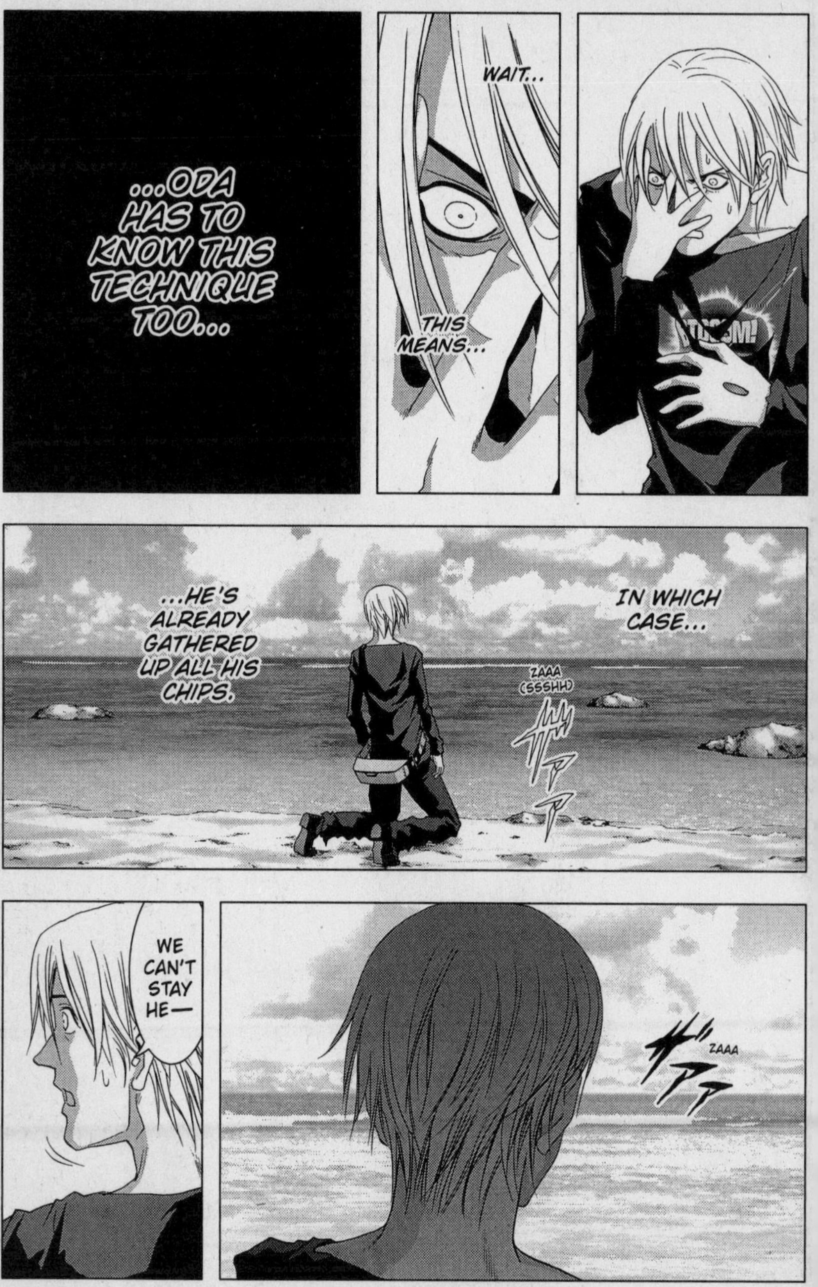
WAIT...
THIS MEANS...
...ODA HAS TO KNOW THIS TECHNIQUE TOO...
IN WHICH CASE...
ZAAA (SSSHH)
...HE'S ALREADY GATHERED UP ALL HIS CHIPS.
ZAAA
WE CAN'T STAY HE—

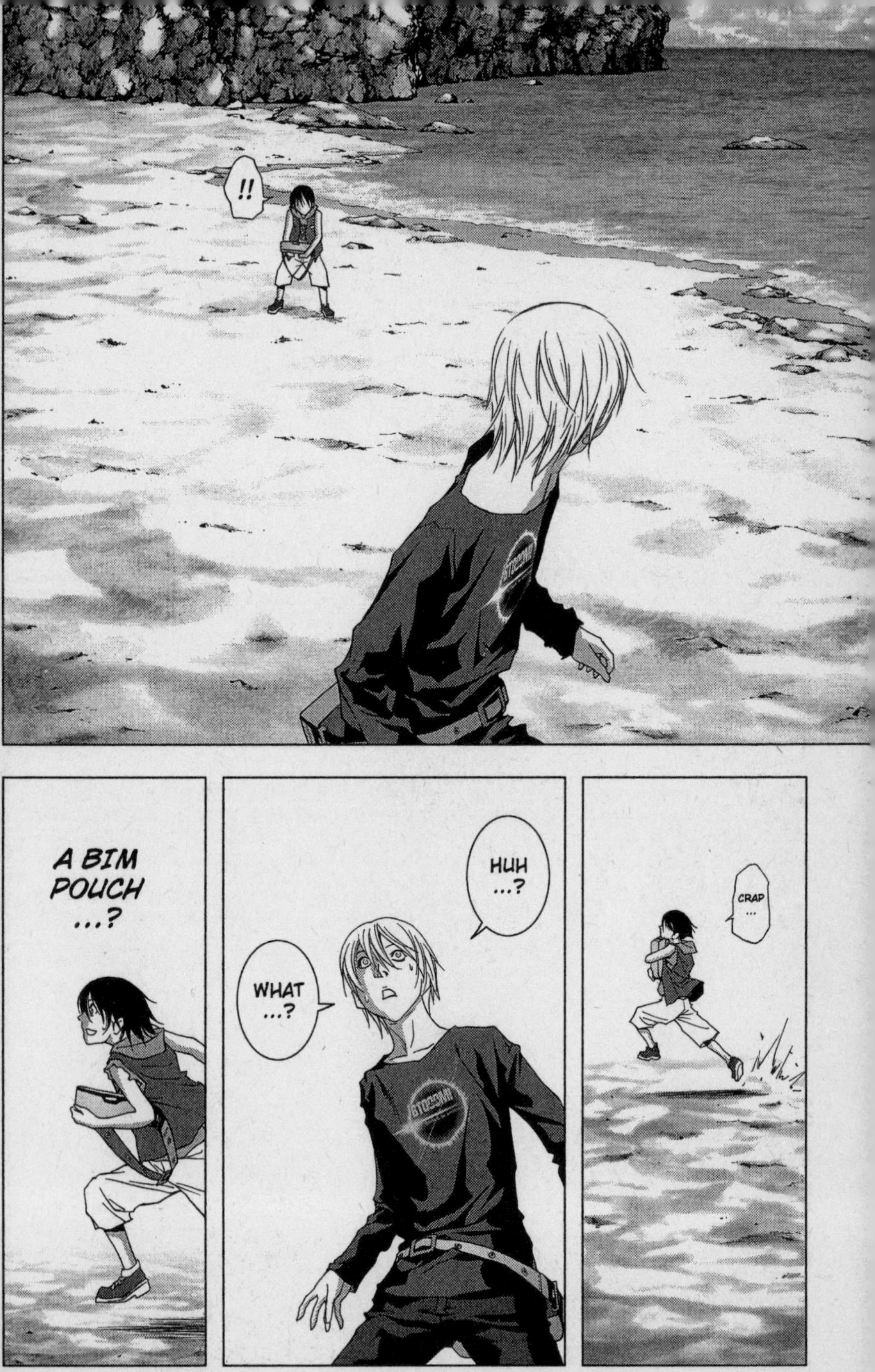
!!
CRAP ...
HUH ...?
WHAT ...?
A BIM POUCH ...?

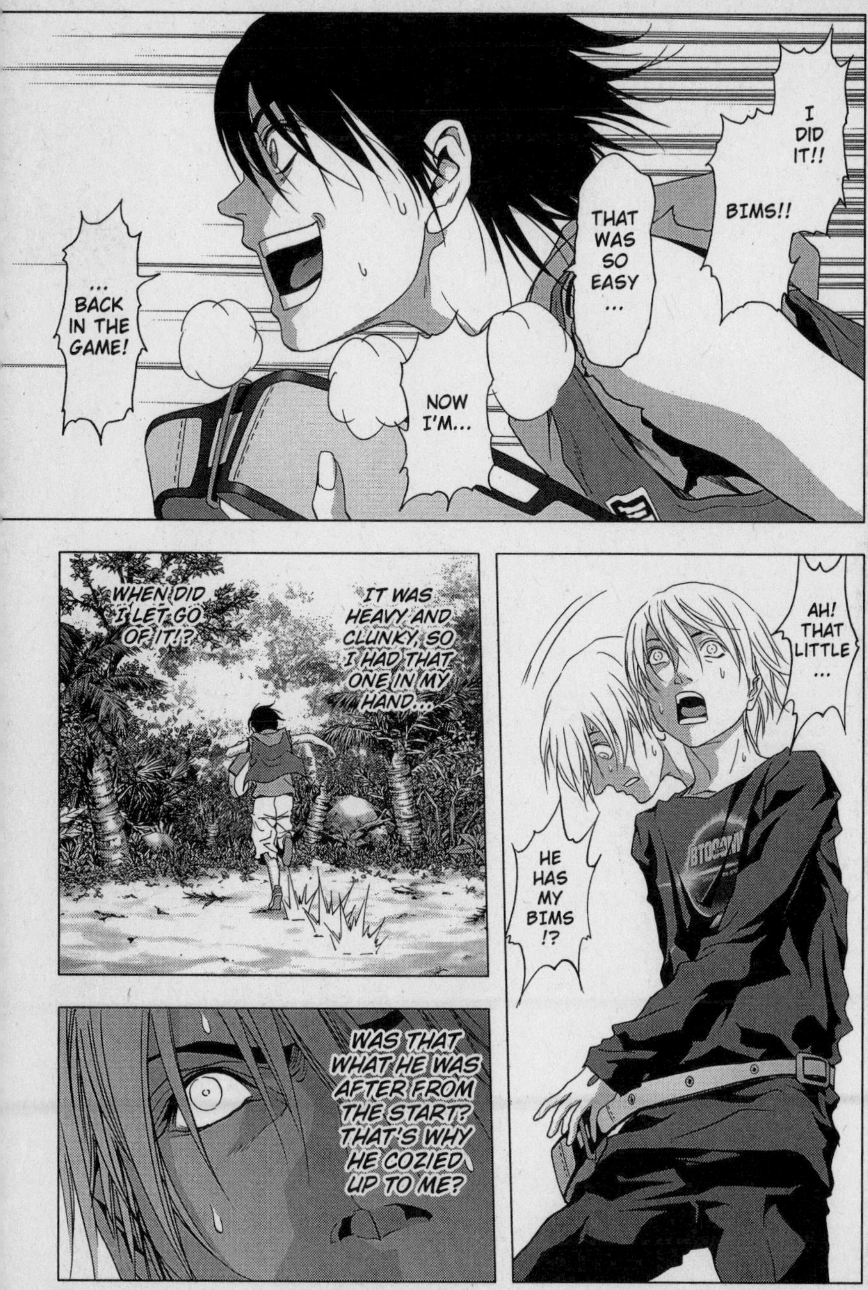
I DID IT!!
BIMS!!
THAT WAS SO EASY...
NOW I'M...
...BACK IN THE GAME!
AH! THAT LITTLE...
HE HAS MY BIMS!?
IT WAS HEAVY AND CLUNKY, SO I HAD THAT ONE IN MY HAND...
WHEN DID I LET GO OF IT!?
WAS THAT WHAT HE WAS AFTER FROM THE START? THAT'S WHY HE COZIED UP TO ME?

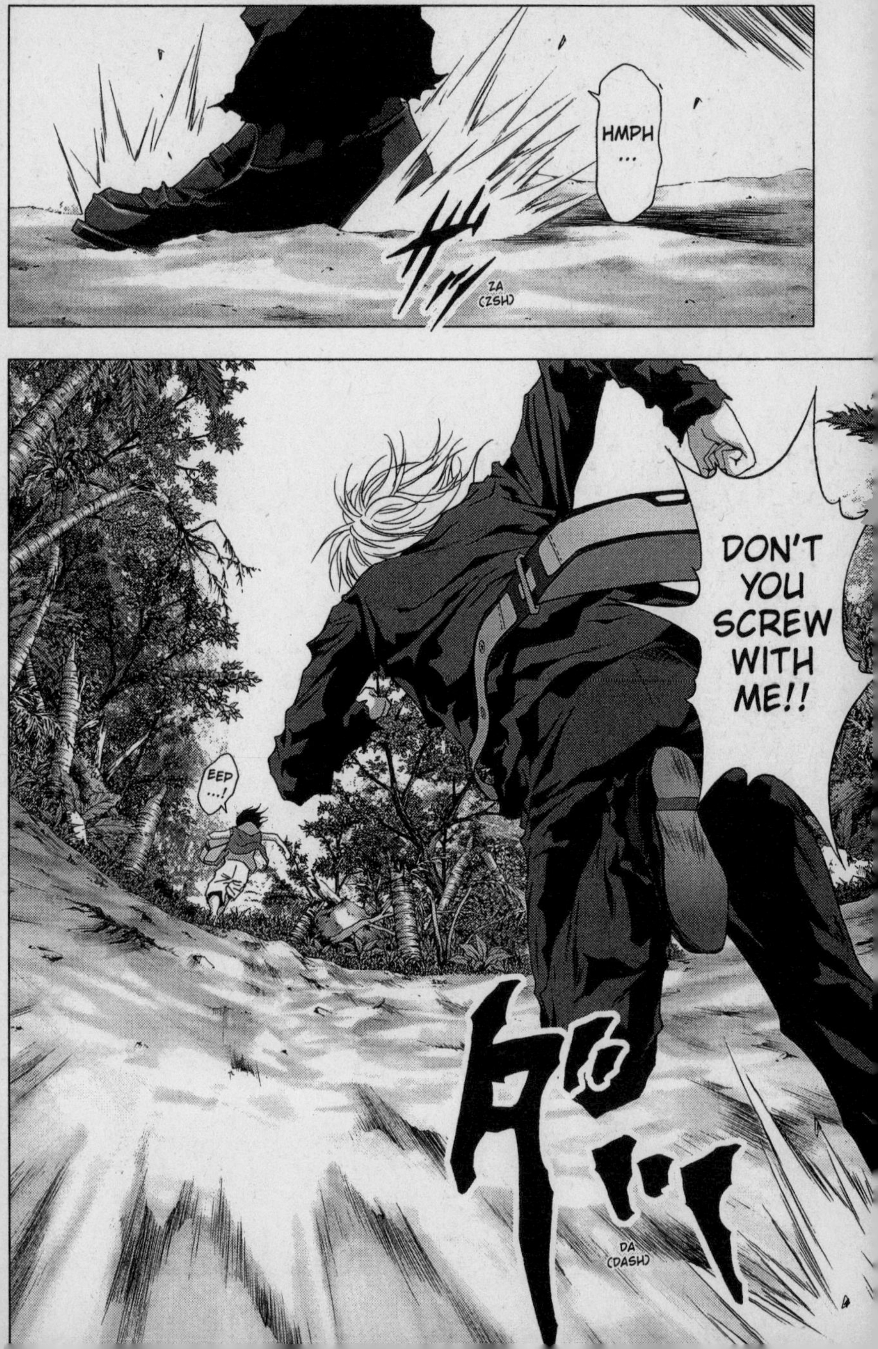
HMPH ...
ZA (ZSH)
DON'T YOU SCREW WITH ME!!
EEP ...!
DA (DASH)

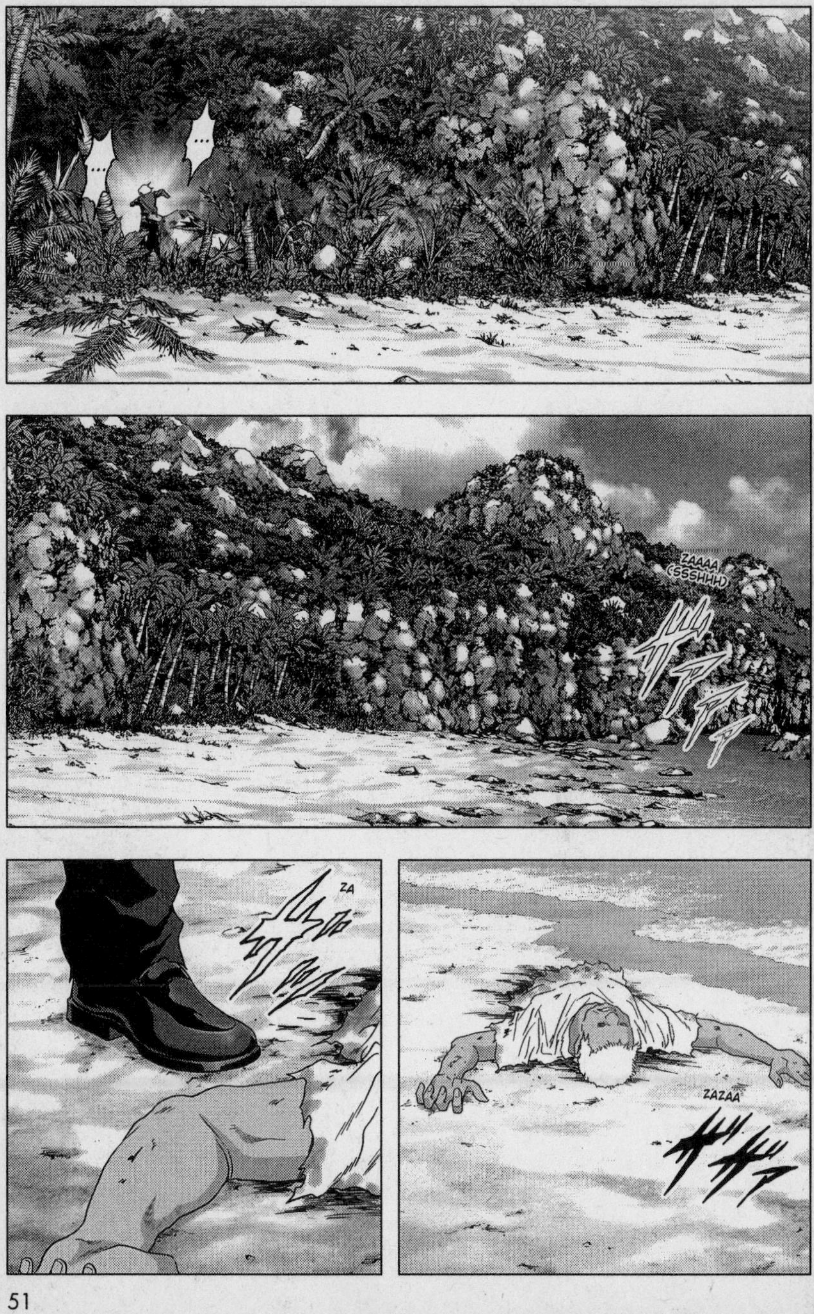
...
...
ZAAAA (SSSHHH)
ZAZAA
ZA

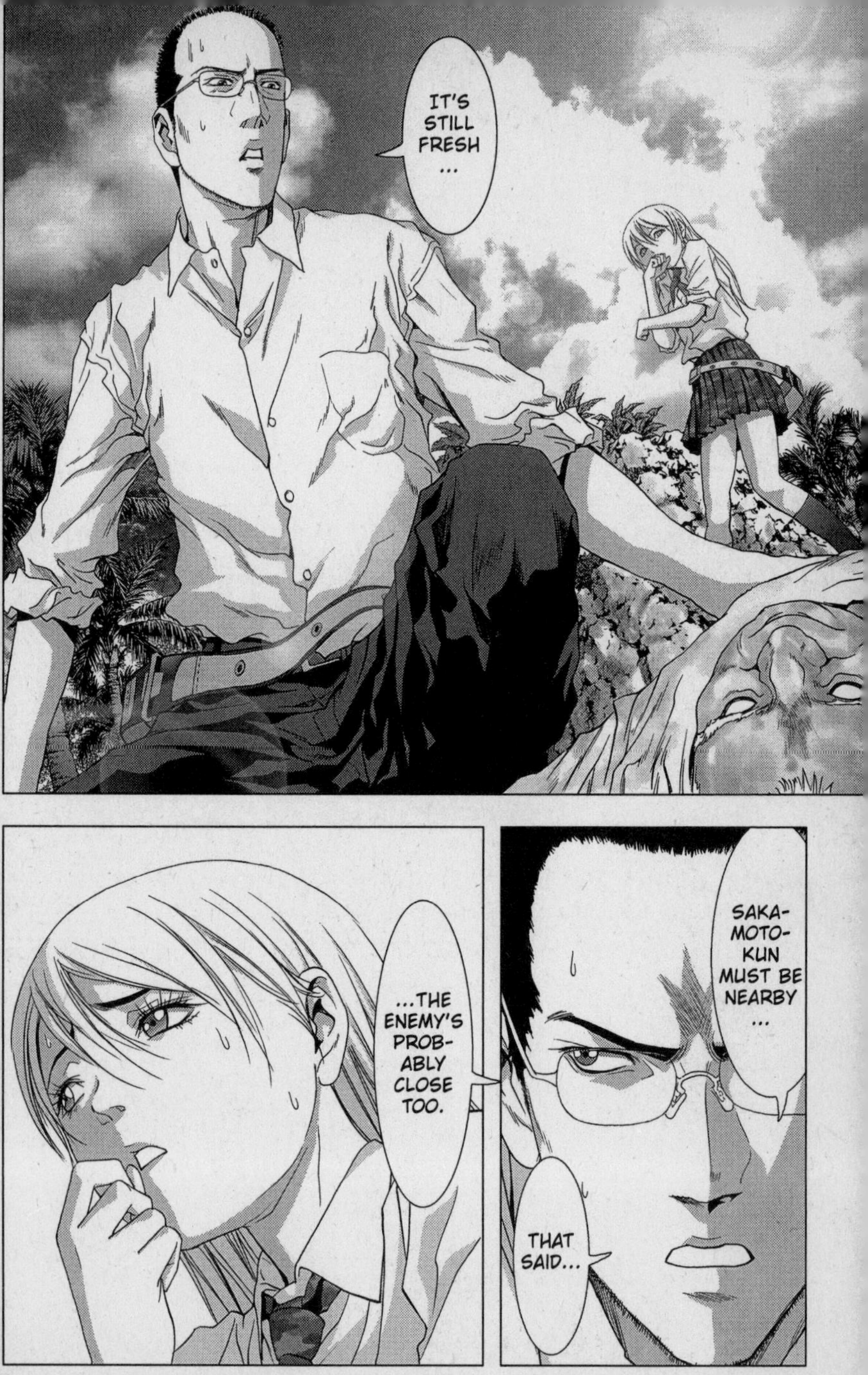
IT'S STILL FRESH...
SAKA-MOTO-KUN MUST BE NEARBY...
THAT SAID...
...THE ENEMY'S PROB-ABLY CLOSE TOO.

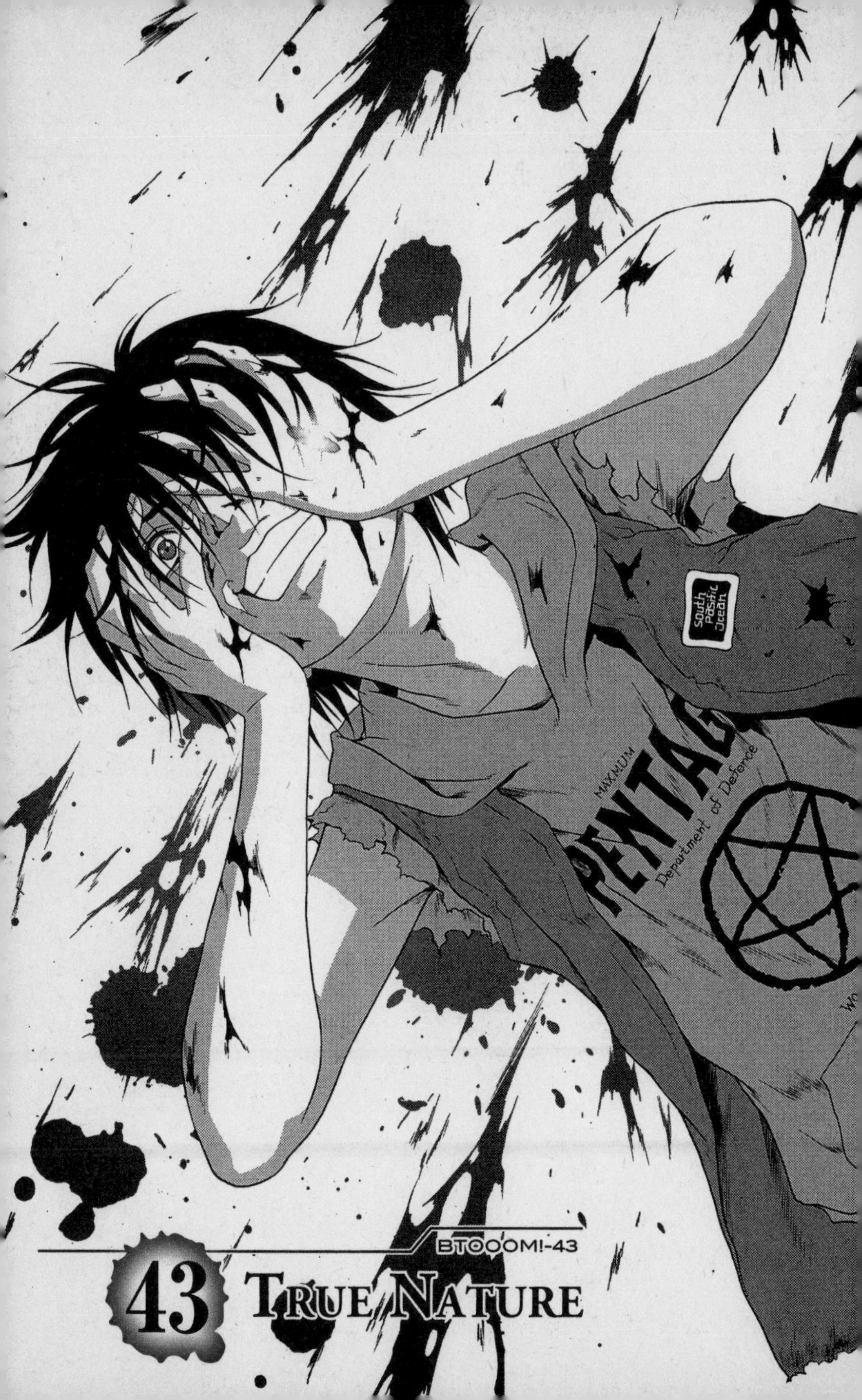
south Pacific Ocean
MAXIMUM
PENTAG
Department of Defence

BTOOOM!-43

43 TRUE NATURE

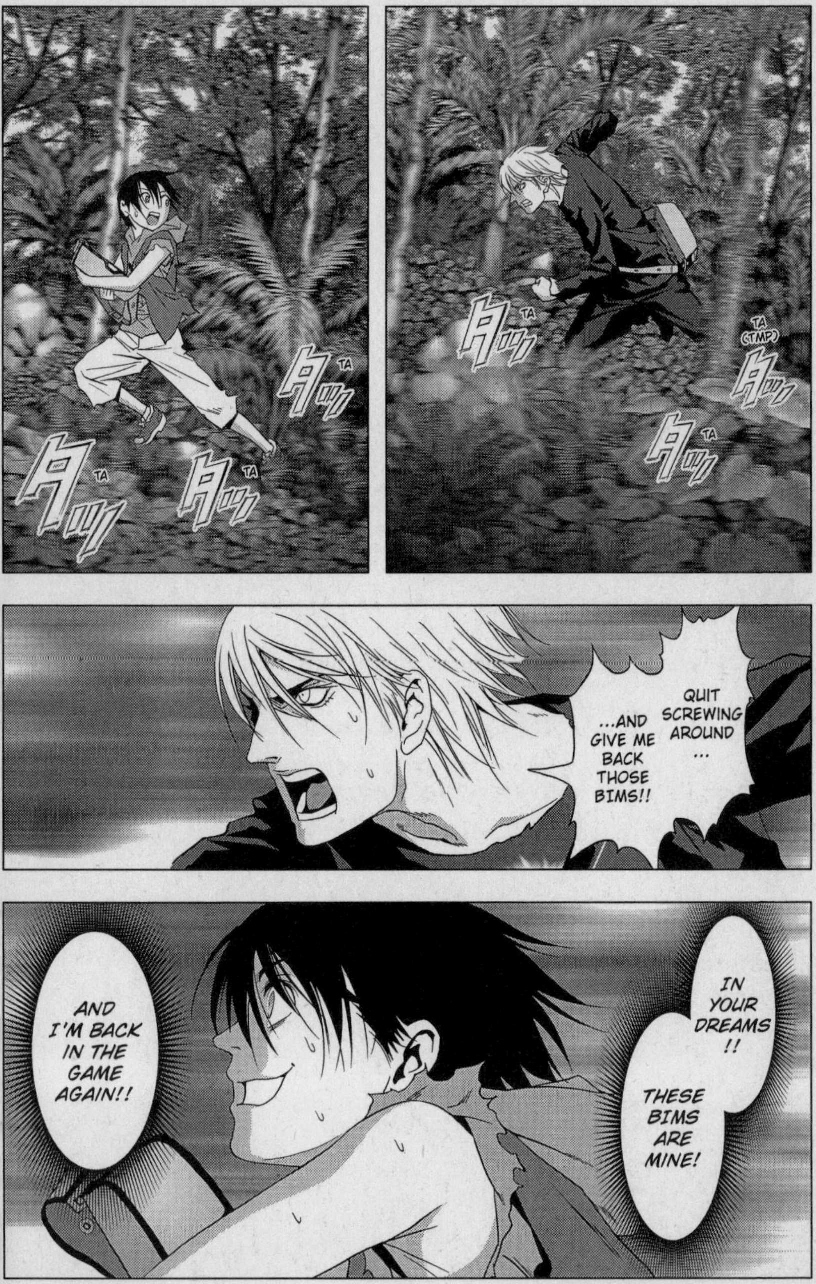
TA (TMP)
TA
TA
TA
TA
TA
QUIT SCREWING AROUND...
...AND GIVE ME BACK THOSE BIMS!!
IN YOUR DREAMS!!
THESE BIMS ARE MINE!
AND I'M BACK IN THE GAME AGAIN!!

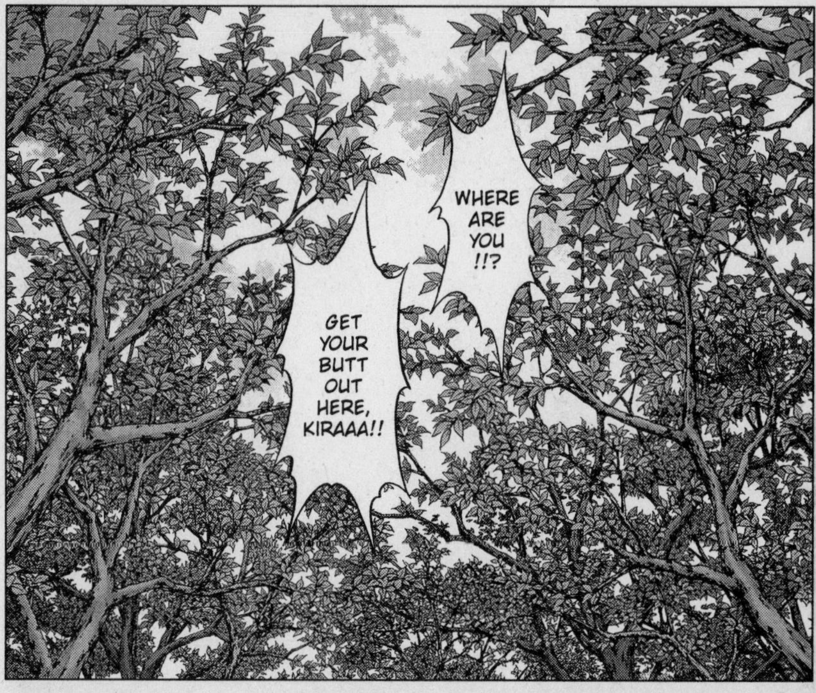
WHERE ARE YOU !!?
GET YOUR BUTT OUT HERE, KIRAAA!!
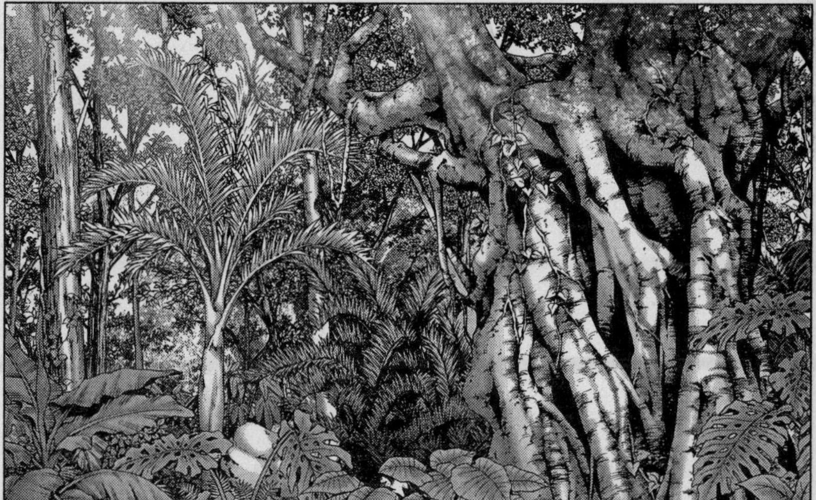

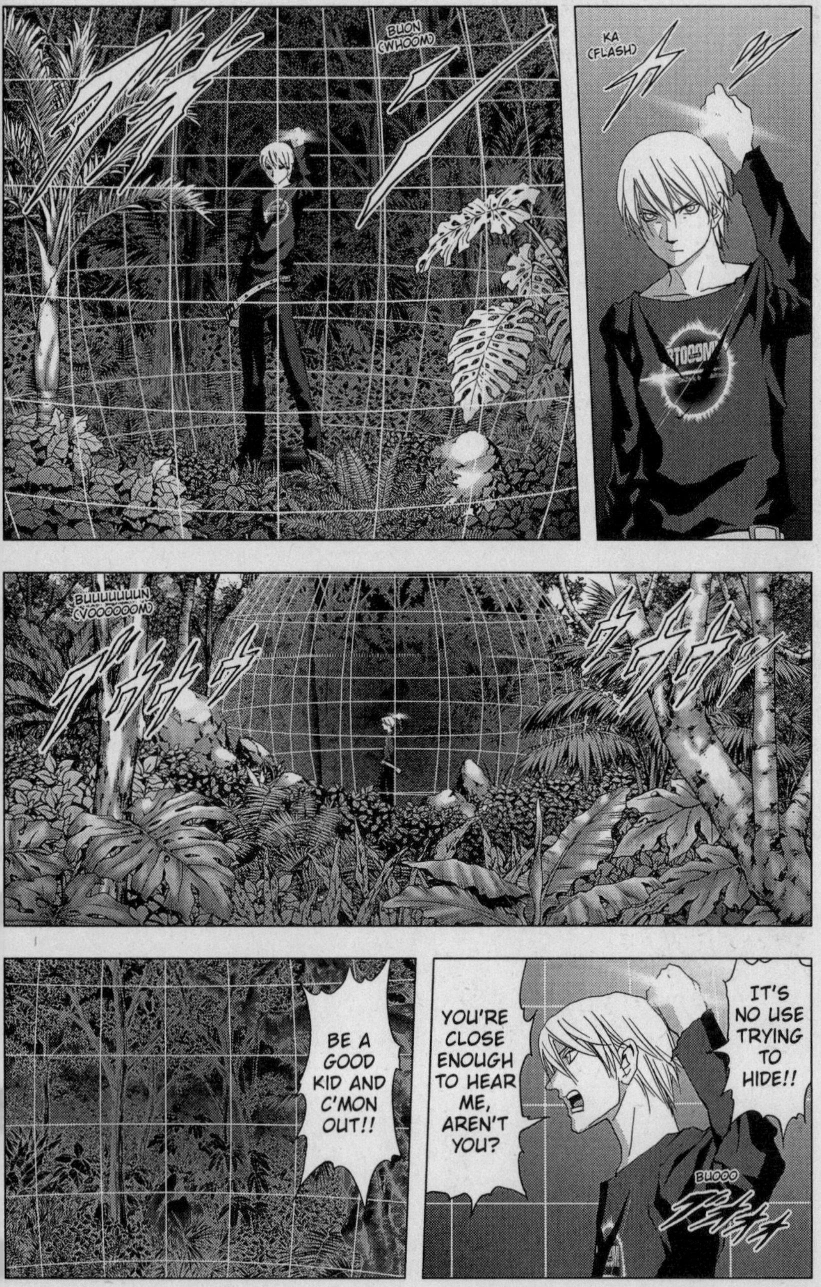
KA (FLASH)
BUON (WHOOM)
BUUUUUUUUN (VOOOOOOOM)
IT'S NO USE TRYING TO HIDE!!
YOU'RE CLOSE ENOUGH TO HEAR ME, AREN'T YOU?
BUOOO
BE A GOOD KID AND C'MON OUT!!

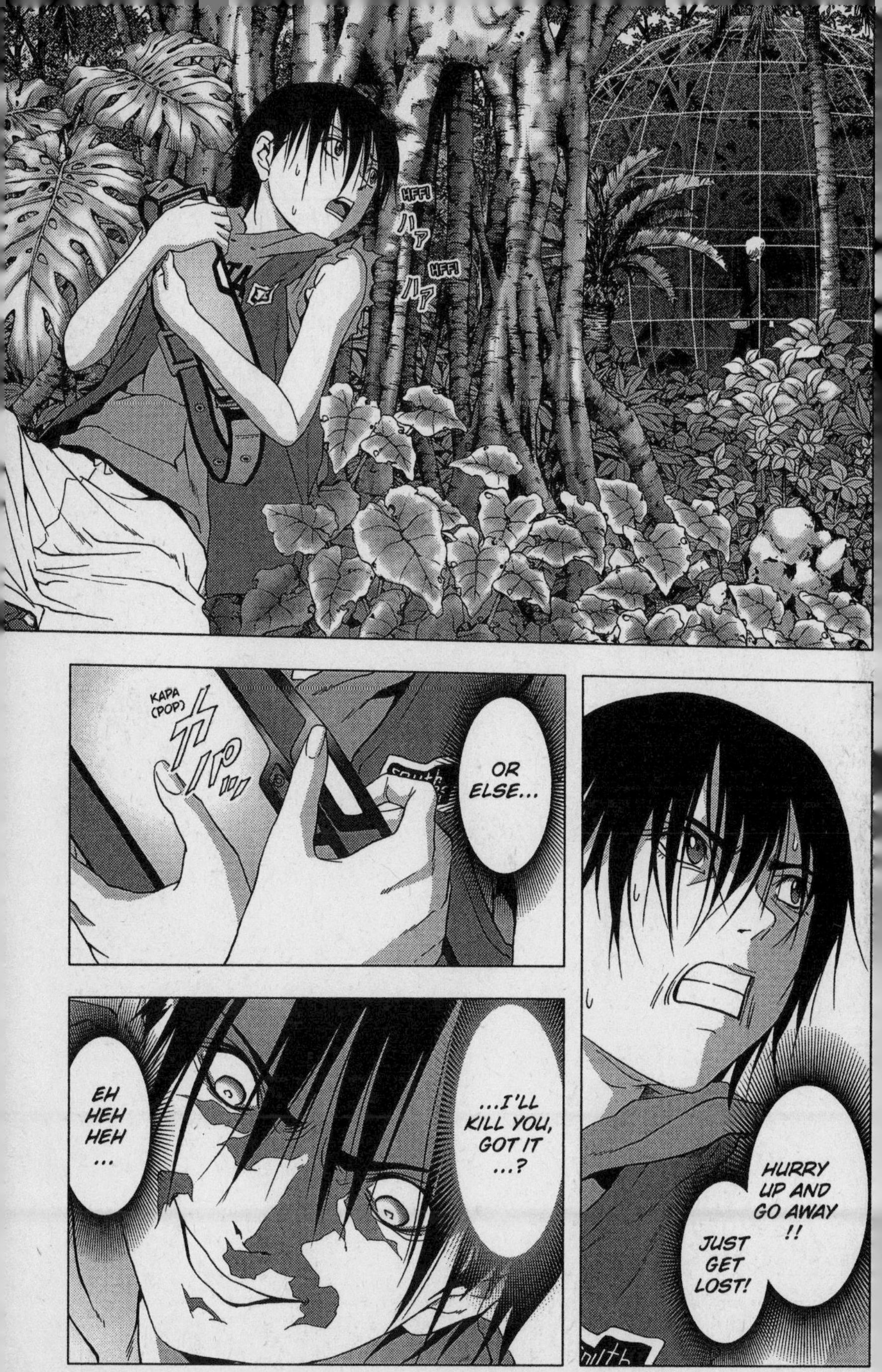
HFF!
ハア
HFF!
ハア
HURRY UP AND GO AWAY !!
JUST GET LOST!
OR ELSE...
KAPA (POP)
カパッ
...I'LL KILL YOU, GOT IT ...?
EH HEH HEH ...

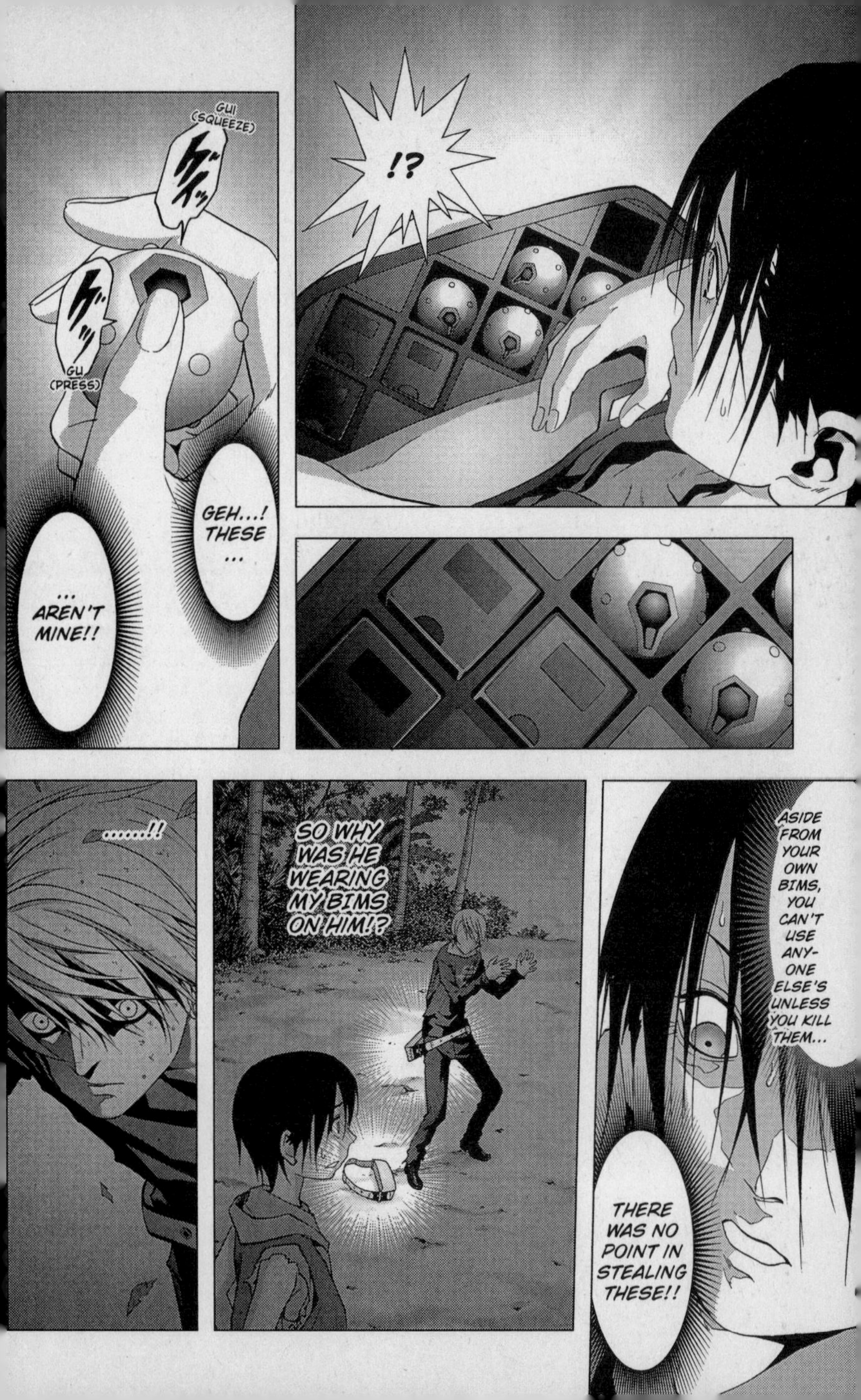
!?
GUI (SQUEEZE)
GU (PRESS)
GEH...! THESE ...
... AREN'T MINE!!
ASIDE FROM YOUR OWN BIMS, YOU CAN'T USE ANYONE ELSE'S UNLESS YOU KILL THEM...
THERE WAS NO POINT IN STEALING THESE!!
SO WHY WAS HE WEARING MY BIMS ON HIM!?
......!!

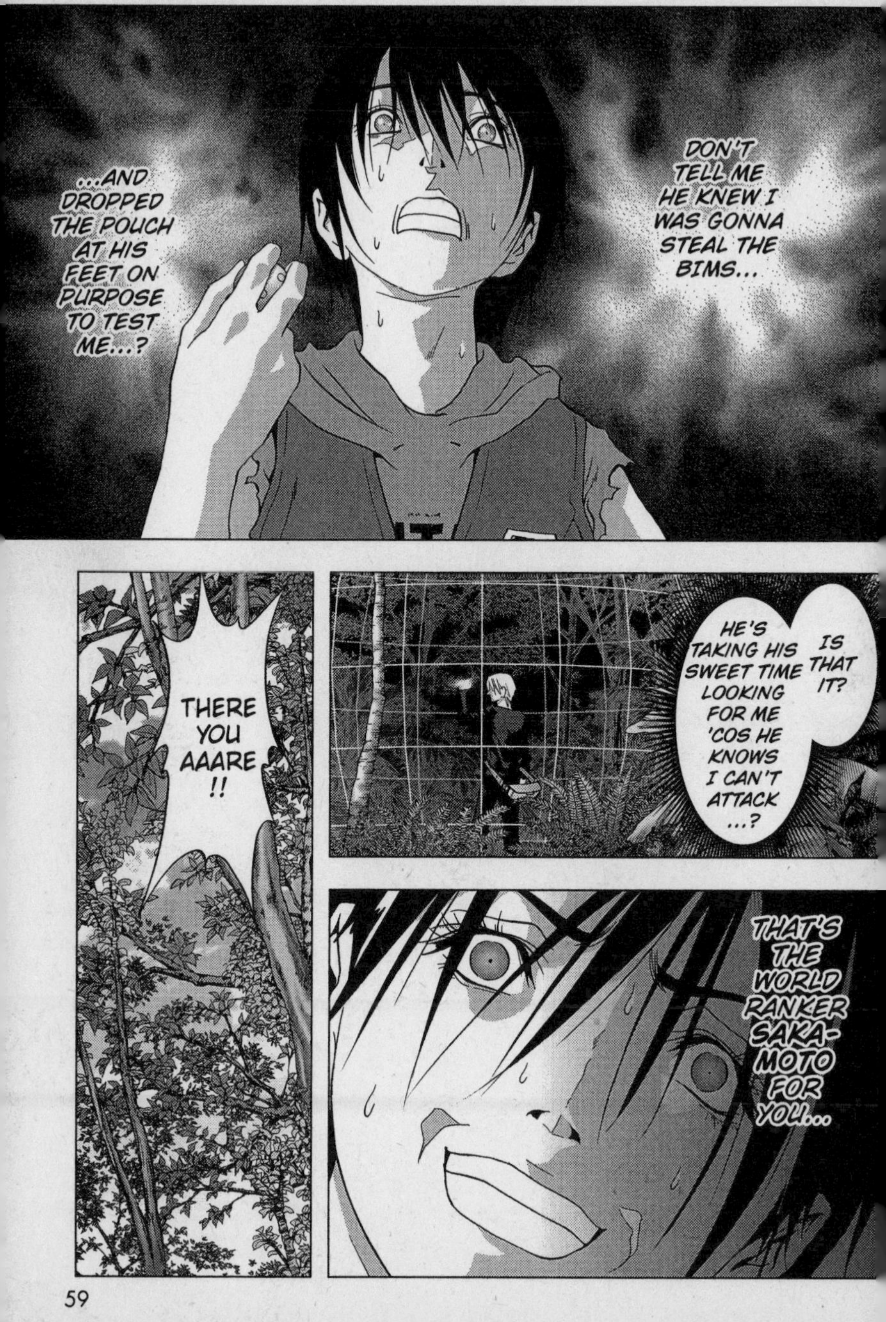
DON'T TELL ME HE KNEW I WAS GONNA STEAL THE BIMS...
...AND DROPPED THE POUCH AT HIS FEET ON PURPOSE TO TEST ME...?
HE'S TAKING HIS SWEET TIME LOOKING FOR ME 'COS HE KNOWS I CAN'T ATTACK...?
IS THAT IT?
THAT'S THE WORLD RANKER SAKA-MOTO FOR YOU...
THERE YOU AAARE!!

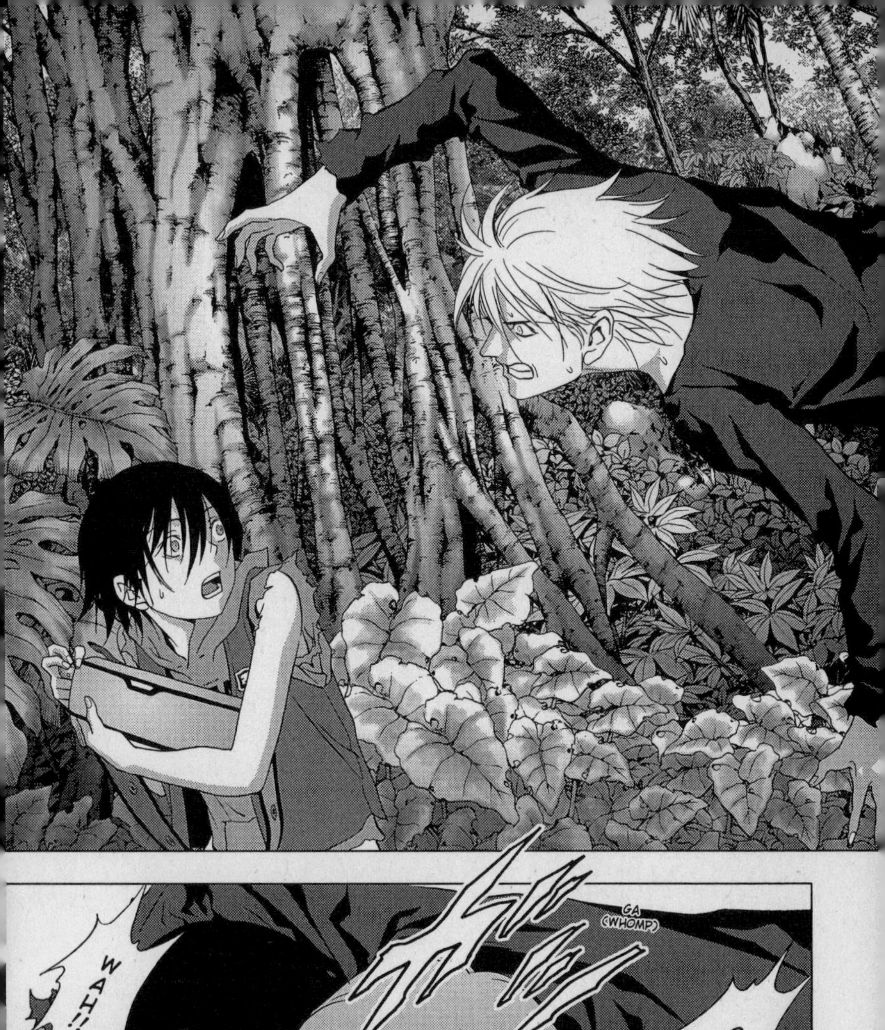

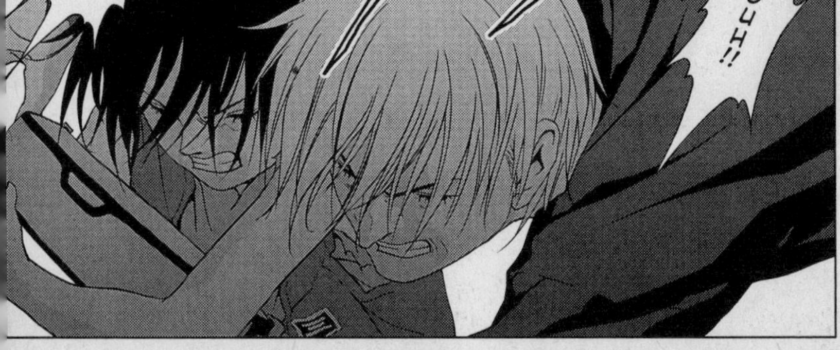
GA
(WHOMP)
GUH!!
WAH!!

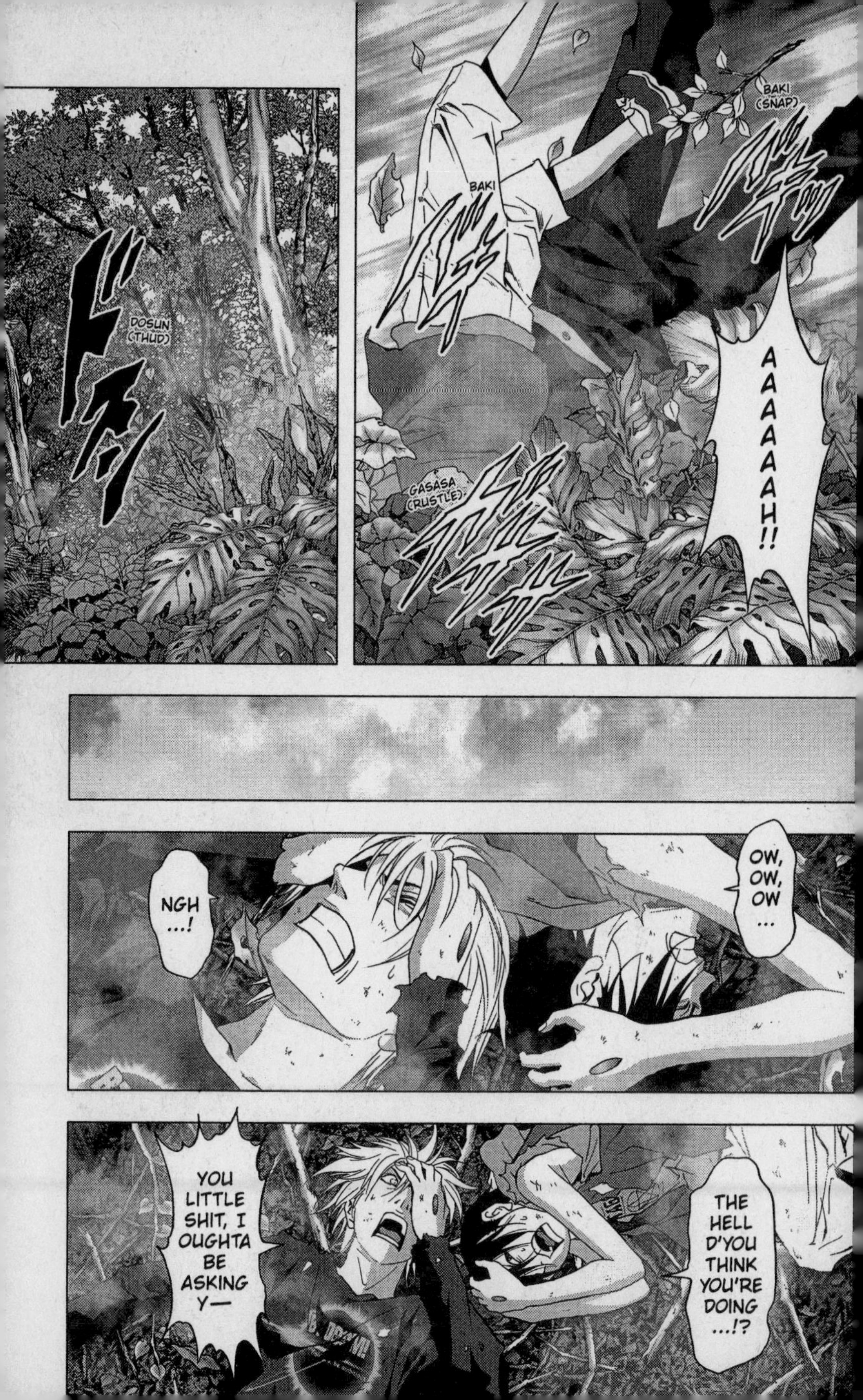
BAKI (SNAP)
BAKI
AAAAAAAH!!
GASASA (RUSTLE)
DOSUN (THUD)
OW, OW, OW ...
NGH ...!
THE HELL D'YOU THINK YOU'RE DOING ...!?
YOU LITTLE SHIT, I OUGHTA BE ASKING Y—

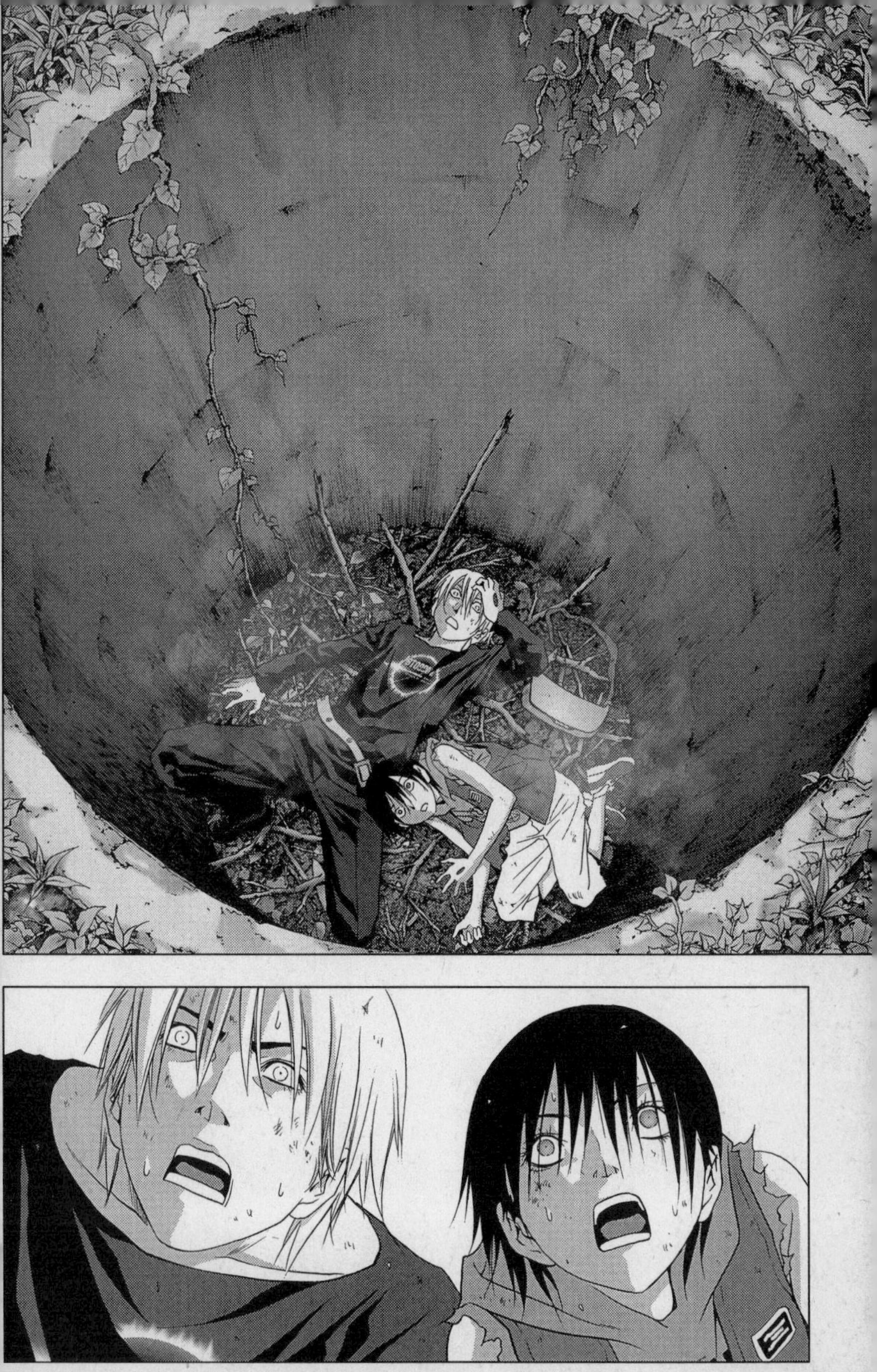

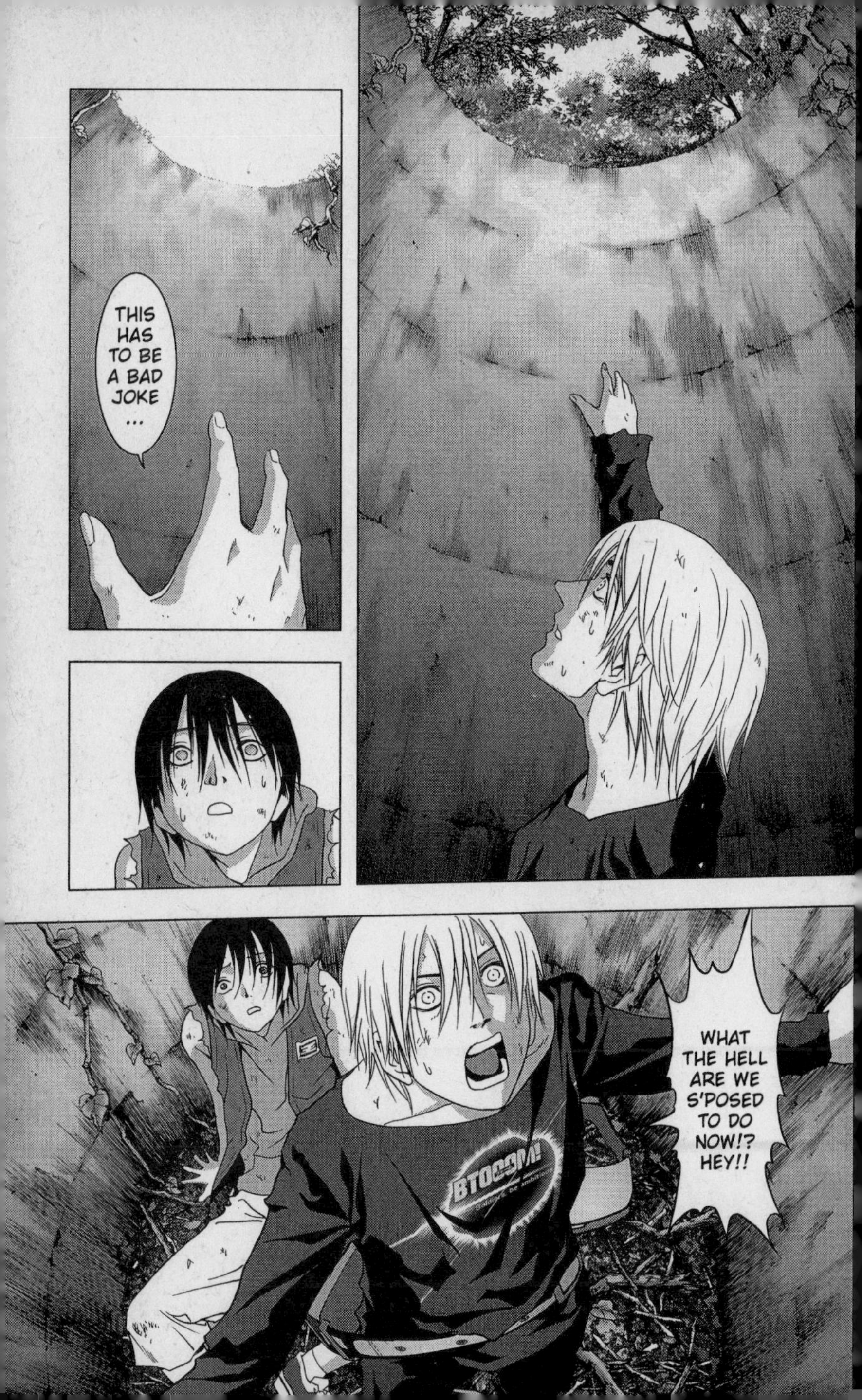
THIS HAS TO BE A BAD JOKE ...
WHAT THE HELL ARE WE S'POSED TO DO NOW!? HEY!!

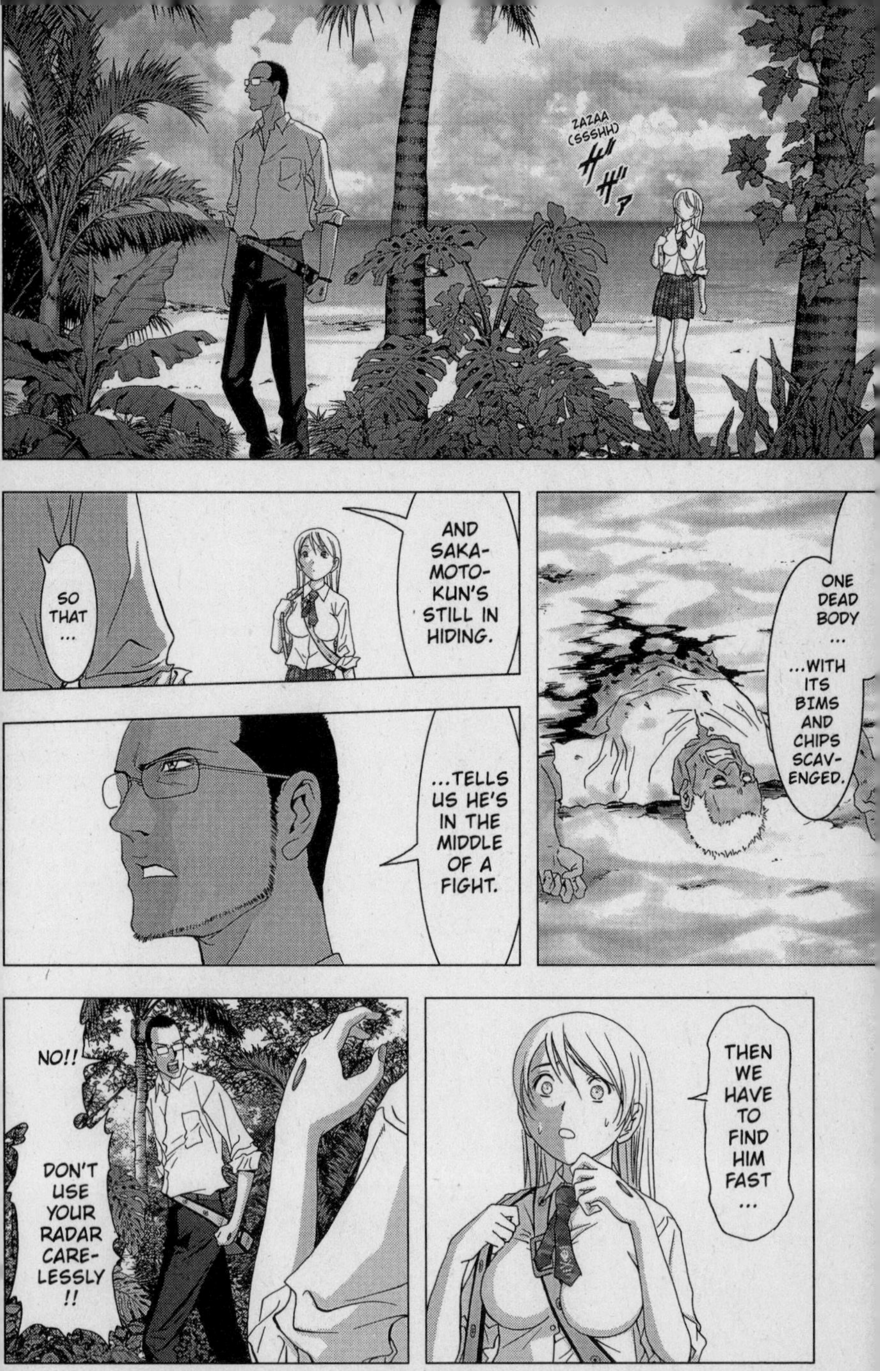
ZAZAA (SSSHH)
ザザァ
ONE DEAD BODY ...
...WITH ITS BIMS AND CHIPS SCAVENGED.
AND SAKAMOTO-KUN'S STILL IN HIDING.
SO THAT ...
...TELLS US HE'S IN THE MIDDLE OF A FIGHT.
THEN WE HAVE TO FIND HIM FAST ...
NO!!
DON'T USE YOUR RADAR CARELESSLY!!

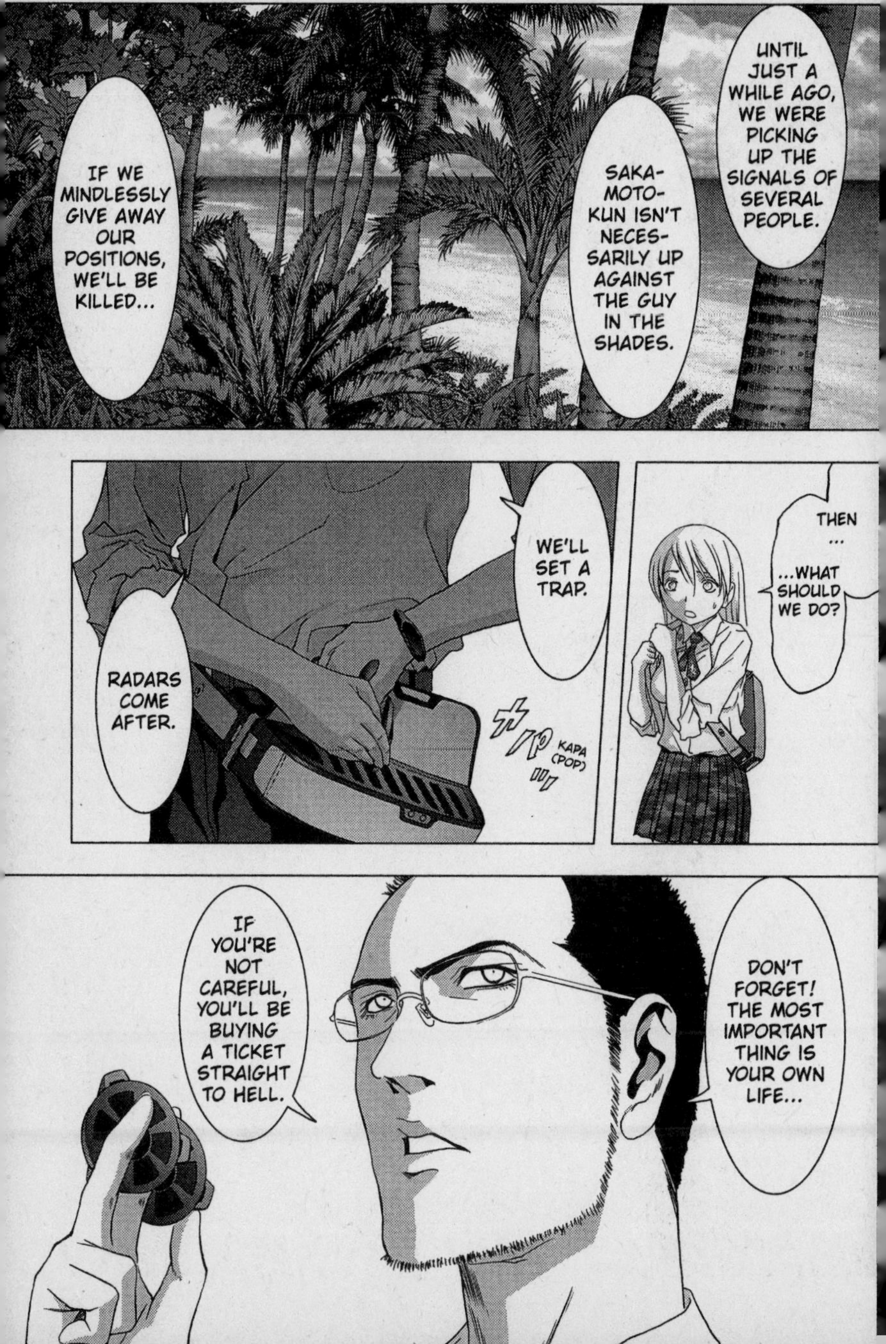
UNTIL JUST A WHILE AGO, WE WERE PICKING UP THE SIGNALS OF SEVERAL PEOPLE.
SAKAMOTO-KUN ISN'T NECESSARILY UP AGAINST THE GUY IN THE SHADES.
IF WE MINDLESSLY GIVE AWAY OUR POSITIONS, WE'LL BE KILLED...
THEN ...
...WHAT SHOULD WE DO?
WE'LL SET A TRAP.
KAPA (POP)
RADARS COME AFTER.
DON'T FORGET! THE MOST IMPORTANT THING IS YOUR OWN LIFE...
IF YOU'RE NOT CAREFUL, YOU'LL BE BUYING A TICKET STRAIGHT TO HELL.

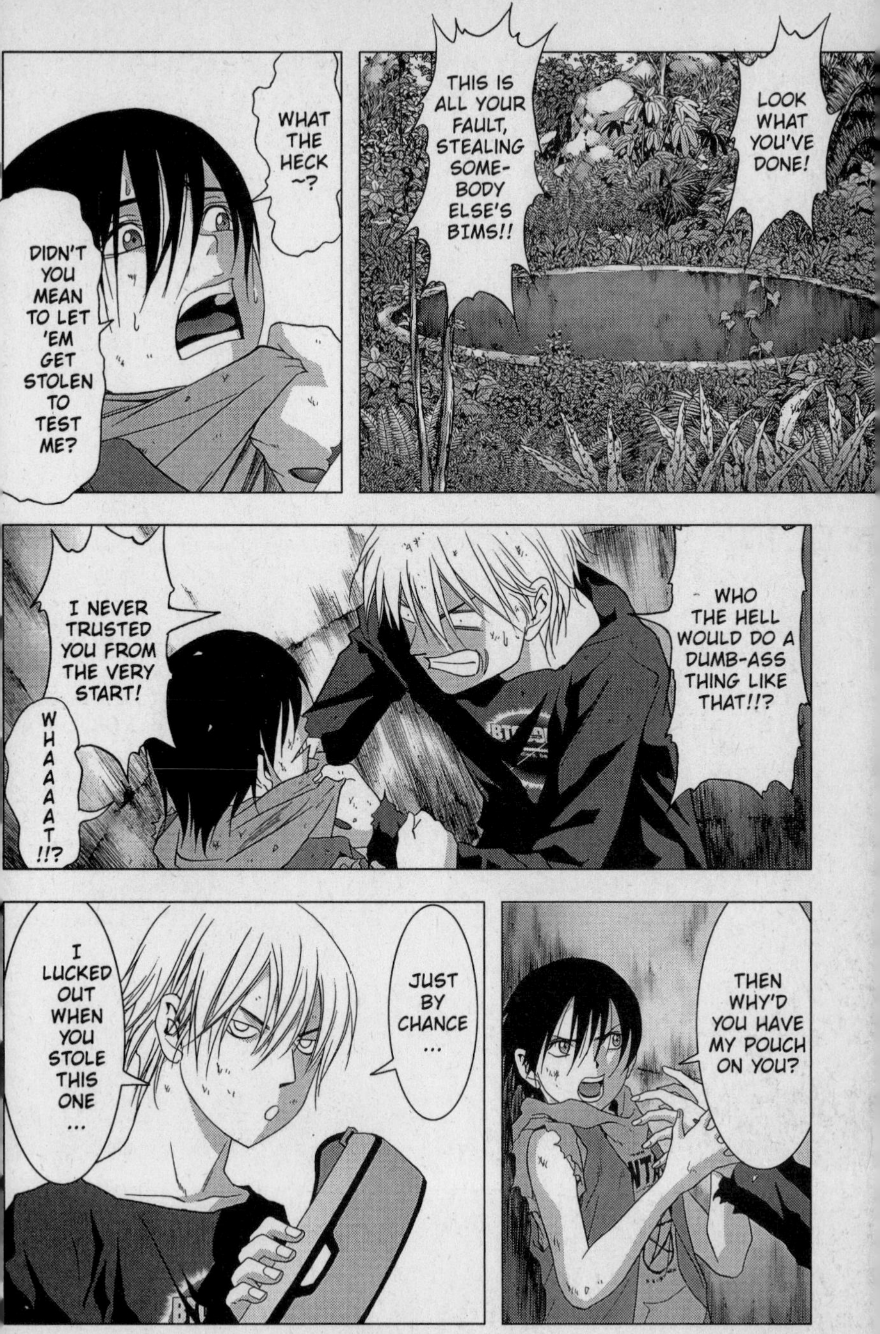
LOOK WHAT YOU'VE DONE!
THIS IS ALL YOUR FAULT, STEALING SOMEBODY ELSE'S BIMS!!
WHAT THE HECK ~?
DIDN'T YOU MEAN TO LET 'EM GET STOLEN TO TEST ME?
WHO THE HELL WOULD DO A DUMB-ASS THING LIKE THAT!!?
I NEVER TRUSTED YOU FROM THE VERY START!
WHAAAAAT!!?
THEN WHY'D YOU HAVE MY POUCH ON YOU?
JUST BY CHANCE ...
I LUCKED OUT WHEN YOU STOLE THIS ONE ...

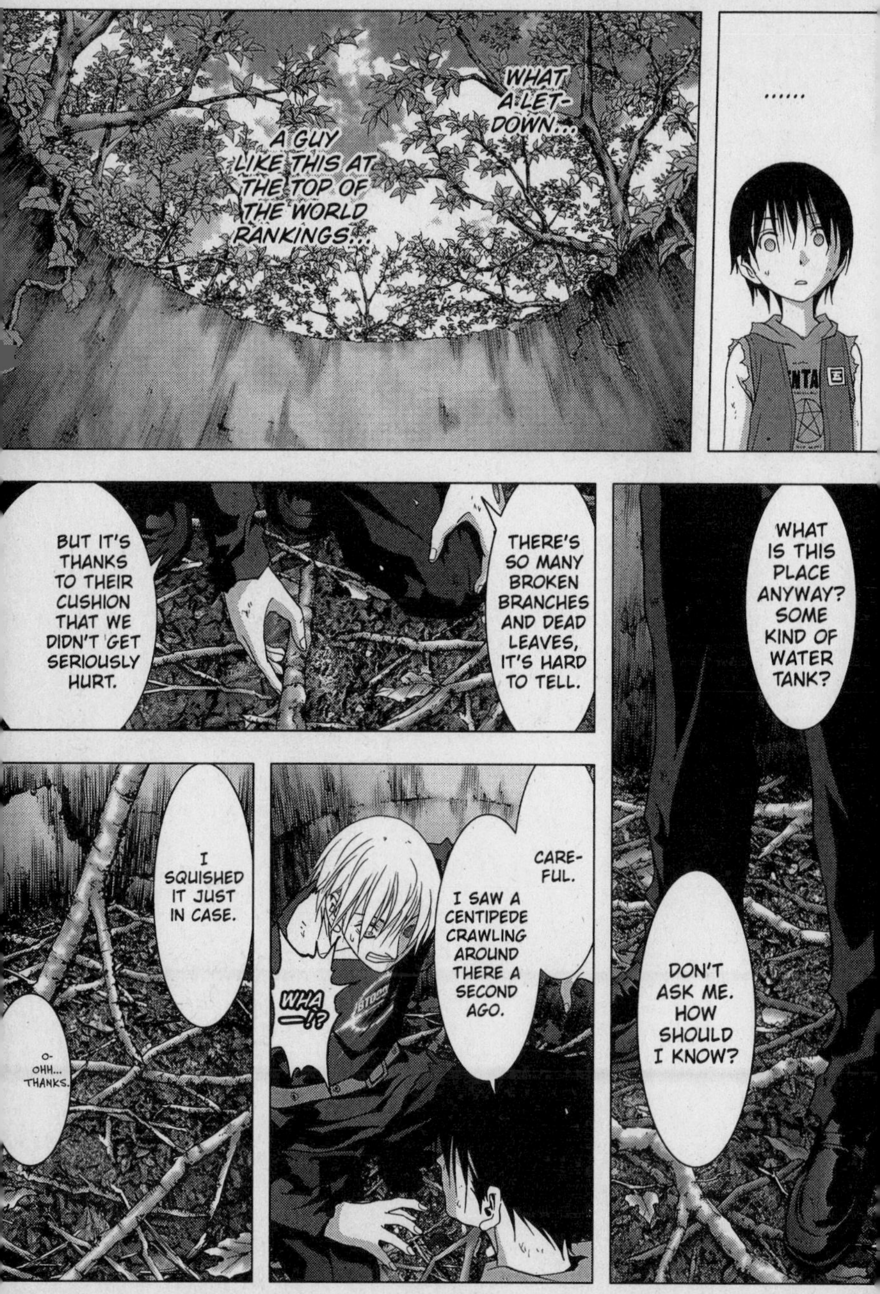
......
WHAT A LET-DOWN...
A GUY LIKE THIS AT THE TOP OF THE WORLD RANKINGS...
WHAT IS THIS PLACE ANYWAY? SOME KIND OF WATER TANK?
DON'T ASK ME. HOW SHOULD I KNOW?
THERE'S SO MANY BROKEN BRANCHES AND DEAD LEAVES, IT'S HARD TO TELL.
BUT IT'S THANKS TO THEIR CUSHION THAT WE DIDN'T GET SERIOUSLY HURT.
CARE-FUL.
I SAW A CENTIPEDE CRAWLING AROUND THERE A SECOND AGO.
WHA—!?
I SQUISHED IT JUST IN CASE.
O-OHH... THANKS.

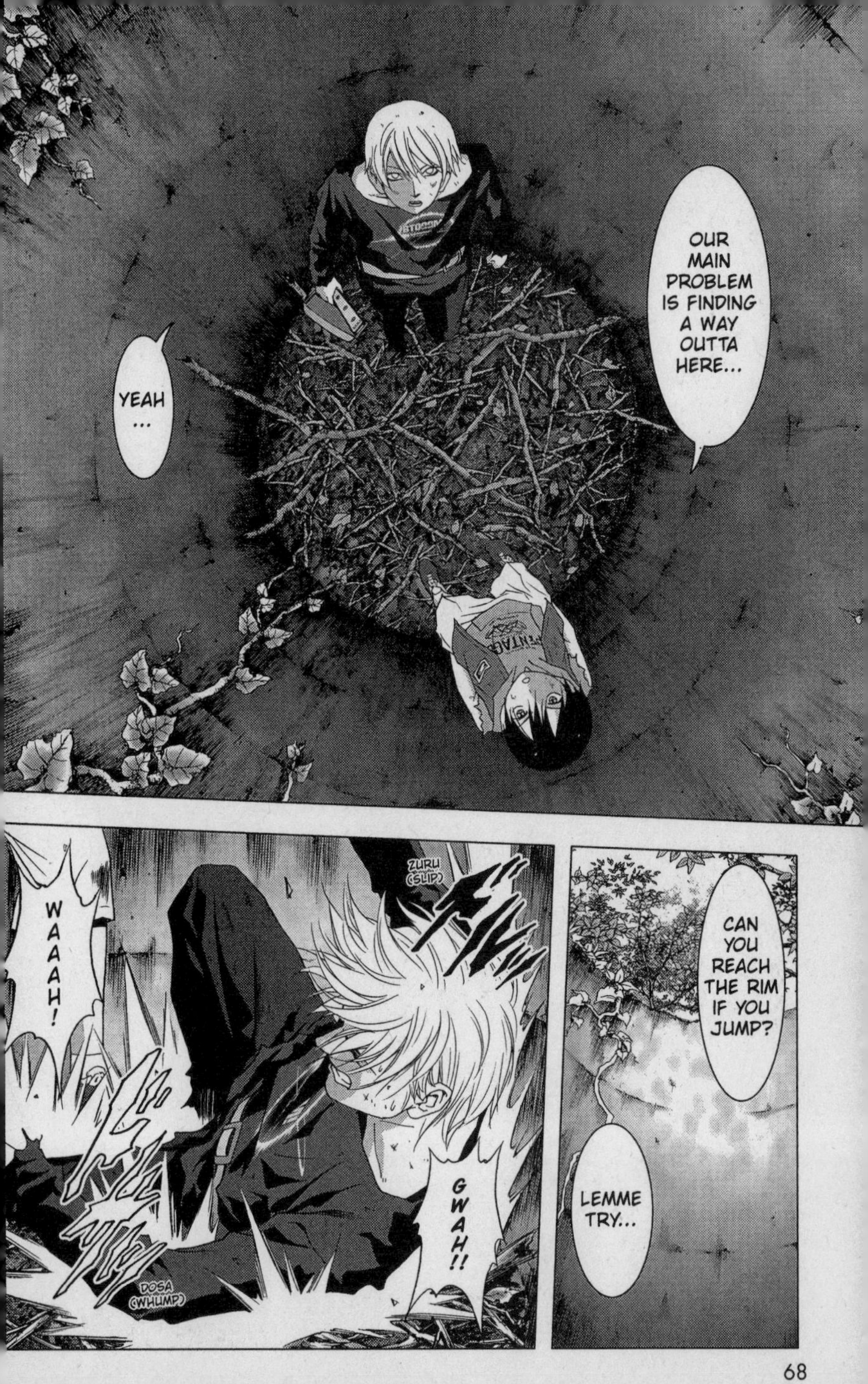
OUR MAIN PROBLEM IS FINDING A WAY OUTTA HERE...
YEAH...
CAN YOU REACH THE RIM IF YOU JUMP?
LEMME TRY...
ZURU (SLIP)
WAAAAH!
GWAH!!
DOSA (WHUMP)

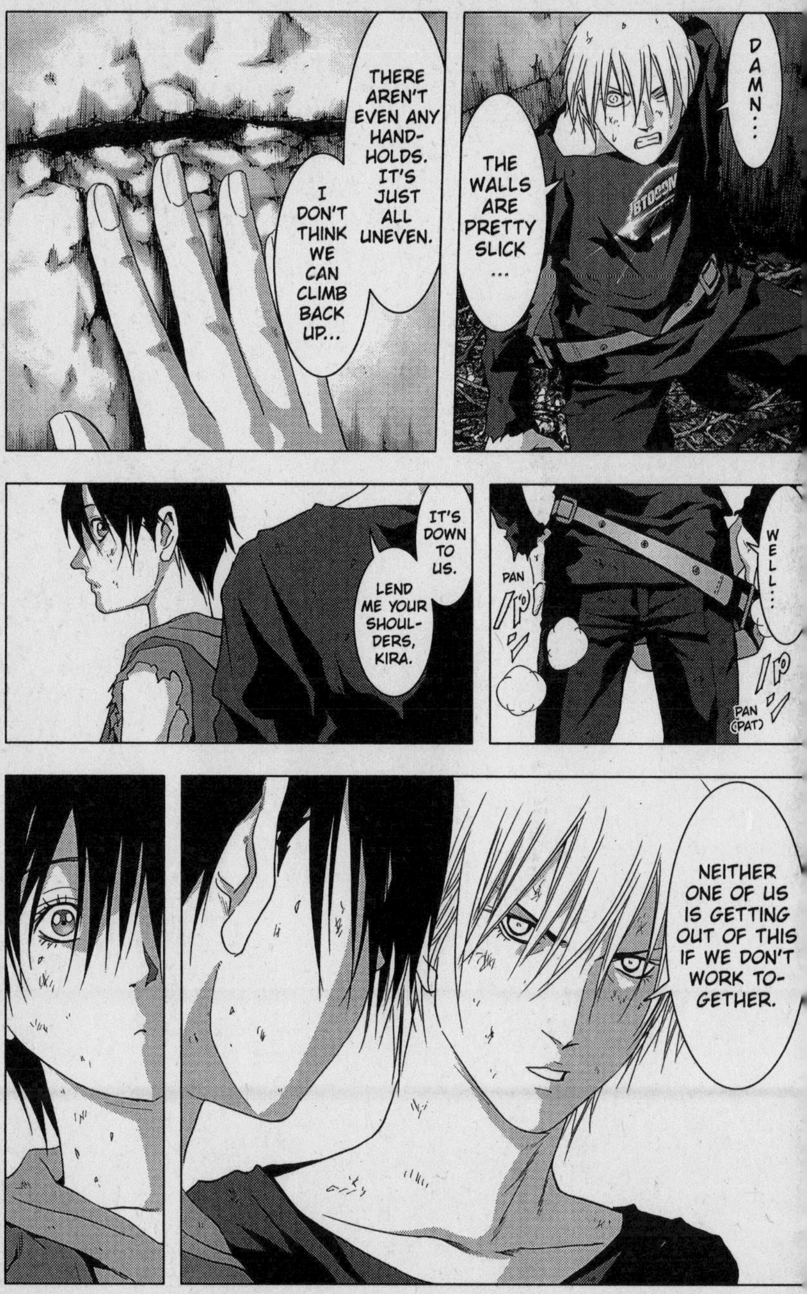
DAMN...
THE WALLS ARE PRETTY SLICK...
THERE AREN'T EVEN ANY HAND-HOLDS. IT'S JUST ALL UNEVEN.
I DON'T THINK WE CAN CLIMB BACK UP...
WELL...
PAN
PAN (PAT)
IT'S DOWN TO US.
LEND ME YOUR SHOUL-DERS, KIRA.
NEITHER ONE OF US IS GETTING OUT OF THIS IF WE DON'T WORK TO-GETHER.

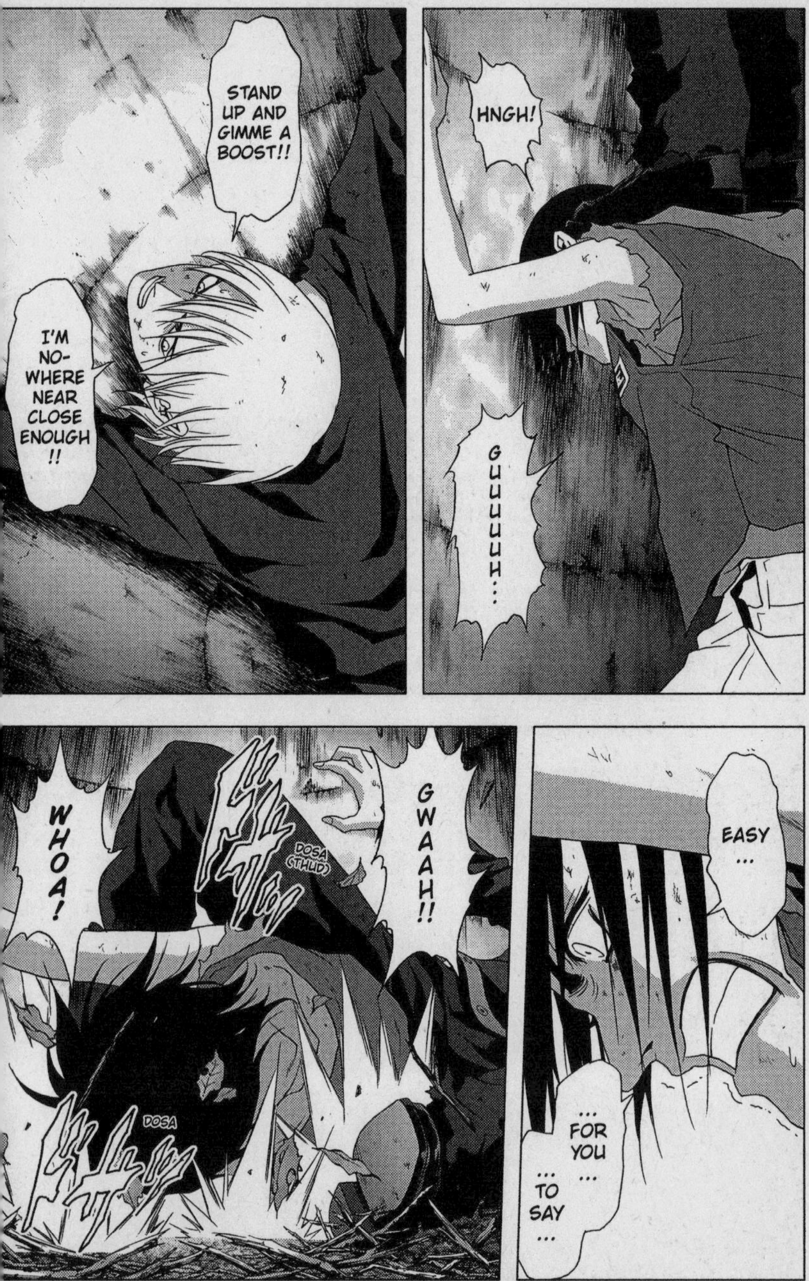
HNGH!
GUUUUUH...
STAND UP AND GIMME A BOOST!!
I'M NO-WHERE NEAR CLOSE ENOUGH!!
EASY...
...FOR YOU...
...TO SAY...
GWAAH!!
DOSA (THUD)
WHOA!
DOSA

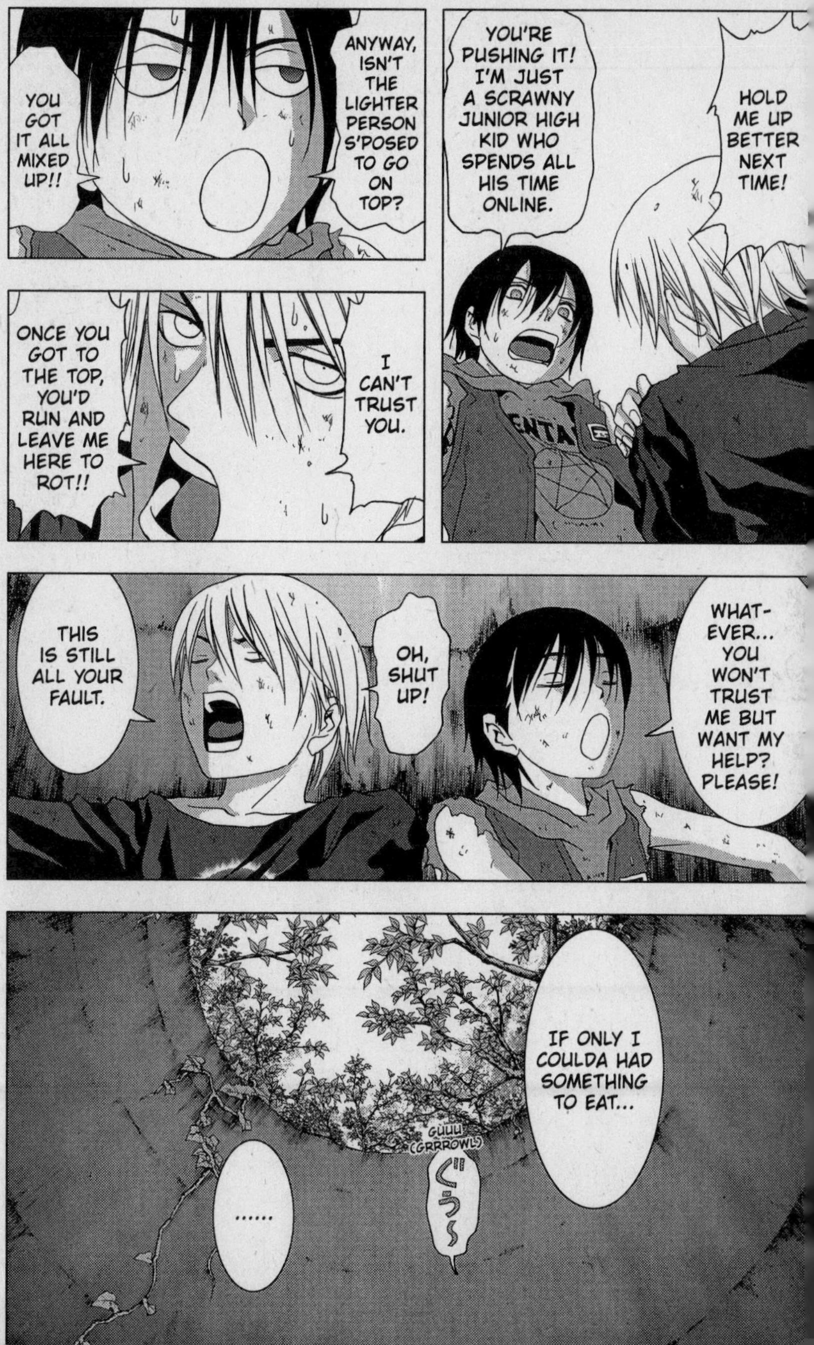
HOLD ME UP BETTER NEXT TIME!
YOU'RE PUSHING IT! I'M JUST A SCRAWNY JUNIOR HIGH KID WHO SPENDS ALL HIS TIME ONLINE.
ANYWAY, ISN'T THE LIGHTER PERSON S'POSED TO GO ON TOP?
YOU GOT IT ALL MIXED UP!!
I CAN'T TRUST YOU.
ONCE YOU GOT TO THE TOP, YOU'D RUN AND LEAVE ME HERE TO ROT!!
WHAT-EVER... YOU WON'T TRUST ME BUT WANT MY HELP? PLEASE!
OH, SHUT UP!
THIS IS STILL ALL YOUR FAULT.
IF ONLY I COULDA HAD SOMETHING TO EAT...
GUUU (GRRROWL)
ぐぅ～
......

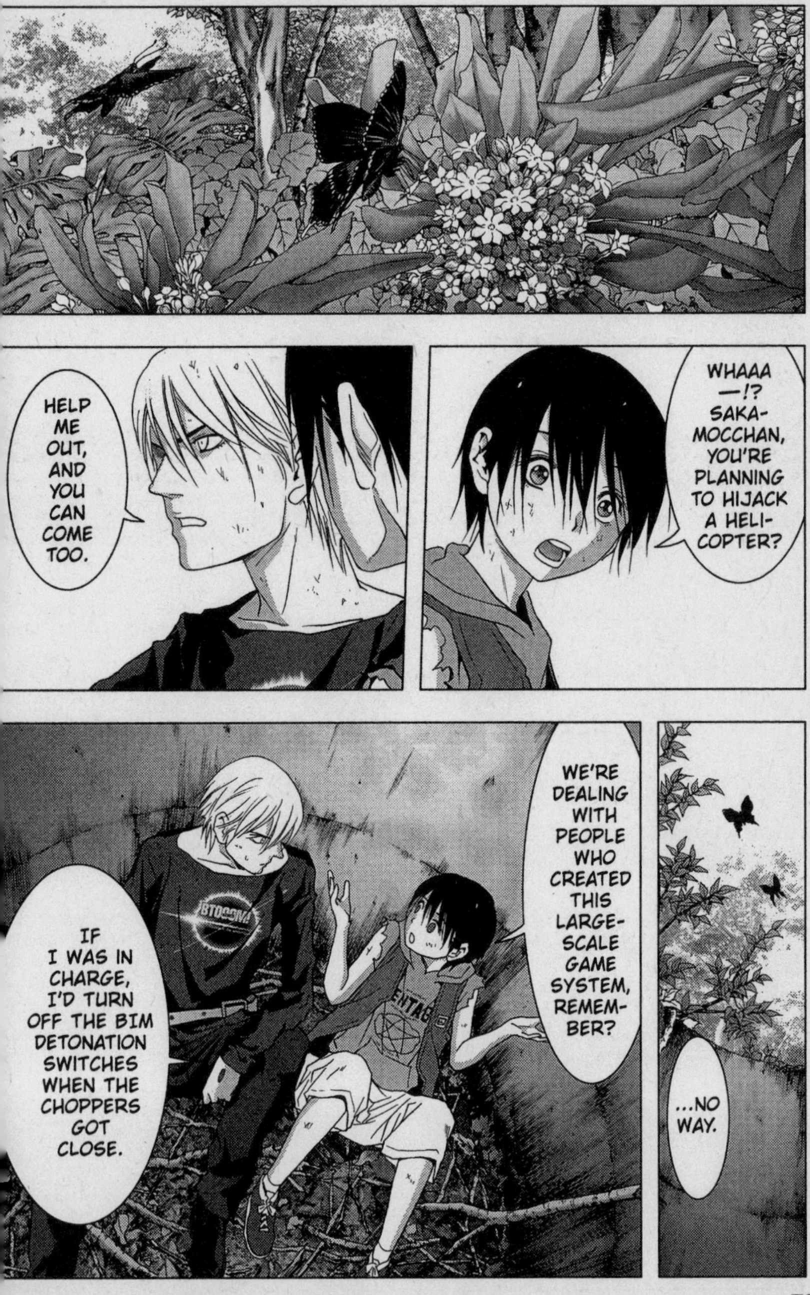
WHAAA—!? SAKA-MOCCHAN, YOU'RE PLANNING TO HIJACK A HELI-COPTER?
HELP ME OUT, AND YOU CAN COME TOO.
...NO WAY.
WE'RE DEALING WITH PEOPLE WHO CREATED THIS LARGE-SCALE GAME SYSTEM, REMEMBER?
IF I WAS IN CHARGE, I'D TURN OFF THE BIM DETONATION SWITCHES WHEN THE CHOPPERS GOT CLOSE.

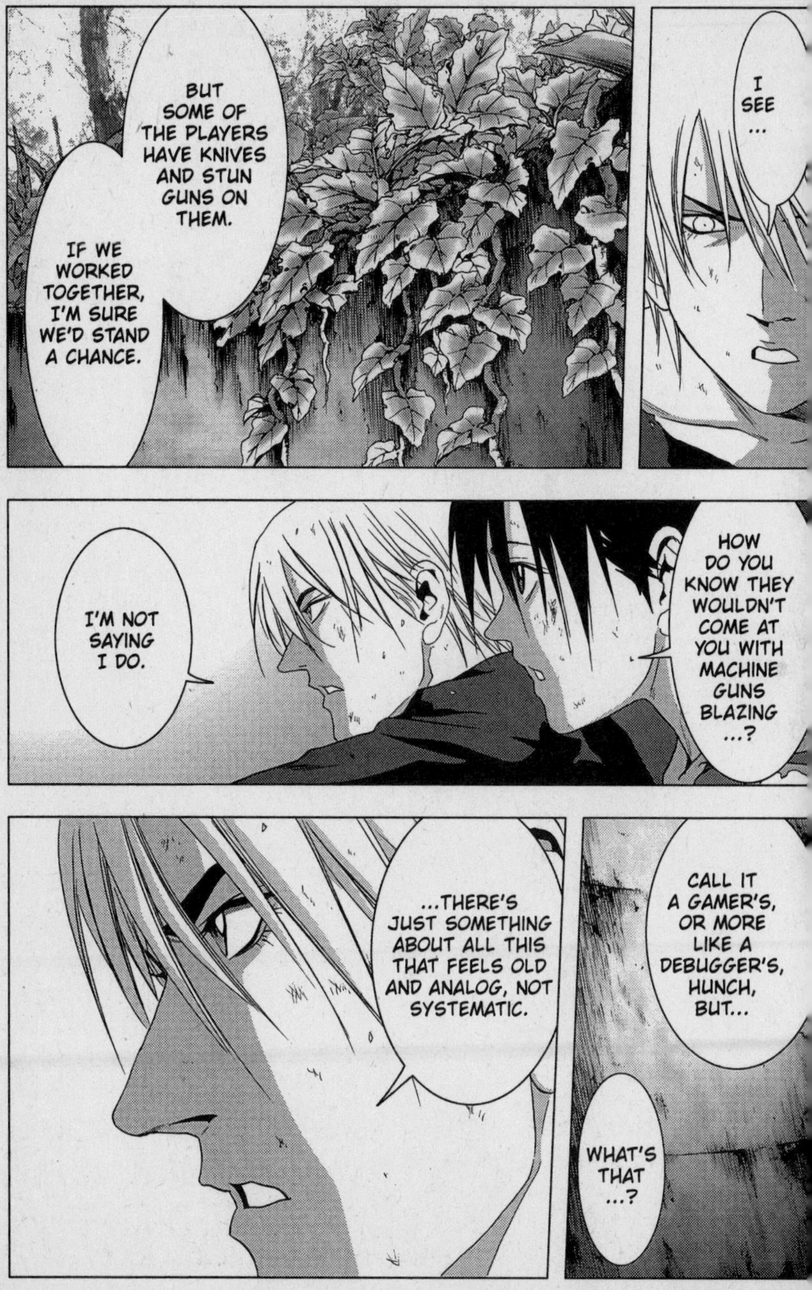
I SEE...
BUT SOME OF THE PLAYERS HAVE KNIVES AND STUN GUNS ON THEM.
IF WE WORKED TOGETHER, I'M SURE WE'D STAND A CHANCE.
HOW DO YOU KNOW THEY WOULDN'T COME AT YOU WITH MACHINE GUNS BLAZING...?
I'M NOT SAYING I DO.
CALL IT A GAMER'S, OR MORE LIKE A DEBUGGER'S, HUNCH, BUT...
WHAT'S THAT...?
...THERE'S JUST SOMETHING ABOUT ALL THIS THAT FEELS OLD AND ANALOG, NOT SYSTEMATIC.

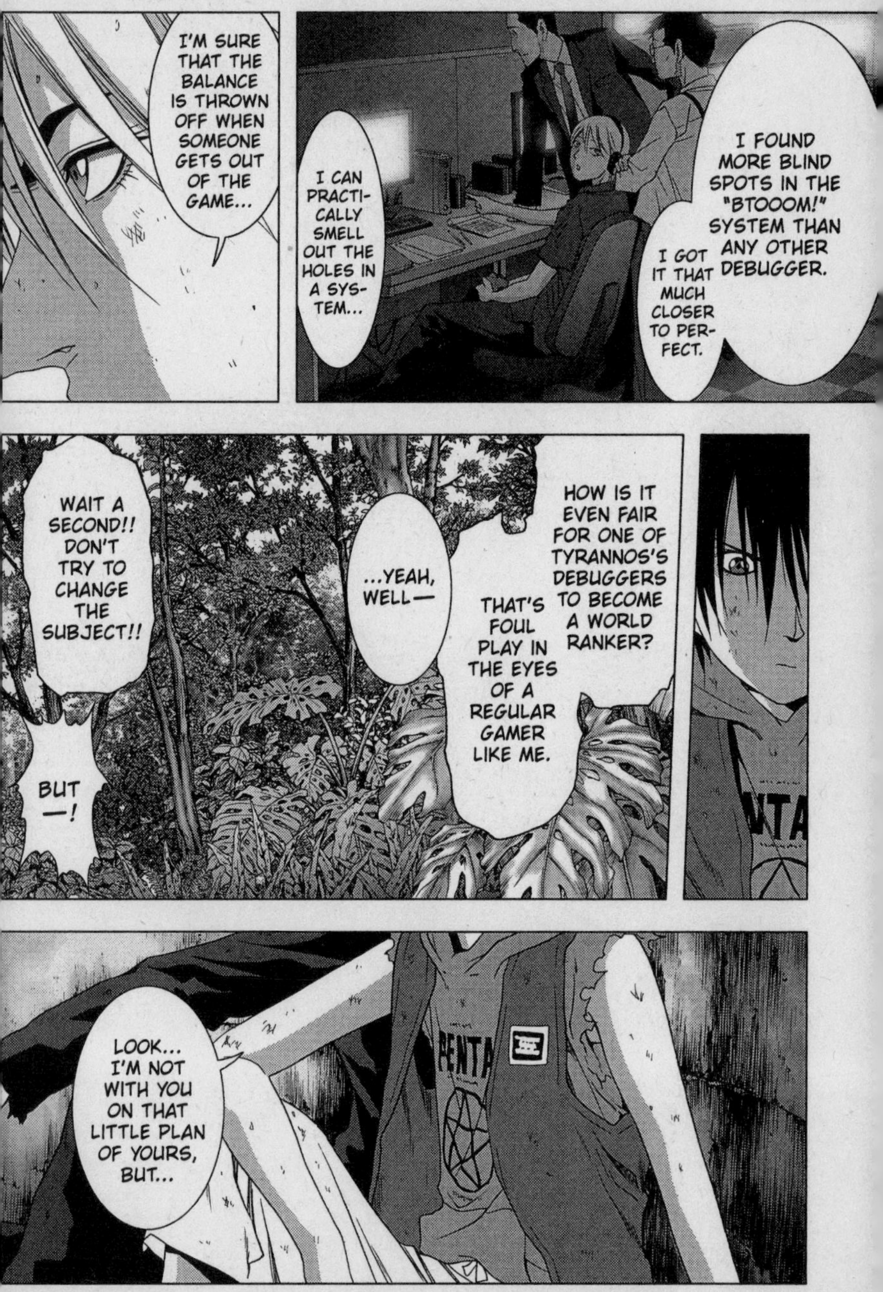
I FOUND MORE BLIND SPOTS IN THE "BTOOOM!" SYSTEM THAN ANY OTHER DEBUGGER.
I GOT IT THAT MUCH CLOSER TO PERFECT.
I CAN PRACTICALLY SMELL OUT THE HOLES IN A SYSTEM...
I'M SURE THAT THE BALANCE IS THROWN OFF WHEN SOMEONE GETS OUT OF THE GAME...
HOW IS IT EVEN FAIR FOR ONE OF TYRANNOS'S DEBUGGERS TO BECOME A WORLD RANKER?
THAT'S FOUL PLAY IN THE EYES OF A REGULAR GAMER LIKE ME.
...YEAH, WELL—
WAIT A SECOND!! DON'T TRY TO CHANGE THE SUBJECT!!
BUT—!
LOOK... I'M NOT WITH YOU ON THAT LITTLE PLAN OF YOURS, BUT...

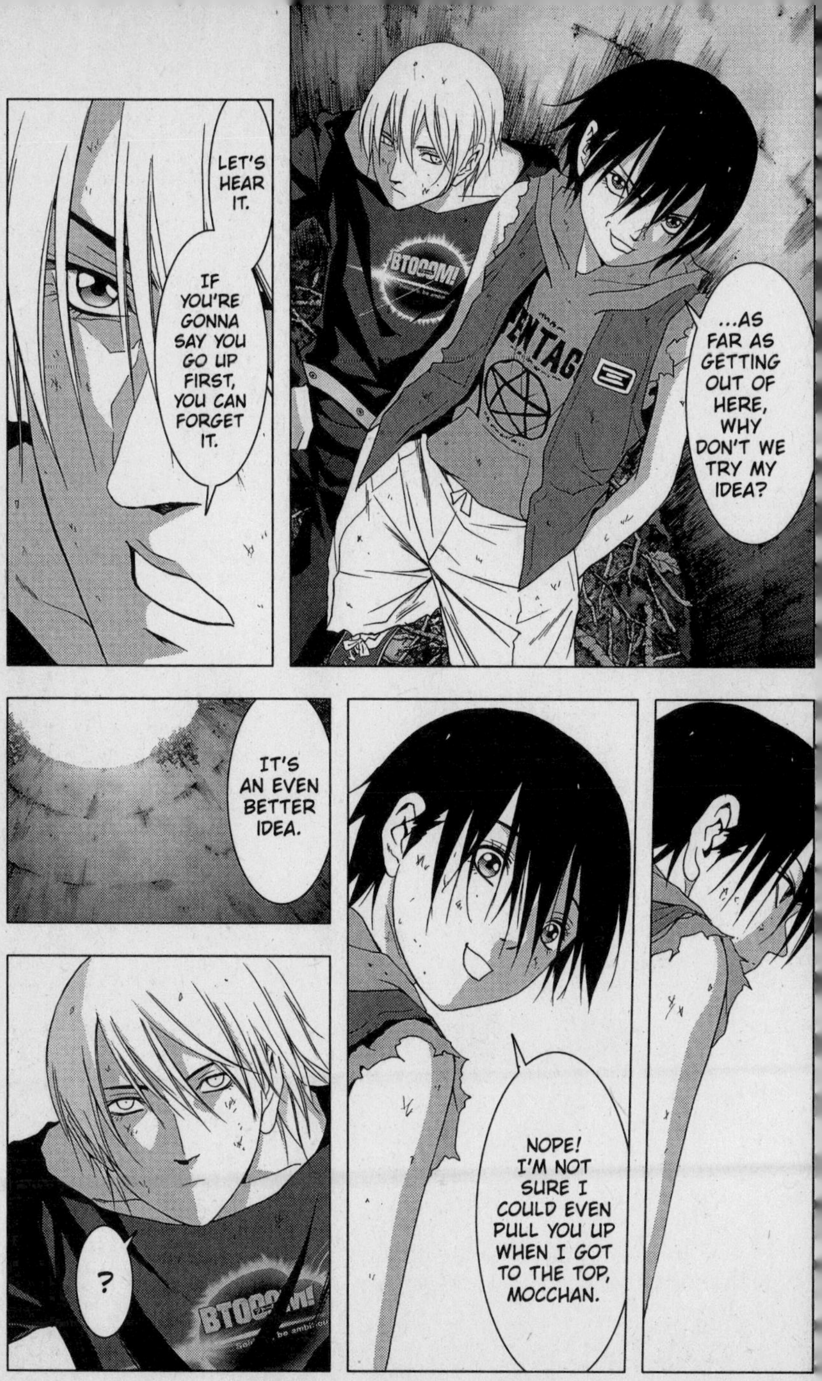
...AS FAR AS GETTING OUT OF HERE, WHY DON'T WE TRY MY IDEA?
LET'S HEAR IT.
IF YOU'RE GONNA SAY YOU GO UP FIRST, YOU CAN FORGET IT.
NOPE! I'M NOT SURE I COULD EVEN PULL YOU UP WHEN I GOT TO THE TOP, MOCCHAN.
IT'S AN EVEN BETTER IDEA.
?

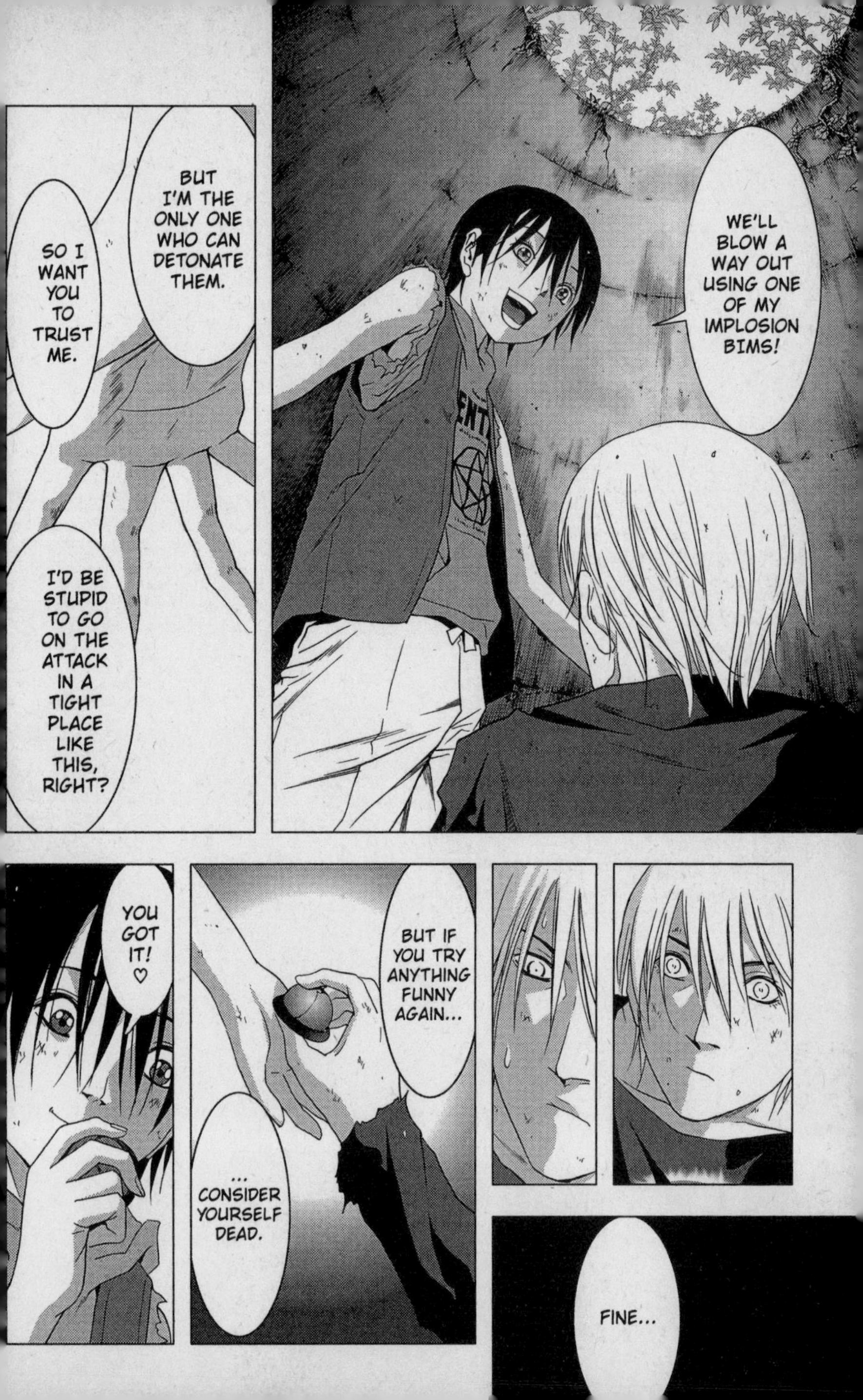

WE'LL BLOW A WAY OUT USING ONE OF MY IMPLOSION BIMS!
BUT I'M THE ONLY ONE WHO CAN DETONATE THEM.
SO I WANT YOU TO TRUST ME.
I'D BE STUPID TO GO ON THE ATTACK IN A TIGHT PLACE LIKE THIS, RIGHT?
FINE...
BUT IF YOU TRY ANYTHING FUNNY AGAIN...
...CONSIDER YOURSELF DEAD.
YOU GOT IT! ♡

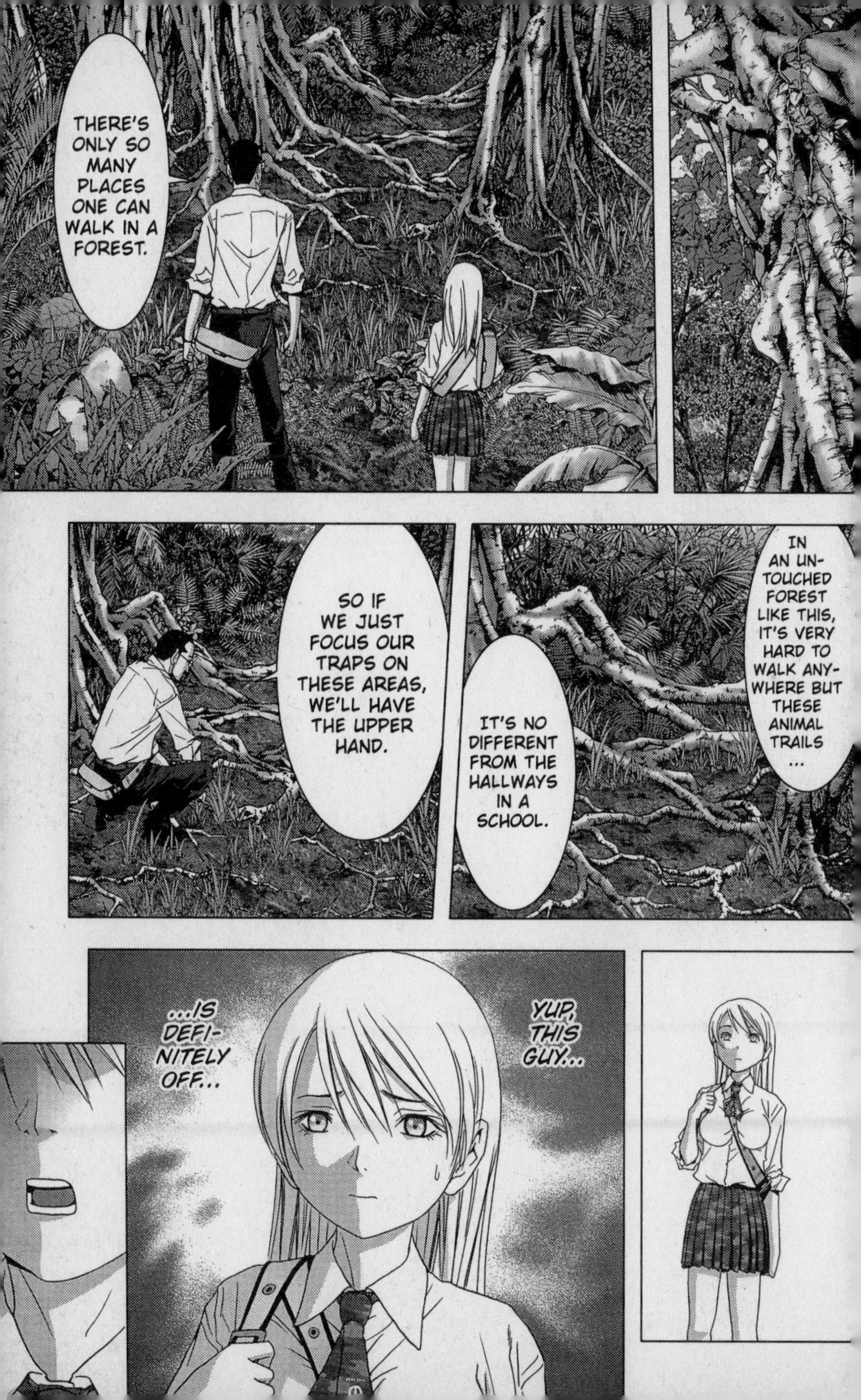
THERE'S ONLY SO MANY PLACES ONE CAN WALK IN A FOREST.
IN AN UN-TOUCHED FOREST LIKE THIS, IT'S VERY HARD TO WALK ANY-WHERE BUT THESE ANIMAL TRAILS ...
IT'S NO DIFFERENT FROM THE HALLWAYS IN A SCHOOL.
SO IF WE JUST FOCUS OUR TRAPS ON THESE AREAS, WE'LL HAVE THE UPPER HAND.
YUP, THIS GUY...
...IS DEFI-NITELY OFF...

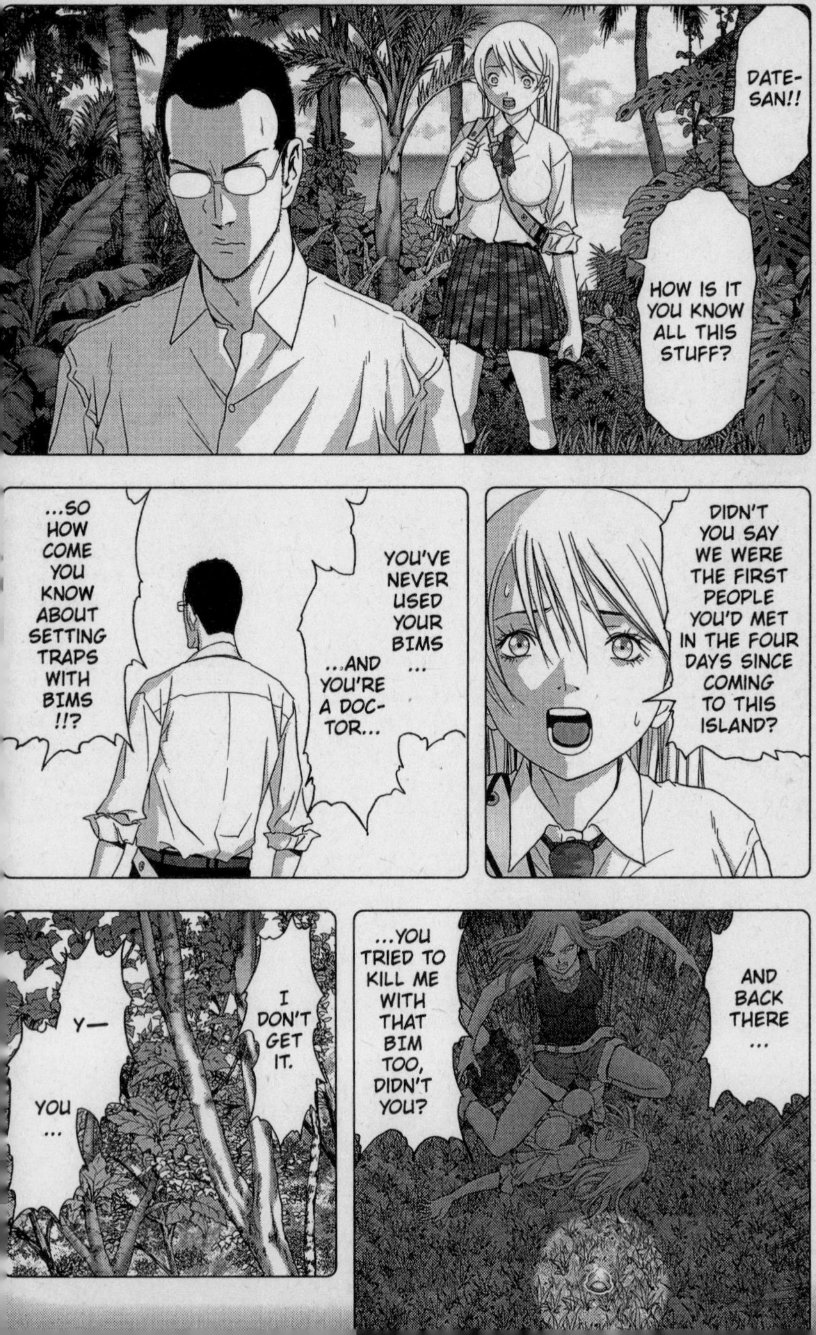
DATE-SAN!!
HOW IS IT YOU KNOW ALL THIS STUFF?
DIDN'T YOU SAY WE WERE THE FIRST PEOPLE YOU'D MET IN THE FOUR DAYS SINCE COMING TO THIS ISLAND?
YOU'VE NEVER USED YOUR BIMS ...
...AND YOU'RE A DOC-TOR...
...SO HOW COME YOU KNOW ABOUT SETTING TRAPS WITH BIMS !!?
AND BACK THERE ...
...YOU TRIED TO KILL ME WITH THAT BIM TOO, DIDN'T YOU?
I DON'T GET IT.
Y—
YOU ...

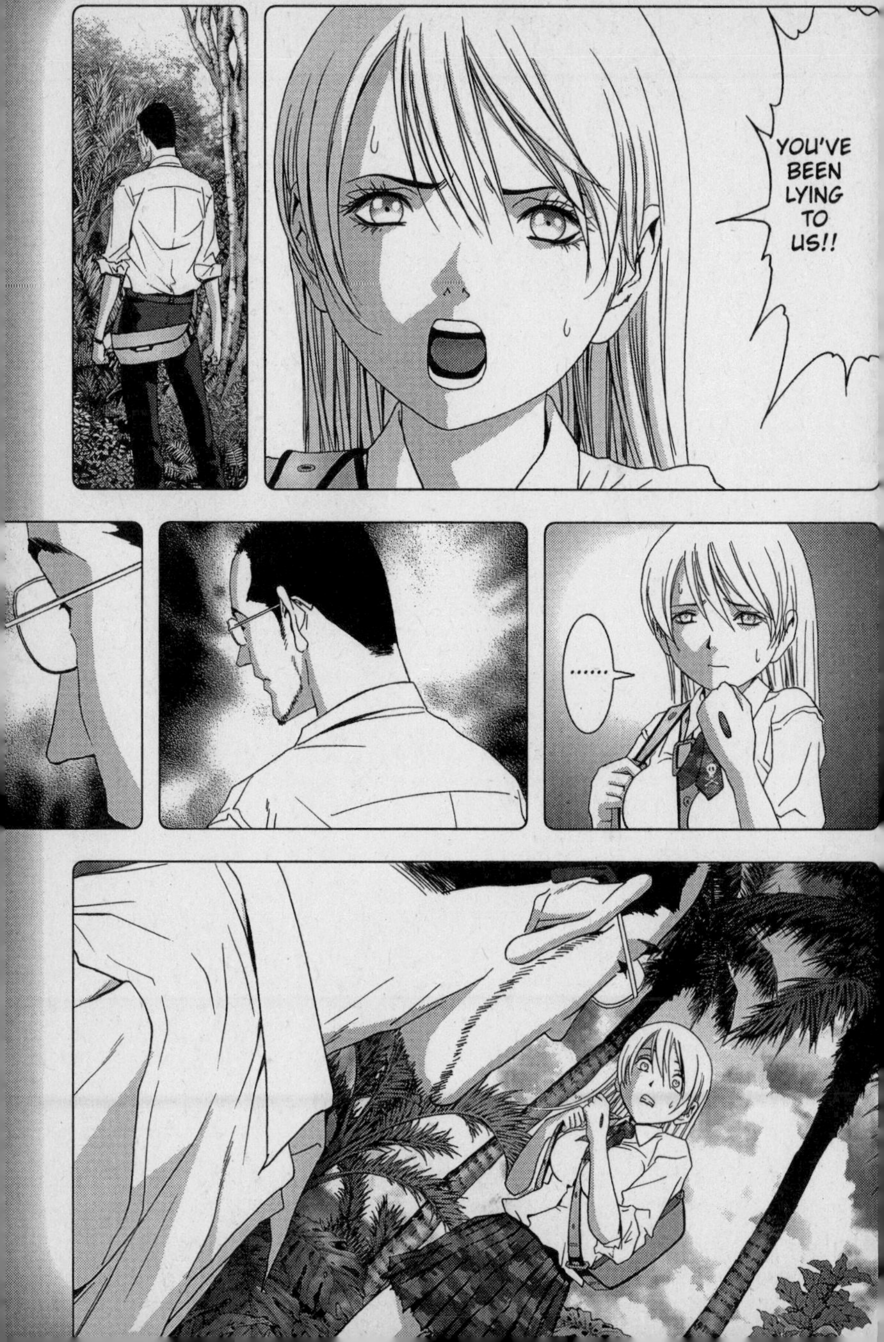
YOU'VE BEEN LYING TO US!!
......

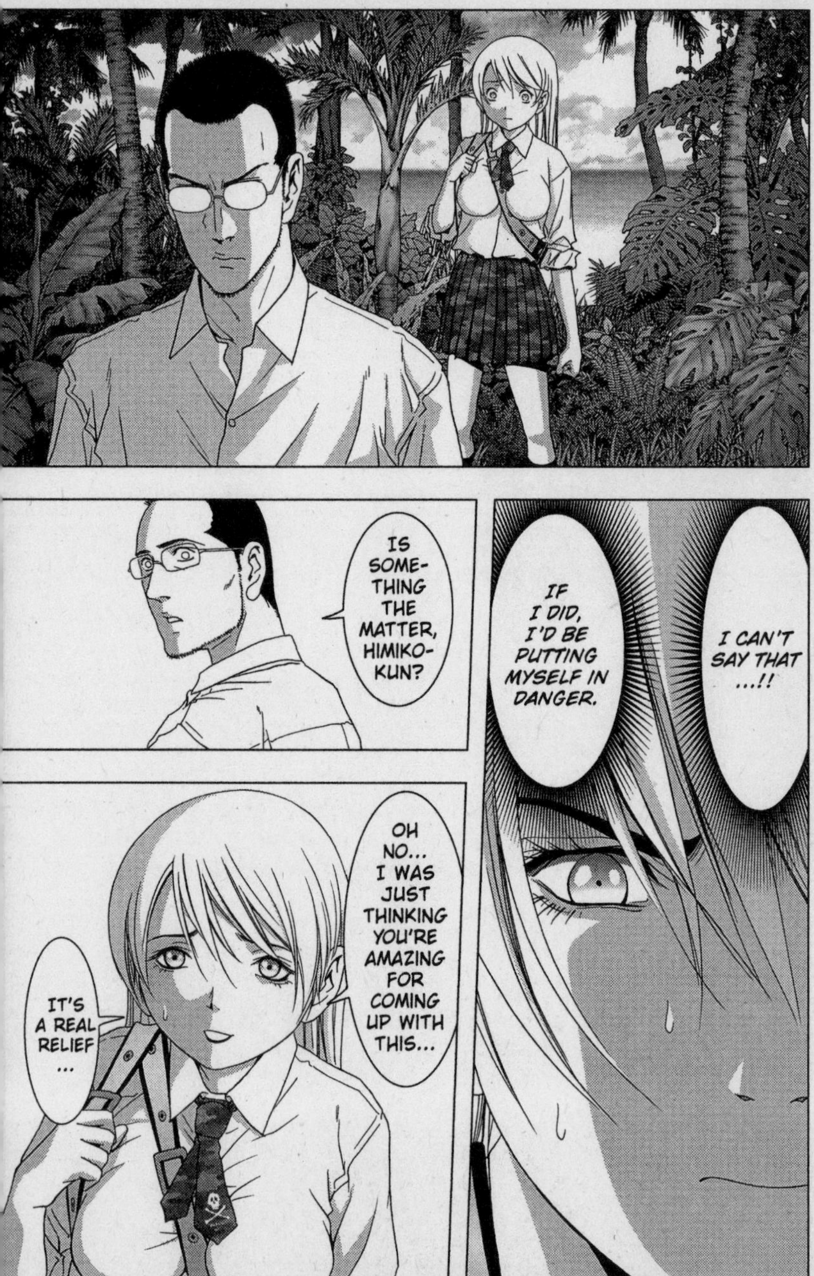
I CAN'T SAY THAT ...!!
IF I DID, I'D BE PUTTING MYSELF IN DANGER.
IS SOMETHING THE MATTER, HIMIKO-KUN?
OH NO... I WAS JUST THINKING YOU'RE AMAZING FOR COMING UP WITH THIS...
IT'S A REAL RELIEF ...

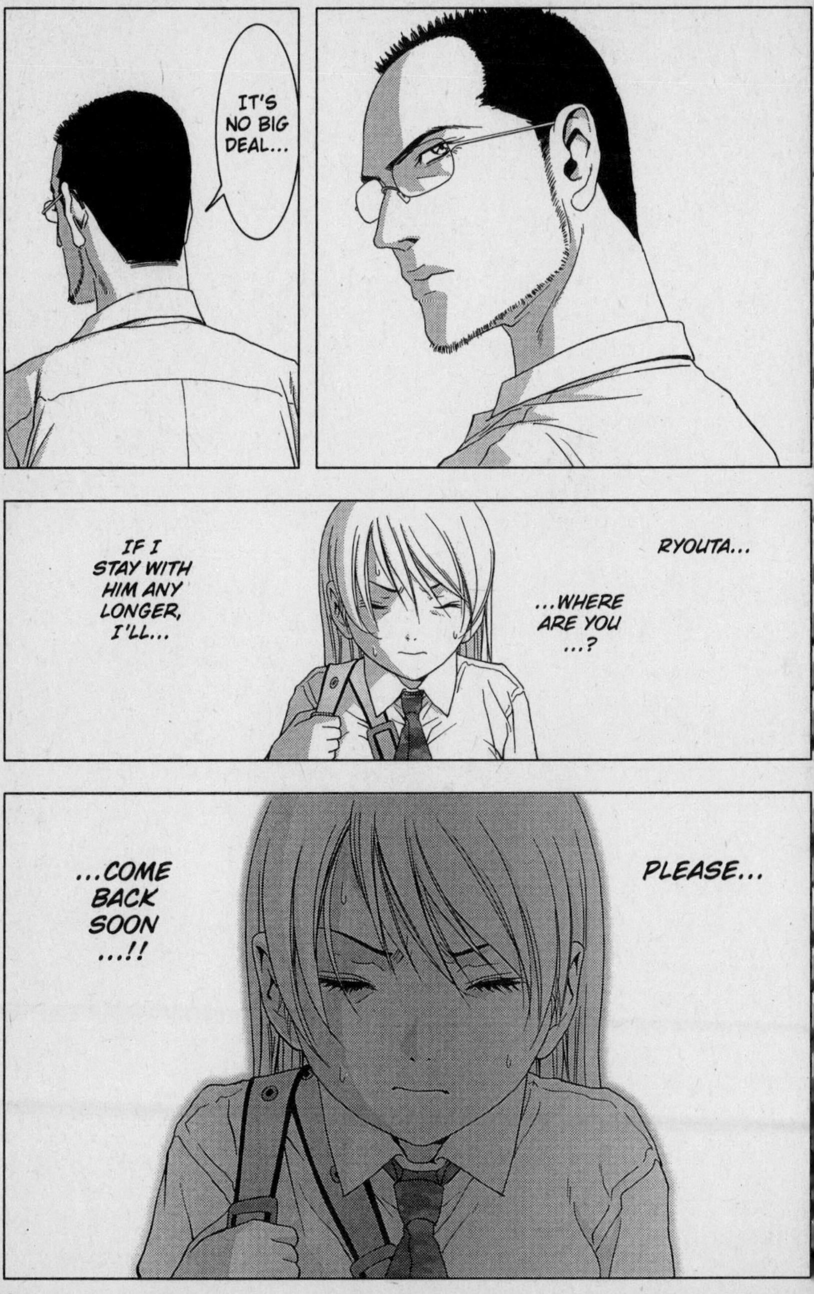
IT'S NO BIG DEAL...
RYOUTA...
...WHERE ARE YOU ...?
IF I STAY WITH HIM ANY LONGER, I'LL...
PLEASE...
...COME BACK SOON ...!!

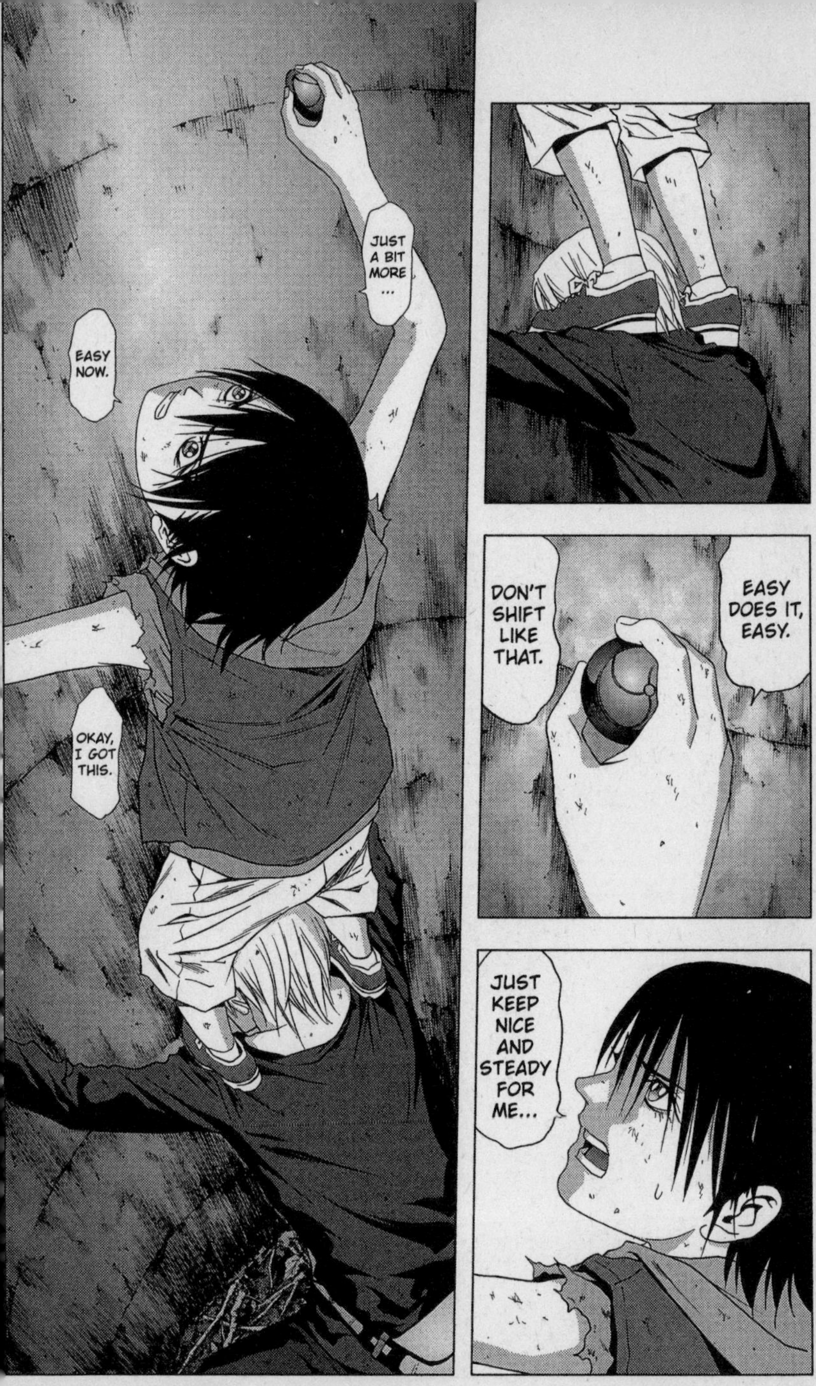
EASY DOES IT, EASY.
DON'T SHIFT LIKE THAT.
JUST KEEP NICE AND STEADY FOR ME...
JUST A BIT MORE...
EASY NOW.
OKAY, I GOT THIS.

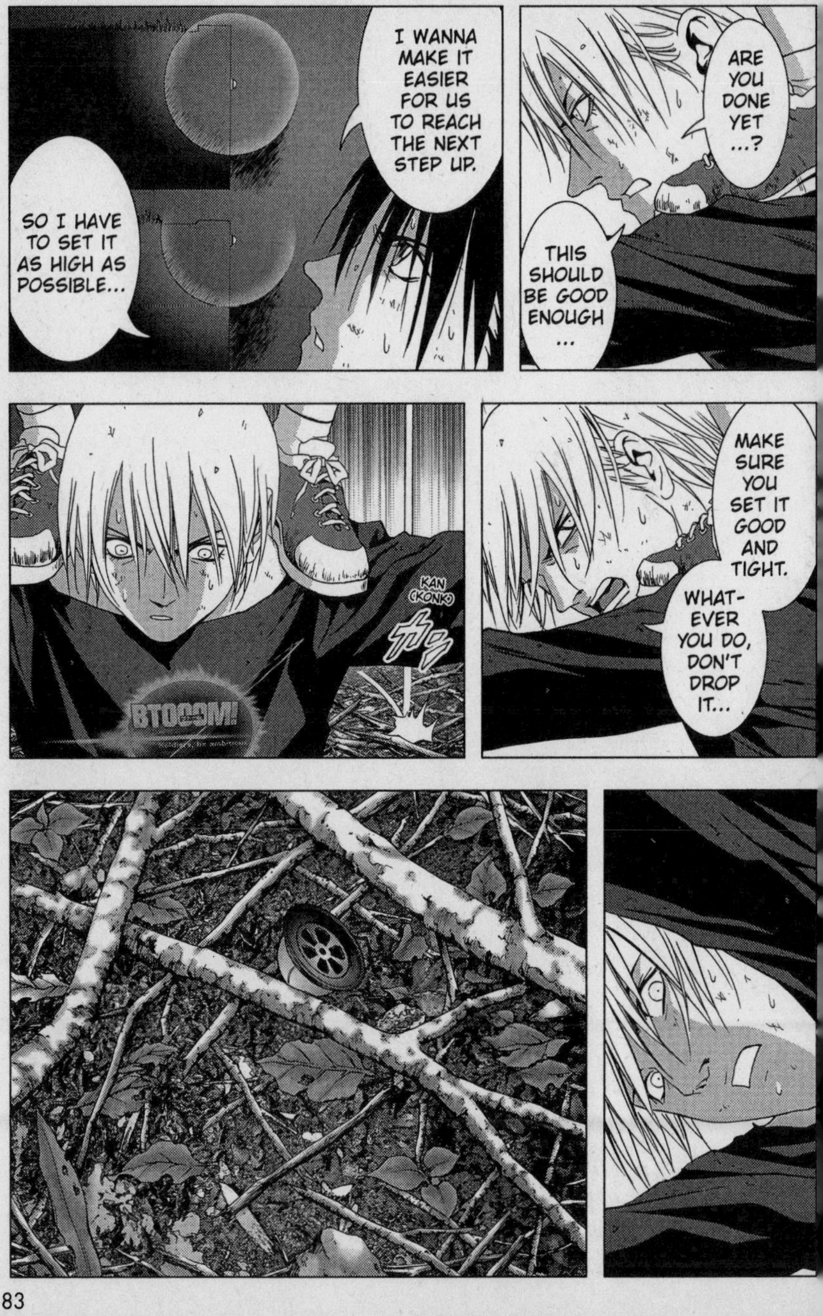
ARE YOU DONE YET ...?
THIS SHOULD BE GOOD ENOUGH ...
I WANNA MAKE IT EASIER FOR US TO REACH THE NEXT STEP UP.
SO I HAVE TO SET IT AS HIGH AS POSSIBLE...
MAKE SURE YOU SET IT GOOD AND TIGHT.
WHAT-EVER YOU DO, DON'T DROP IT...
KAN (KONK)

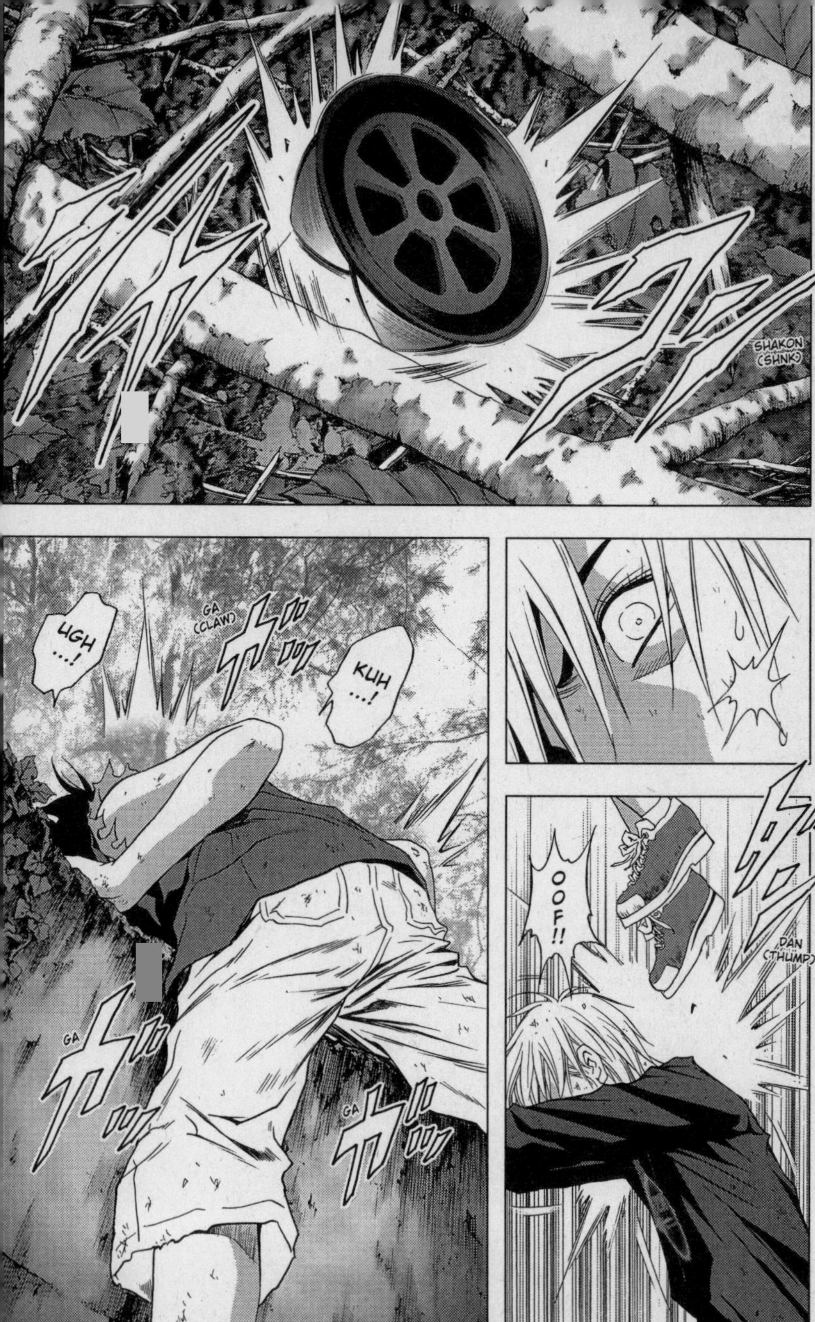
SHAKON (SHNK)
OOF!!
DAN (THUMP)
KUH ...!
GA (CLAW)
UGH ...!
GA
GA

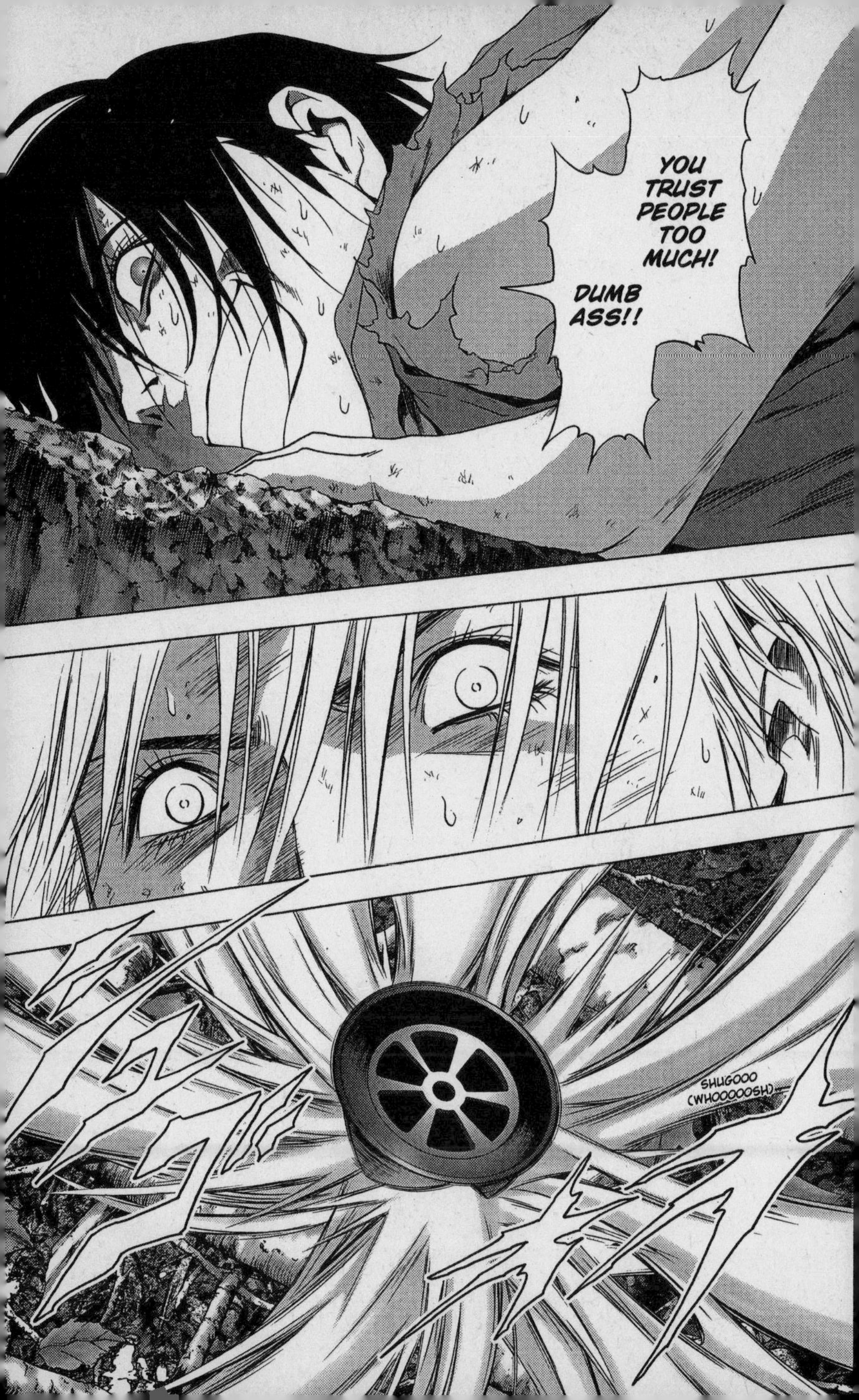
YOU TRUST PEOPLE TOO MUCH!
DUMB ASS!!
SHUGOOO (WHOOOOOSH)

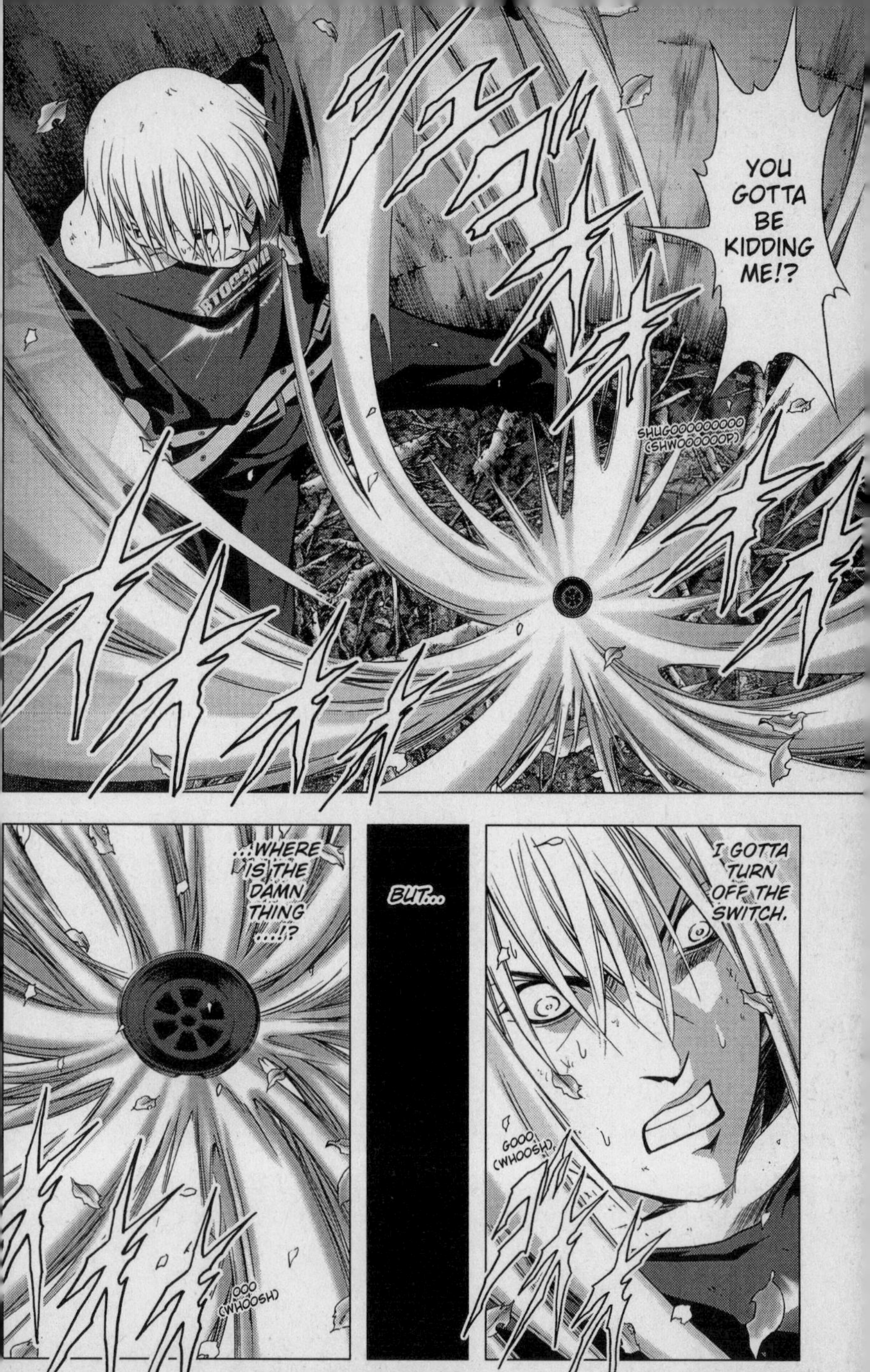
YOU GOTTA BE KIDDING ME!?
SHUGOOOOOOOOOO (SHWOOOOOOOP)
I GOTTA TURN OFF THE SWITCH.
GOOO (WHOOSH)
BUT...
...WHERE IS THE DAMN THING ...!?
OOO (WHOOSH)

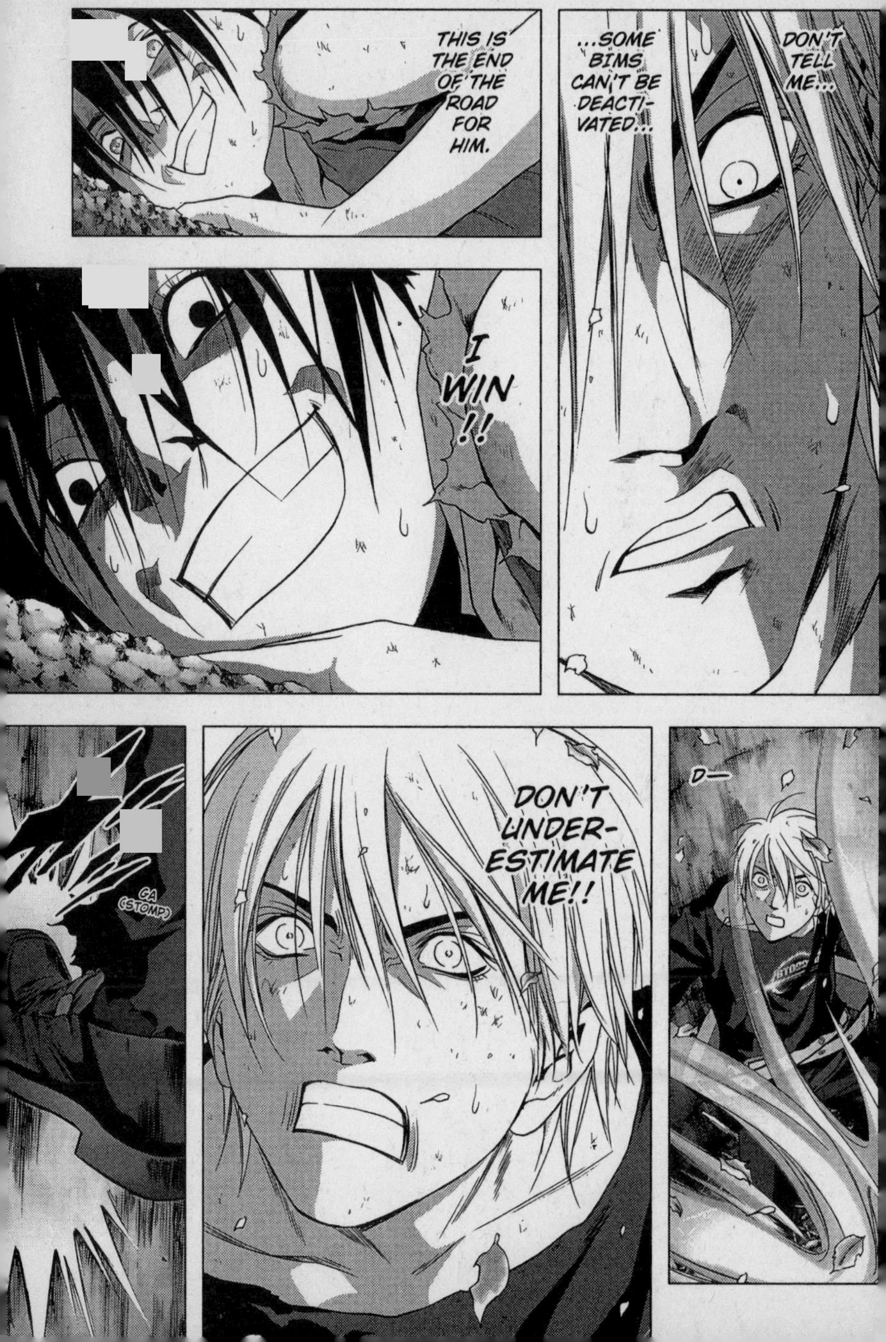
DON'T TELL ME...
...SOME BIMS CAN'T BE DEACTIVATED...
THIS IS THE END OF THE ROAD FOR HIM.
I WIN!!
D—
DON'T UNDER-ESTIMATE ME!!
GA (STOMP)

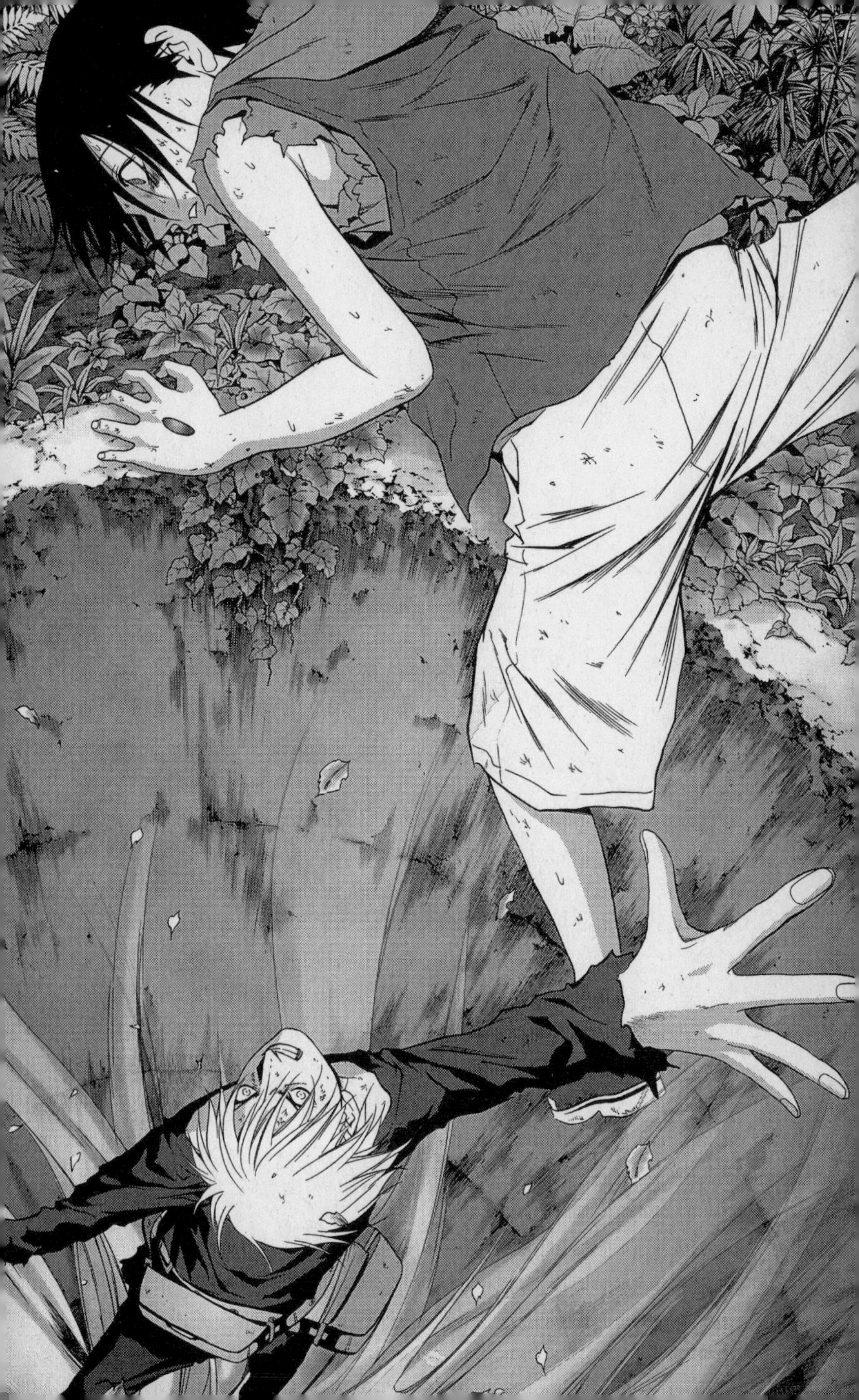

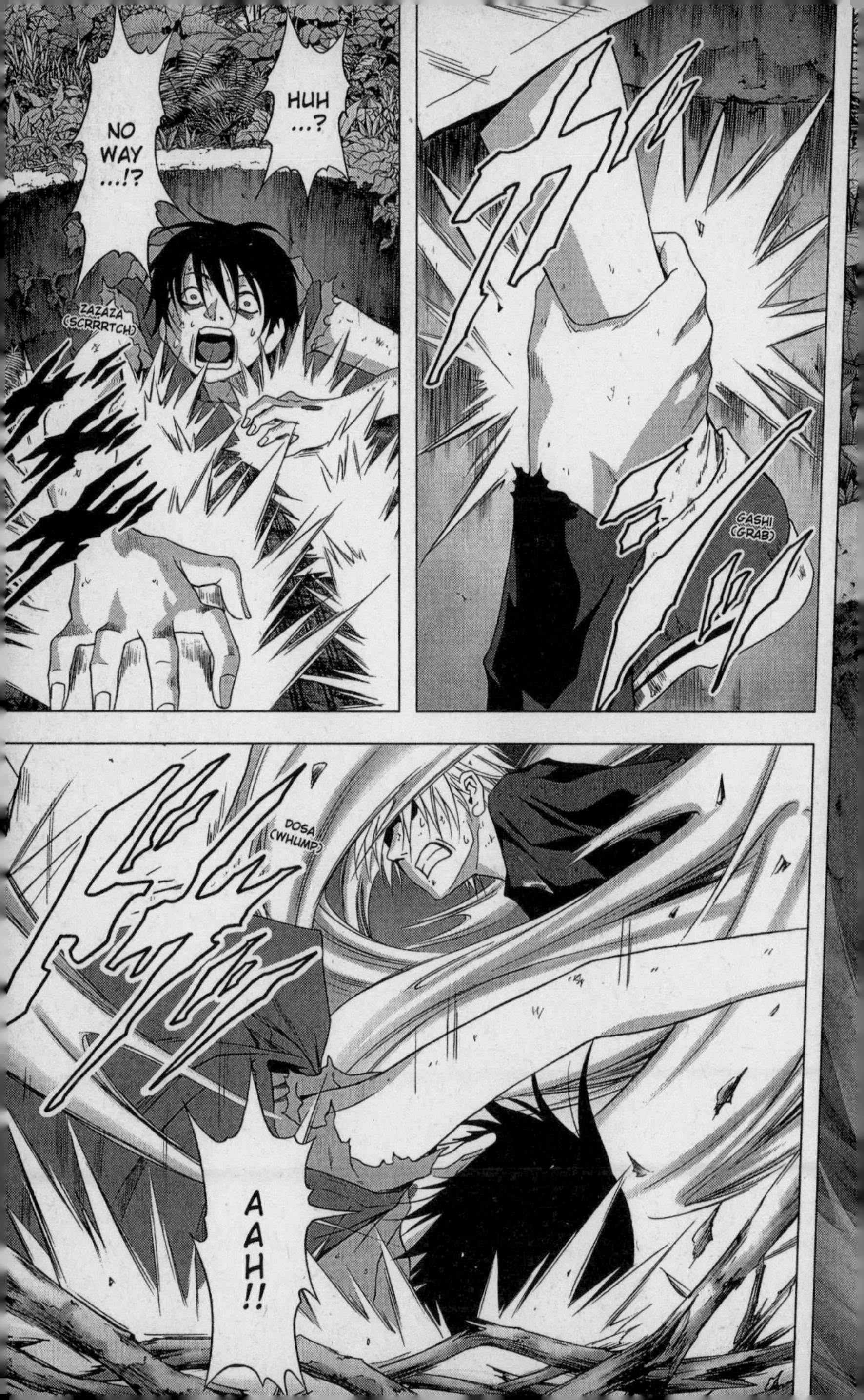
HUH ...?
NO WAY ...!?
ZAZAZA (SCRRRTCH)
GASHI (GRAB)
DOSA (WHUMP)
AAAH!!

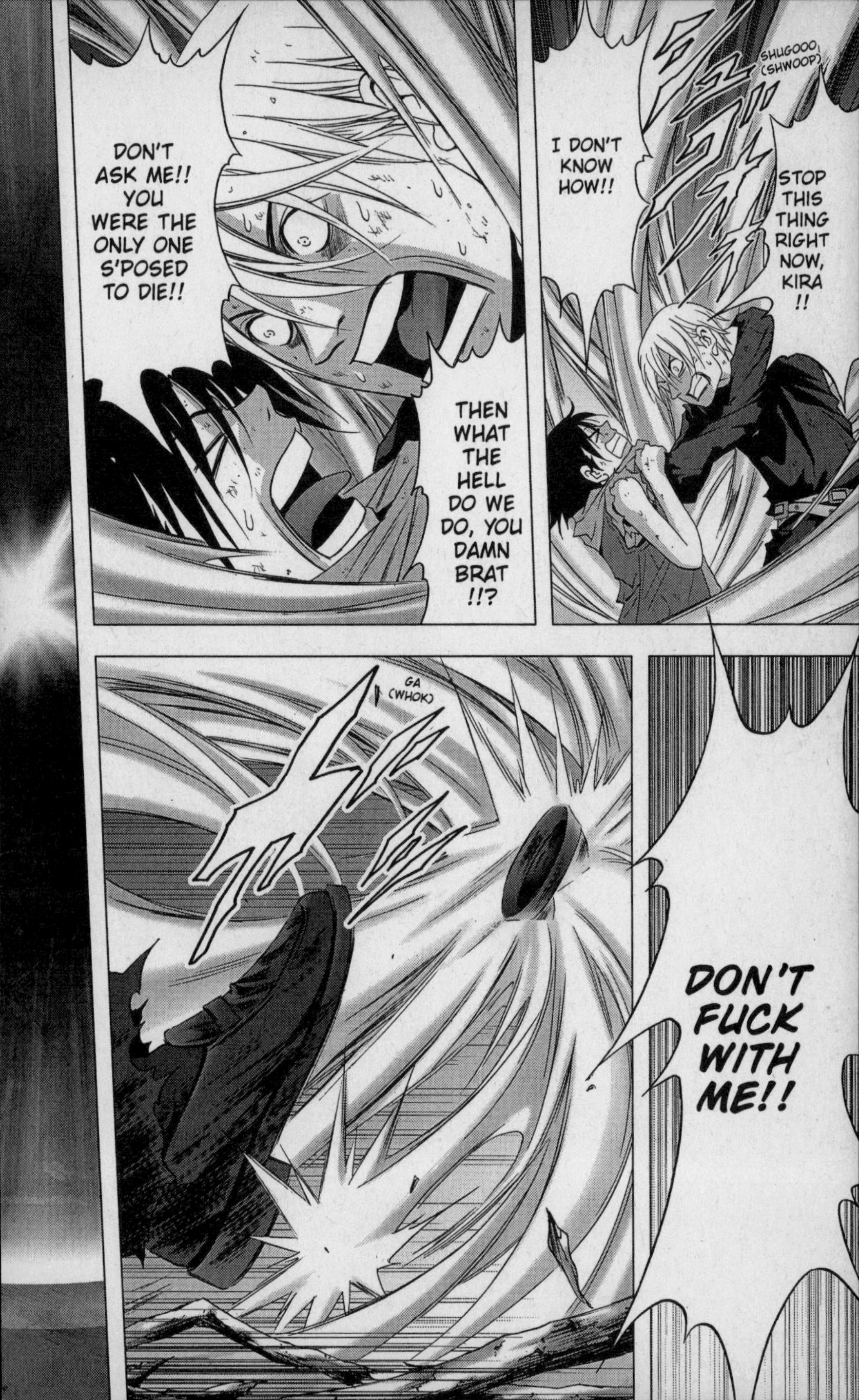
SHUGOOO (SHWOOP)
STOP THIS THING RIGHT NOW, KIRA !!
I DON'T KNOW HOW!!
THEN WHAT THE HELL DO WE DO, YOU DAMN BRAT !!?
DON'T ASK ME!! YOU WERE THE ONLY ONE S'POSED TO DIE!!
DON'T FUCK WITH ME!!
GA (WHOK)

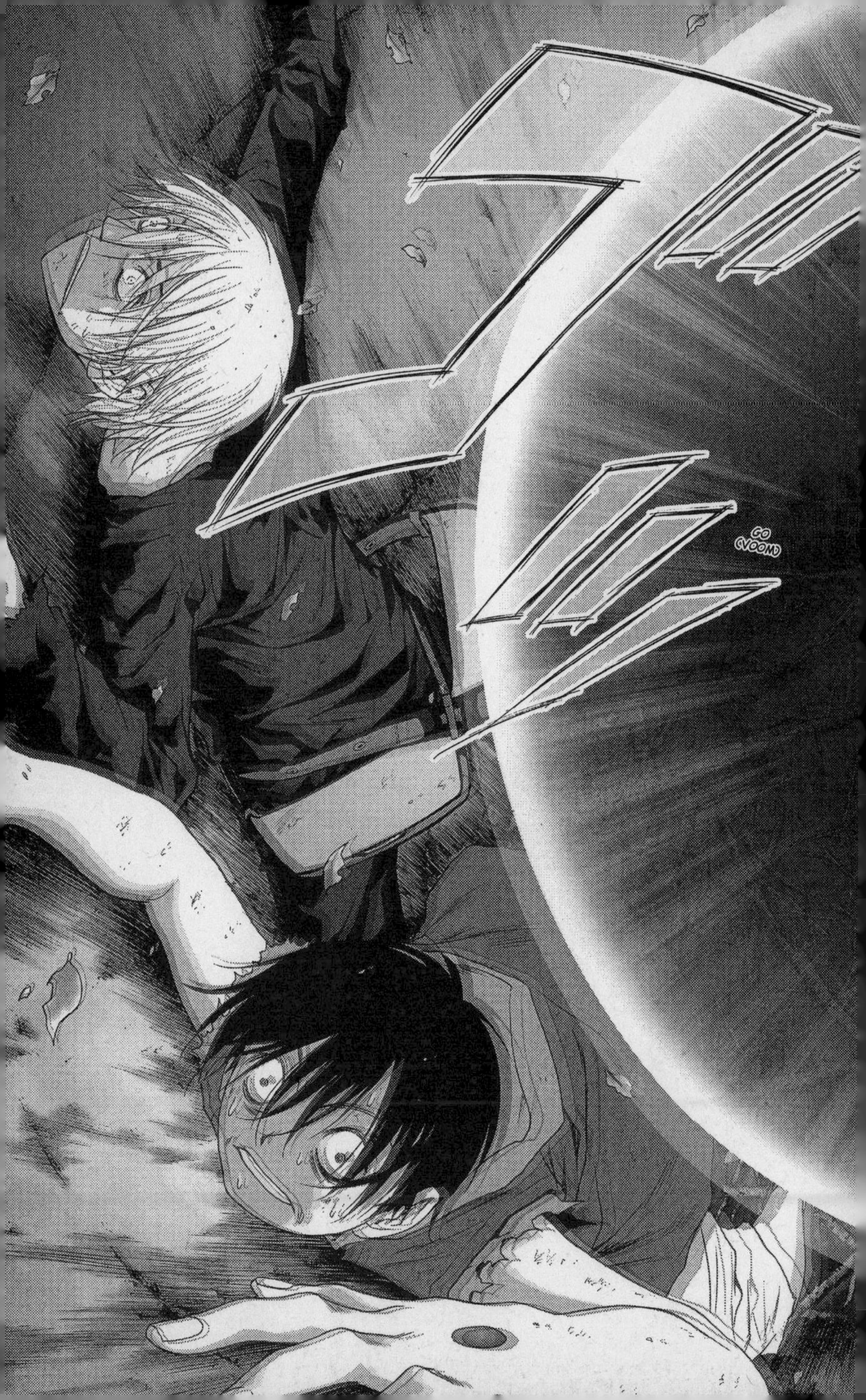
GO
(VOOM)

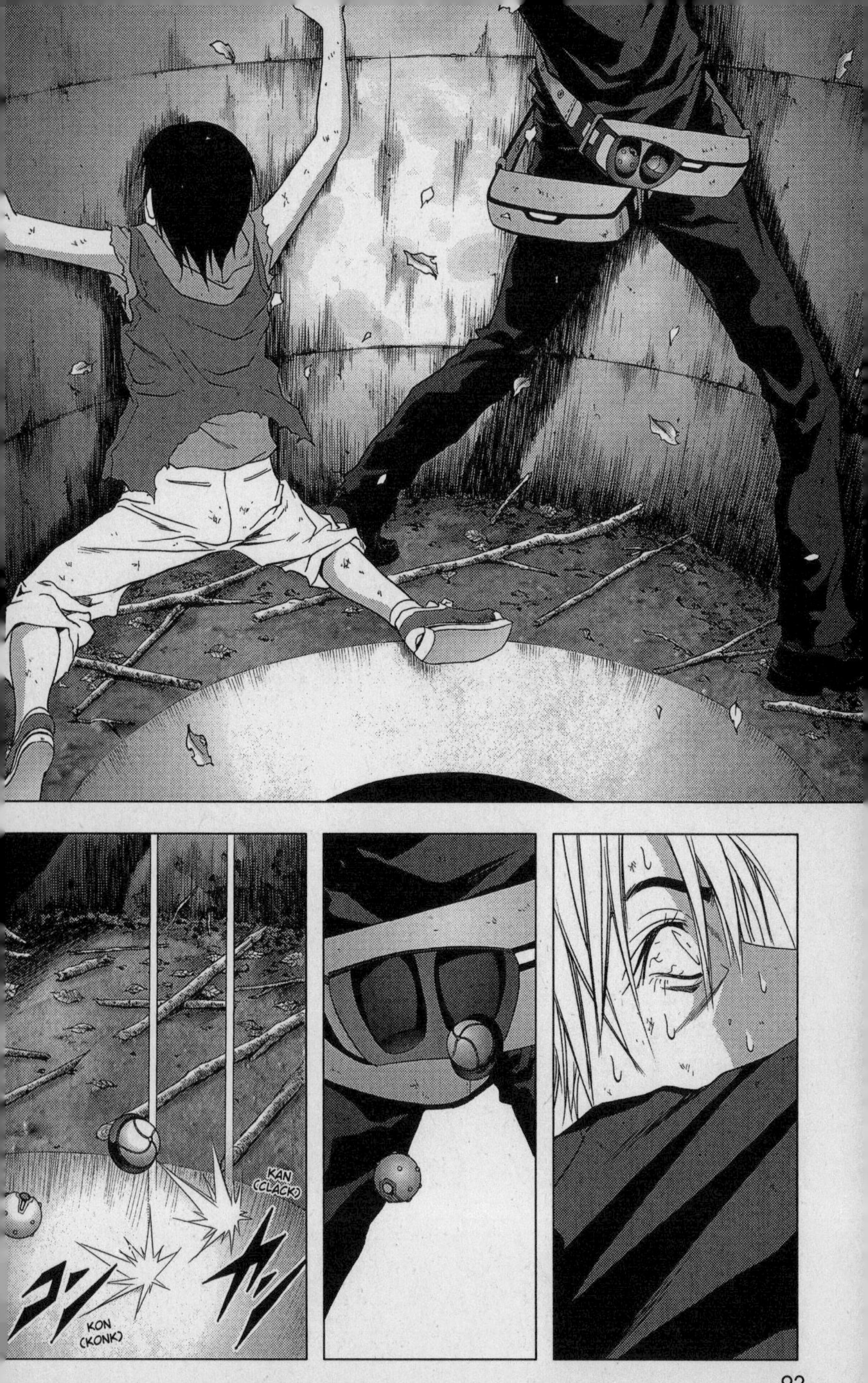
KAN
(CLACK)
KON
(KONK)

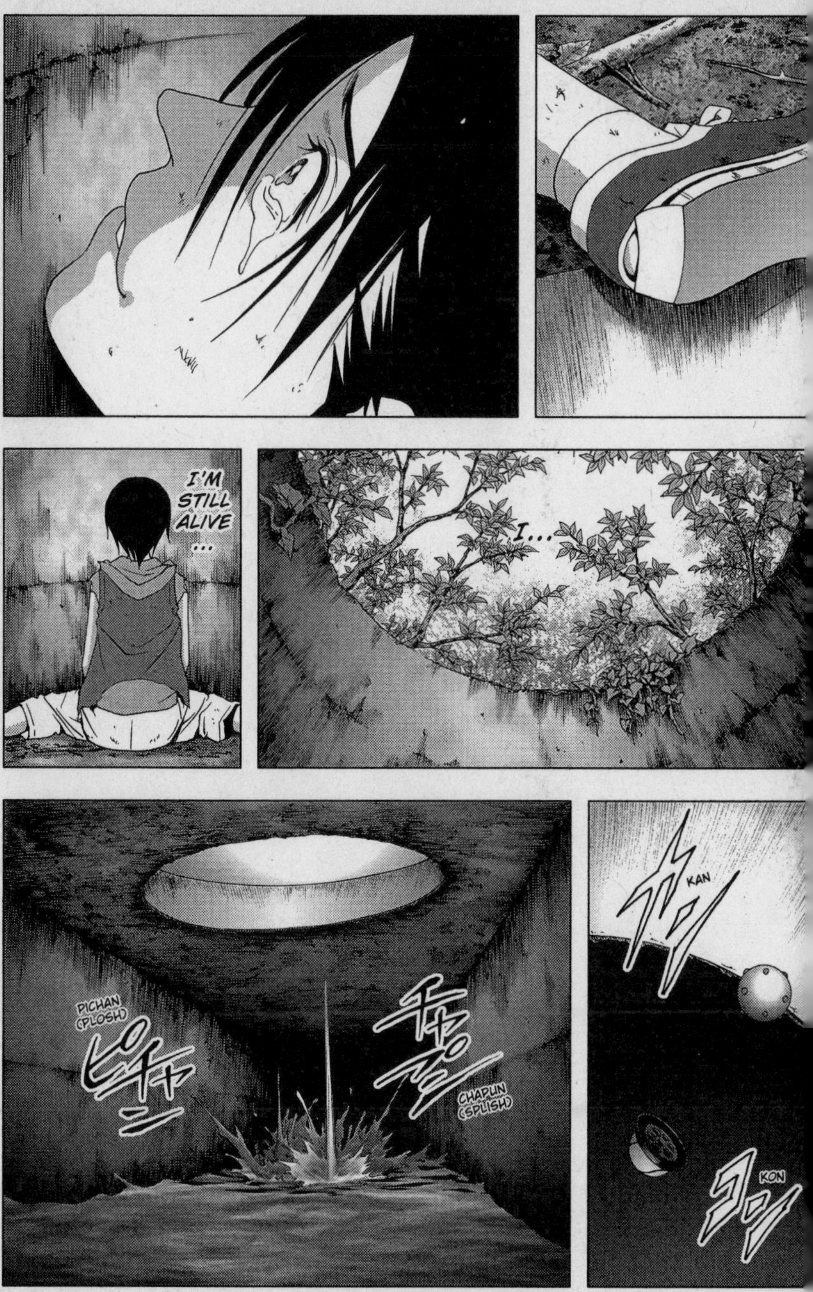
I...
I'M STILL ALIVE ...
KAN
KON
CHAPUN (SPLISH)
PICHAN (PLOSH)

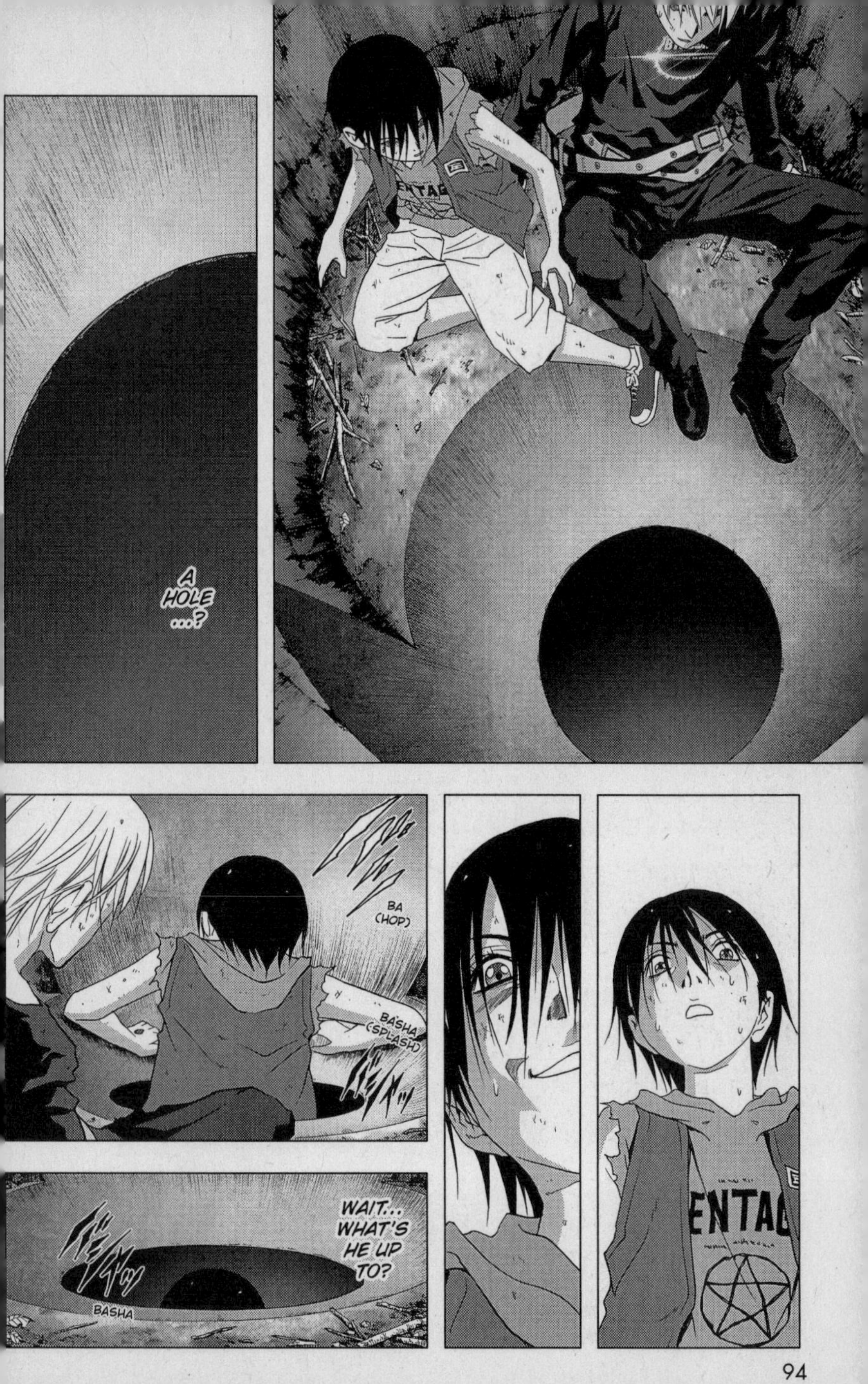
A HOLE ...?
BA (HOP)
BASHA (SPLASH)
WAIT... WHAT'S HE UP TO?
BASHA

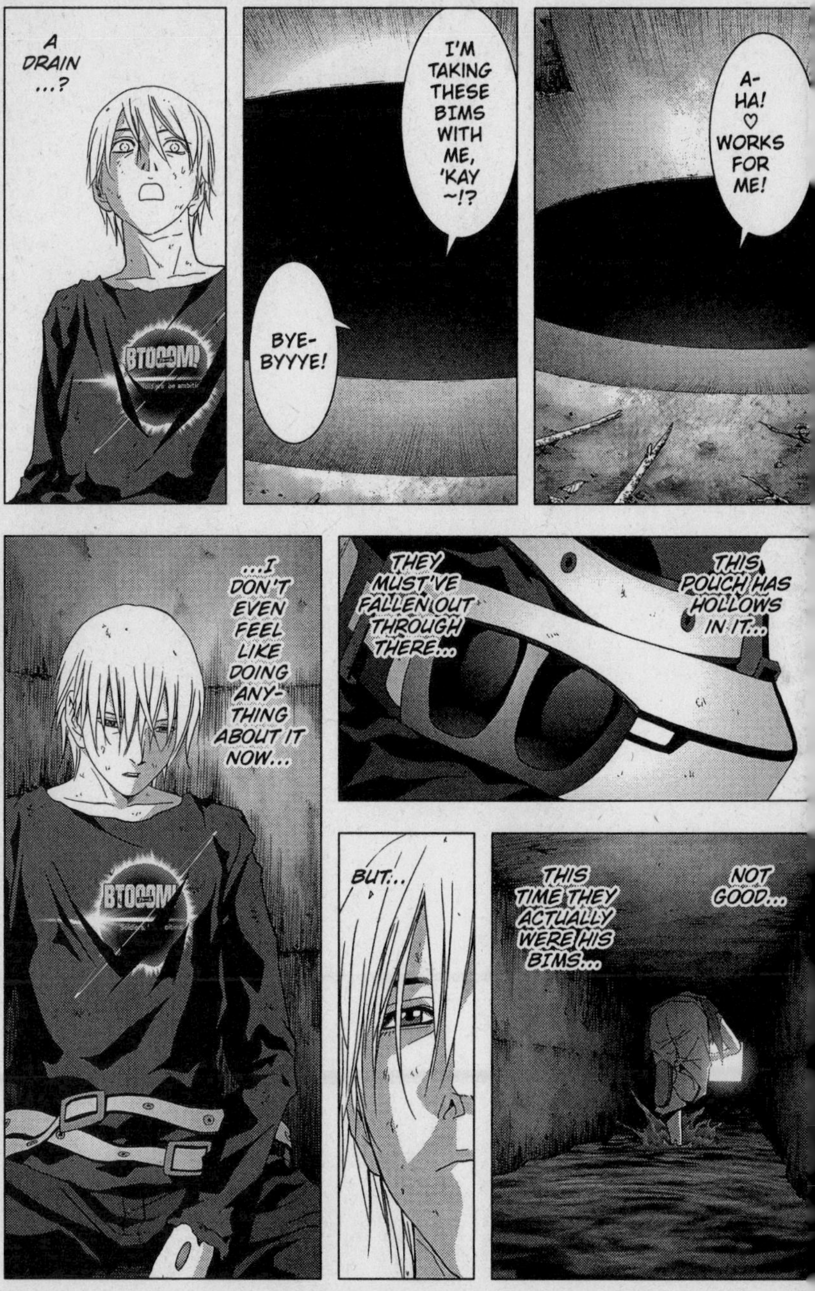
A-HA! ♡ WORKS FOR ME!
I'M TAKING THESE BIMS WITH ME, 'KAY~!?
BYE-BYYYE!
A DRAIN ...?
THIS POUCH HAS HOLLOWS IN IT...
THEY MUST'VE FALLEN OUT THROUGH THERE...
NOT GOOD...
THIS TIME THEY ACTUALLY WERE HIS BIMS...
BUT...
...I DON'T EVEN FEEL LIKE DOING ANY-THING ABOUT IT NOW...

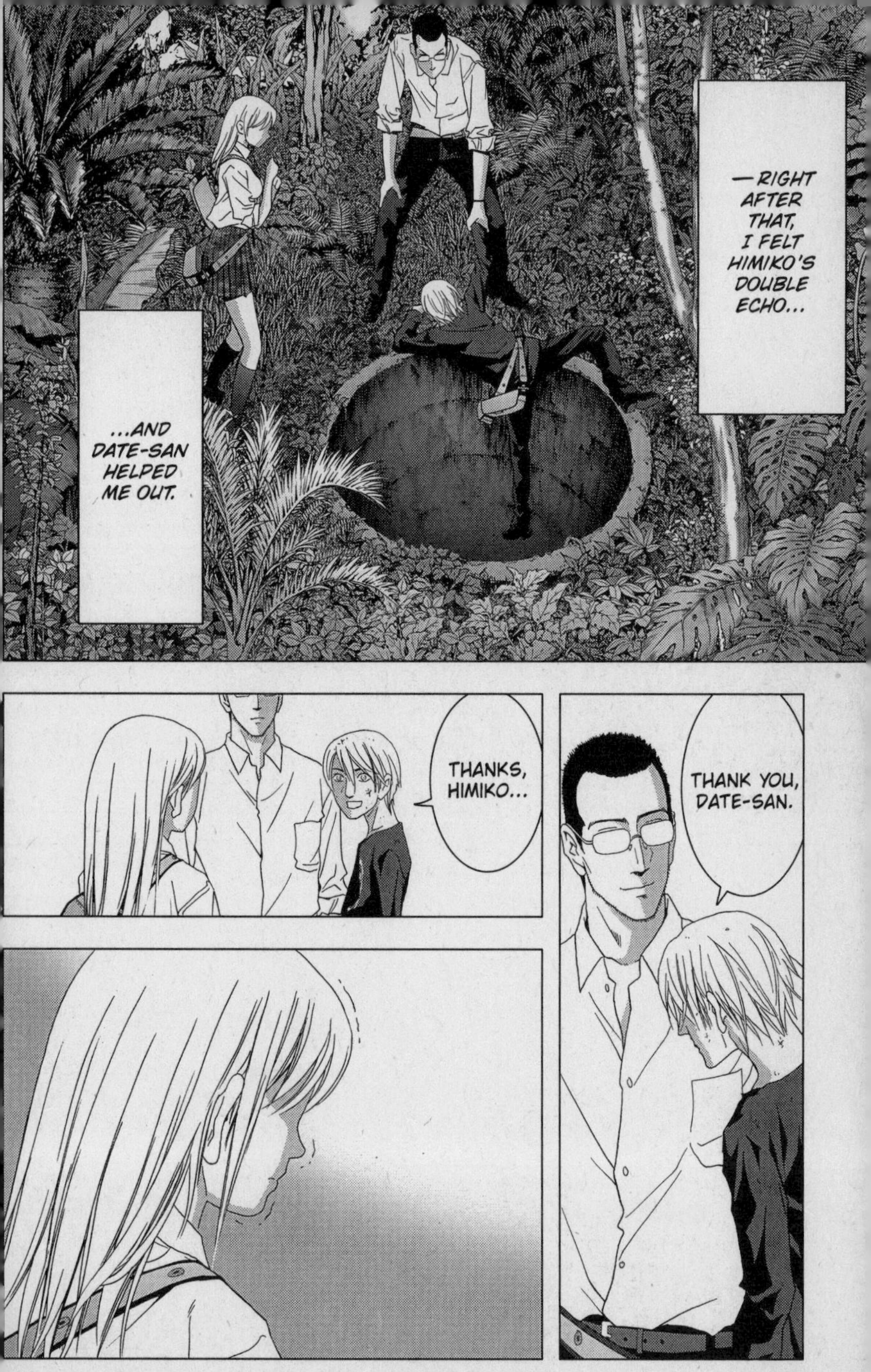
—RIGHT AFTER THAT, I FELT HIMIKO'S DOUBLE ECHO...
...AND DATE-SAN HELPED ME OUT.
THANK YOU, DATE-SAN.
THANKS, HIMIKO...

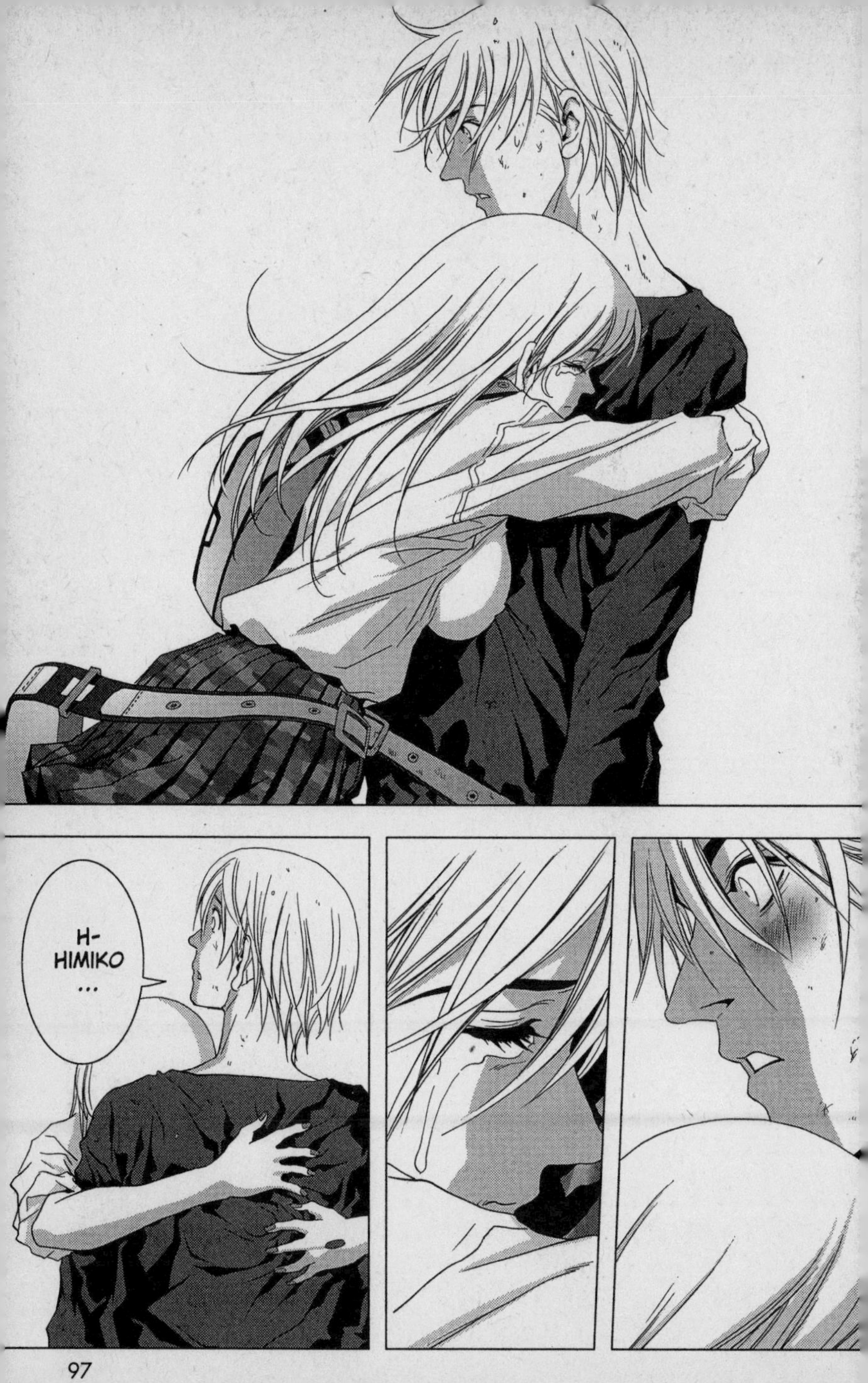
H-HIMIKO ...

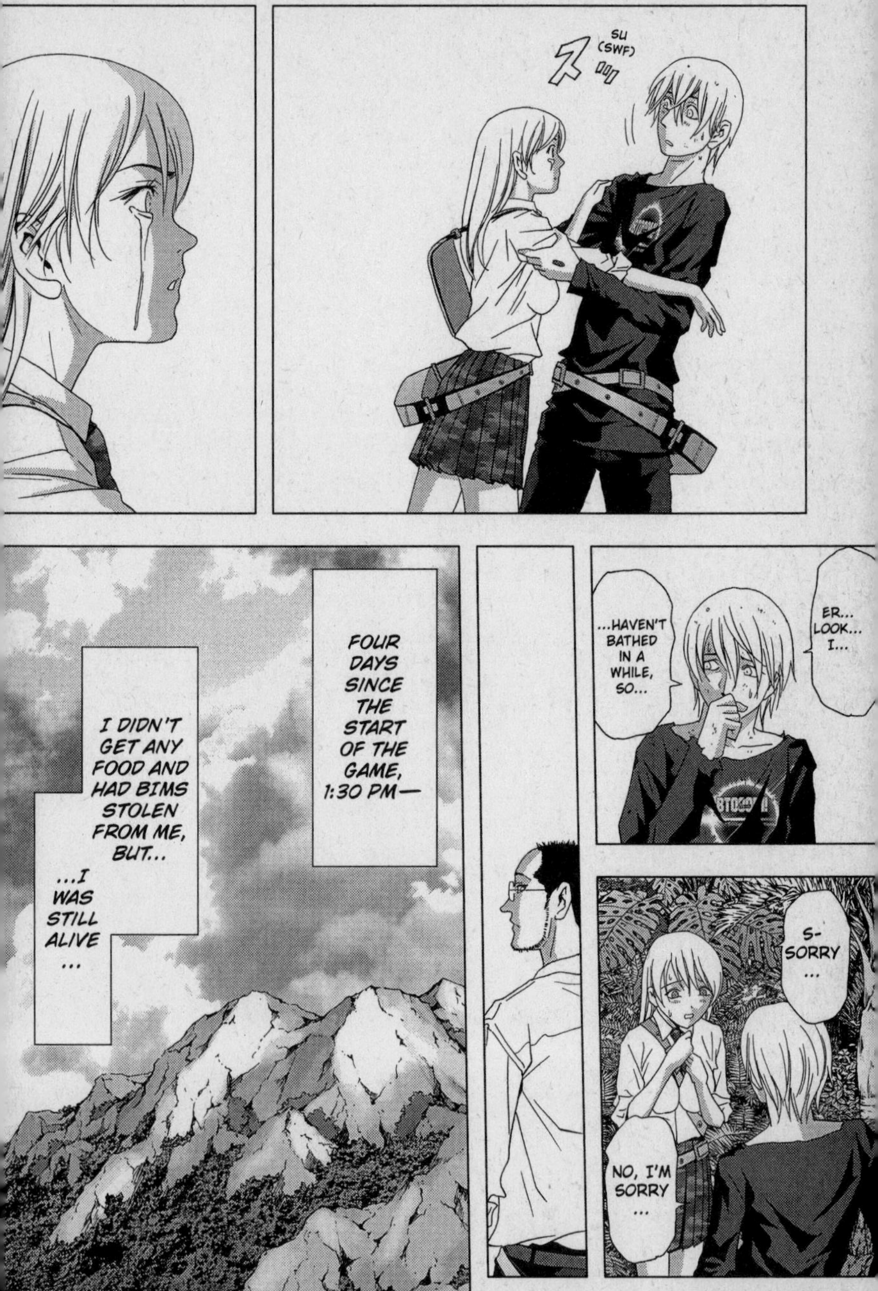
SU (SWF)
ER... LOOK... I...
...HAVEN'T BATHED IN A WHILE, SO...
S-SORRY...
NO, I'M SORRY...
FOUR DAYS SINCE THE START OF THE GAME, 1:30 PM—
I DIDN'T GET ANY FOOD AND HAD BIMS STOLEN FROM ME, BUT...
...I WAS STILL ALIVE...

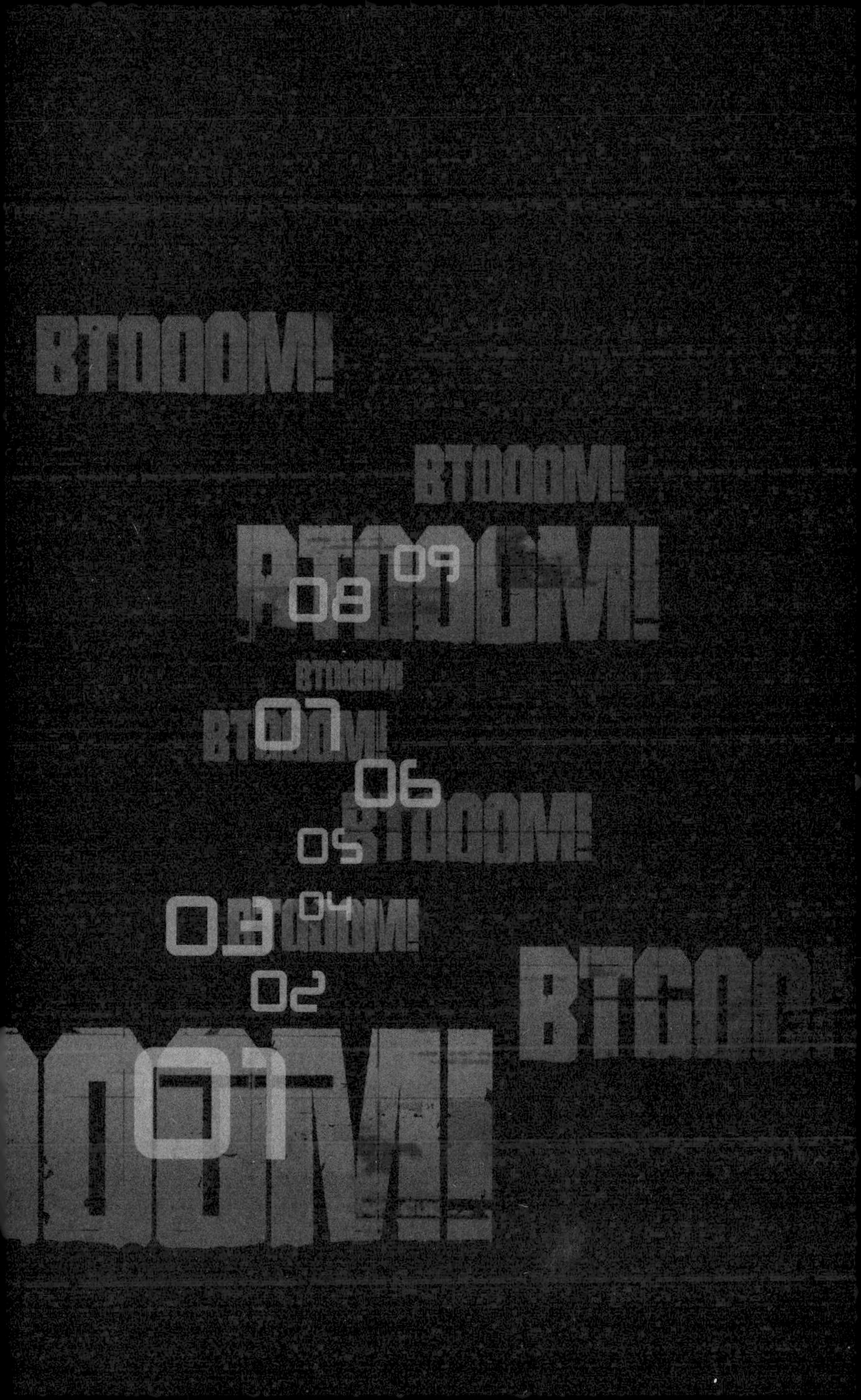
BTOOOM!
BTOOOM!
09
08
BTOOOM!
07
06
05
04
03
02
01

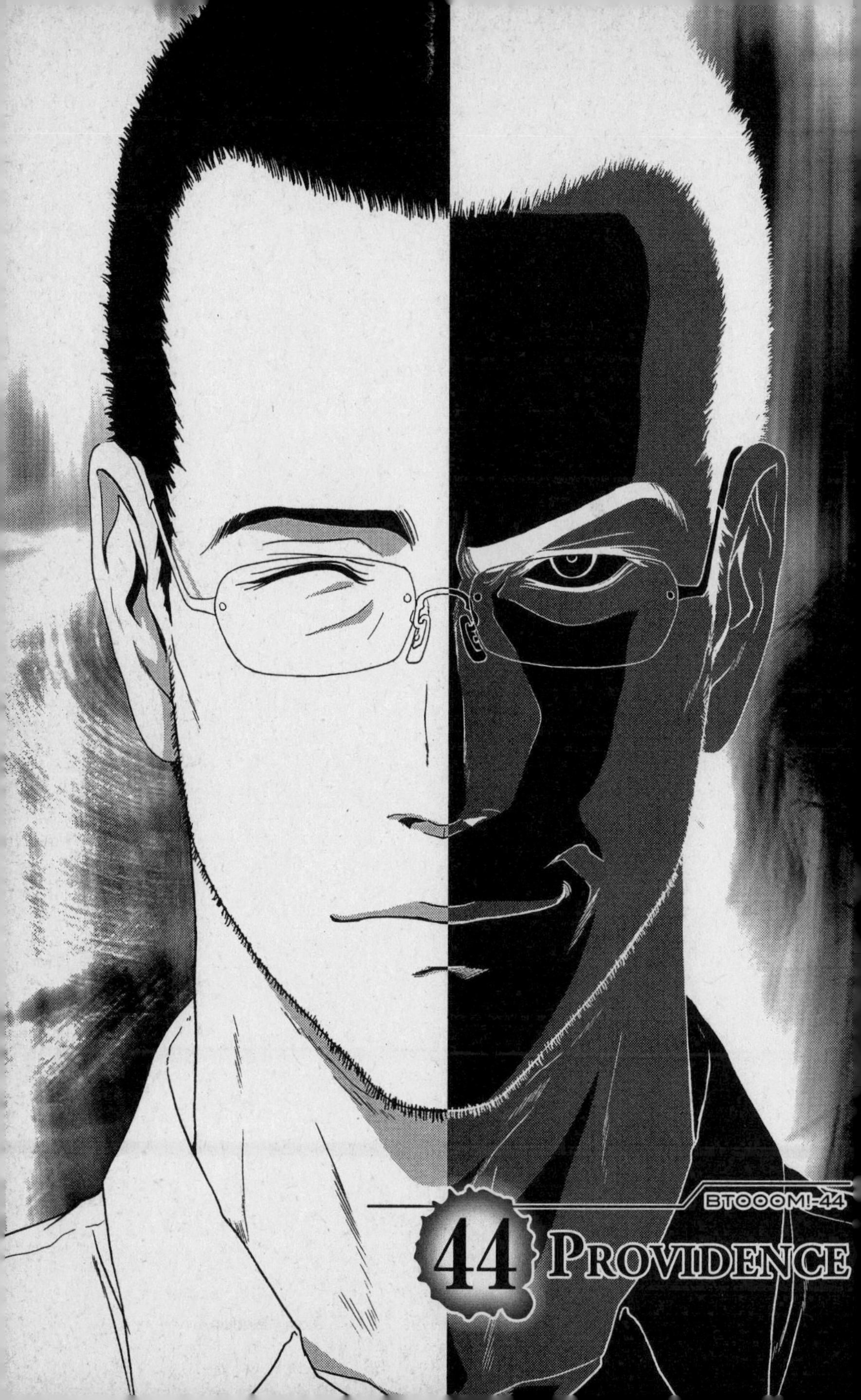
BTOOOM!-44
44 PROVIDENCE

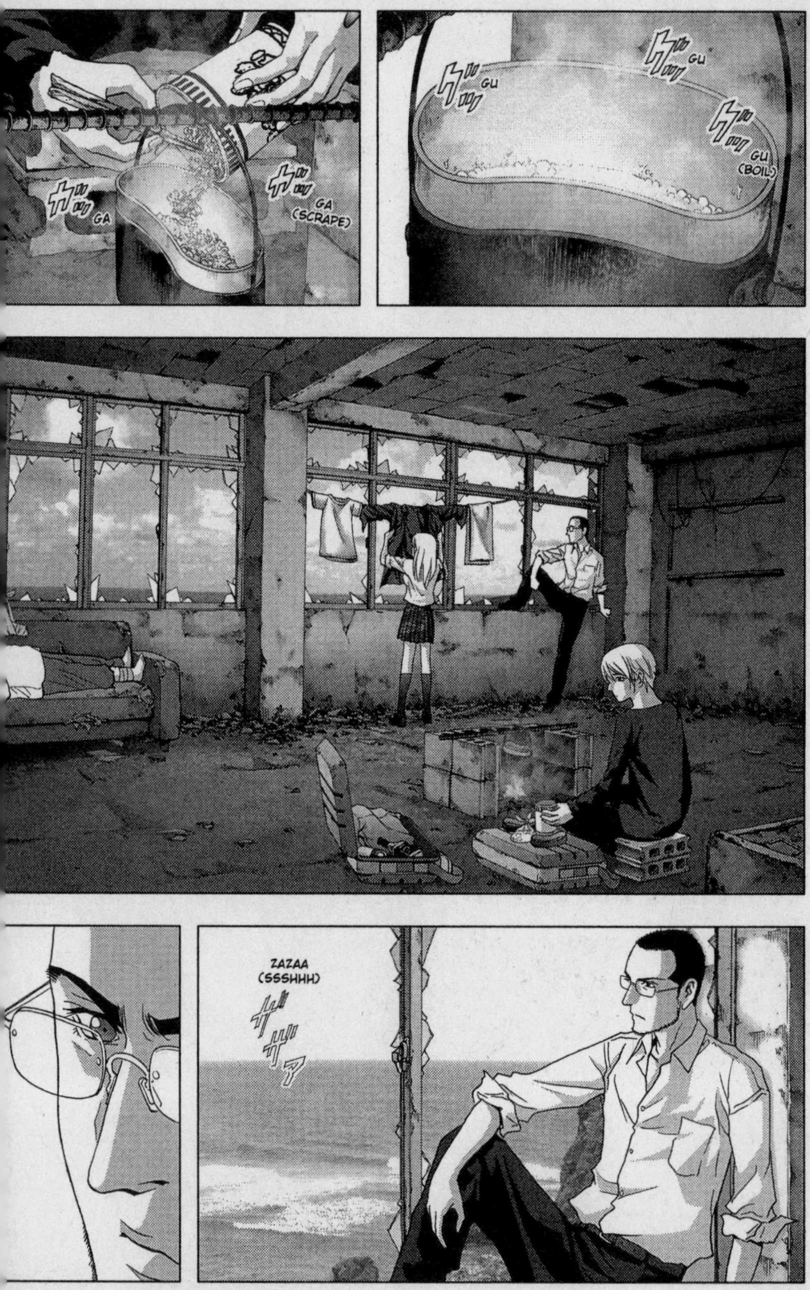
GU
GU
GU
(BOIL)
GA
(SCRAPE)
GA
ZAZAA
(SSSHHH)

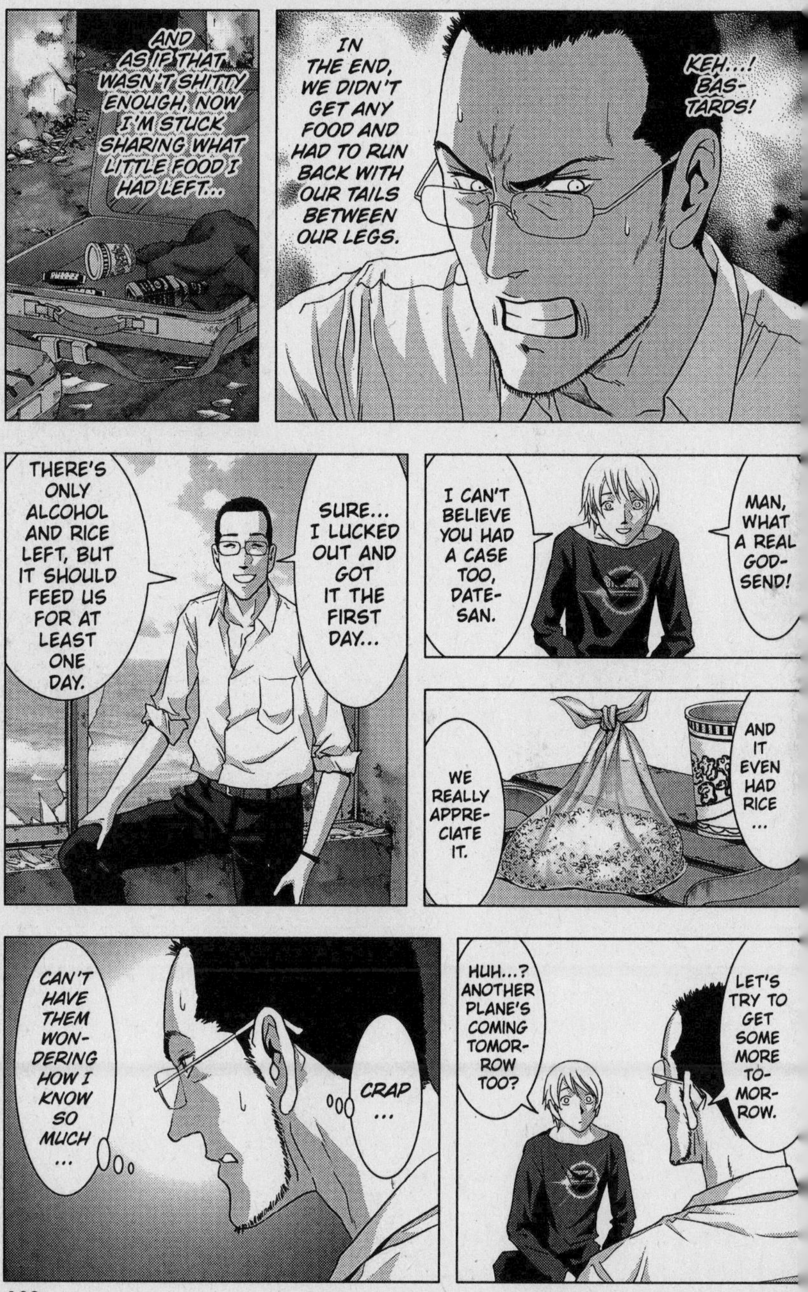
KEH...! BASTARDS!
IN THE END, WE DIDN'T GET ANY FOOD AND HAD TO RUN BACK WITH OUR TAILS BETWEEN OUR LEGS.
AND AS IF THAT WASN'T SHITTY ENOUGH, NOW I'M STUCK SHARING WHAT LITTLE FOOD I HAD LEFT...
MAN, WHAT A REAL GODSEND!
I CAN'T BELIEVE YOU HAD A CASE TOO, DATE-SAN.
AND IT EVEN HAD RICE...
WE REALLY APPRECIATE IT.
SURE... I LUCKED OUT AND GOT IT THE FIRST DAY...
THERE'S ONLY ALCOHOL AND RICE LEFT, BUT IT SHOULD FEED US FOR AT LEAST ONE DAY.
LET'S TRY TO GET SOME MORE TOMORROW.
HUH...? ANOTHER PLANE'S COMING TOMORROW TOO?
CRAP...
CAN'T HAVE THEM WONDERING HOW I KNOW SO MUCH...

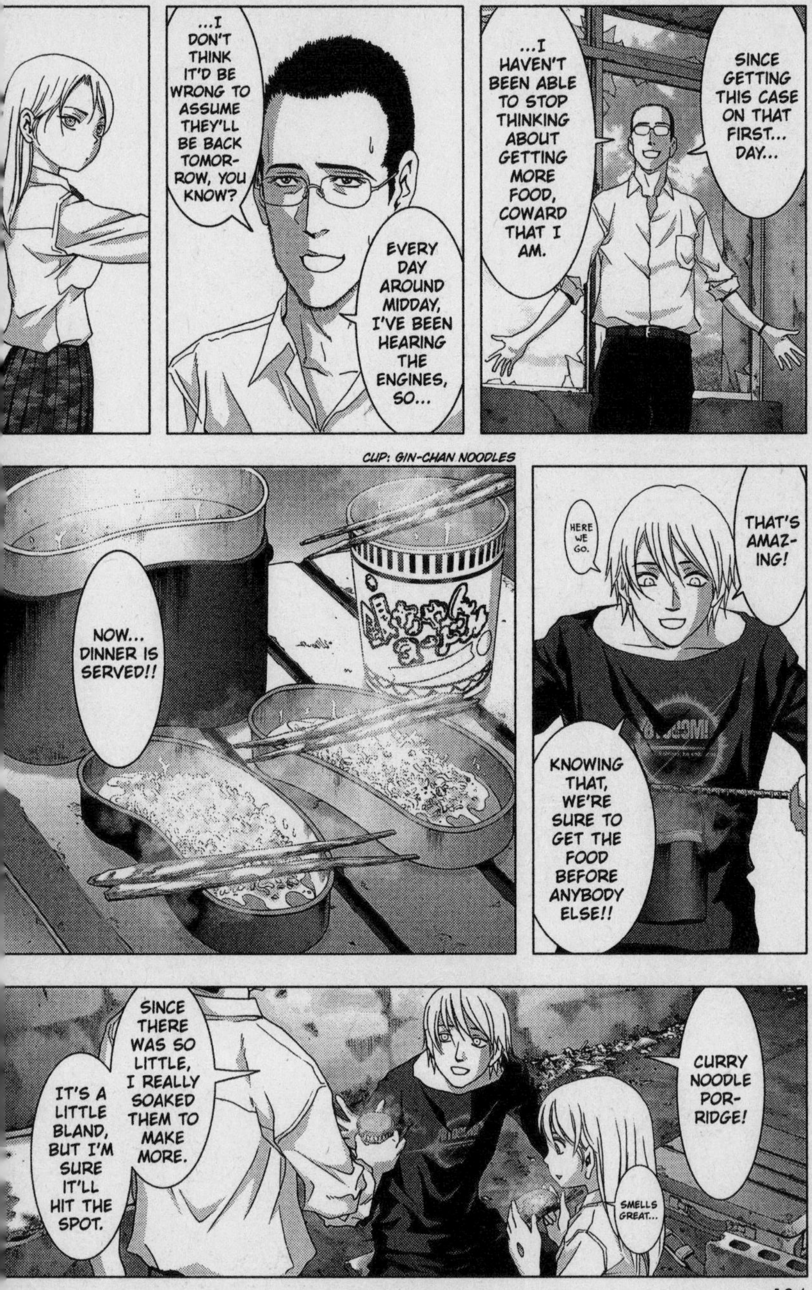
SINCE GETTING THIS CASE ON THAT FIRST... DAY...
...I HAVEN'T BEEN ABLE TO STOP THINKING ABOUT GETTING MORE FOOD, COWARD THAT I AM.
EVERY DAY AROUND MIDDAY, I'VE BEEN HEARING THE ENGINES, SO...
...I DON'T THINK IT'D BE WRONG TO ASSUME THEY'LL BE BACK TOMOR-ROW, YOU KNOW?
THAT'S AMAZ-ING!
HERE WE GO.
KNOWING THAT, WE'RE SURE TO GET THE FOOD BEFORE ANYBODY ELSE!!
CUP: GIN-CHAN NOODLES
NOW... DINNER IS SERVED!!
CURRY NOODLE POR-RIDGE!
SMELLS GREAT...
SINCE THERE WAS SO LITTLE, I REALLY SOAKED THEM TO MAKE MORE.
IT'S A LITTLE BLAND, BUT I'M SURE IT'LL HIT THE SPOT.

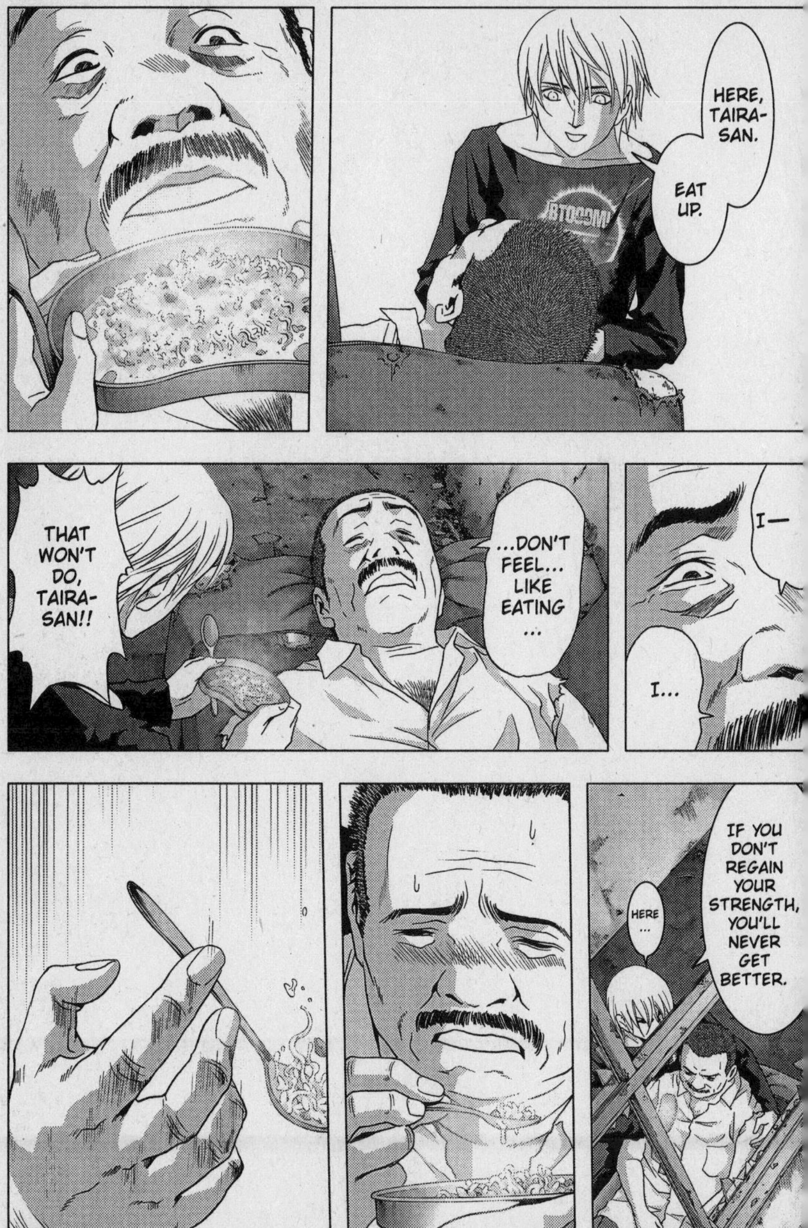
HERE, TAIRA-SAN.
EAT UP.
BTOOOM!
I—
I...
...DON'T FEEL... LIKE EATING ...
THAT WON'T DO, TAIRA-SAN!!
IF YOU DON'T REGAIN YOUR STRENGTH, YOU'LL NEVER GET BETTER.
HERE ...

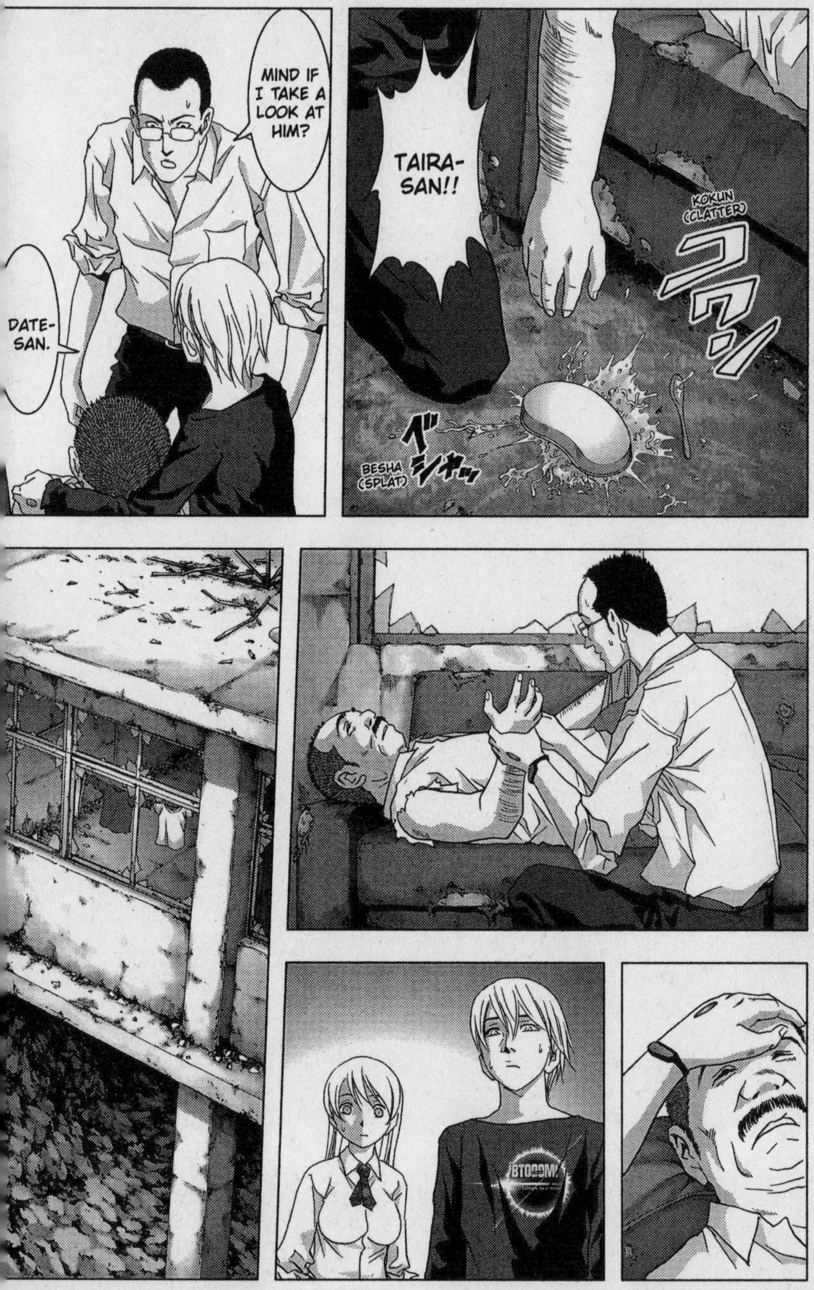
TAIRA-SAN!!
KOKUN (CLATTER)
BESHA (SPLAT)
MIND IF I TAKE A LOOK AT HIM?
DATE-SAN.

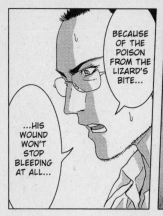

THIS IS BAD...
BECAUSE OF THE POISON FROM THE LIZARD'S BITE...
...HIS WOUND WON'T STOP BLEEDING AT ALL...
POISON...?
BUT ON TV THEY SAID THAT KOMODO DRAGONS AREN'T POISONOUS...
THAT'S AN OUTDATED THEORY.
THE BITE OF THE KOMODO IS DEFINITELY VENOMOUS.
AND THE LARGE LIZARDS ON THIS ISLAND ARE PROBABLY NO EXCEPTION...
THE FACT THAT HIS BLEEDING WON'T STOP IS PROOF OF THAT.
IF HE DOESN'T GET THE ANTIVENOM AND FORMAL MEDICAL CARE RIGHT AWAY, HIS LIFE WILL BE IN DANGER.

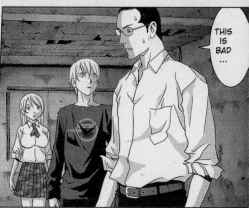

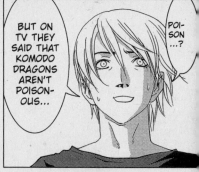

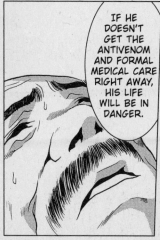

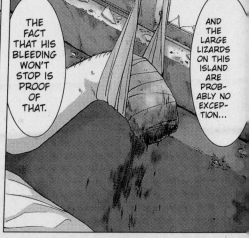

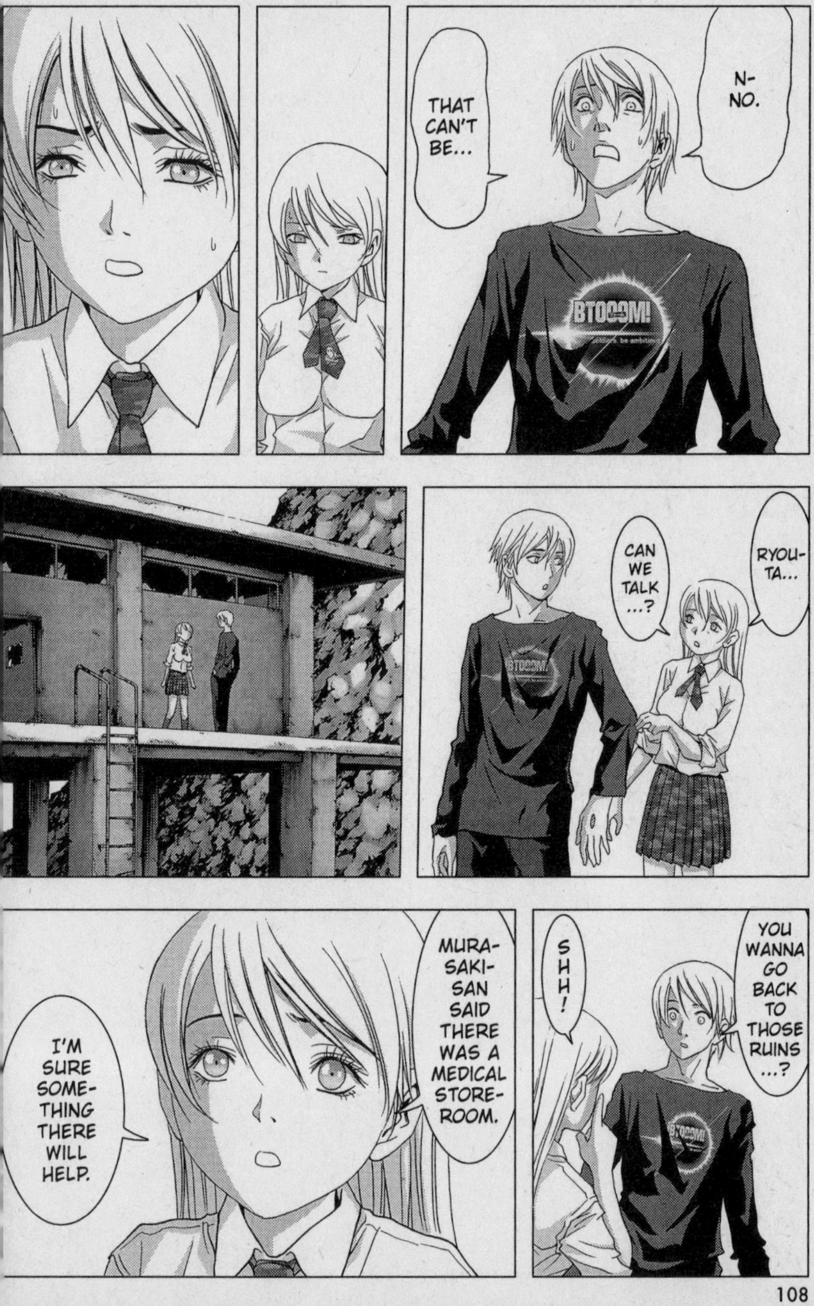
N-NO.
THAT CAN'T BE...
BTOOOM!
RYOU-TA...
CAN WE TALK ...?
YOU WANNA GO BACK TO THOSE RUINS ...?
SHH!
MURA-SAKI-SAN SAID THERE WAS A MEDICAL STORE-ROOM.
I'M SURE SOME-THING THERE WILL HELP.

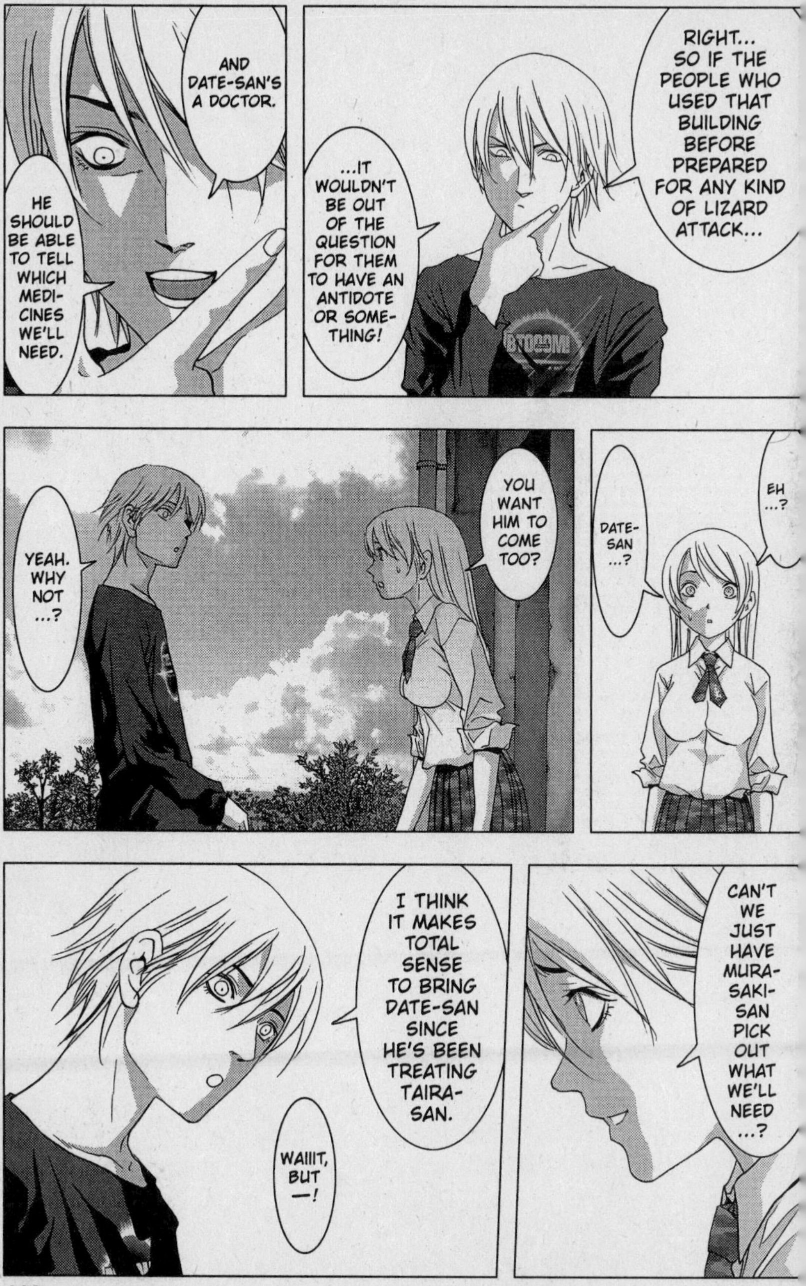
RIGHT... SO IF THE PEOPLE WHO USED THAT BUILDING BEFORE PREPARED FOR ANY KIND OF LIZARD ATTACK...
...IT WOULDN'T BE OUT OF THE QUESTION FOR THEM TO HAVE AN ANTIDOTE OR SOME-THING!
AND DATE-SAN'S A DOCTOR.
HE SHOULD BE ABLE TO TELL WHICH MEDI-CINES WE'LL NEED.
EH ...?
DATE-SAN ...?
YOU WANT HIM TO COME TOO?
YEAH. WHY NOT ...?
CAN'T WE JUST HAVE MURA-SAKI-SAN PICK OUT WHAT WE'LL NEED ...?
I THINK IT MAKES TOTAL SENSE TO BRING DATE-SAN SINCE HE'S BEEN TREATING TAIRA-SAN.
WAIIIT, BUT —!

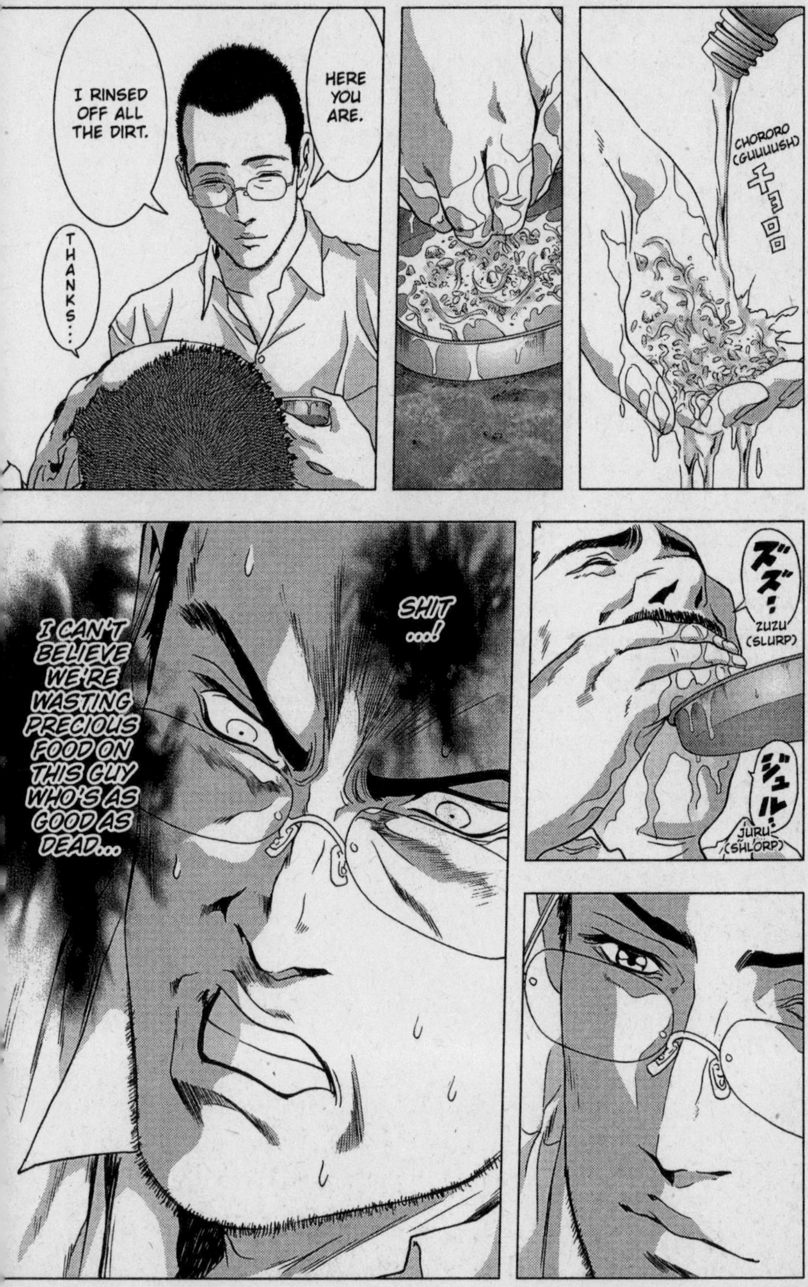
CHORORO (GUUUUSH)
チョロロ
HERE YOU ARE.
I RINSED OFF ALL THE DIRT.
THANKS...
ズズー
ZUZU (SLURP)
ジュル
JURU (SHLORP)
SHIT...!
I CAN'T BELIEVE WE'RE WASTING PRECIOUS FOOD ON THIS GUY WHO'S AS GOOD AS DEAD...

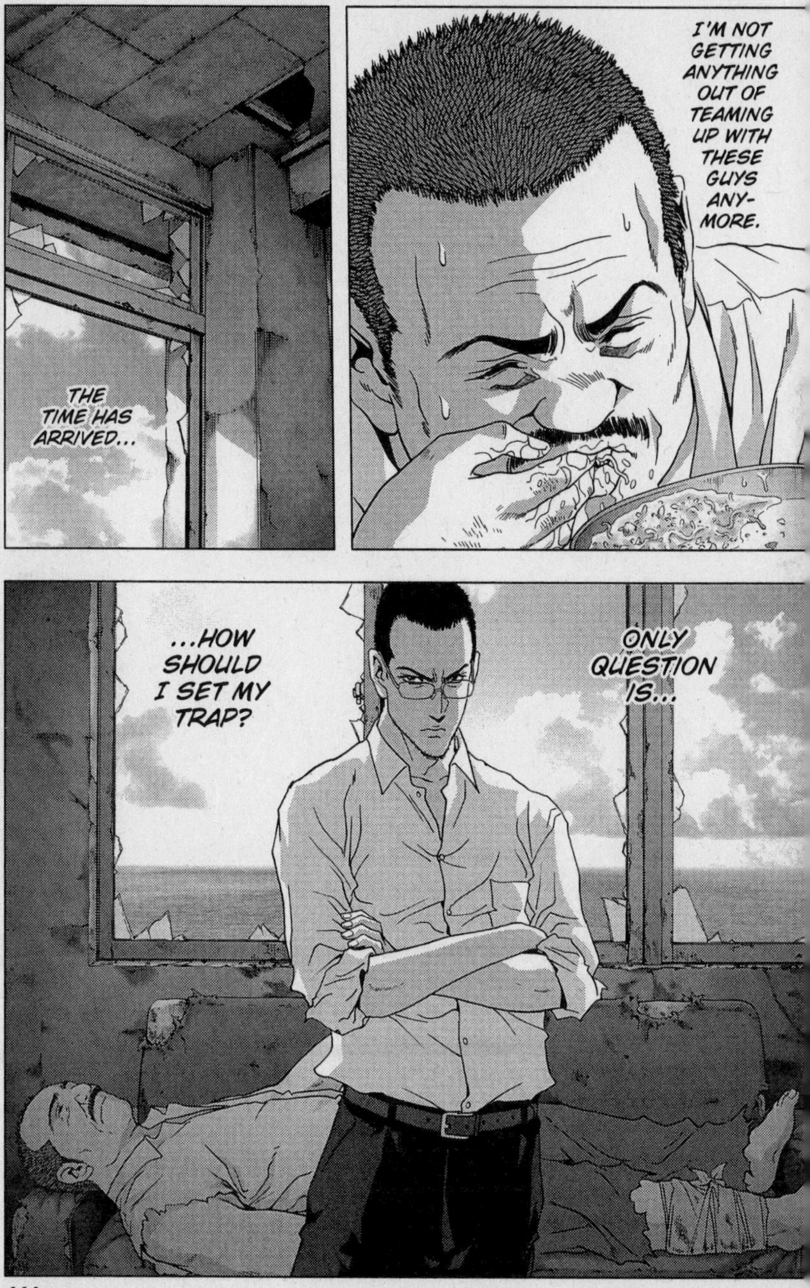
I'M NOT GETTING ANYTHING OUT OF TEAMING UP WITH THESE GUYS ANY-MORE.
THE TIME HAS ARRIVED...
ONLY QUESTION IS...
...HOW SHOULD I SET MY TRAP?

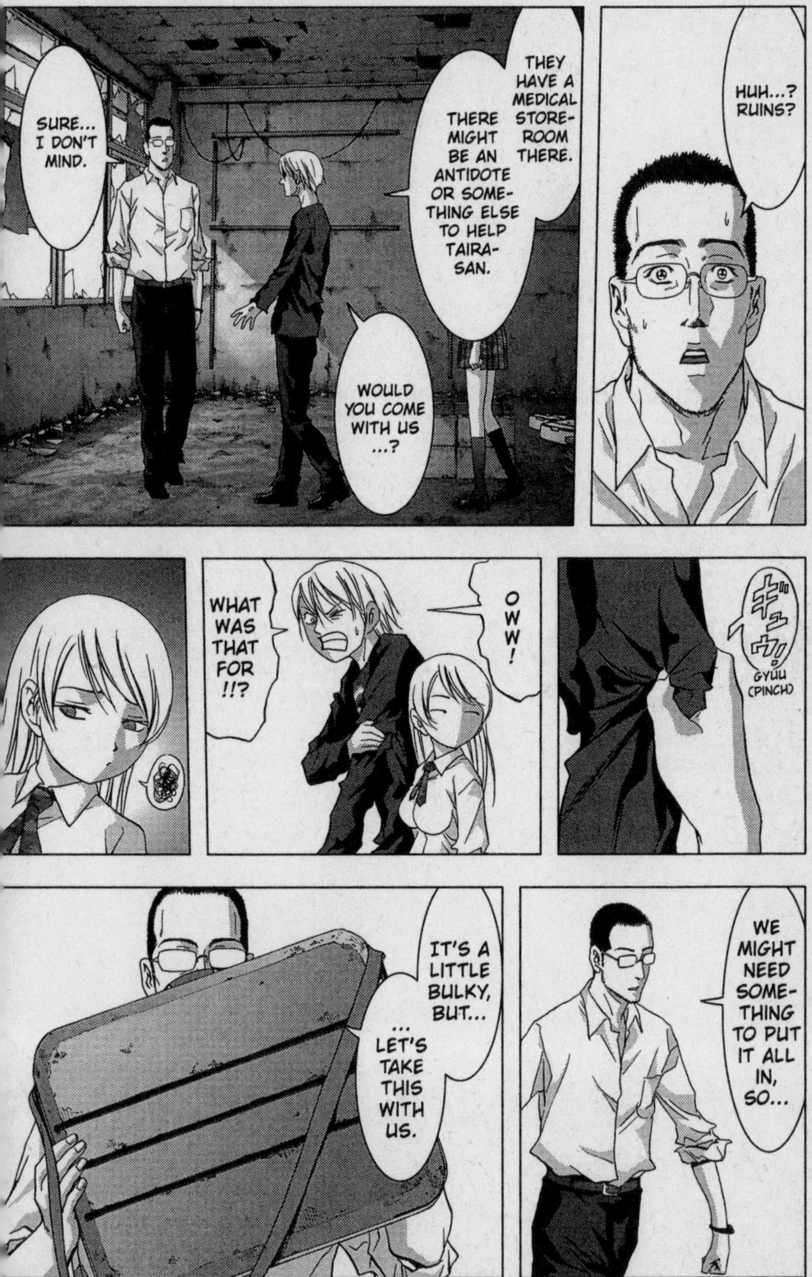
HUH...? RUINS?
THEY HAVE A MEDICAL STORE-ROOM THERE.
THERE MIGHT BE AN ANTIDOTE OR SOME-THING ELSE TO HELP TAIRA-SAN.
WOULD YOU COME WITH US ...?
SURE... I DON'T MIND.
ギュウ!
GYUU (PINCH)
OWW!
WHAT WAS THAT FOR !!?
WE MIGHT NEED SOME-THING TO PUT IT ALL IN, SO...
IT'S A LITTLE BULKY, BUT...
... LET'S TAKE THIS WITH US.

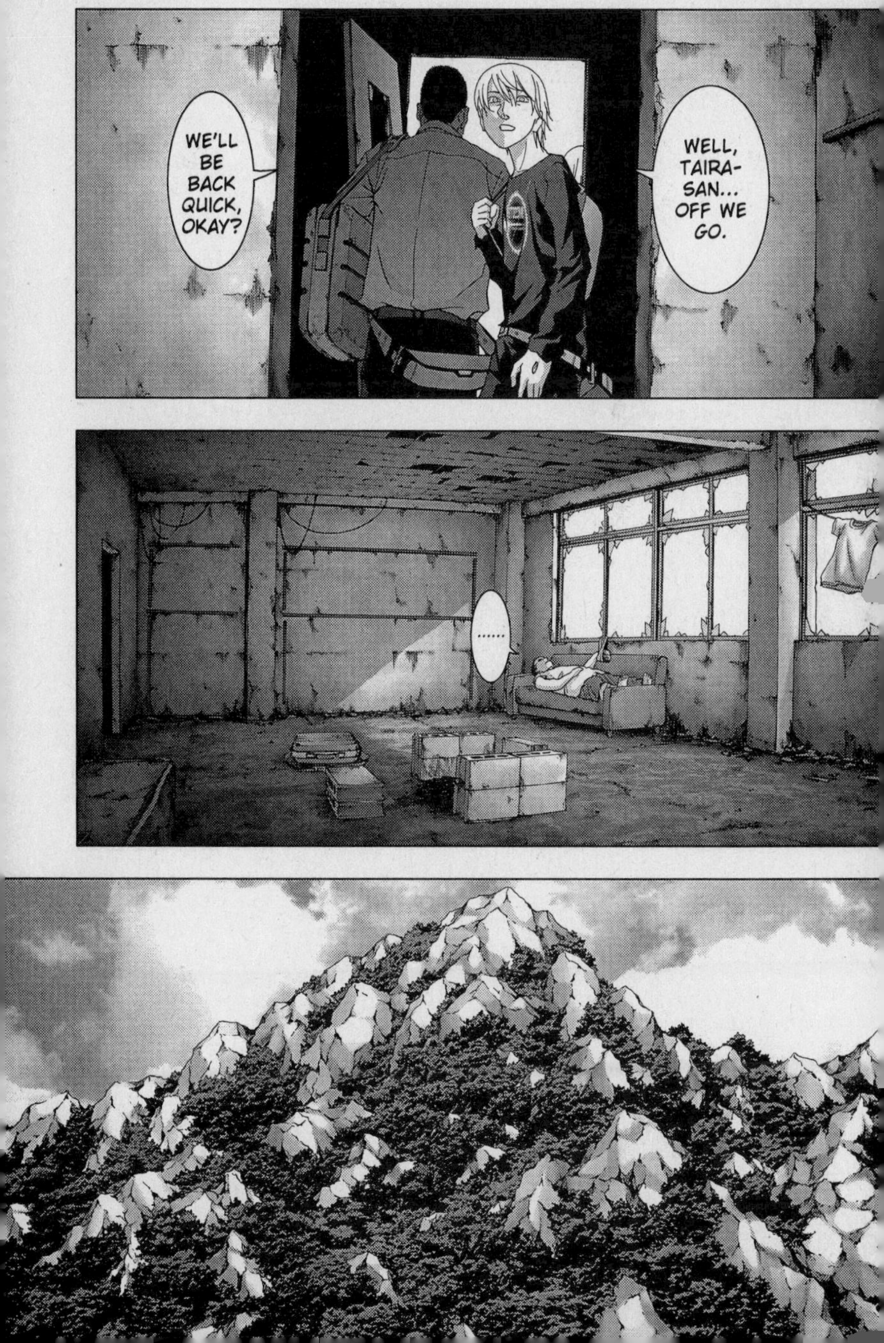
WELL, TAIRA-SAN... OFF WE GO.
WE'LL BE BACK QUICK, OKAY?
......

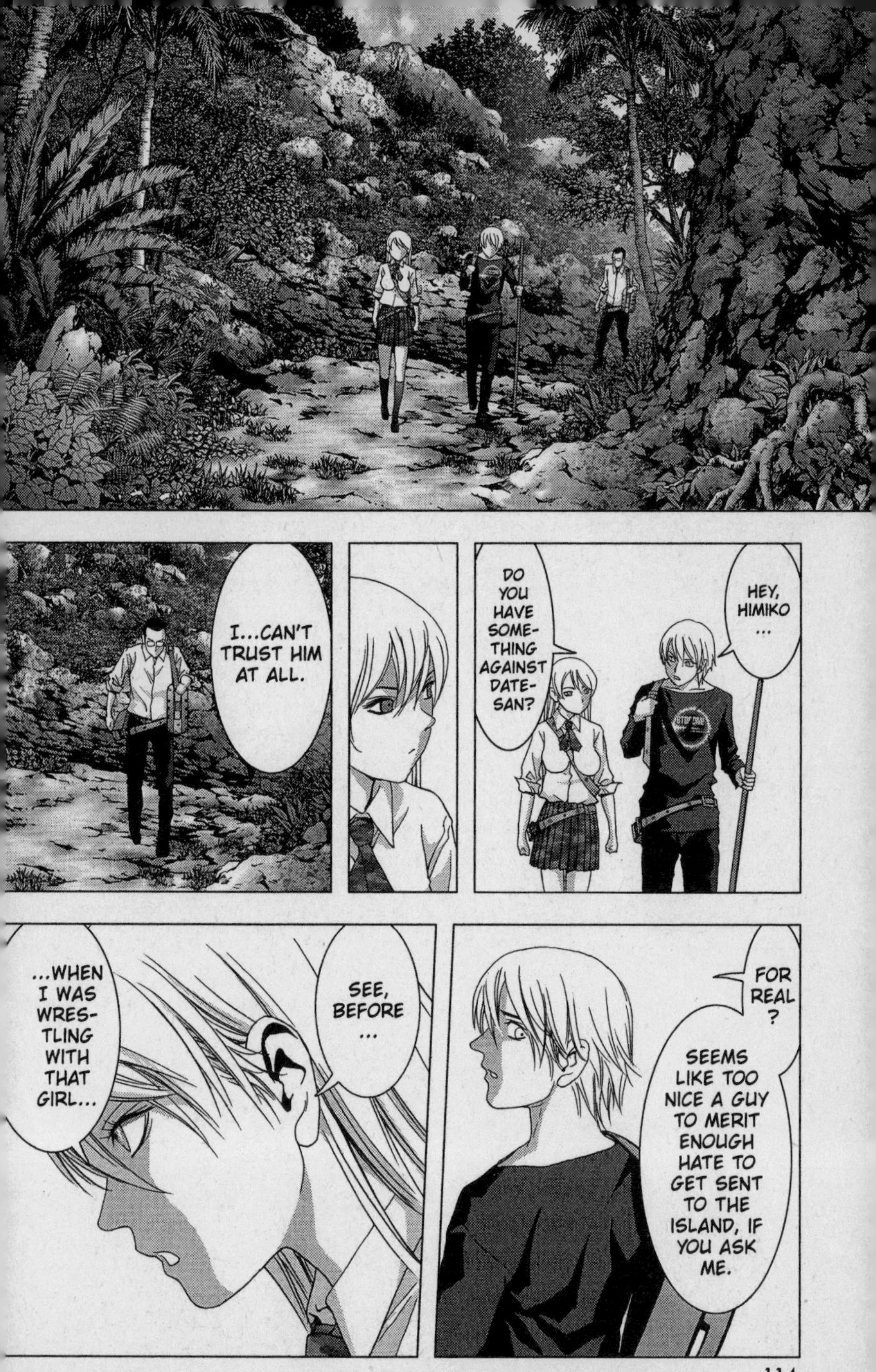
HEY, HIMIKO...
DO YOU HAVE SOMETHING AGAINST DATE-SAN?
I...CAN'T TRUST HIM AT ALL.
FOR REAL?
SEEMS LIKE TOO NICE A GUY TO MERIT ENOUGH HATE TO GET SENT TO THE ISLAND, IF YOU ASK ME.
SEE, BEFORE...
...WHEN I WAS WRESTLING WITH THAT GIRL...

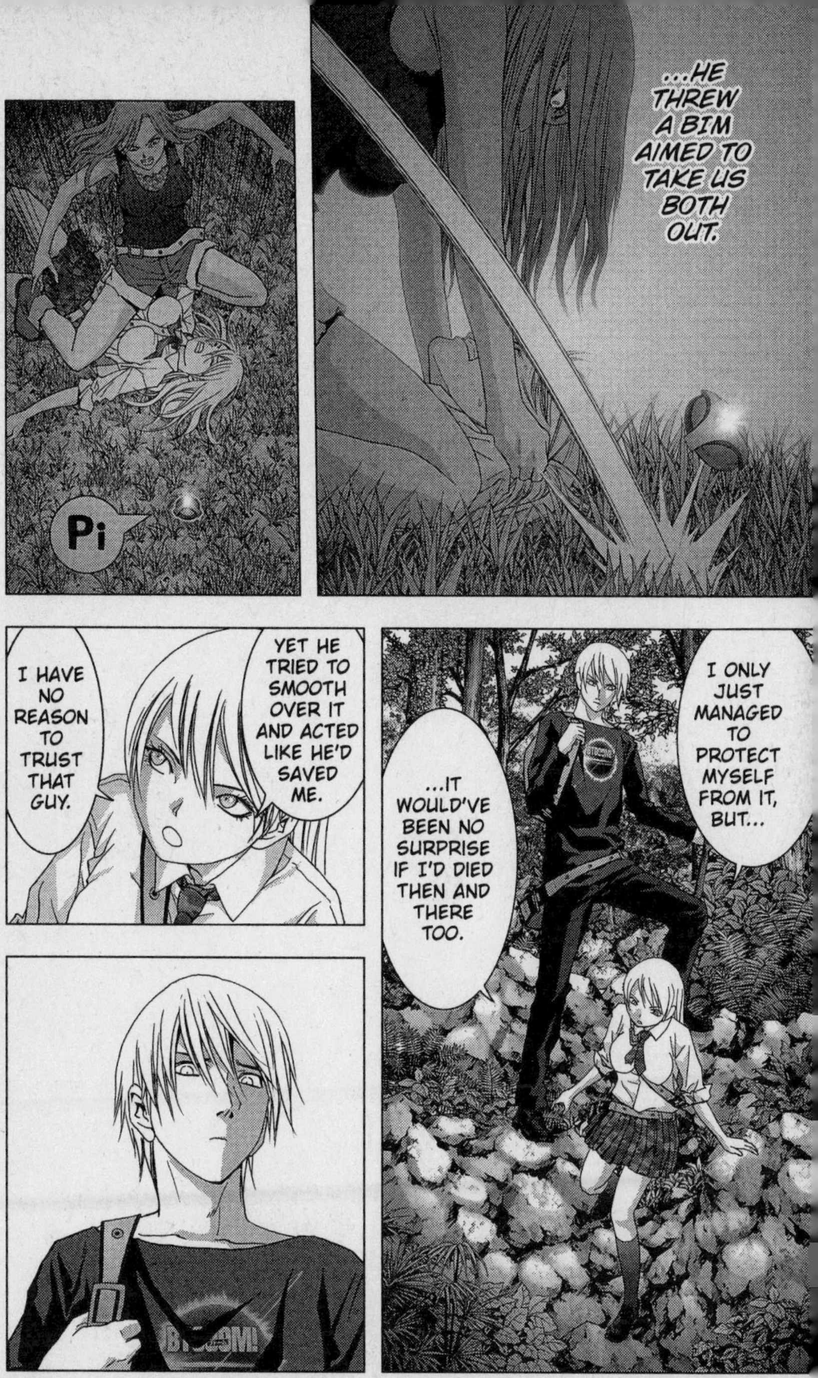
...HE THREW A BIM AIMED TO TAKE US BOTH OUT.
Pi
I ONLY JUST MANAGED TO PROTECT MYSELF FROM IT, BUT...
...IT WOULD'VE BEEN NO SURPRISE IF I'D DIED THEN AND THERE TOO.
YET HE TRIED TO SMOOTH OVER IT AND ACTED LIKE HE'D SAVED ME.
I HAVE NO REASON TO TRUST THAT GUY.

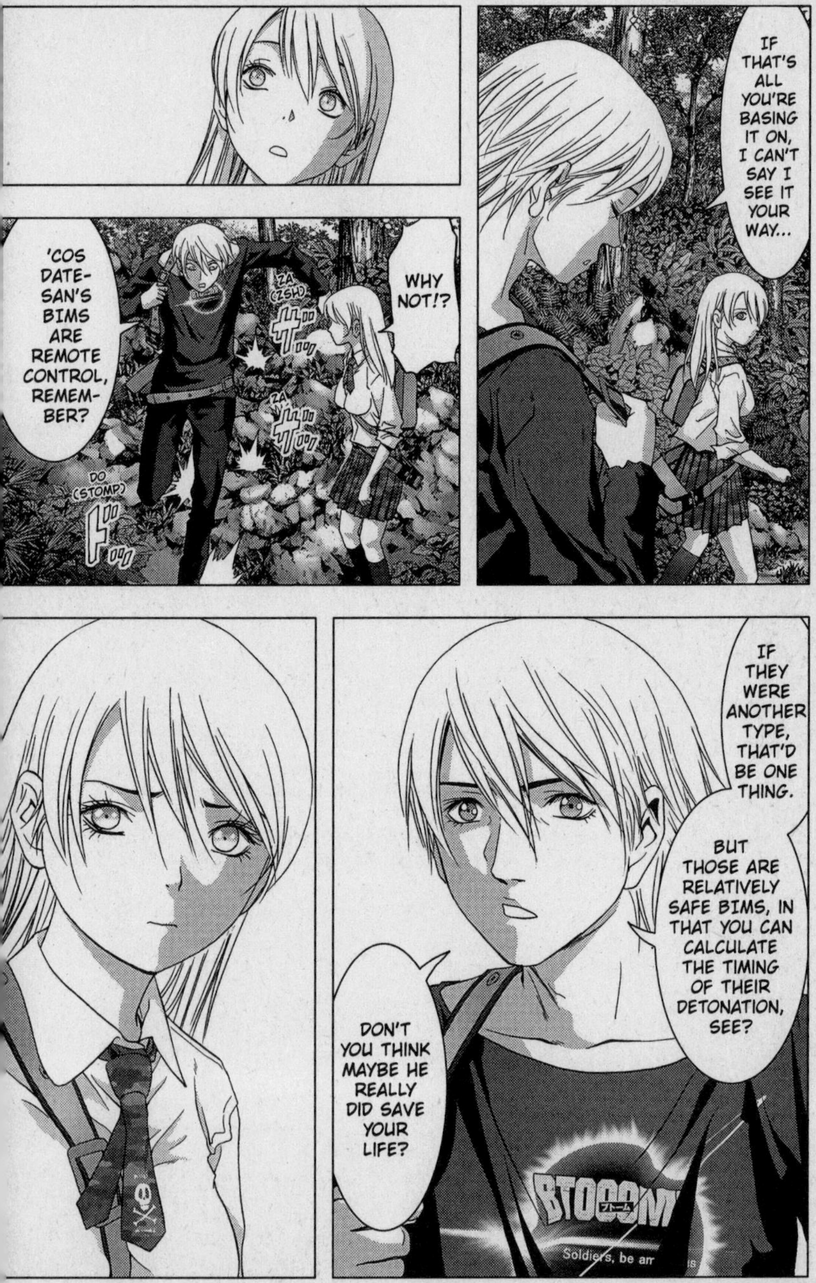
IF THAT'S ALL YOU'RE BASING IT ON, I CAN'T SAY I SEE IT YOUR WAY...
WHY NOT!?
'COS DATE-SAN'S BIMS ARE REMOTE CONTROL, REMEMBER?
ZA (ZSH)
ZA
DO (STOMP)
IF THEY WERE ANOTHER TYPE, THAT'D BE ONE THING.
BUT THOSE ARE RELATIVELY SAFE BIMS, IN THAT YOU CAN CALCULATE THE TIMING OF THEIR DETONATION, SEE?
DON'T YOU THINK MAYBE HE REALLY DID SAVE YOUR LIFE?
BTOOOM

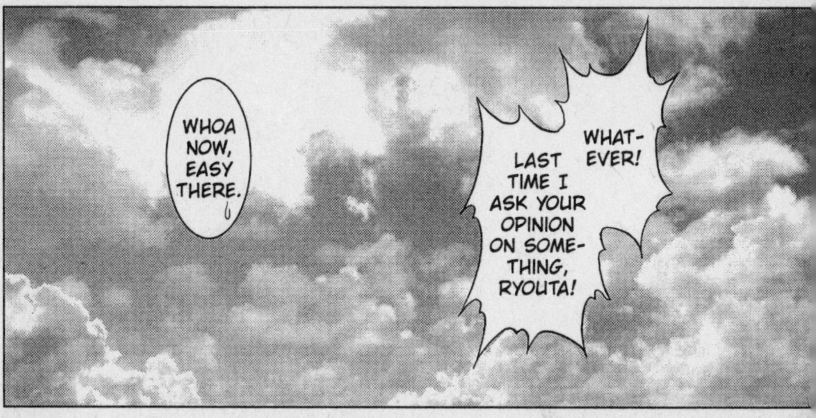
WHATEVER!
LAST TIME I ASK YOUR OPINION ON SOMETHING, RYOUTA!
WHOA NOW, EASY THERE.

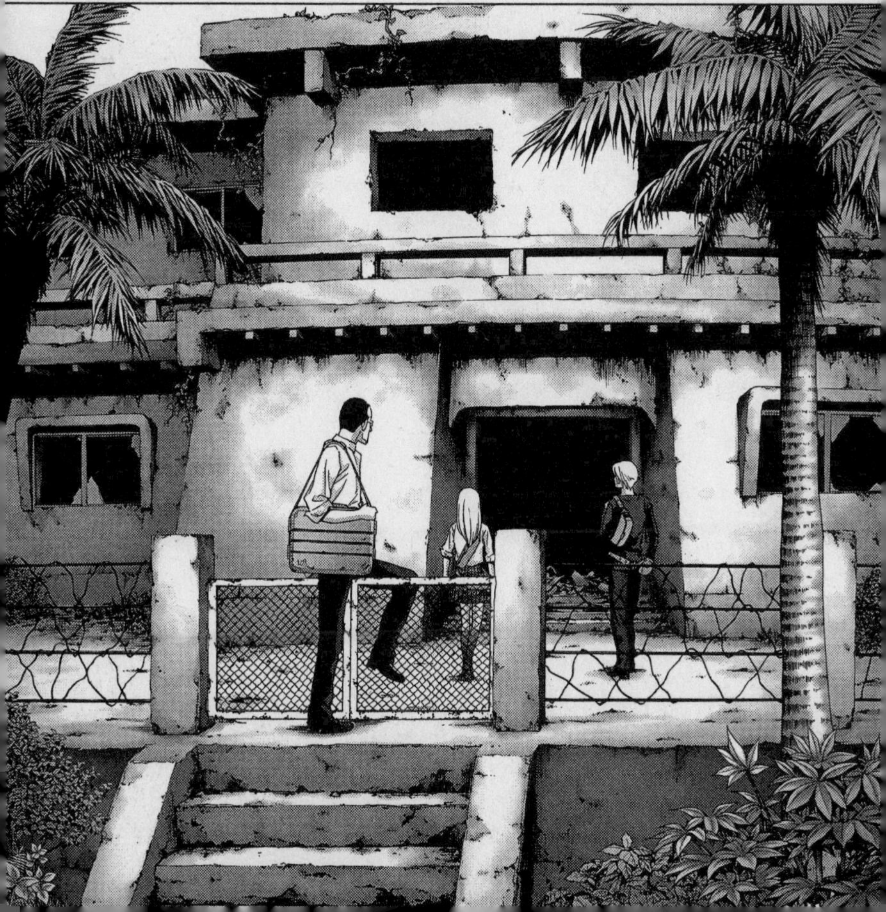

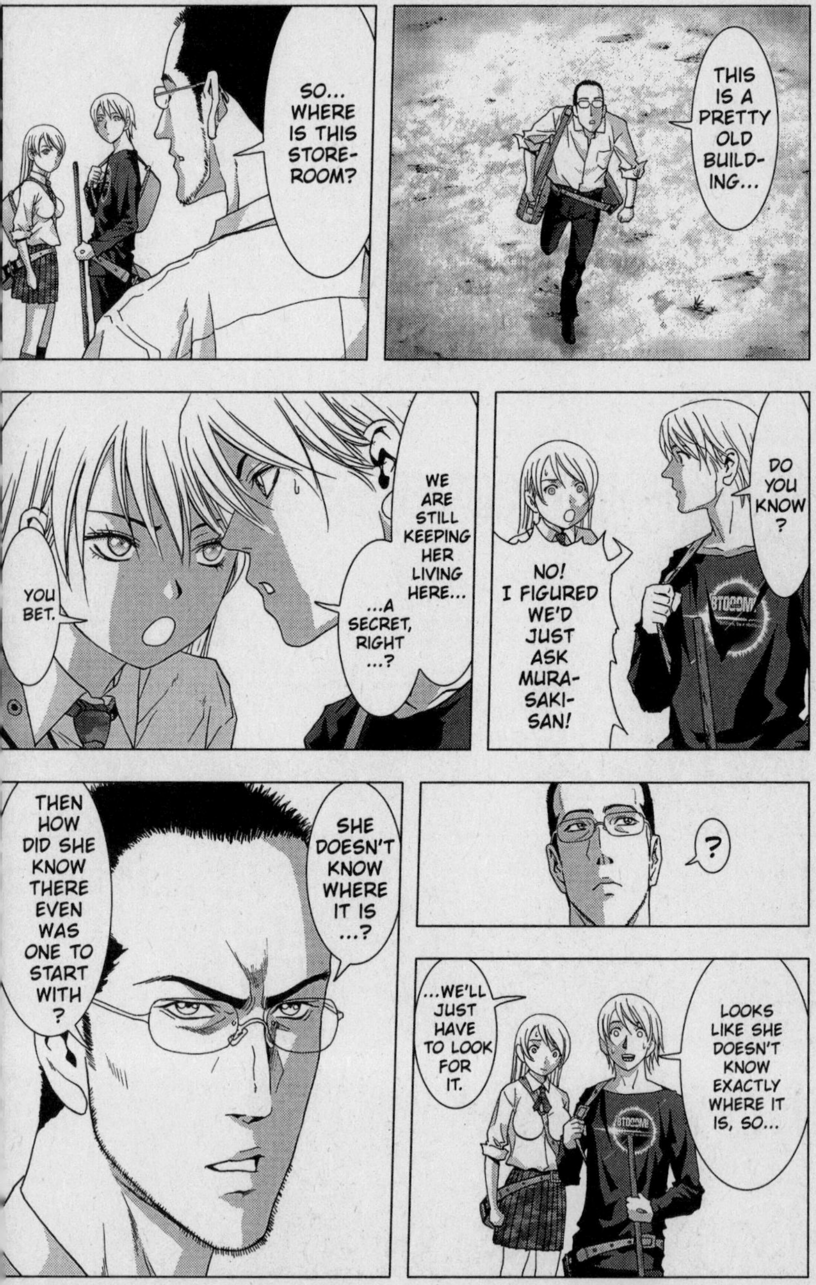
THIS IS A PRETTY OLD BUILDING...
SO... WHERE IS THIS STOREROOM?
DO YOU KNOW ?
NO! I FIGURED WE'D JUST ASK MURASAKI-SAN!
WE ARE STILL KEEPING HER LIVING HERE...
...A SECRET, RIGHT ...?
YOU BET.
?
LOOKS LIKE SHE DOESN'T KNOW EXACTLY WHERE IT IS, SO...
...WE'LL JUST HAVE TO LOOK FOR IT.
SHE DOESN'T KNOW WHERE IT IS ...?
THEN HOW DID SHE KNOW THERE EVEN WAS ONE TO START WITH ?

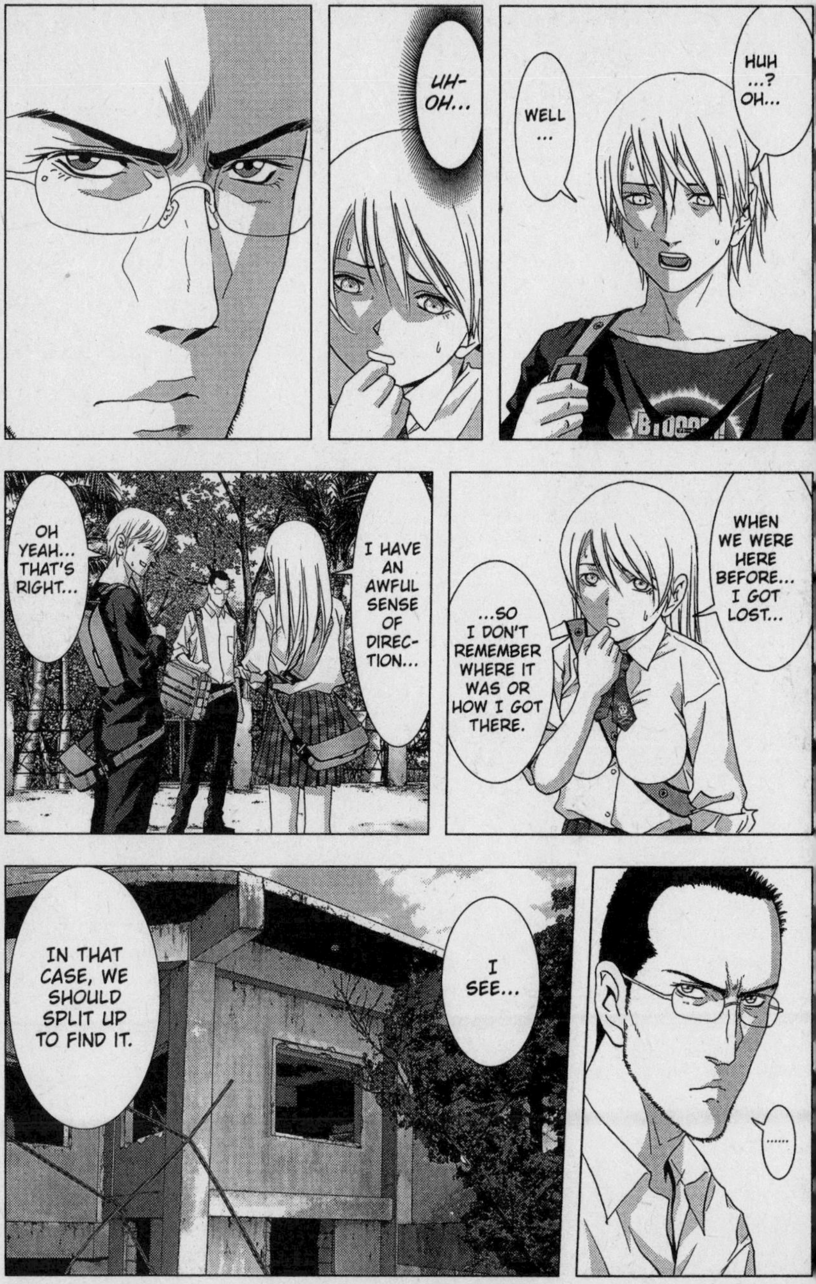
HUH ...? OH...
WELL ...
UH- OH...
WHEN WE WERE HERE BEFORE... I GOT LOST...
...SO I DON'T REMEMBER WHERE IT WAS OR HOW I GOT THERE.
I HAVE AN AWFUL SENSE OF DIRECTION...
OH YEAH... THAT'S RIGHT...
......
I SEE...
IN THAT CASE, WE SHOULD SPLIT UP TO FIND IT.

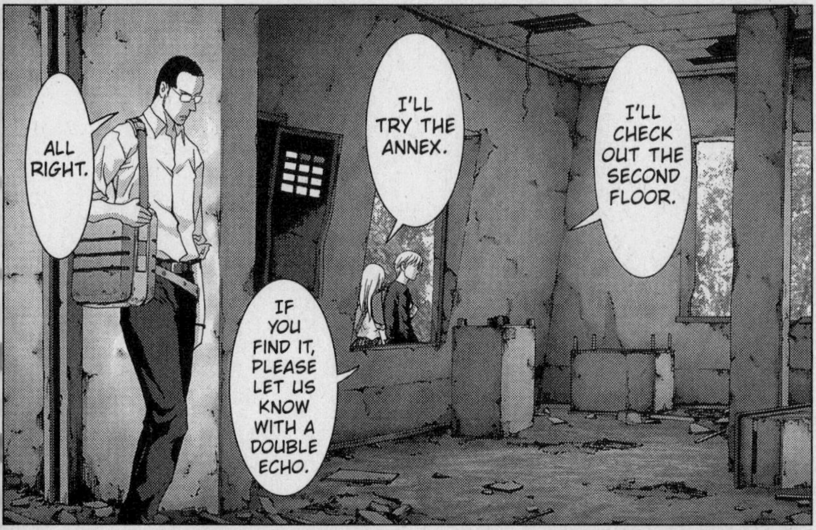
I'LL CHECK OUT THE SECOND FLOOR.
I'LL TRY THE ANNEX.
IF YOU FIND IT, PLEASE LET US KNOW WITH A DOUBLE ECHO.
ALL RIGHT.
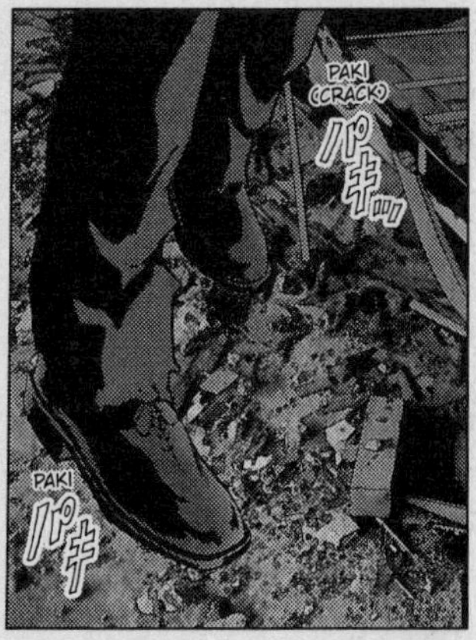
PAKI (CRACK)
パキッ
PAKI
パキ
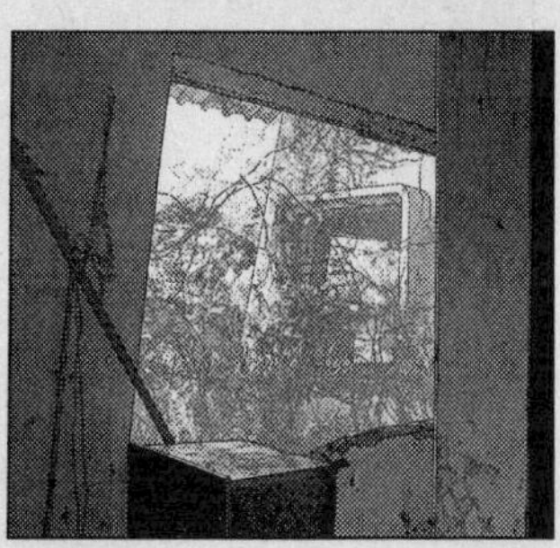
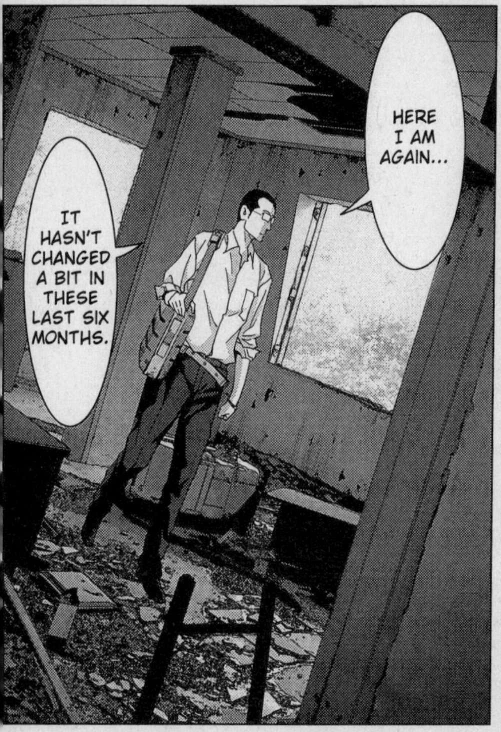
HERE I AM AGAIN...
IT HASN'T CHANGED A BIT IN THESE LAST SIX MONTHS.

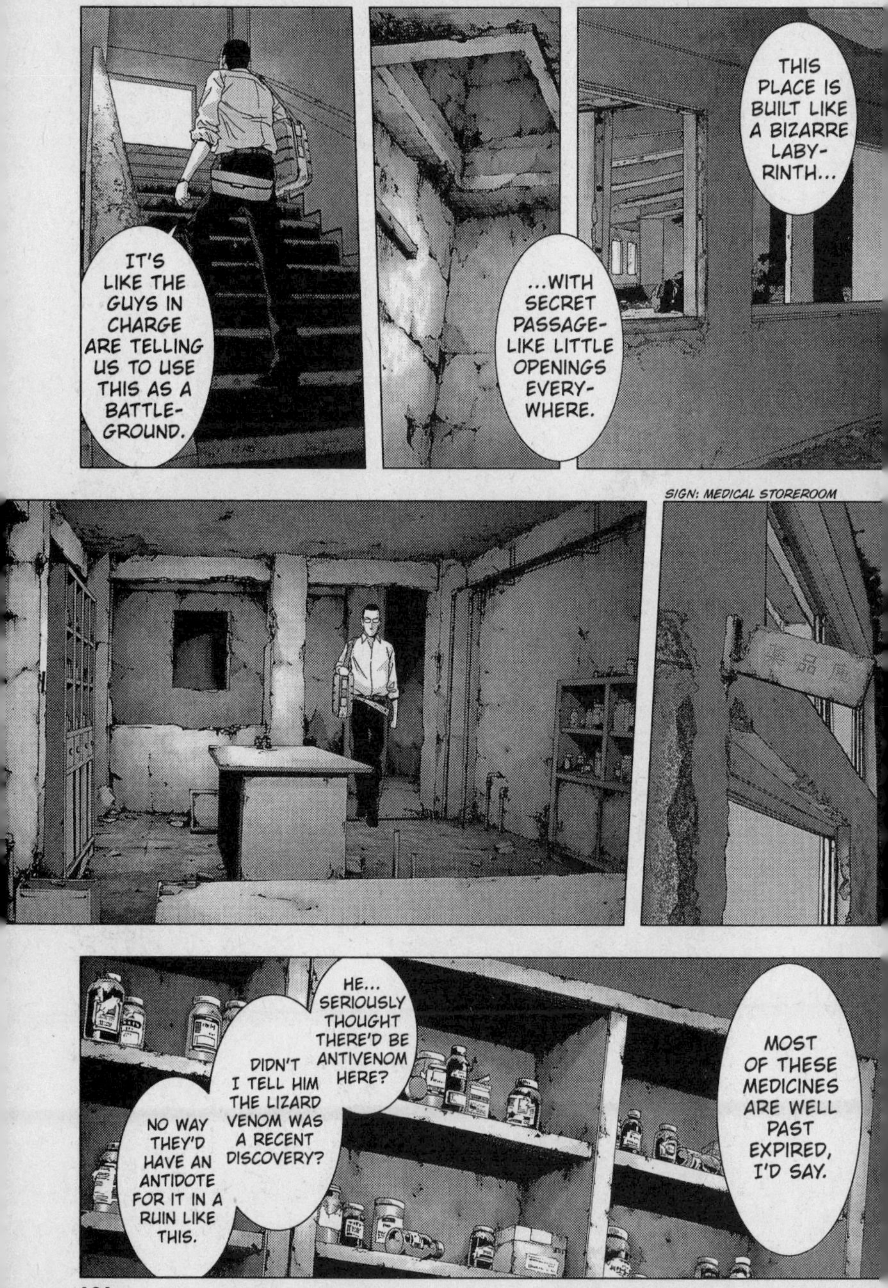
THIS PLACE IS BUILT LIKE A BIZARRE LABY-RINTH...
...WITH SECRET PASSAGE-LIKE LITTLE OPENINGS EVERY-WHERE.
IT'S LIKE THE GUYS IN CHARGE ARE TELLING US TO USE THIS AS A BATTLE-GROUND.
SIGN: MEDICAL STOREROOM
MOST OF THESE MEDICINES ARE WELL PAST EXPIRED, I'D SAY.
HE... SERIOUSLY THOUGHT THERE'D BE ANTIVENOM HERE?
DIDN'T I TELL HIM THE LIZARD VENOM WAS A RECENT DISCOVERY?
NO WAY THEY'D HAVE AN ANTIDOTE FOR IT IN A RUIN LIKE THIS.

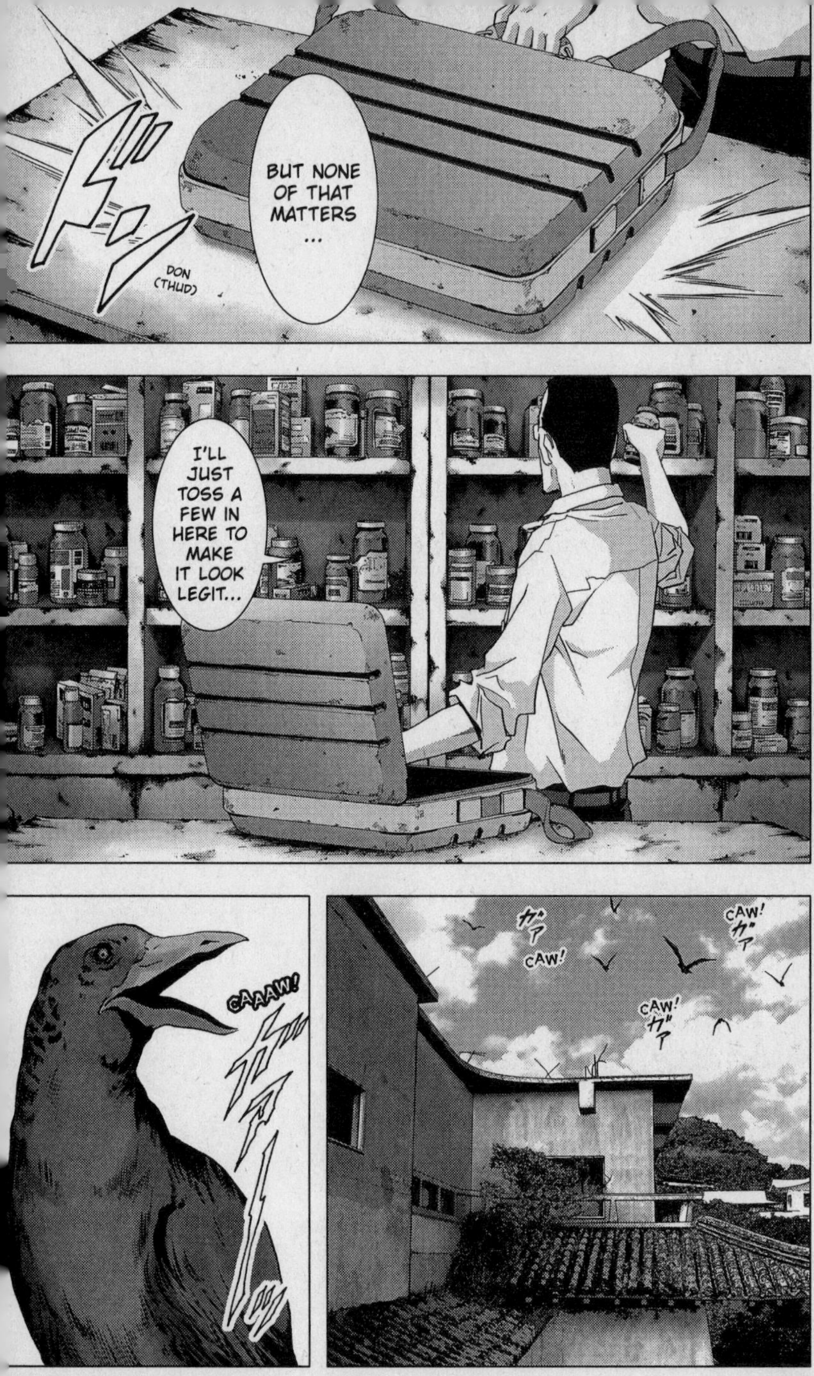
BUT NONE OF THAT MATTERS ...
DON (THUD)
I'LL JUST TOSS A FEW IN HERE TO MAKE IT LOOK LEGIT...
CAW!
ガア
ガア
CAW!
CAW!
ガア
CAAAW!

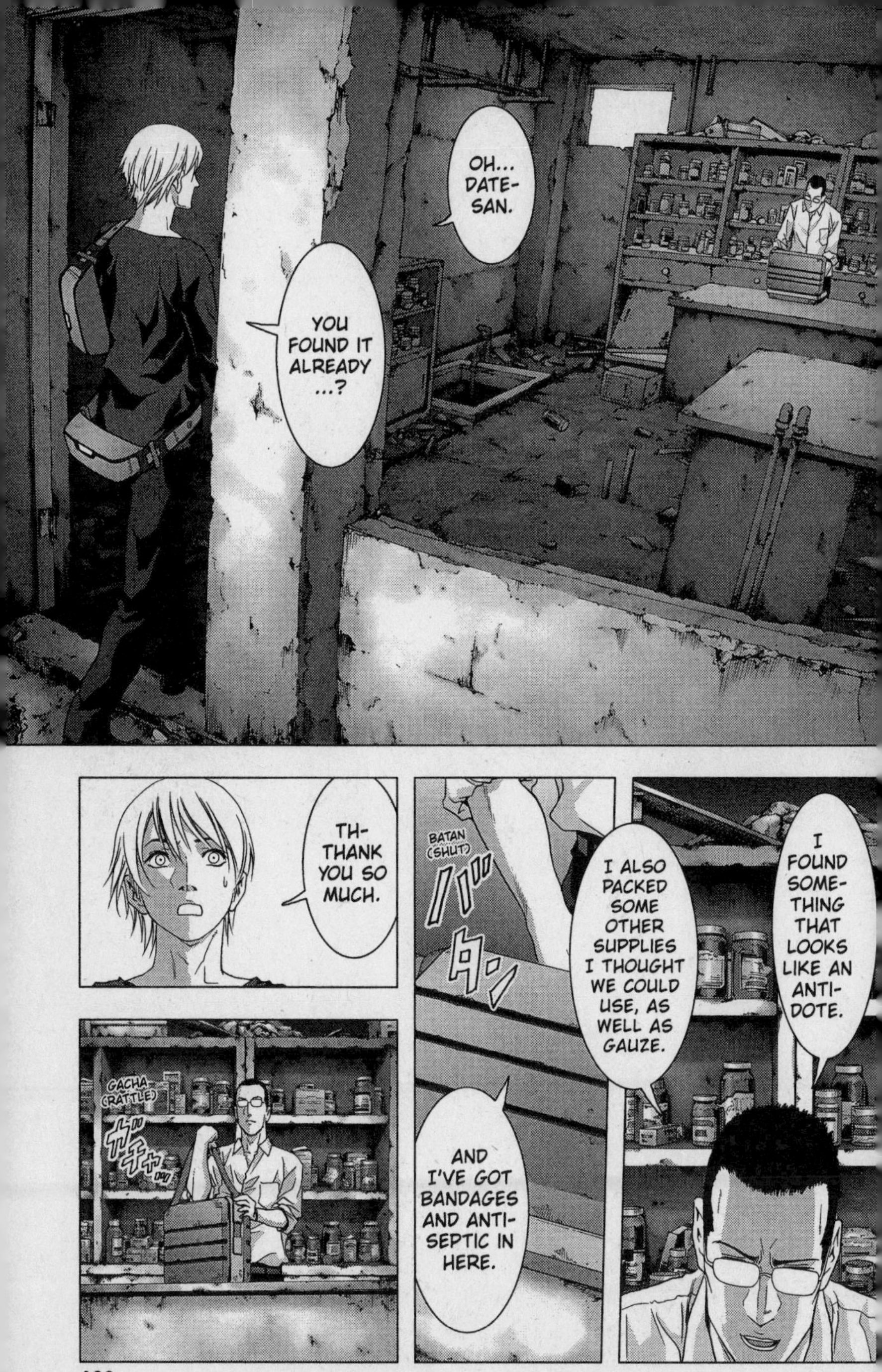
OH... DATE-SAN.
YOU FOUND IT ALREADY ...?
I FOUND SOMETHING THAT LOOKS LIKE AN ANTIDOTE.
I ALSO PACKED SOME OTHER SUPPLIES I THOUGHT WE COULD USE, AS WELL AS GAUZE.
BATAN (SHUT)
AND I'VE GOT BANDAGES AND ANTISEPTIC IN HERE.
TH-THANK YOU SO MUCH.
GACHA (RATTLE)

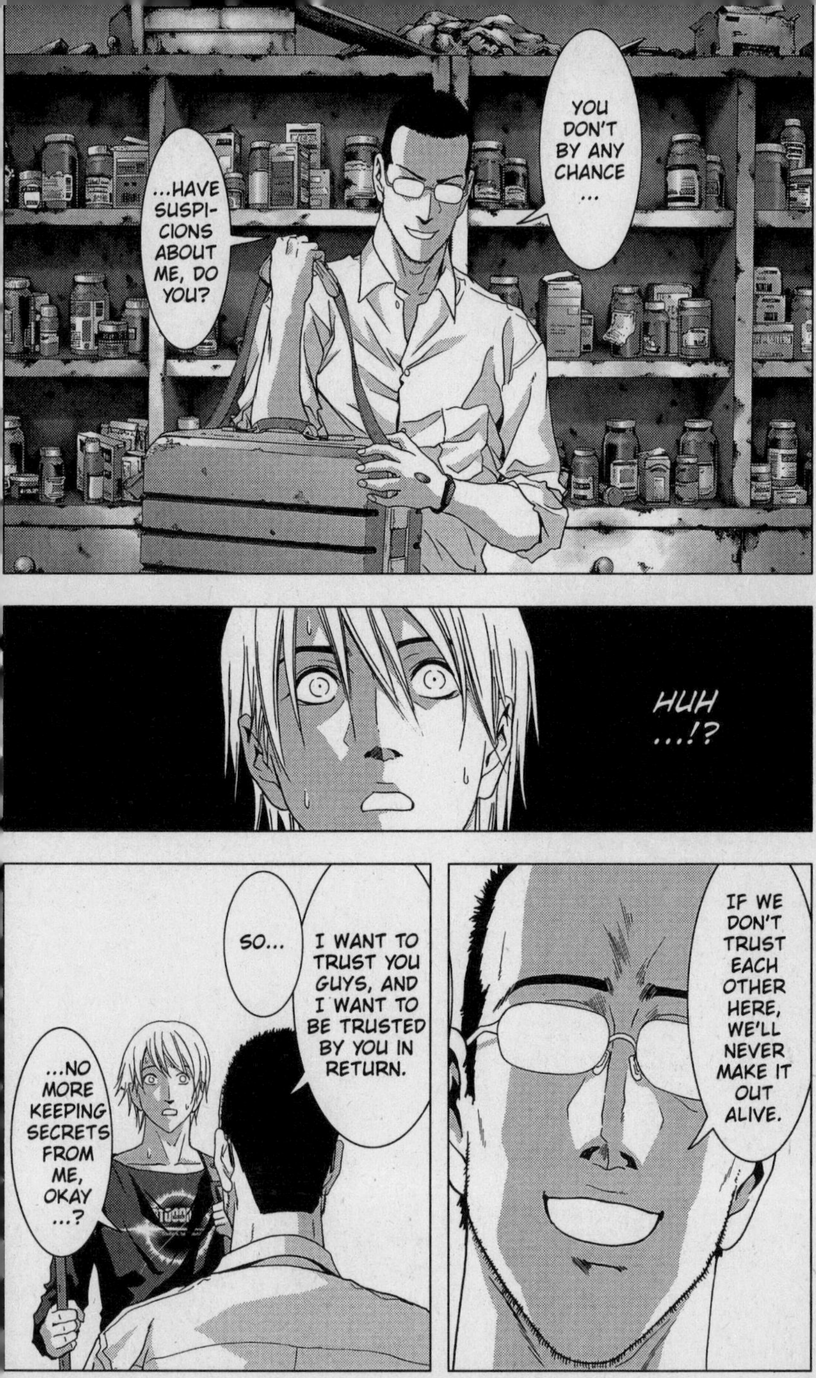
YOU DON'T BY ANY CHANCE ...
...HAVE SUSPICIONS ABOUT ME, DO YOU?
HUH ...!?
IF WE DON'T TRUST EACH OTHER HERE, WE'LL NEVER MAKE IT OUT ALIVE.
I WANT TO TRUST YOU GUYS, AND I WANT TO BE TRUSTED BY YOU IN RETURN.
SO...
...NO MORE KEEPING SECRETS FROM ME, OKAY ...?

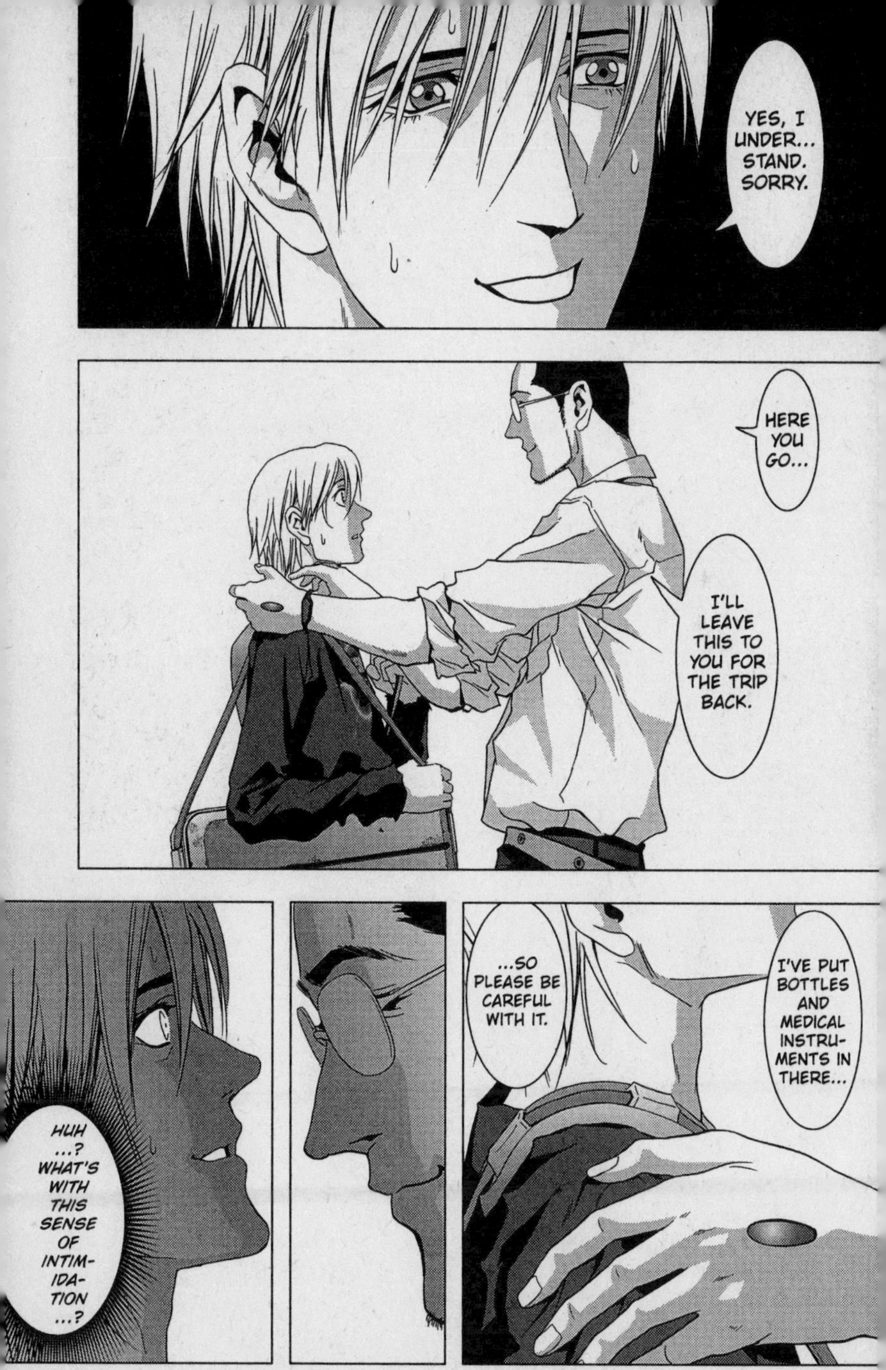
YES, I UNDER... STAND. SORRY.
HERE YOU GO...
I'LL LEAVE THIS TO YOU FOR THE TRIP BACK.
I'VE PUT BOTTLES AND MEDICAL INSTRU-MENTS IN THERE...
...SO PLEASE BE CAREFUL WITH IT.
HUH ...? WHAT'S WITH THIS SENSE OF INTIM-IDA-TION ...?

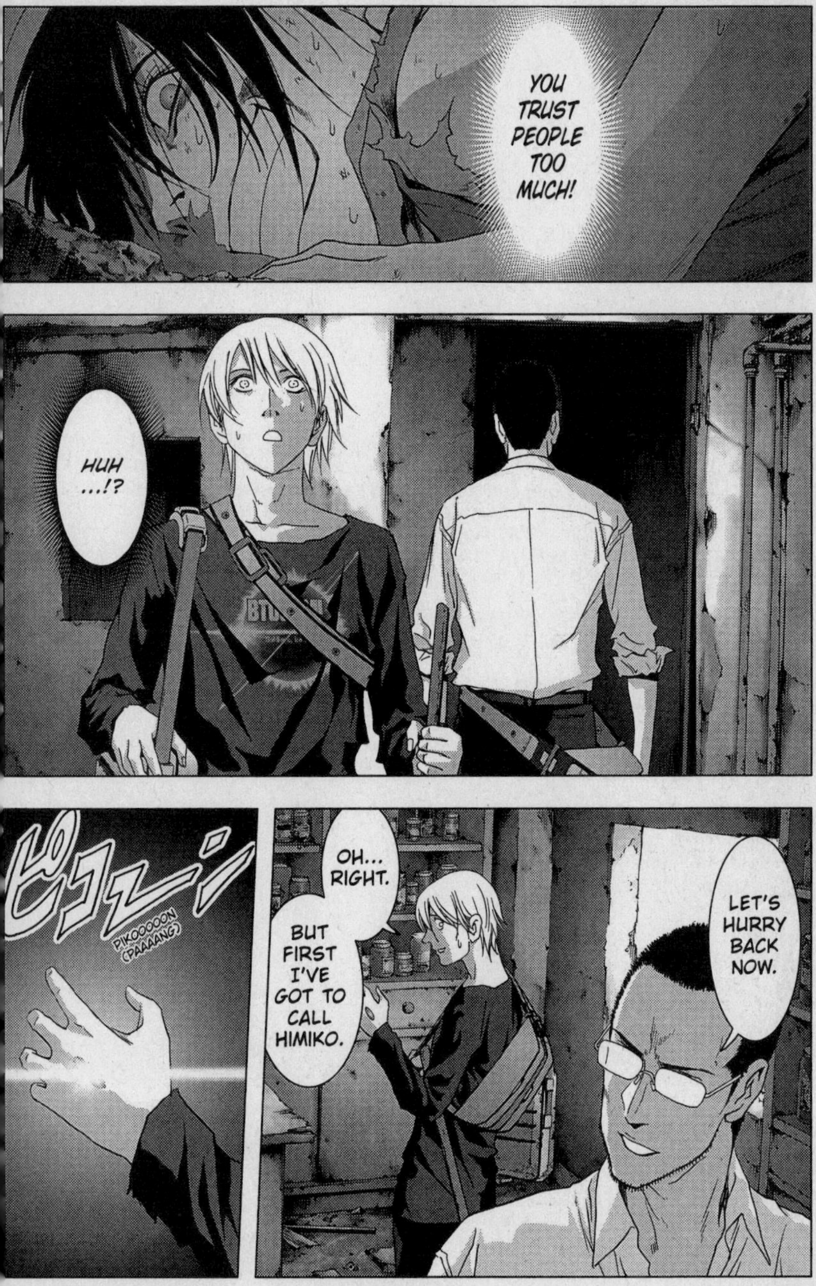
YOU TRUST PEOPLE TOO MUCH!
HUH ...!?
LET'S HURRY BACK NOW.
OH... RIGHT.
BUT FIRST I'VE GOT TO CALL HIMIKO.
PIKOOOOON (PAAAANG)

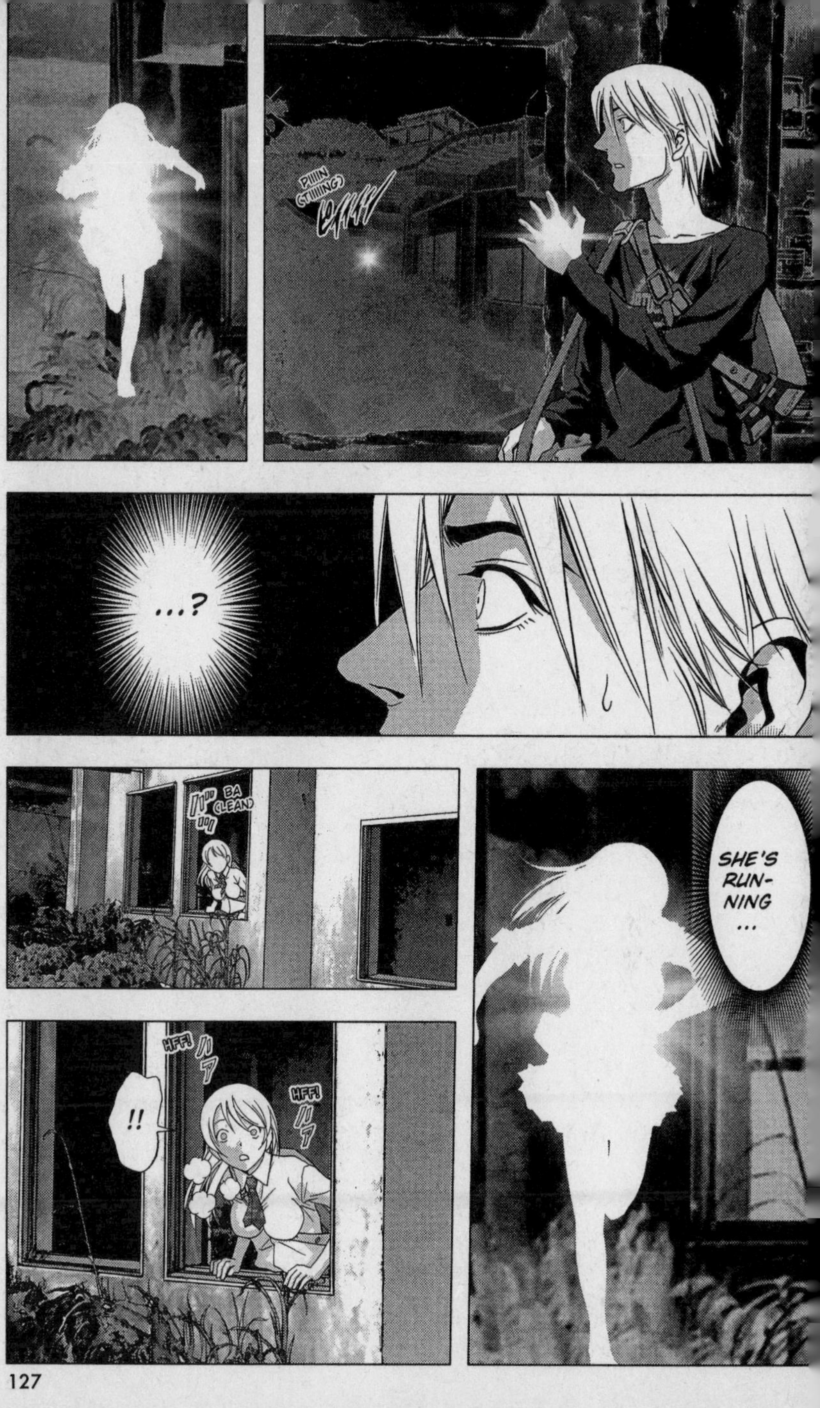
PIIIIN (STIIIING)
...?
SHE'S RUN-NING ...
BA (CLEAN)
HFF!
HFF!
!!

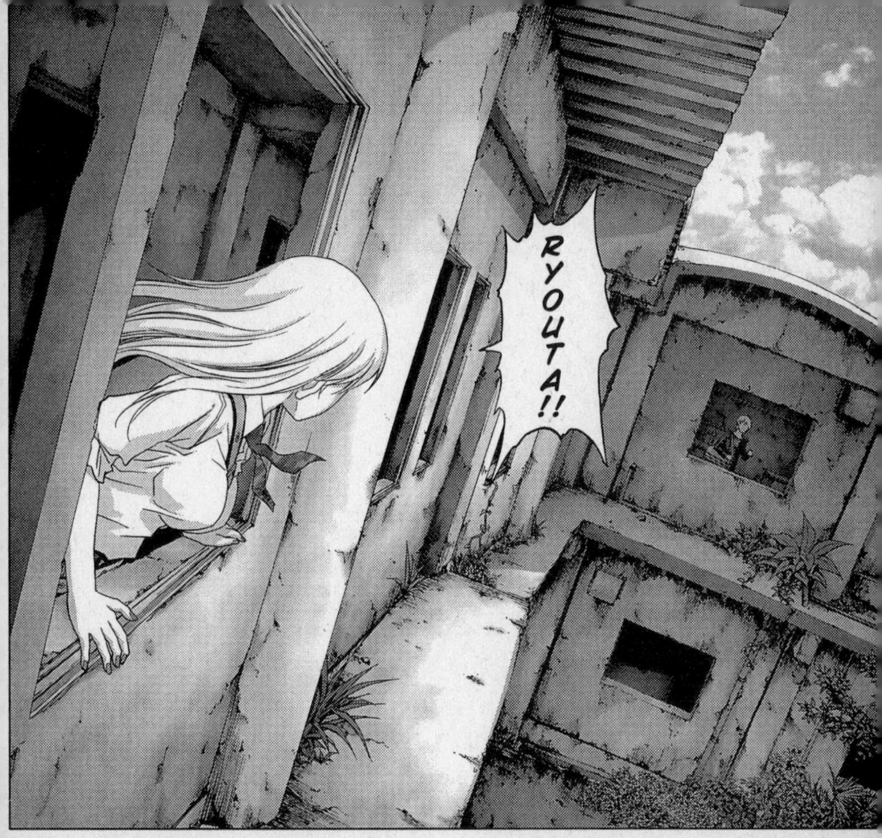
RYOUTA!!
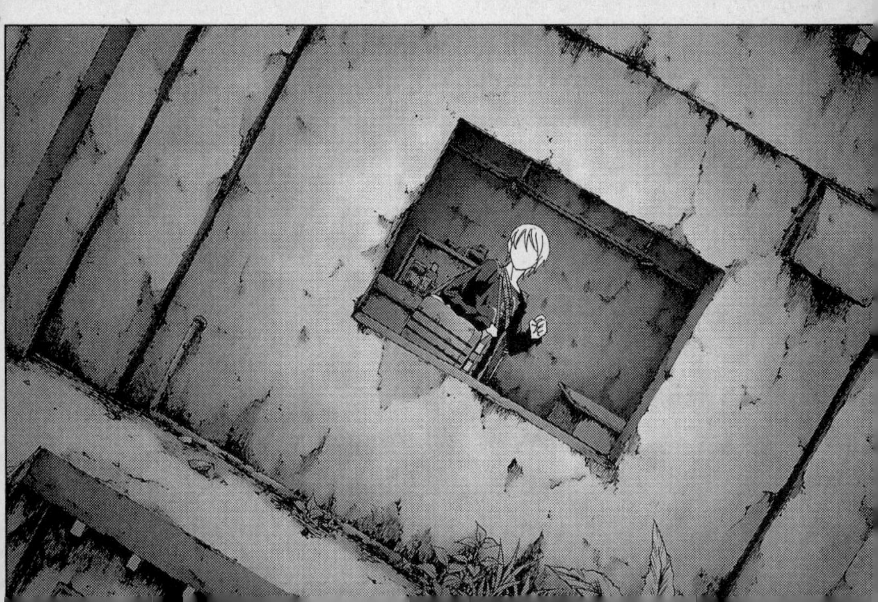

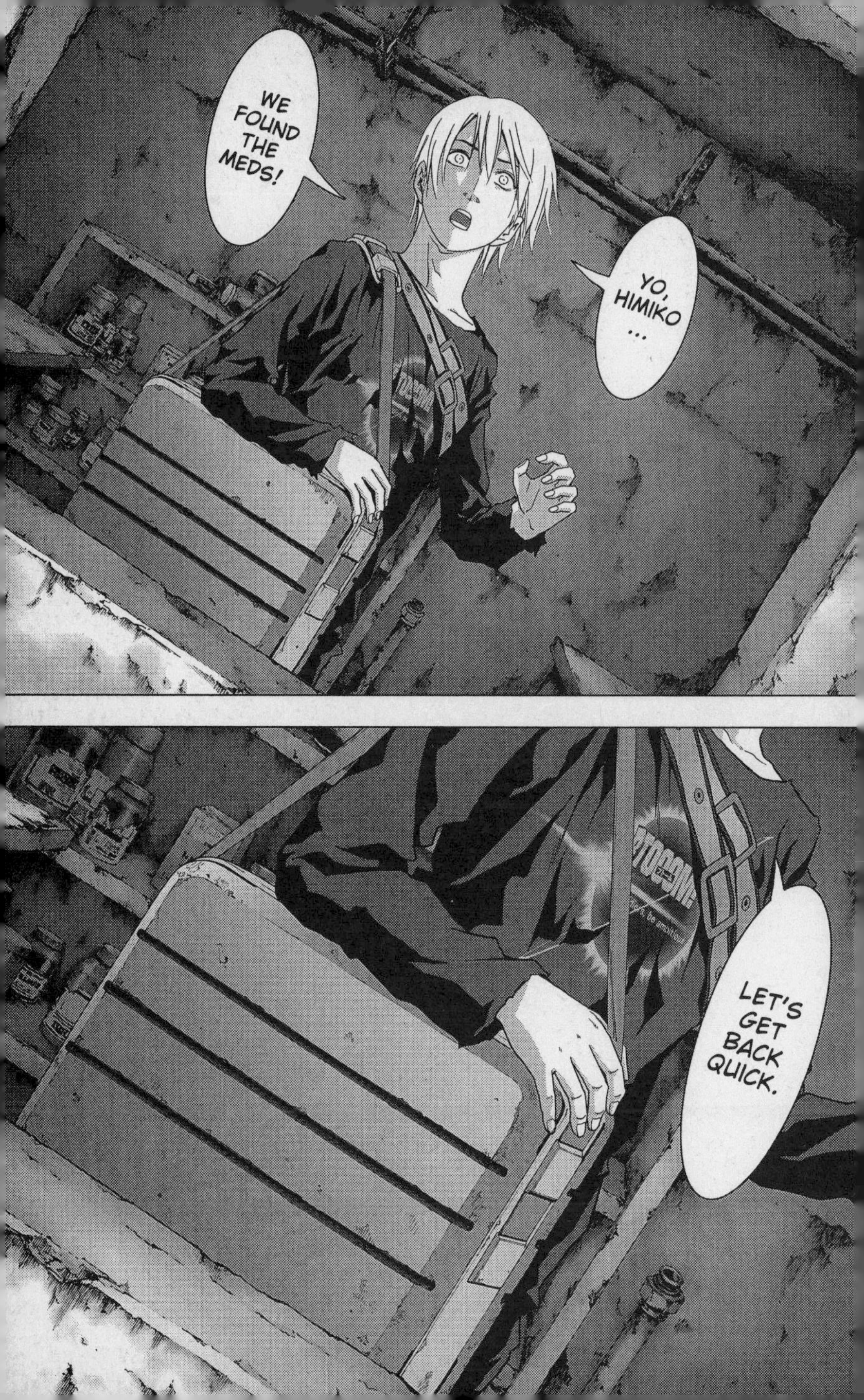
YO, HIMIKO ...
WE FOUND THE MEDS!
LET'S GET BACK QUICK.

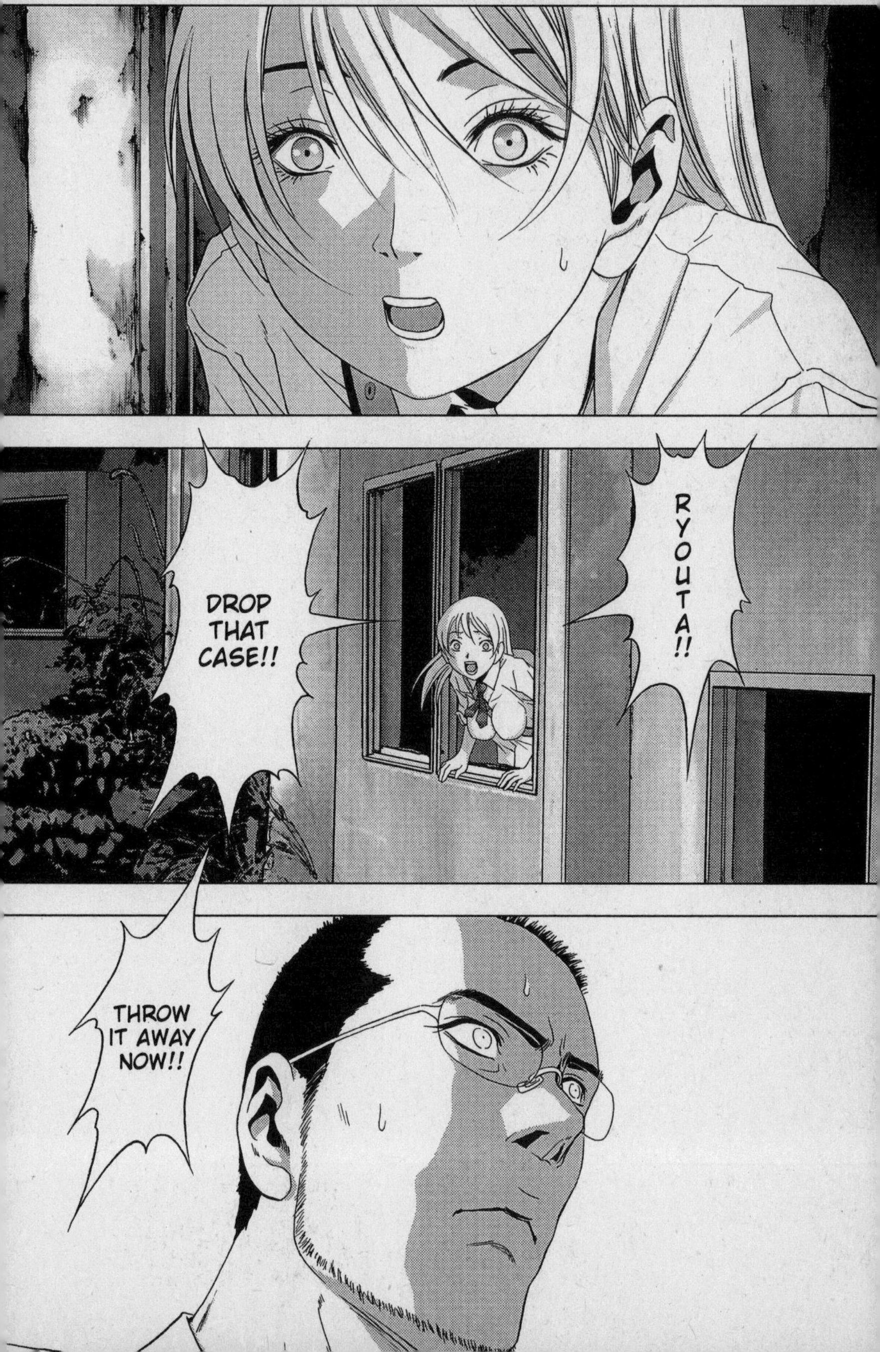
RYOUTA!!
DROP THAT CASE!!
THROW IT AWAY NOW!!

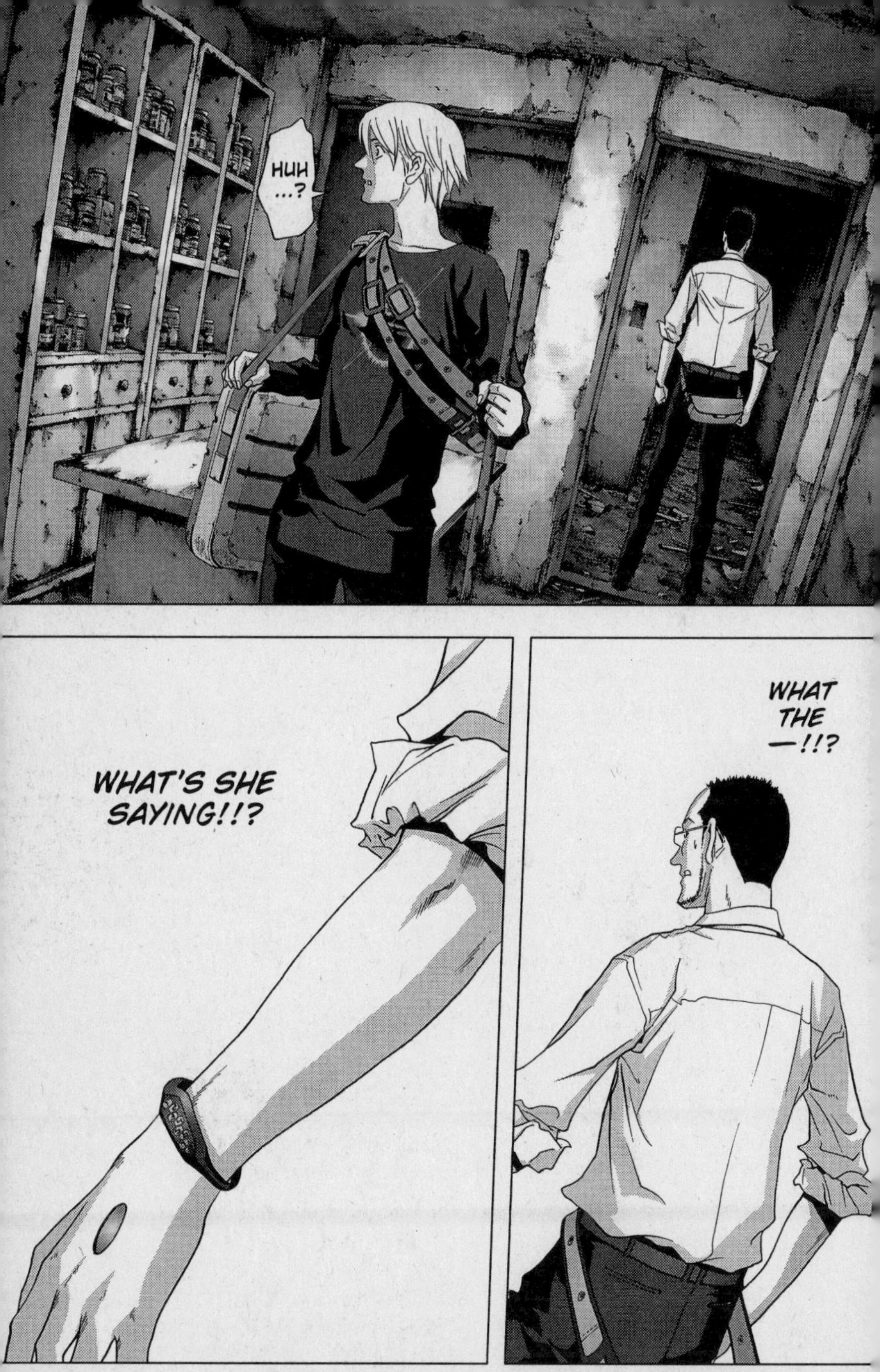
HUH ...?
WHAT THE —!!?
WHAT'S SHE SAYING!!?

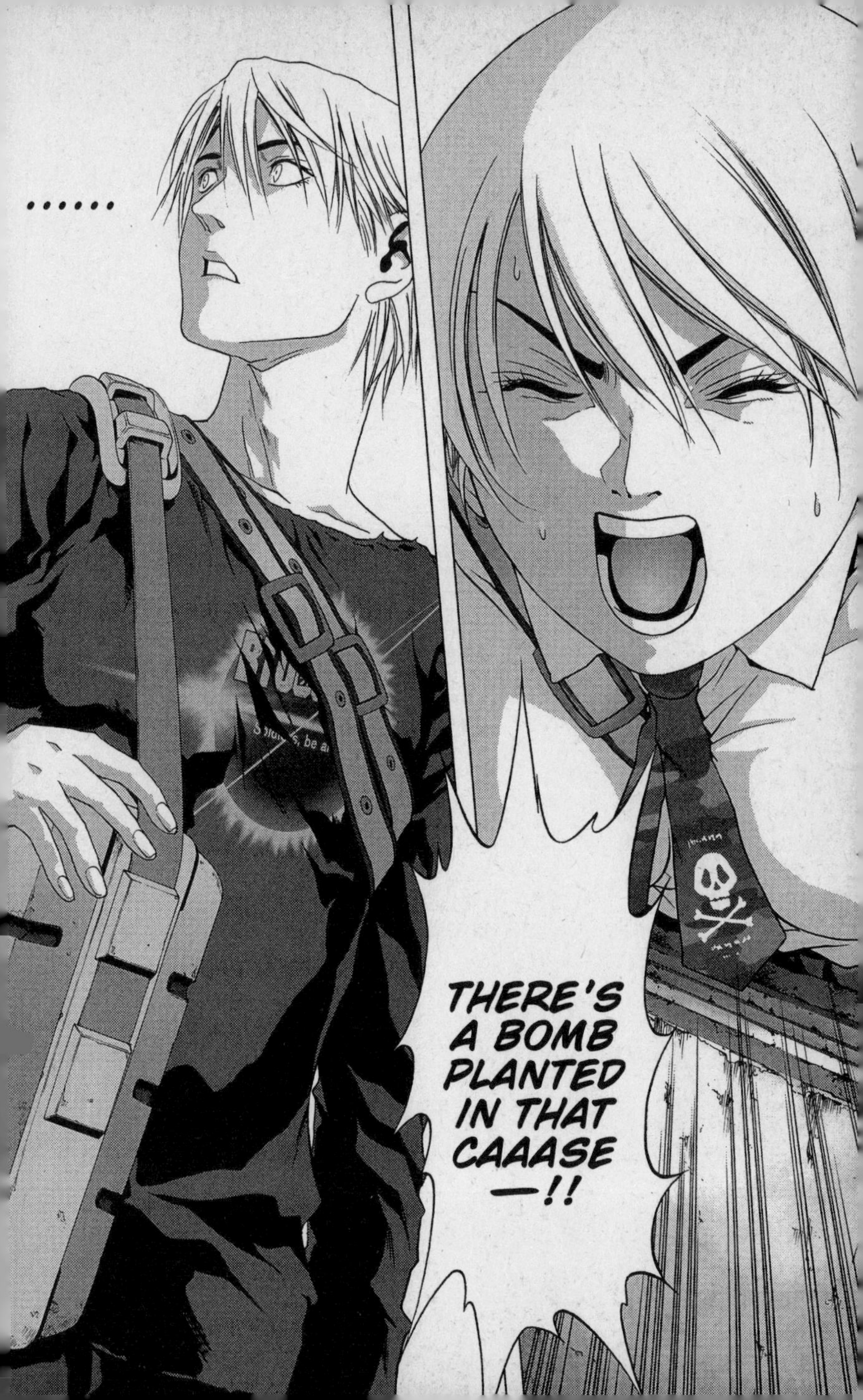
THERE'S A BOMB PLANTED IN THAT CAAASE—!!
......

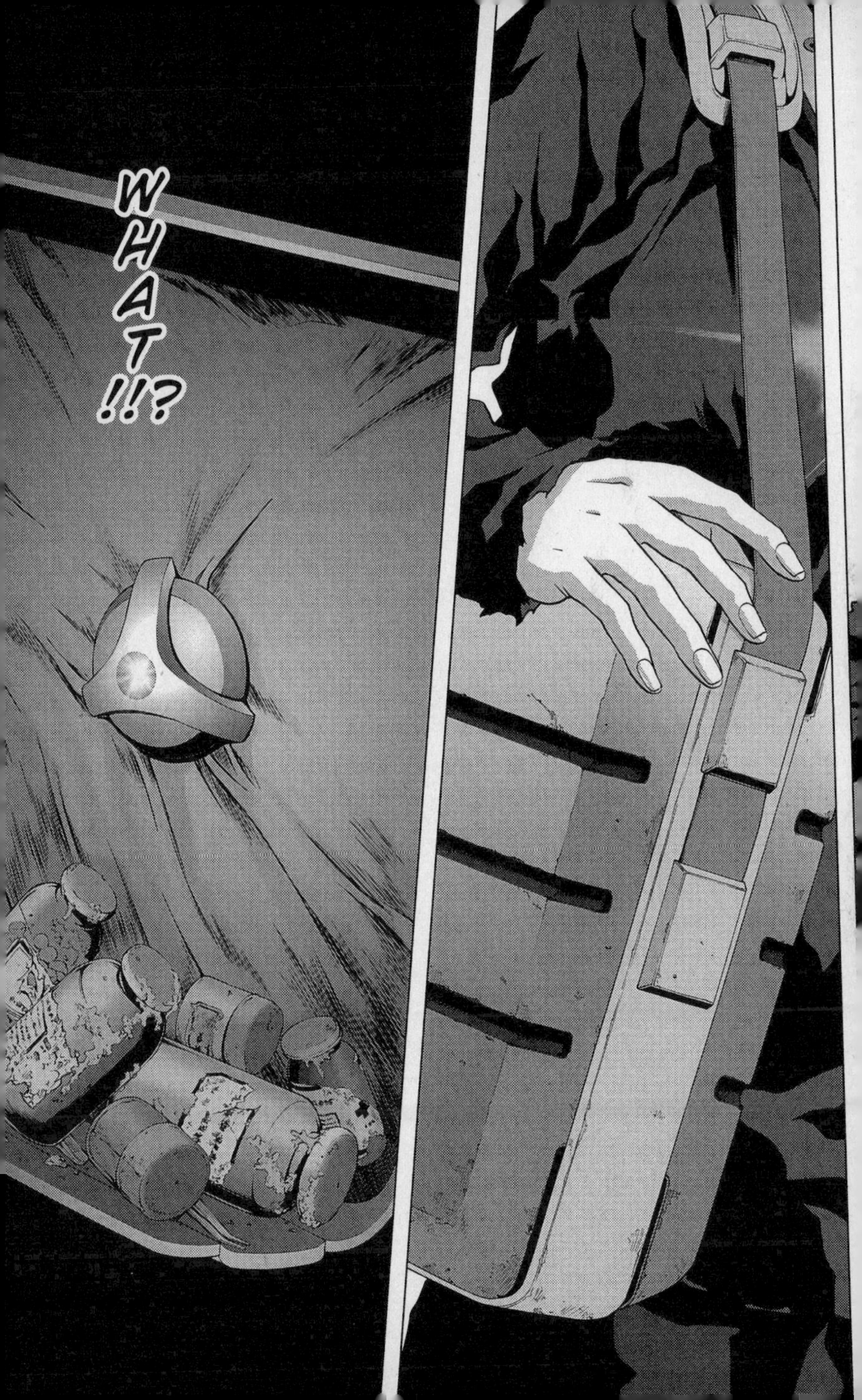
WHAT!!?

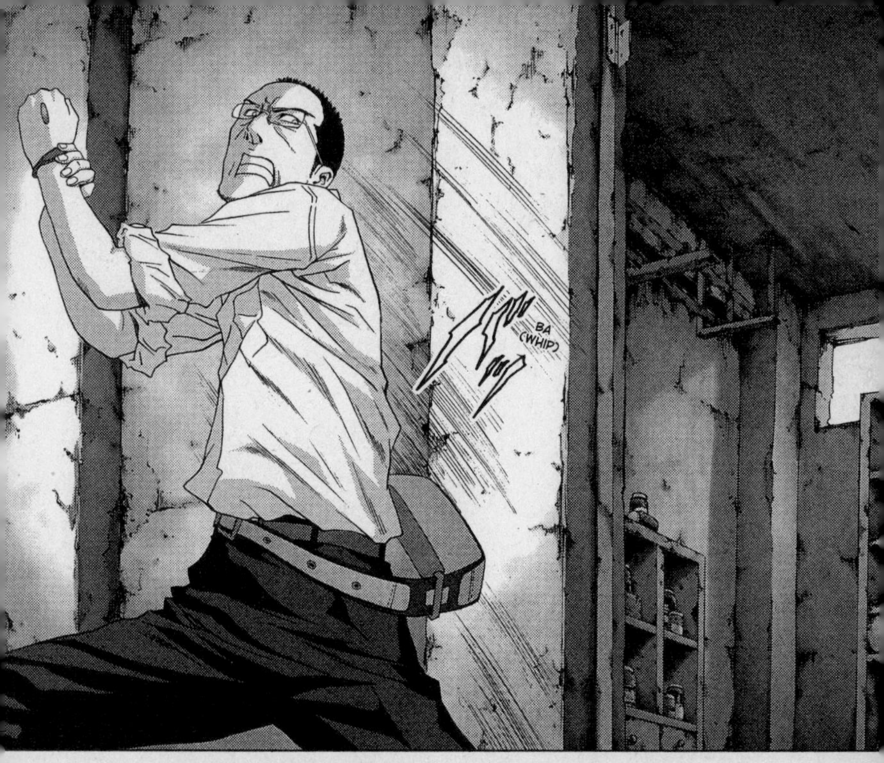
BA
(WHIP)
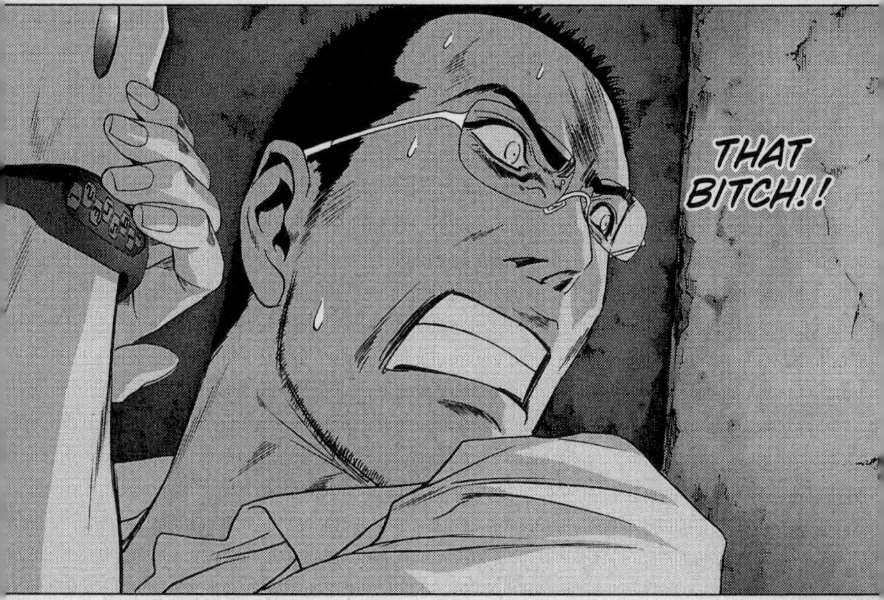
THAT BITCH!!

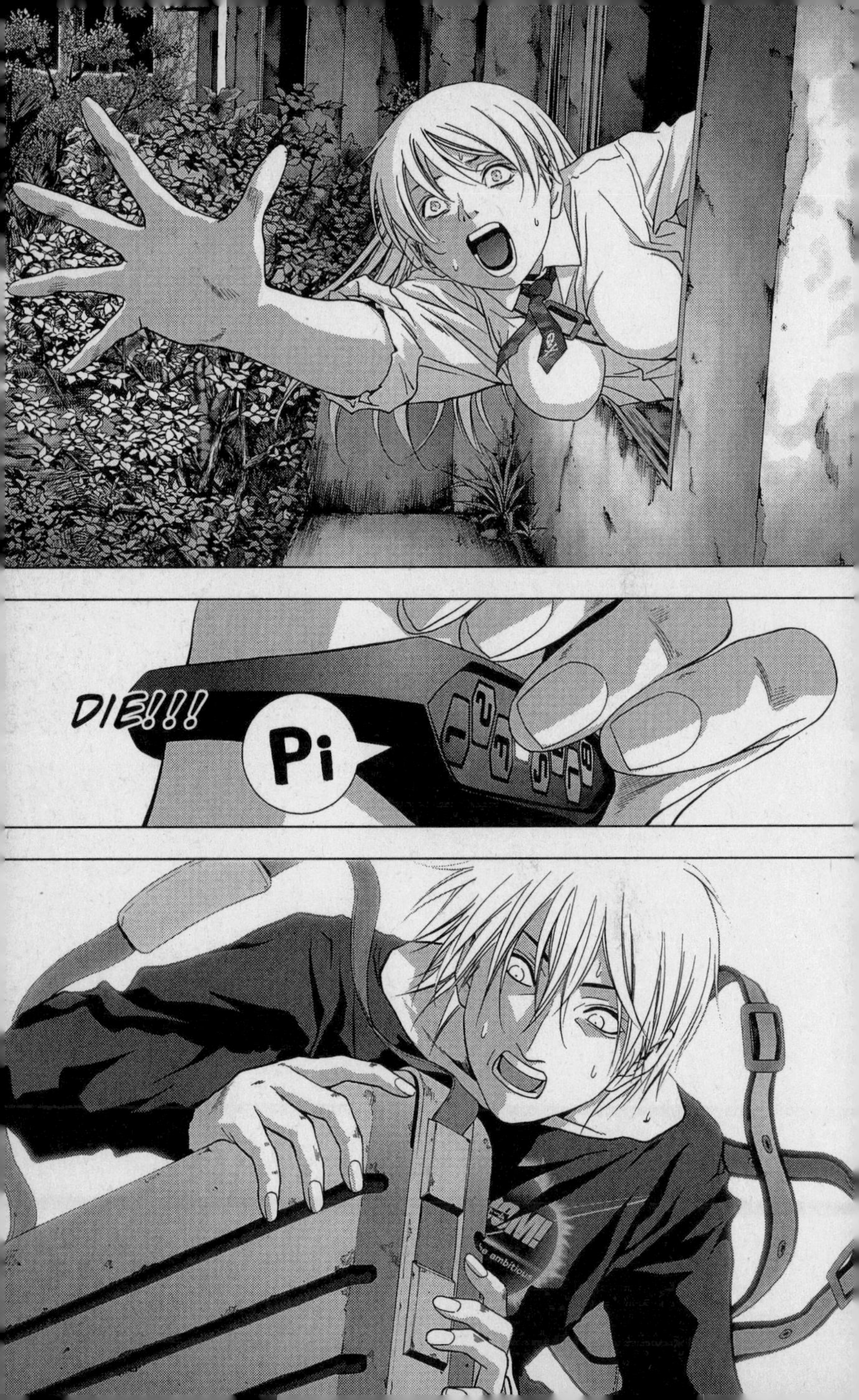
Pi
DIE!!!

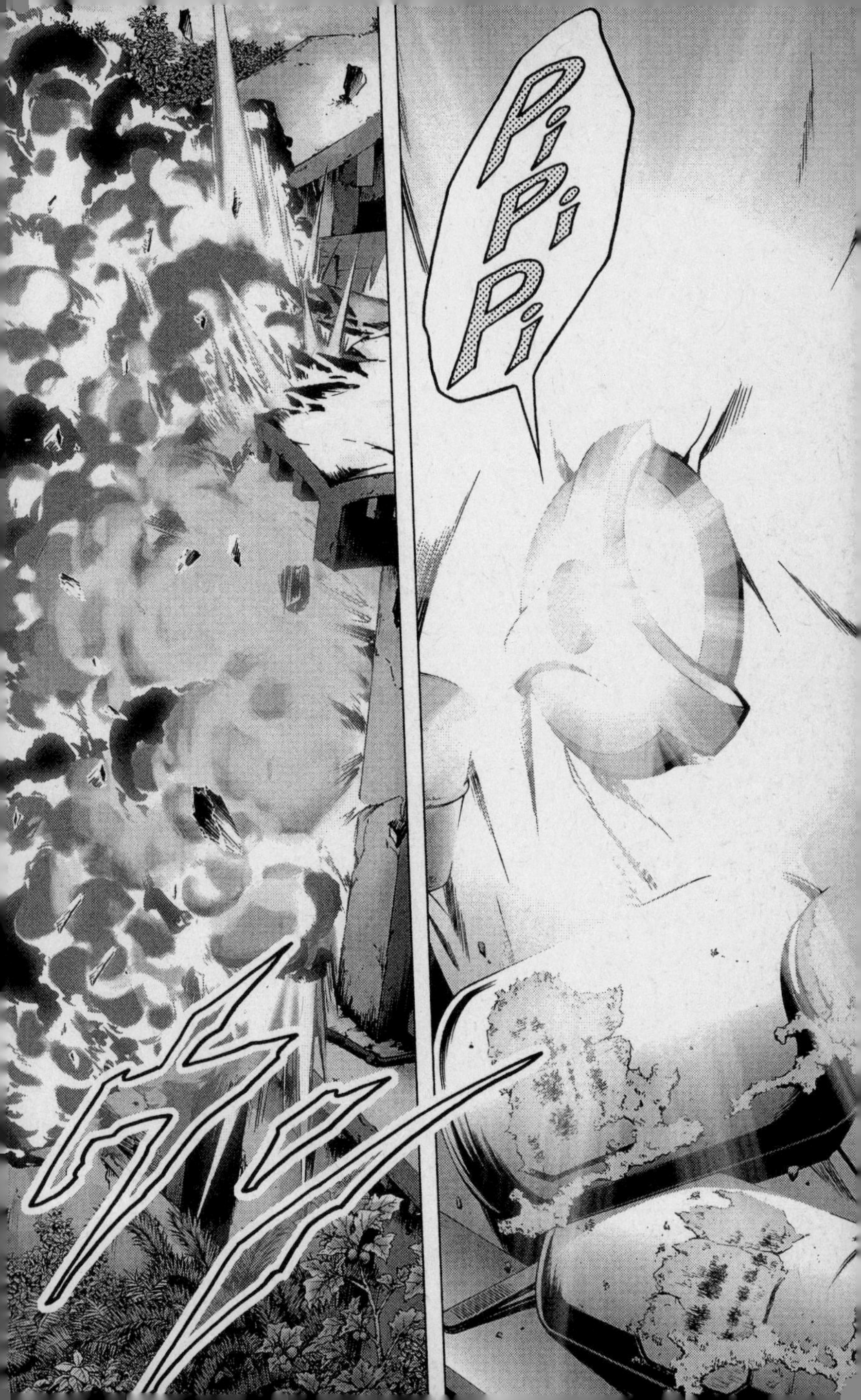
PiPiPi

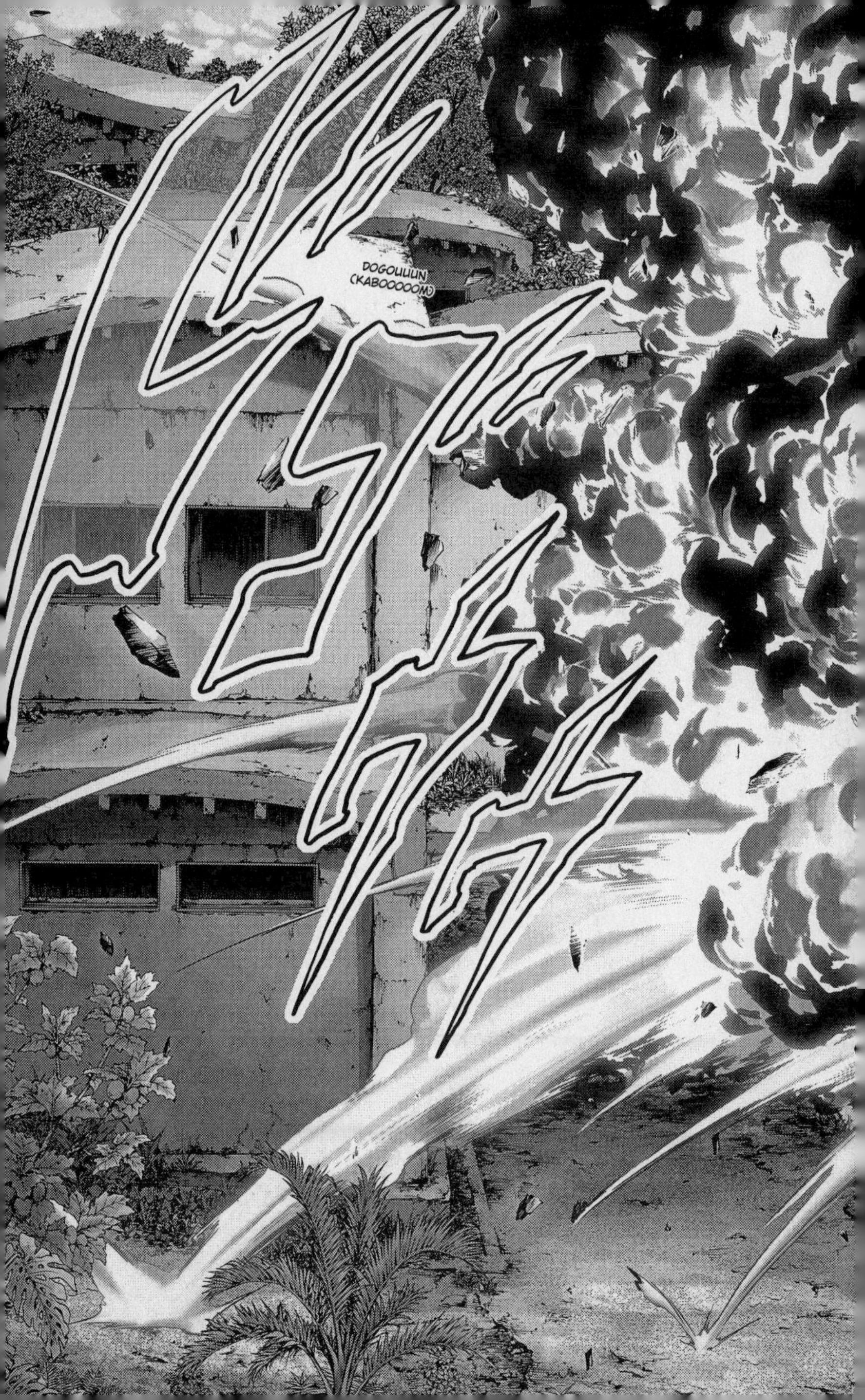
DOGOUUUN
(KABOOOOOM)

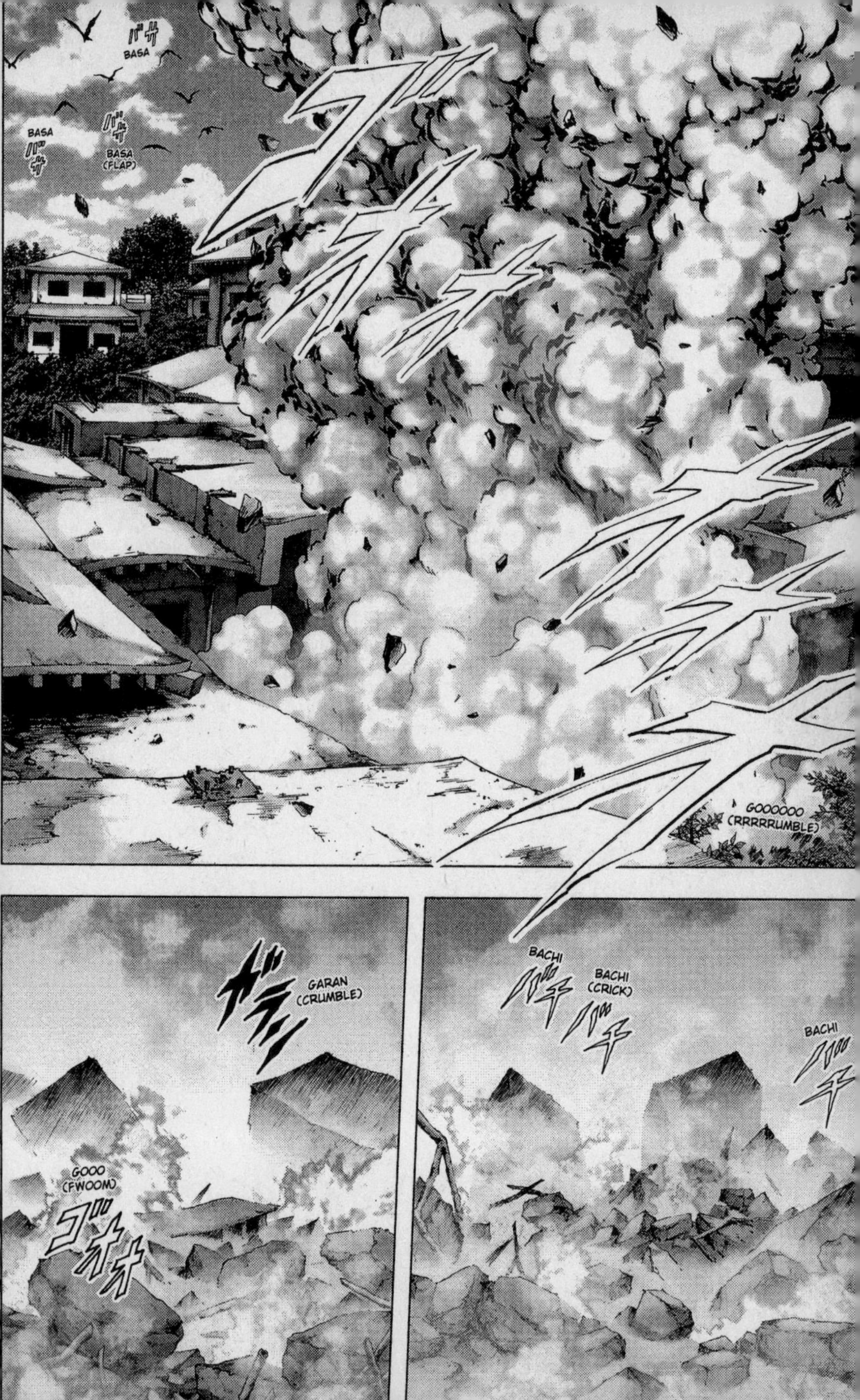
BASA
BASA
BASA (FLAP)
GOOOOOO (RRRRRUMBLE)
BACHI
BACHI (CRICK)
BACHI
GARAN (CRUMBLE)
GOOO (FWOOM)

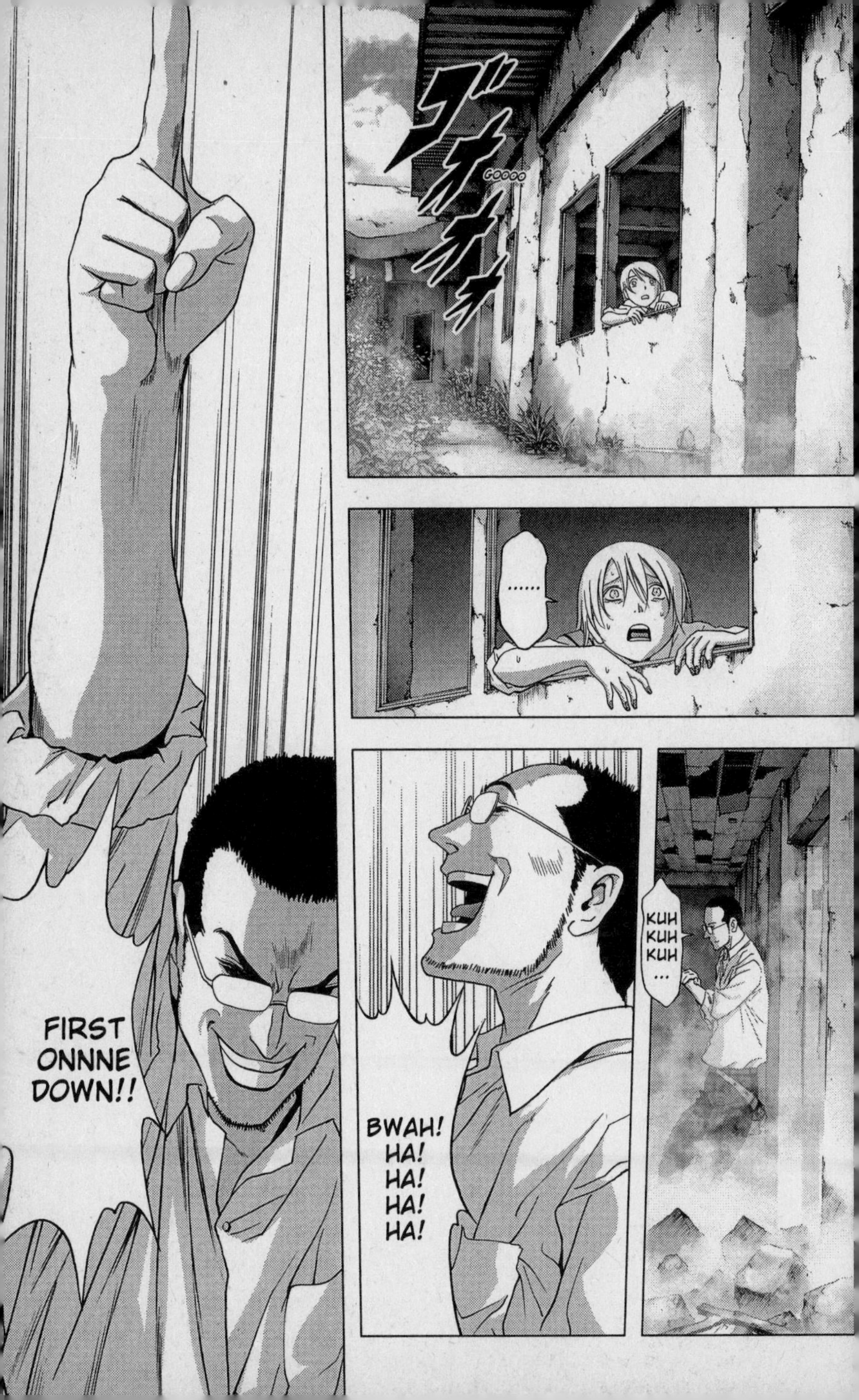
GOOOO
......
KUH KUH KUH ...
BWAH! HA! HA! HA! HA!
FIRST ONNNE DOWN!!

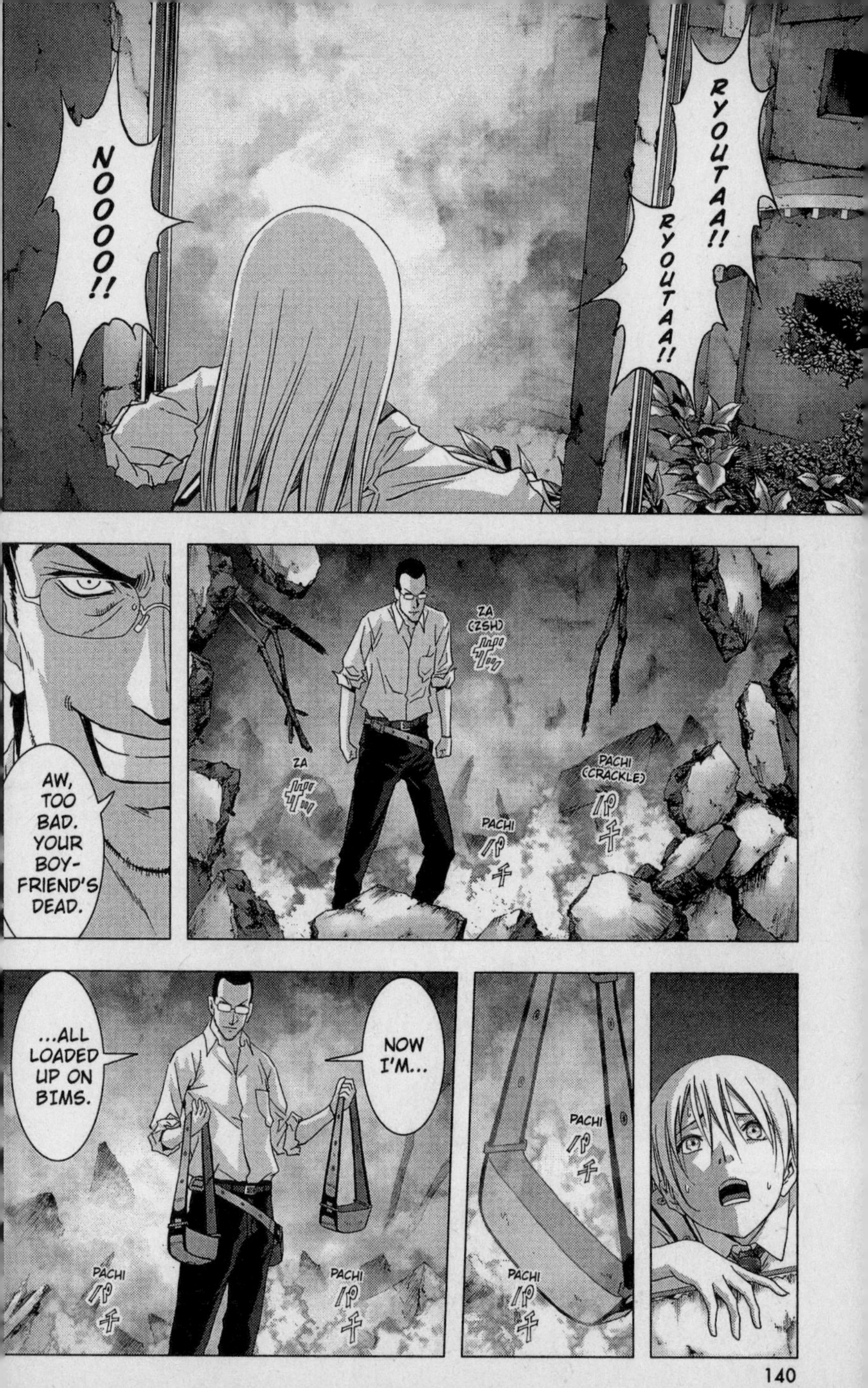
RYOUTAA!!
RYOUTAA!!
NOOOOO!!
ZA (ZSH)
PACHI (CRACKLE)
PACHI
ZA
AW, TOO BAD. YOUR BOY-FRIEND'S DEAD.
PACHI
PACHI
NOW I'M...
...ALL LOADED UP ON BIMS.
PACHI
PACHI

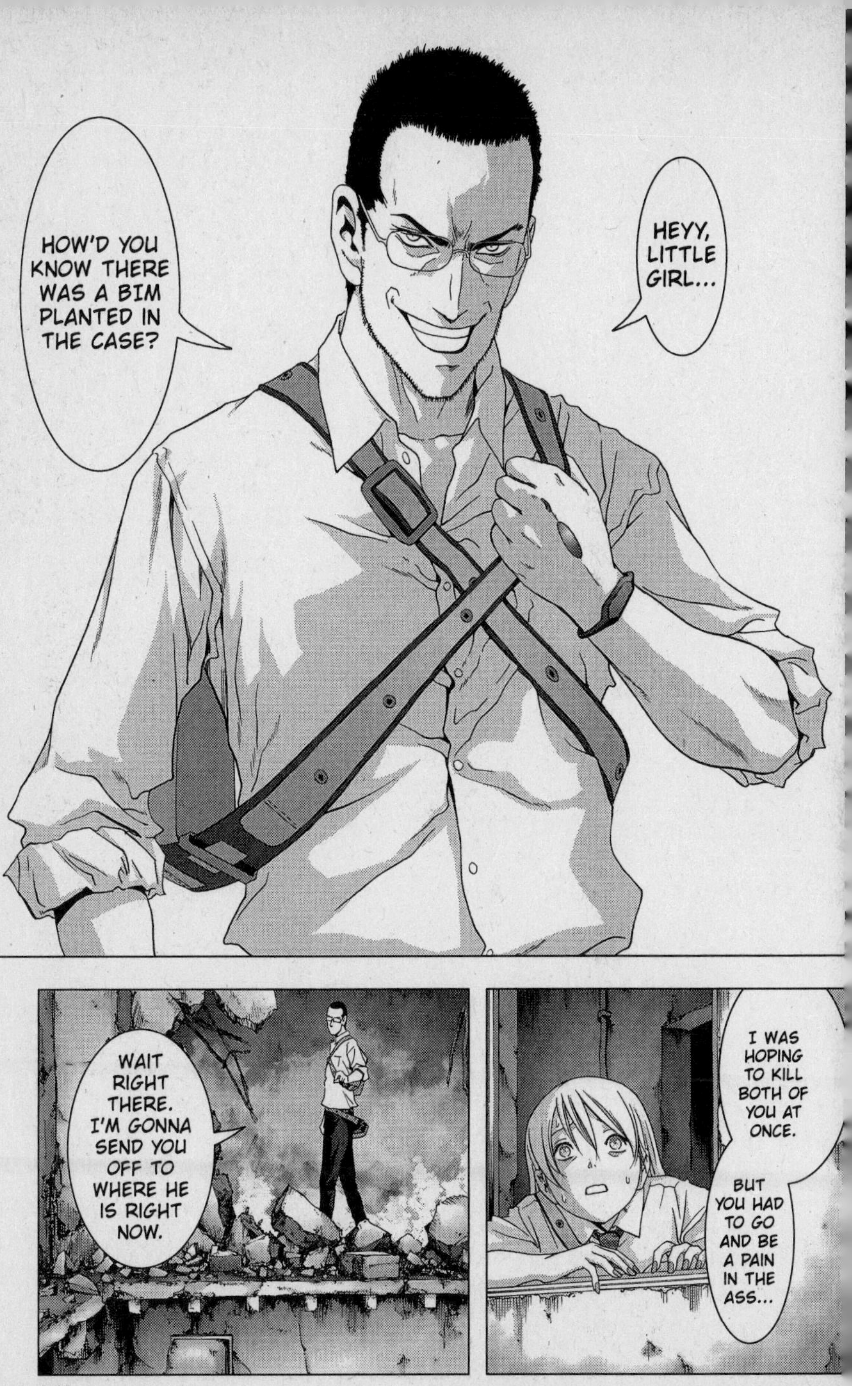
HEYY, LITTLE GIRL...
HOW'D YOU KNOW THERE WAS A BIM PLANTED IN THE CASE?
I WAS HOPING TO KILL BOTH OF YOU AT ONCE.
BUT YOU HAD TO GO AND BE A PAIN IN THE ASS...
WAIT RIGHT THERE. I'M GONNA SEND YOU OFF TO WHERE HE IS RIGHT NOW.

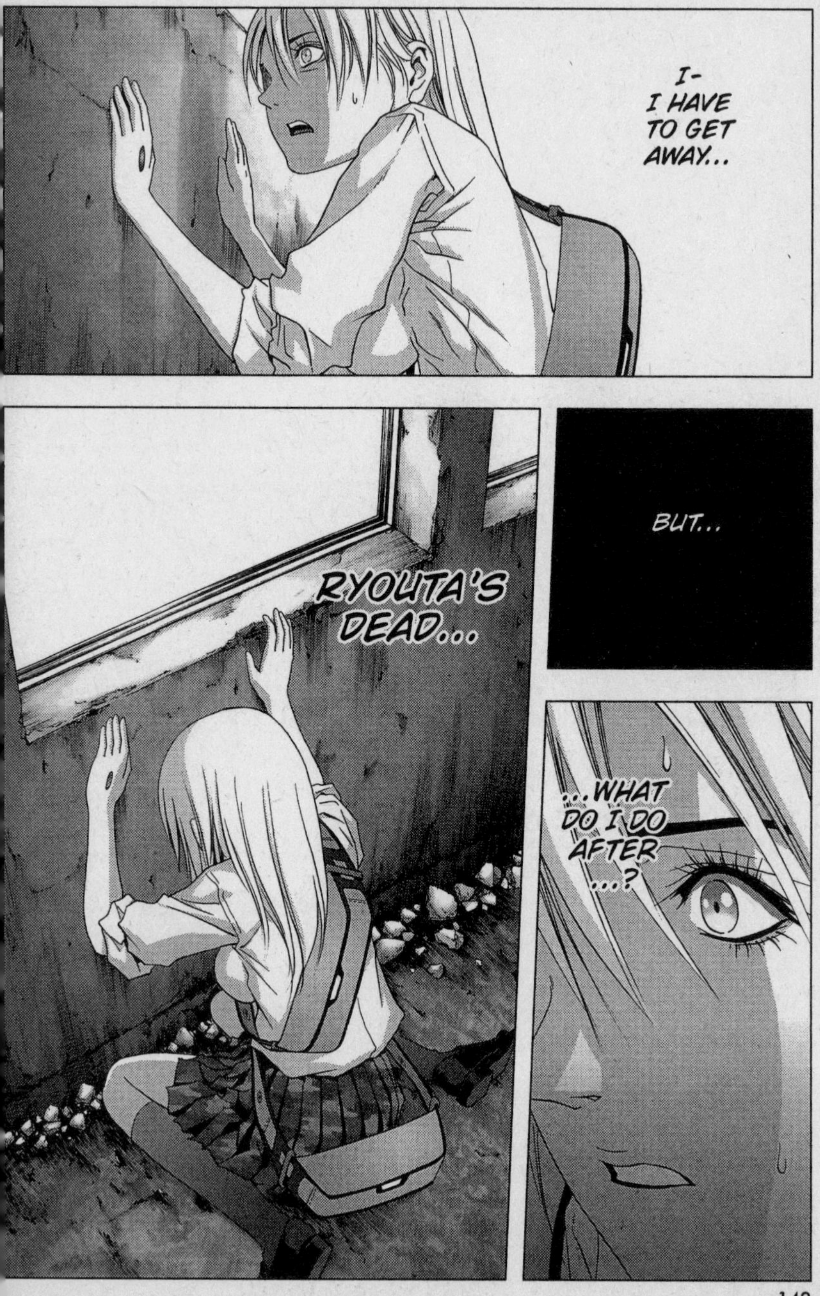
I-
I HAVE TO GET AWAY...
BUT...
...WHAT DO I DO AFTER ...?
RYOUTA'S DEAD...

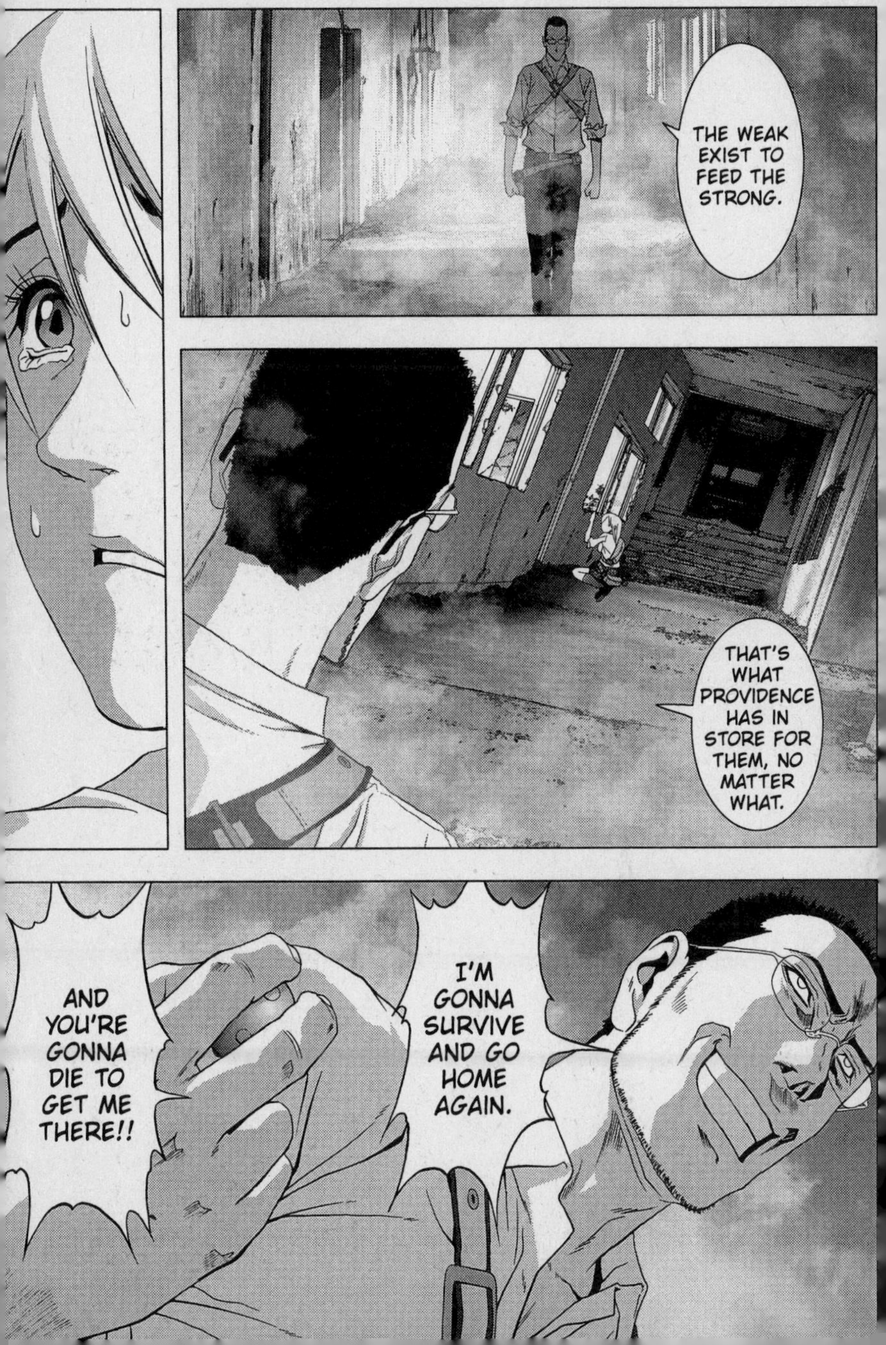
THE WEAK EXIST TO FEED THE STRONG.
THAT'S WHAT PROVIDENCE HAS IN STORE FOR THEM, NO MATTER WHAT.
I'M GONNA SURVIVE AND GO HOME AGAIN.
AND YOU'RE GONNA DIE TO GET ME THERE!!

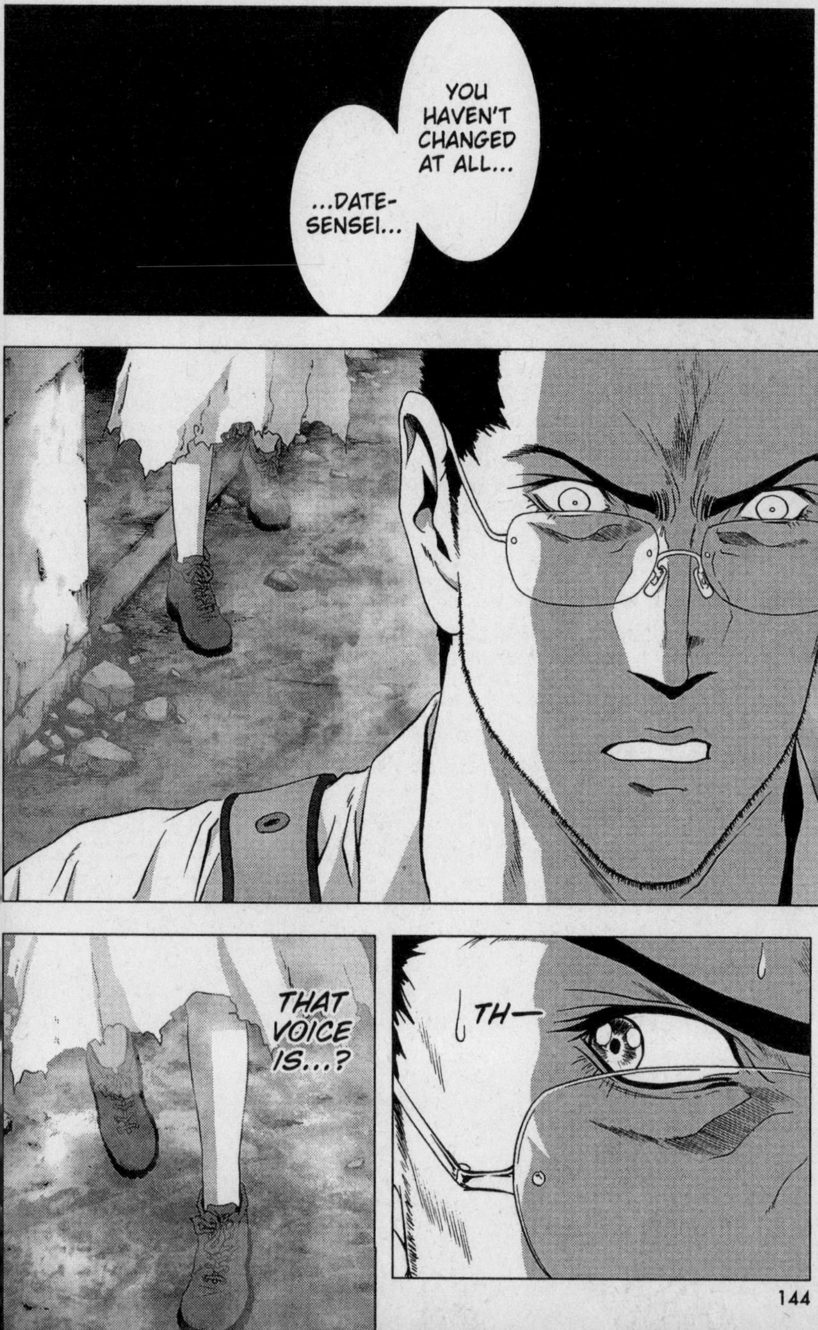
YOU HAVEN'T CHANGED AT ALL...
...DATE-SENSEI...
TH—
THAT VOICE IS...?

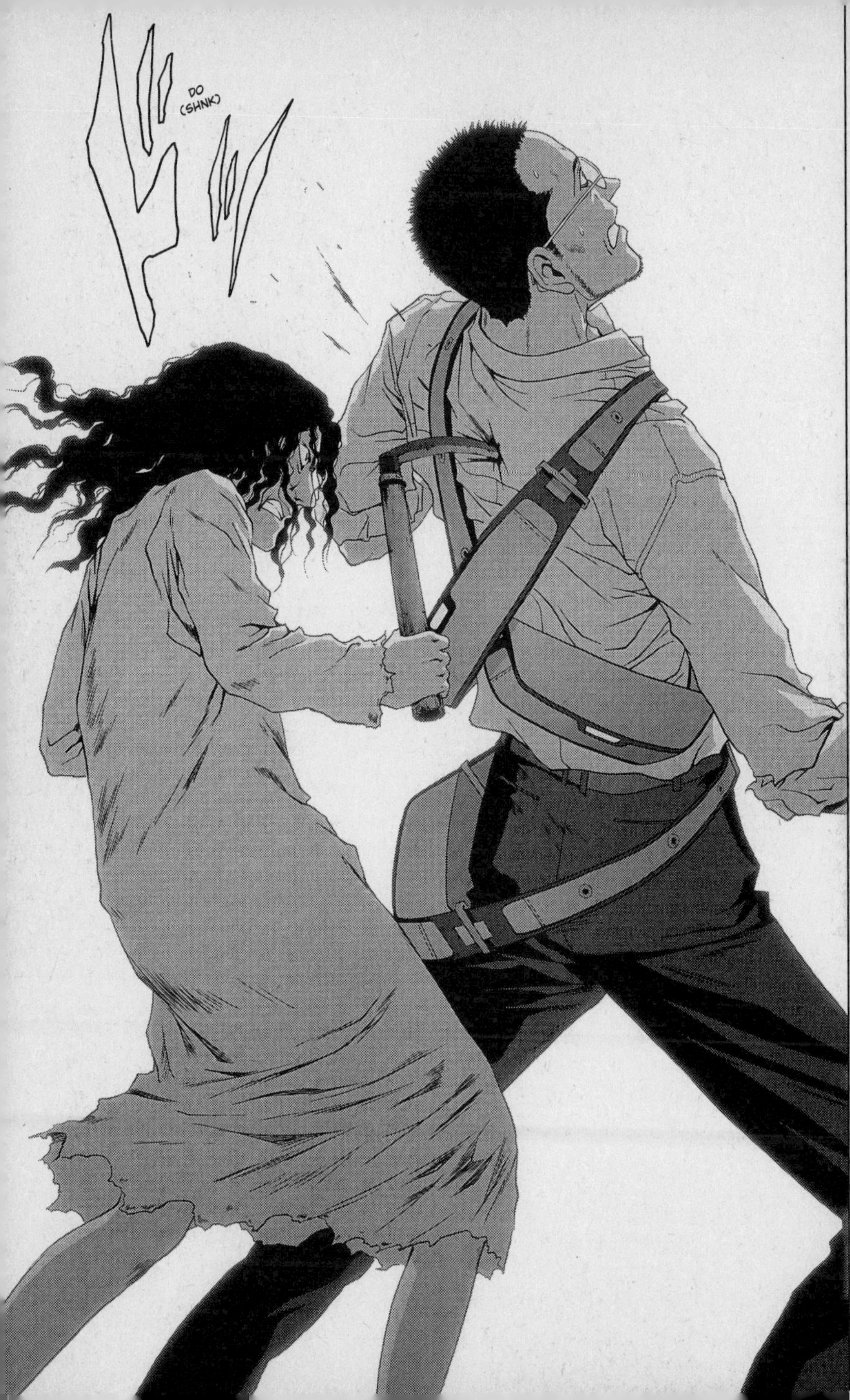
DO
(SHNK)

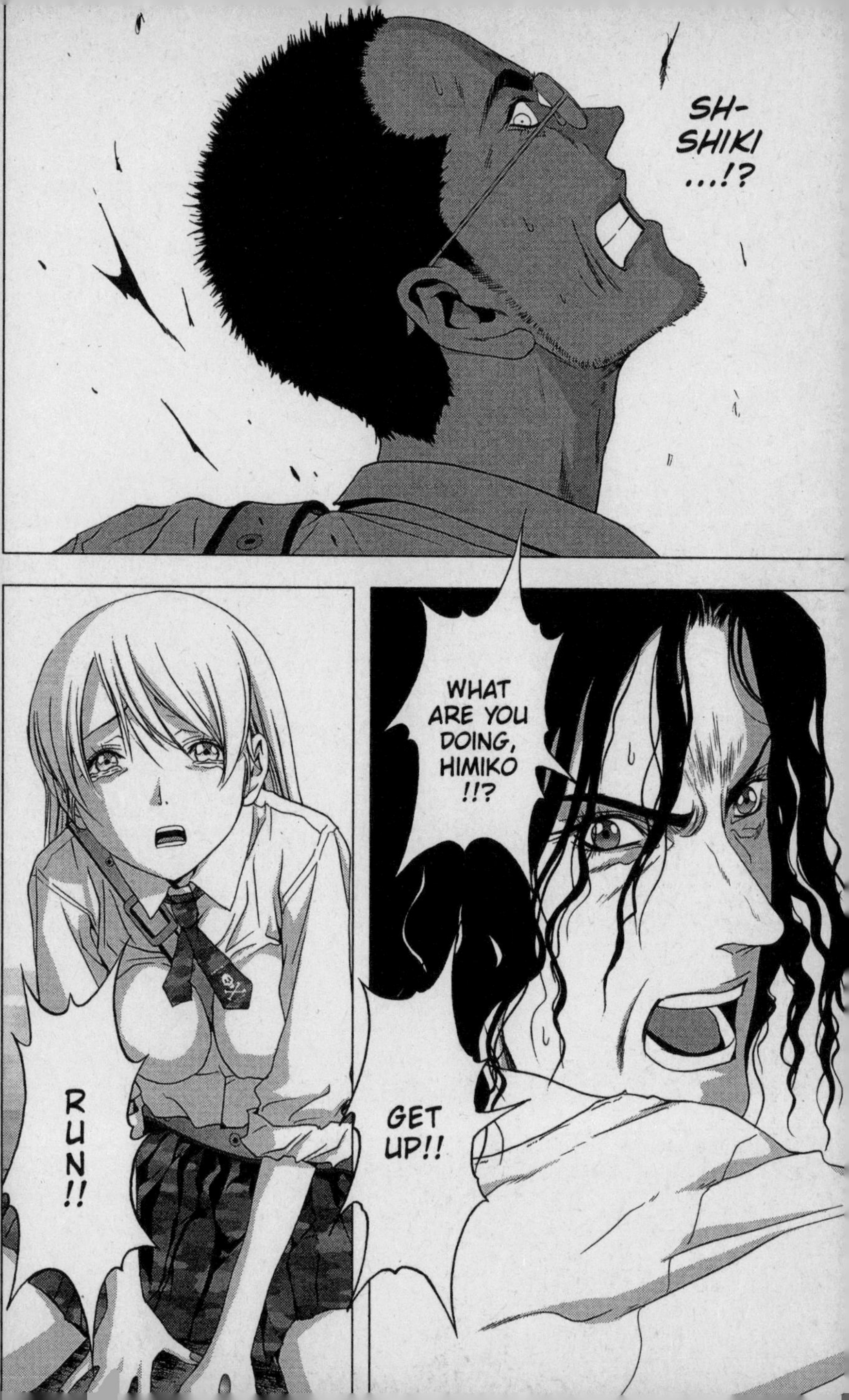
SH-SHIKI ...!?
WHAT ARE YOU DOING, HIMIKO !!?
GET UP!!
RUN!!

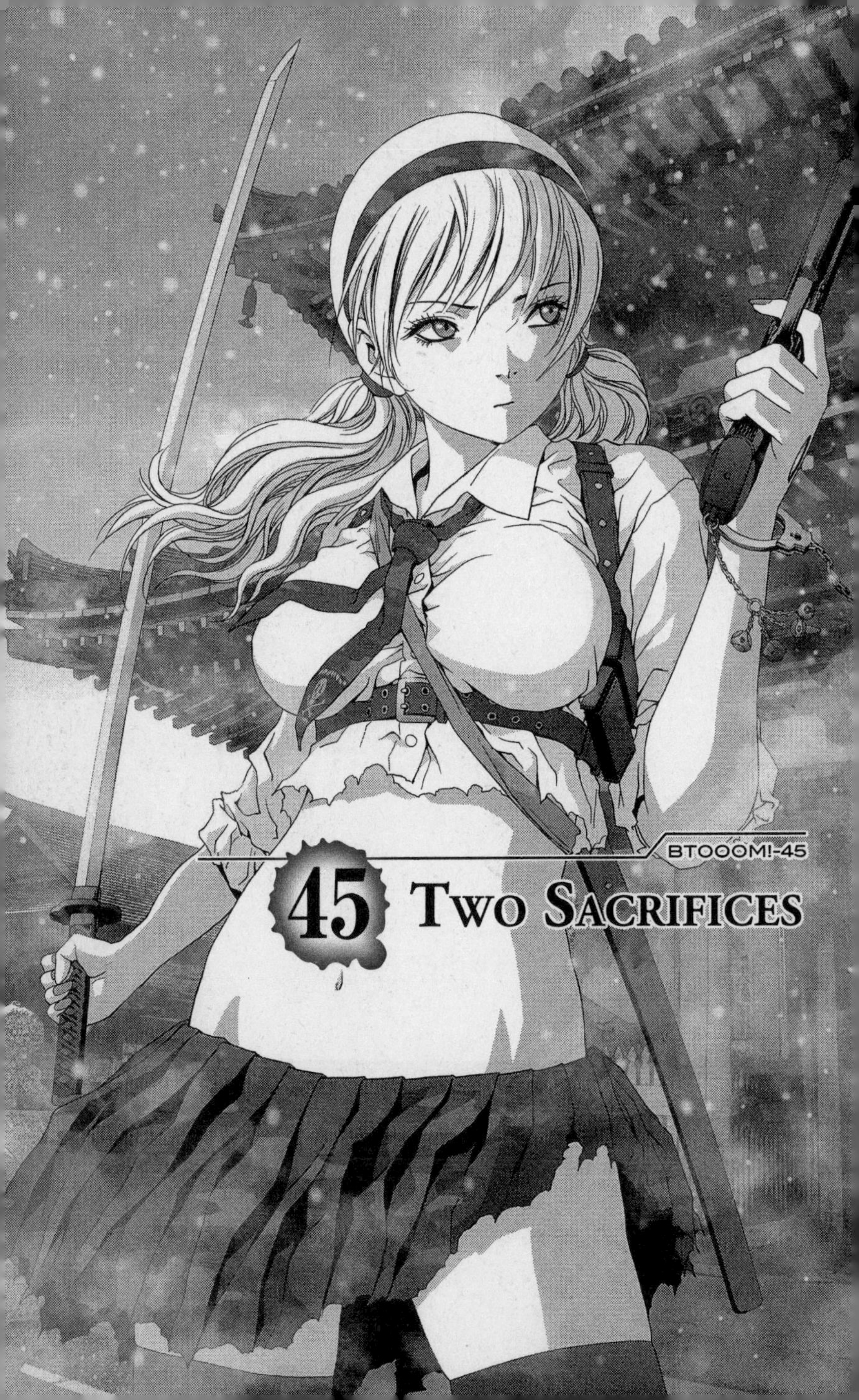
BTOOOM!-45
45 Two Sacrifices

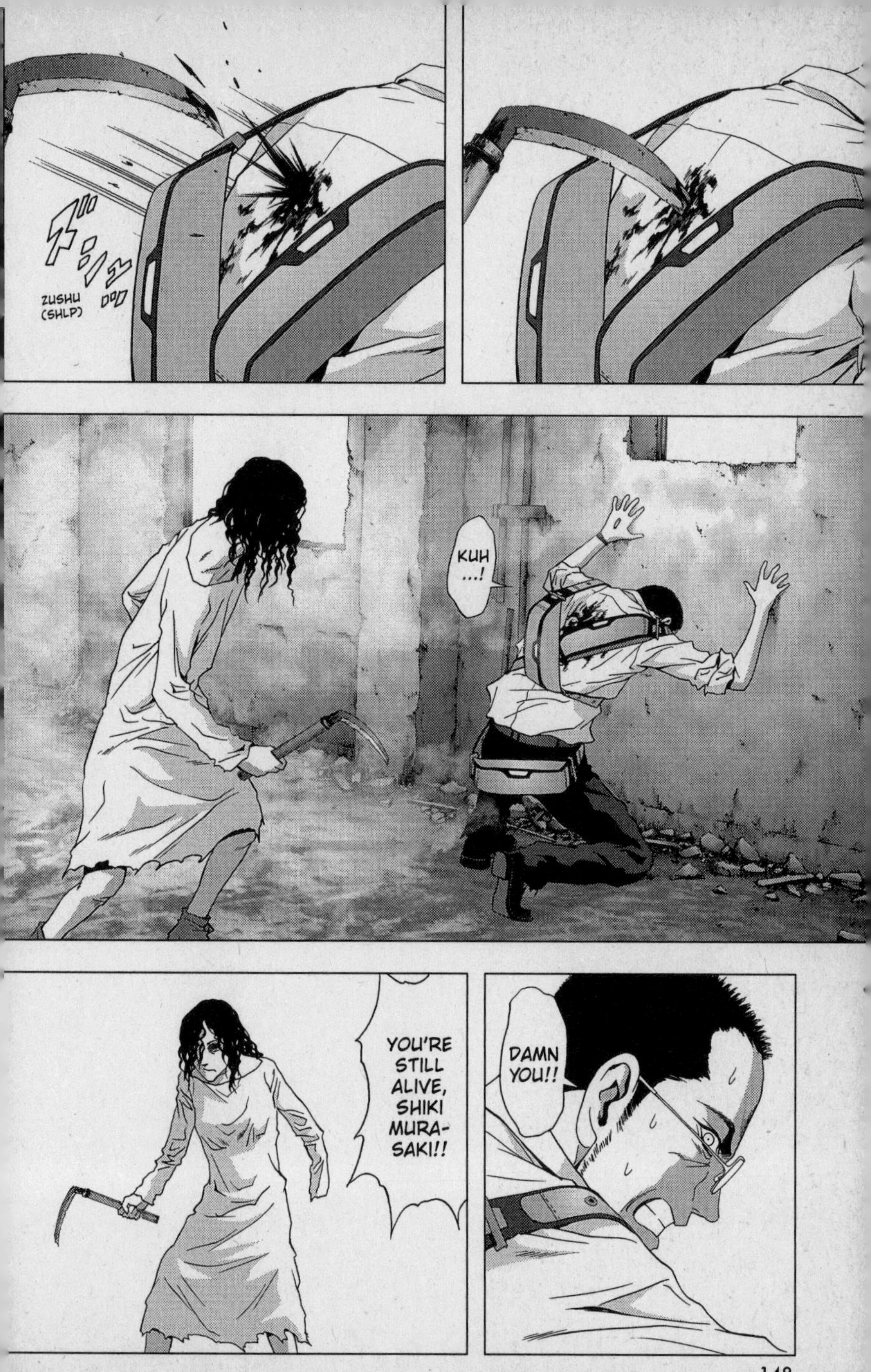
ZUSHU
(SHLP)
KUH...!
DAMN YOU!!
YOU'RE STILL ALIVE, SHIKI MURASAKI!!

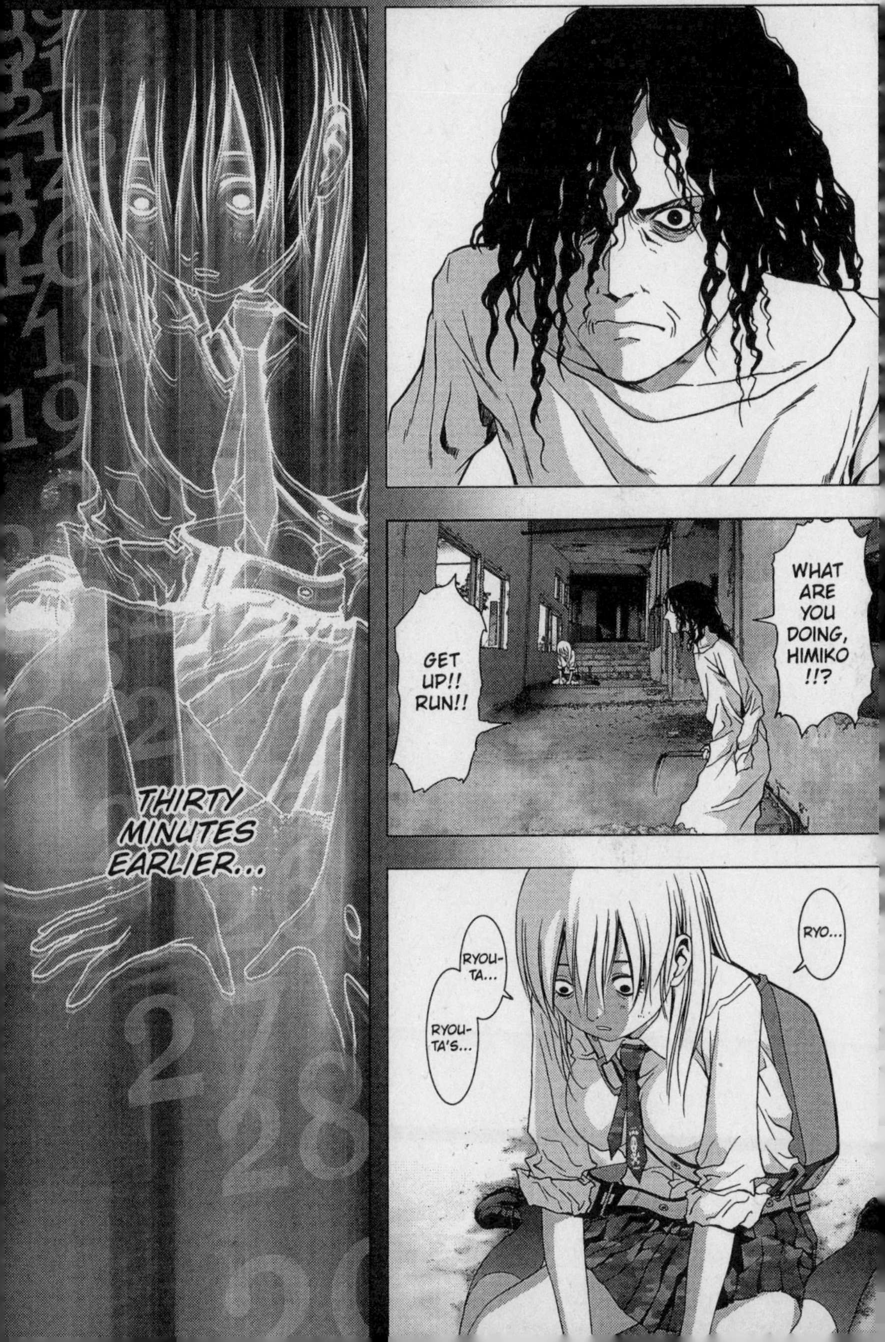
WHAT ARE YOU DOING, HIMIKO!!?
GET UP!! RUN!!
RYO...
RYOU-TA...
RYOU-TA'S...
THIRTY MINUTES EARLIER...

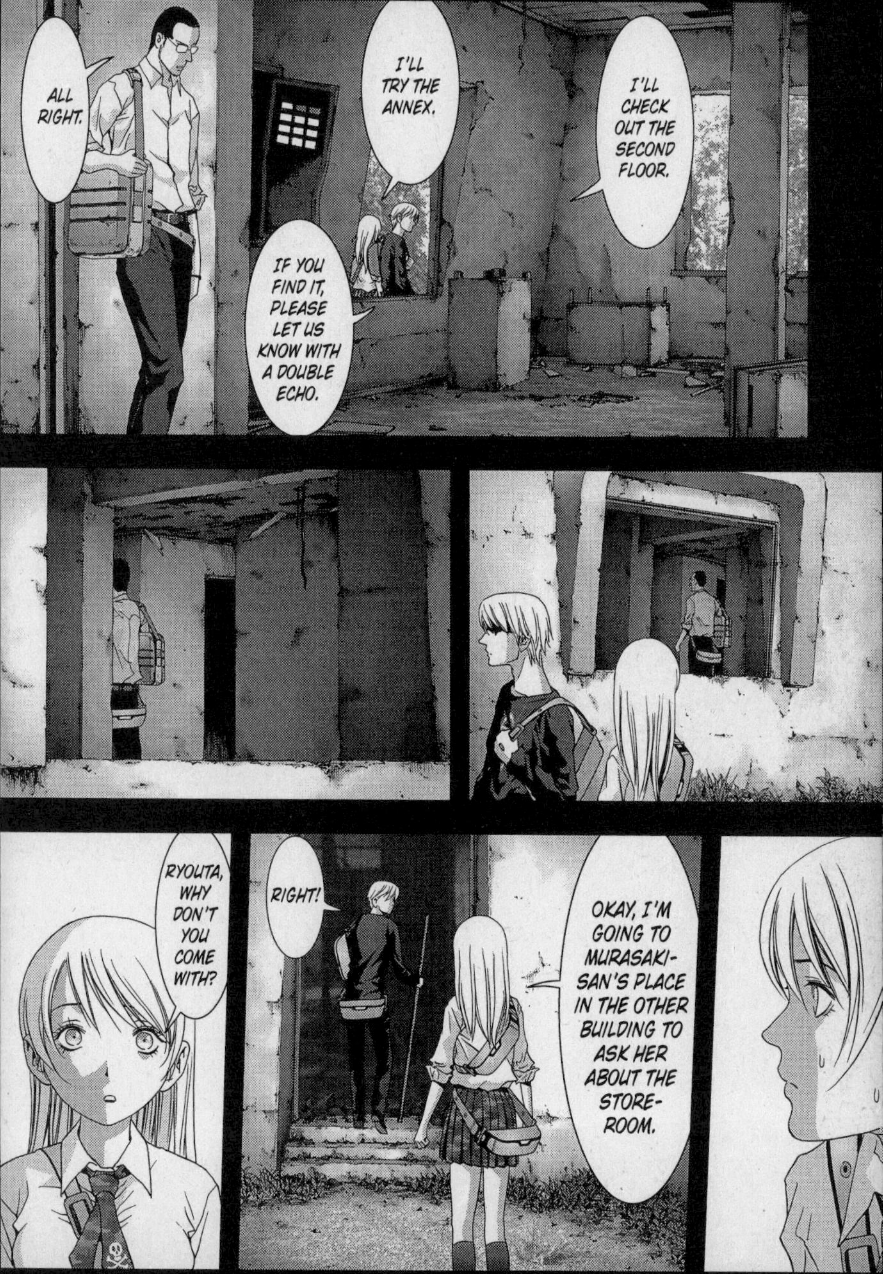
I'LL CHECK OUT THE SECOND FLOOR.
I'LL TRY THE ANNEX.
IF YOU FIND IT, PLEASE LET US KNOW WITH A DOUBLE ECHO.
ALL RIGHT.
OKAY, I'M GOING TO MURASAKI-SAN'S PLACE IN THE OTHER BUILDING TO ASK HER ABOUT THE STORE-ROOM.
RIGHT!
RYOUTA, WHY DON'T YOU COME WITH?

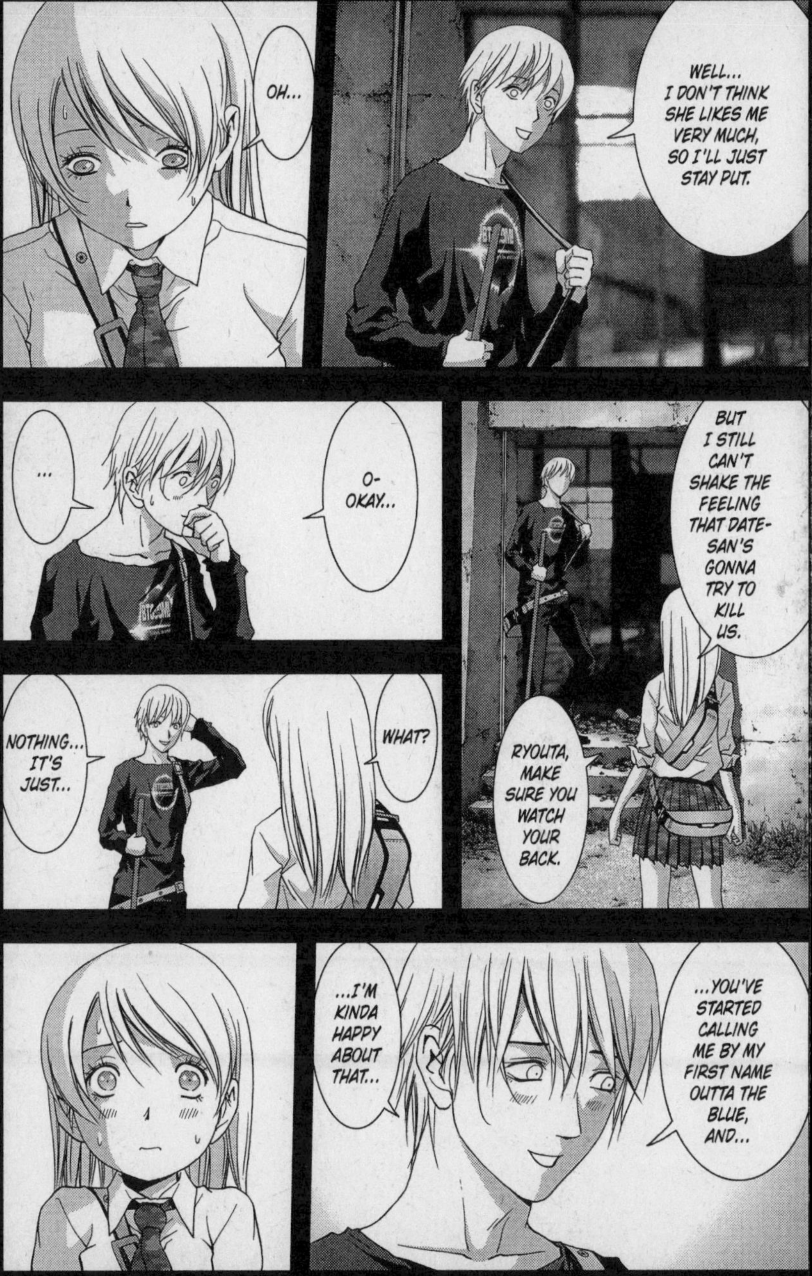
WELL... I DON'T THINK SHE LIKES ME VERY MUCH, SO I'LL JUST STAY PUT.
OH...
BUT I STILL CAN'T SHAKE THE FEELING THAT DATE-SAN'S GONNA TRY TO KILL US.
RYOUTA, MAKE SURE YOU WATCH YOUR BACK.
O-OKAY...
...
WHAT?
NOTHING... IT'S JUST...
...YOU'VE STARTED CALLING ME BY MY FIRST NAME OUTTA THE BLUE, AND...
...I'M KINDA HAPPY ABOUT THAT...

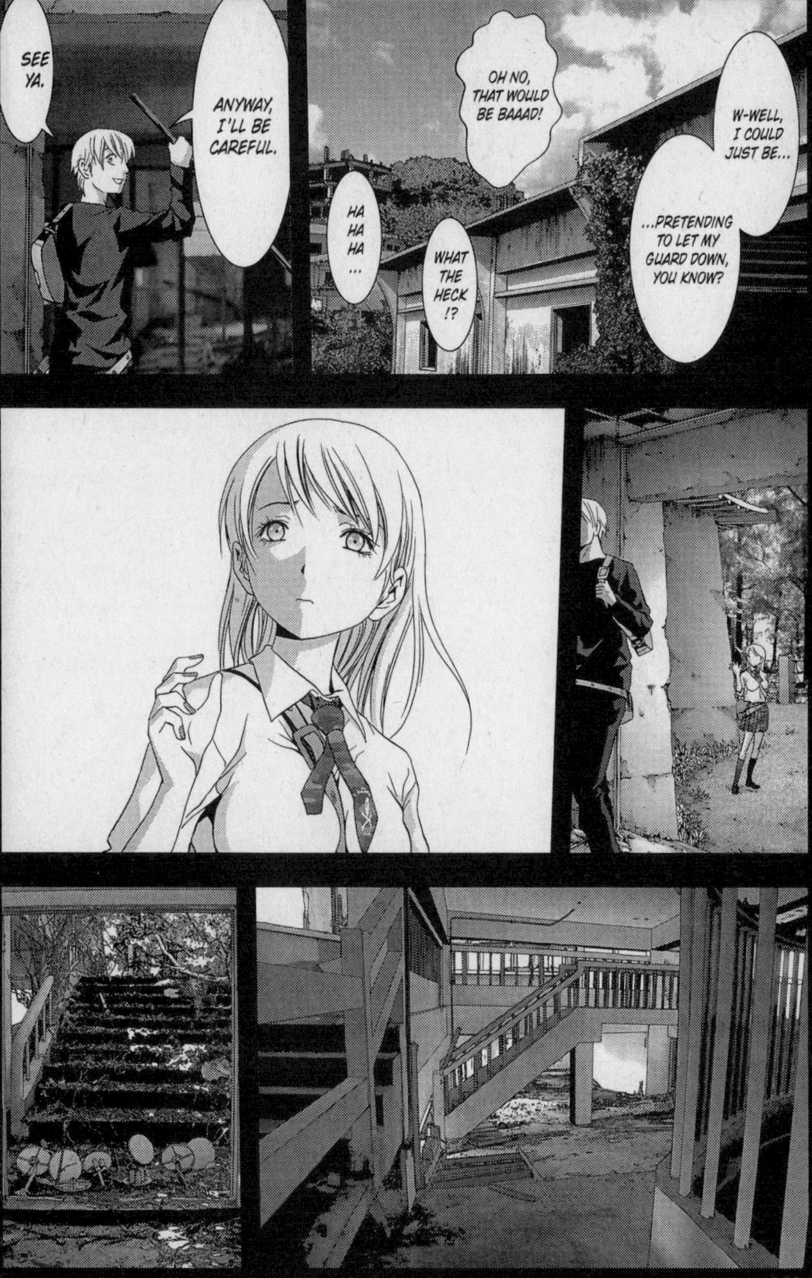
W-WELL, I COULD JUST BE...
...PRETENDING TO LET MY GUARD DOWN, YOU KNOW?
OH NO, THAT WOULD BE BAAAD!
WHAT THE HECK !?
HA HA HA ...
ANYWAY, I'LL BE CAREFUL.
SEE YA.

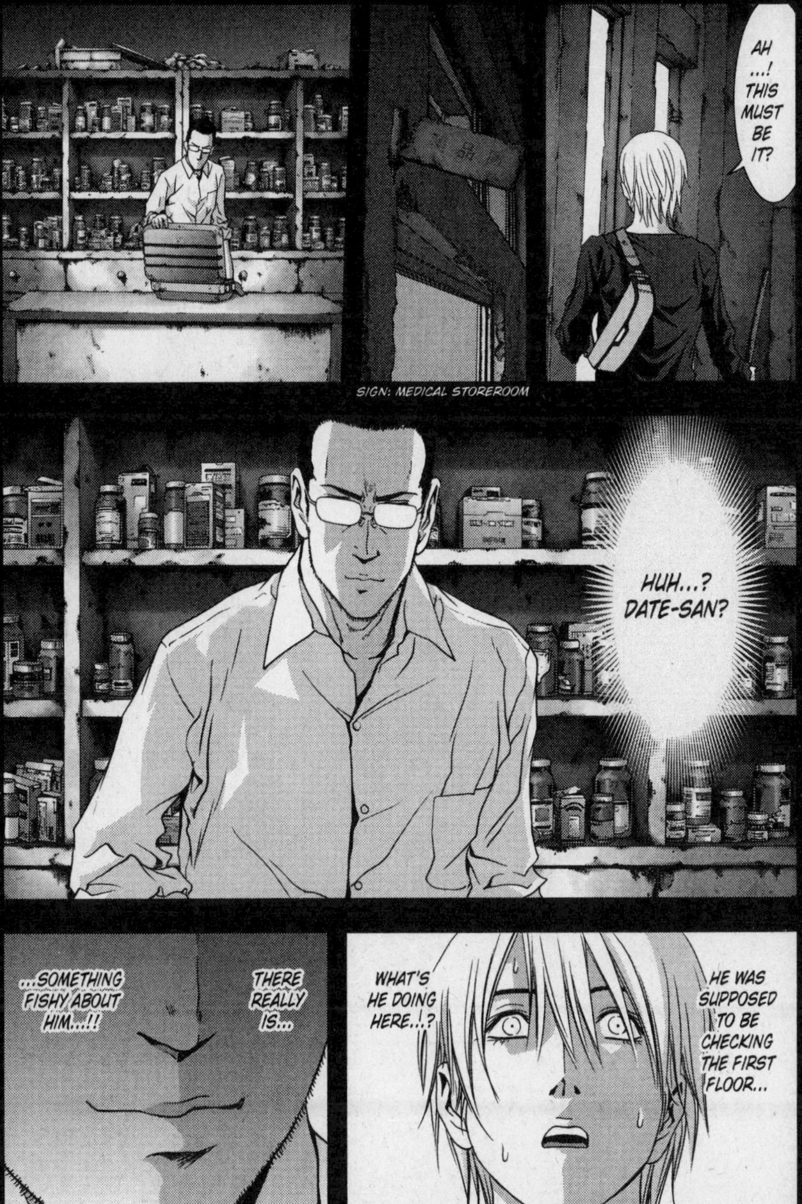
AH ...! THIS MUST BE IT?
SIGN: MEDICAL STOREROOM
HUH...? DATE-SAN?
HE WAS SUPPOSED TO BE CHECKING THE FIRST FLOOR...
WHAT'S HE DOING HERE..!?
THERE REALLY IS...
...SOMETHING FISHY ABOUT HIM...!!

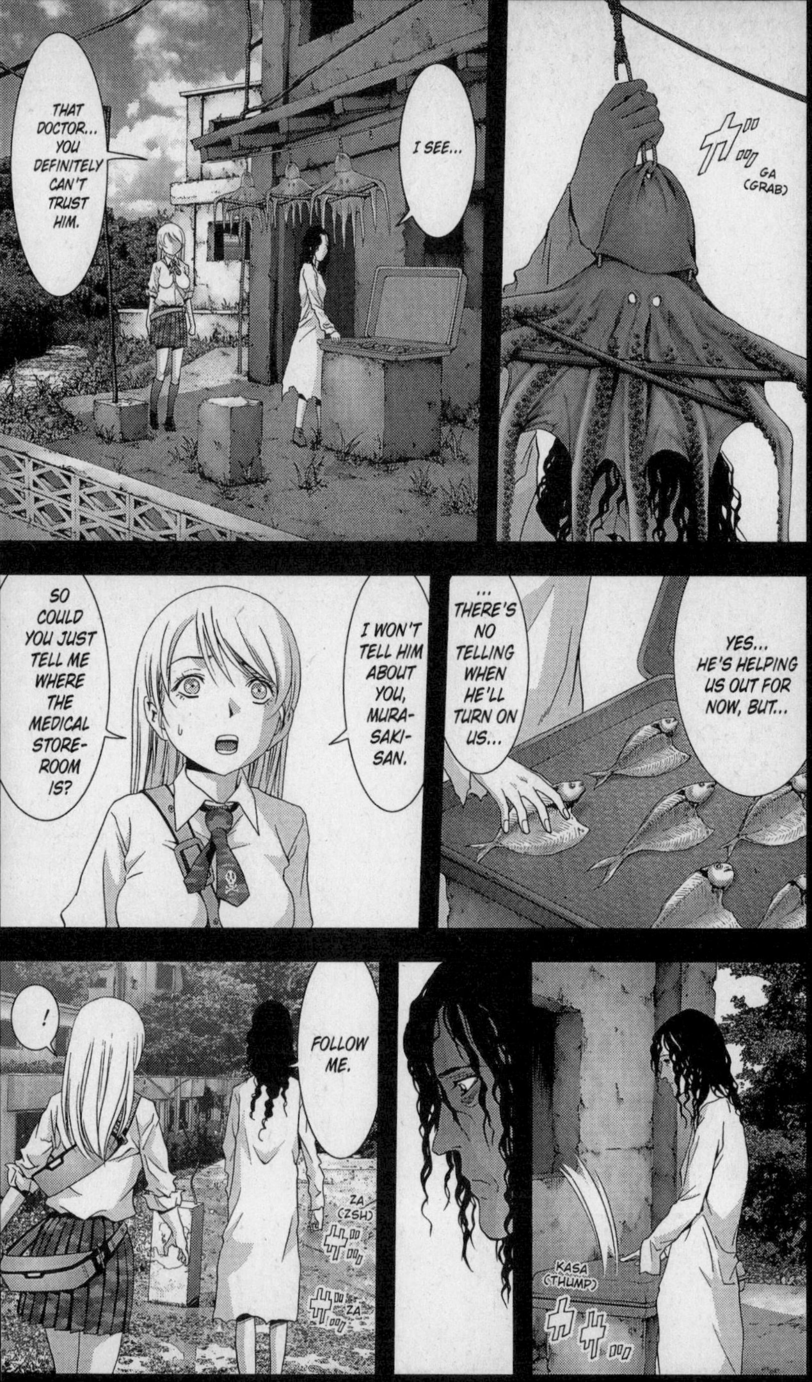
GA
(GRAB)
I SEE...
THAT DOCTOR... YOU DEFINITELY CAN'T TRUST HIM.
YES... HE'S HELPING US OUT FOR NOW, BUT...
... THERE'S NO TELLING WHEN HE'LL TURN ON US...
I WON'T TELL HIM ABOUT YOU, MURASAKI-SAN.
SO COULD YOU JUST TELL ME WHERE THE MEDICAL STOREROOM IS?
KASA
(THUMP)
FOLLOW ME.
!
ZA
(ZSH)
ZA

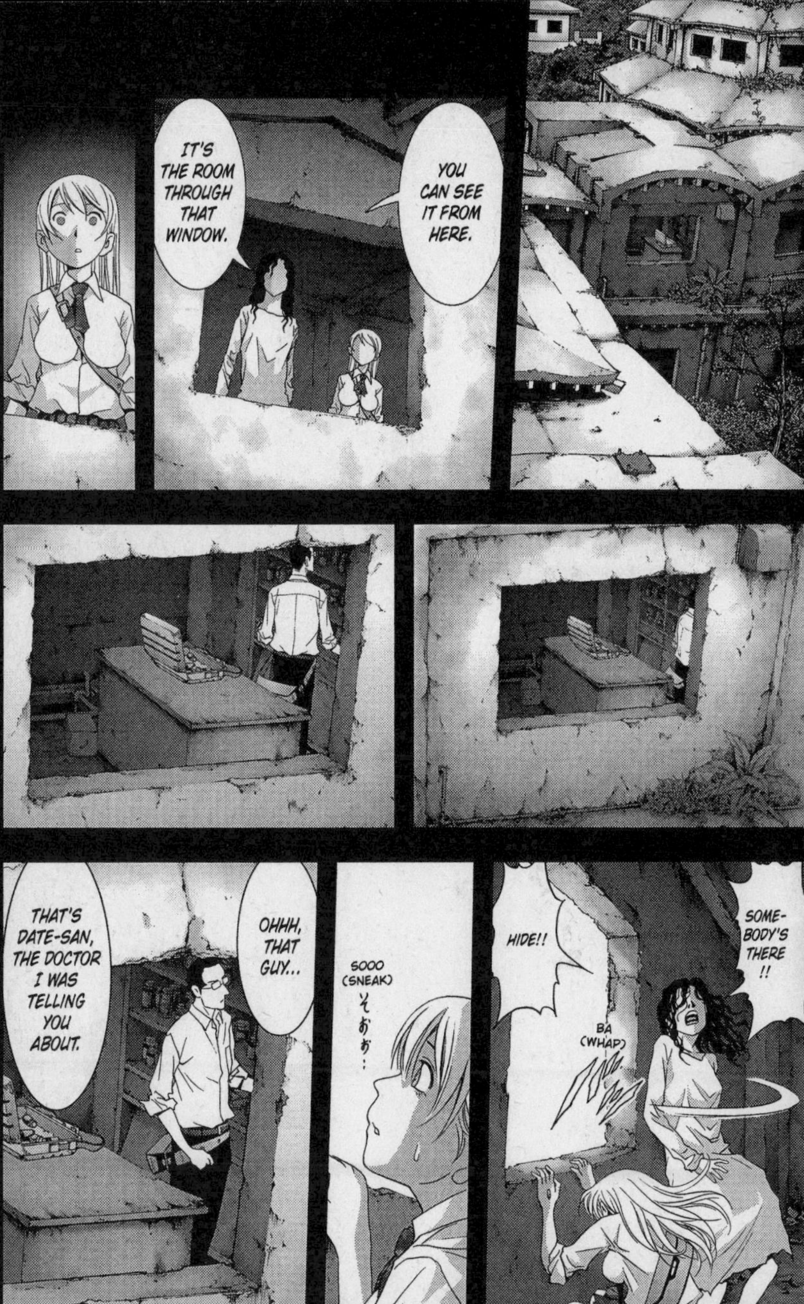
YOU CAN SEE IT FROM HERE.
IT'S THE ROOM THROUGH THAT WINDOW.
SOME-BODY'S THERE!!
HIDE!!
BA (WHAP)
SOOO (SNEAK)
そぉぉ…
OHHH, THAT GUY...
THAT'S DATE-SAN, THE DOCTOR I WAS TELLING YOU ABOUT.

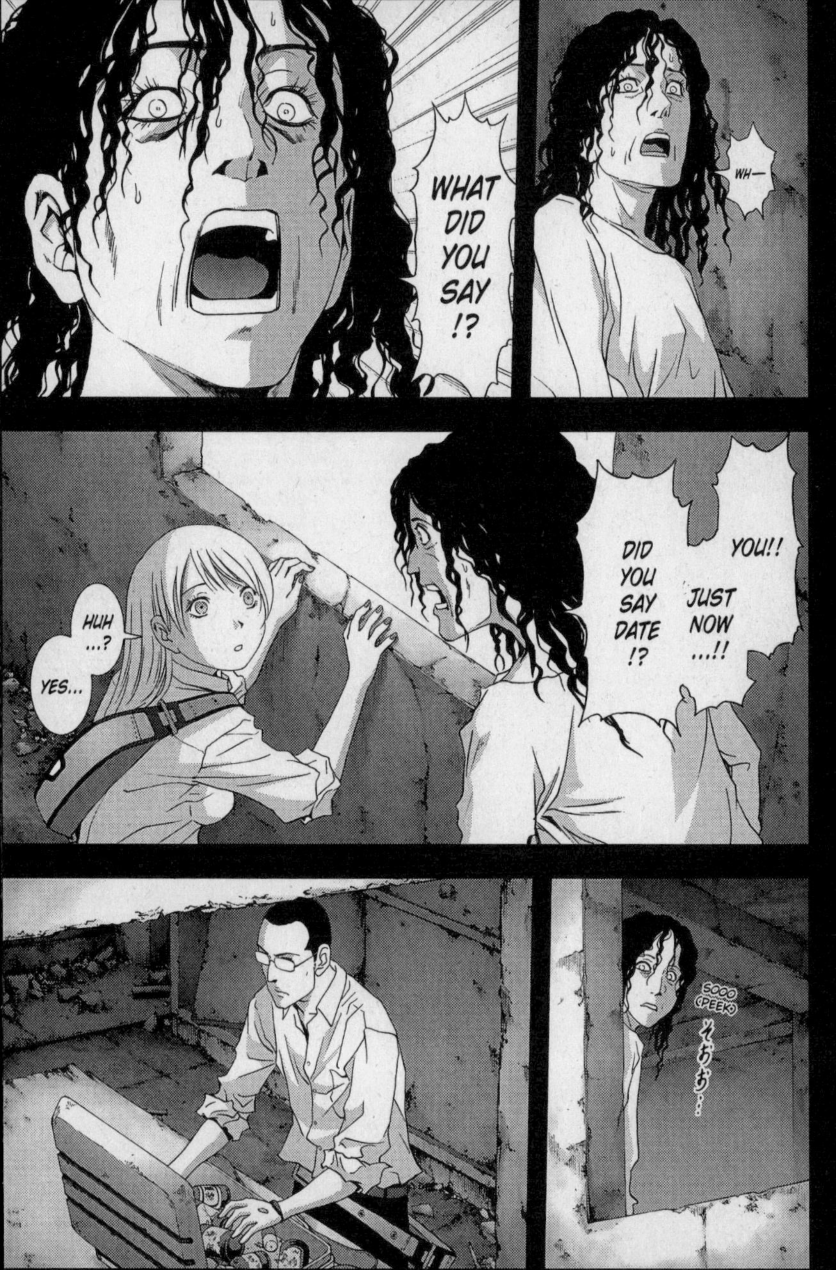
WH—
WHAT DID YOU SAY !?
YOU!! JUST NOW ...!!
DID YOU SAY DATE !?
HUH ...?
YES...
SOOO (PEEK)
そおぉ・・・

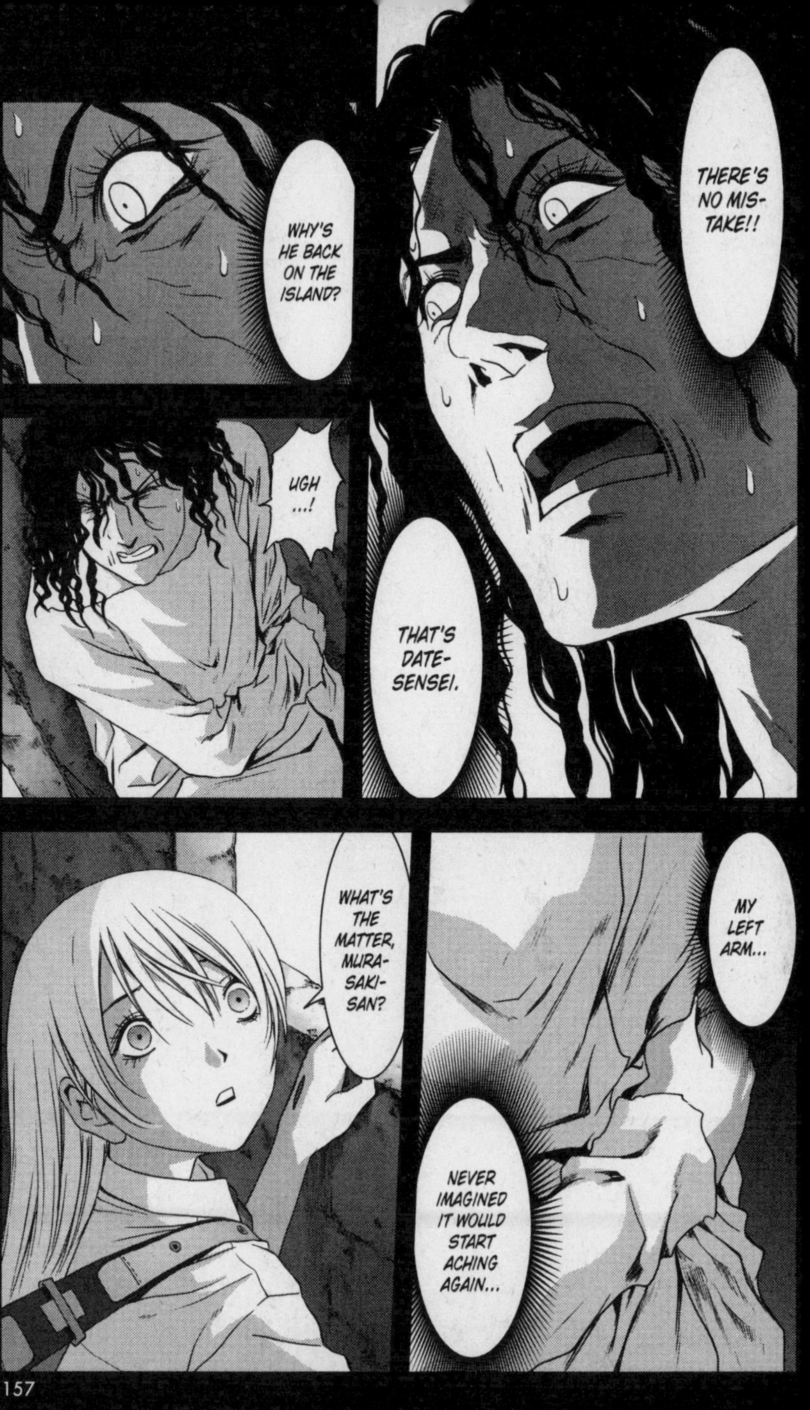
THERE'S NO MIS-TAKE!!
THAT'S DATE-SENSEI.
WHY'S HE BACK ON THE ISLAND?
UGH ...!
MY LEFT ARM...
NEVER IMAGINED IT WOULD START ACHING AGAIN...
WHAT'S THE MATTER, MURA-SAKI-SAN?

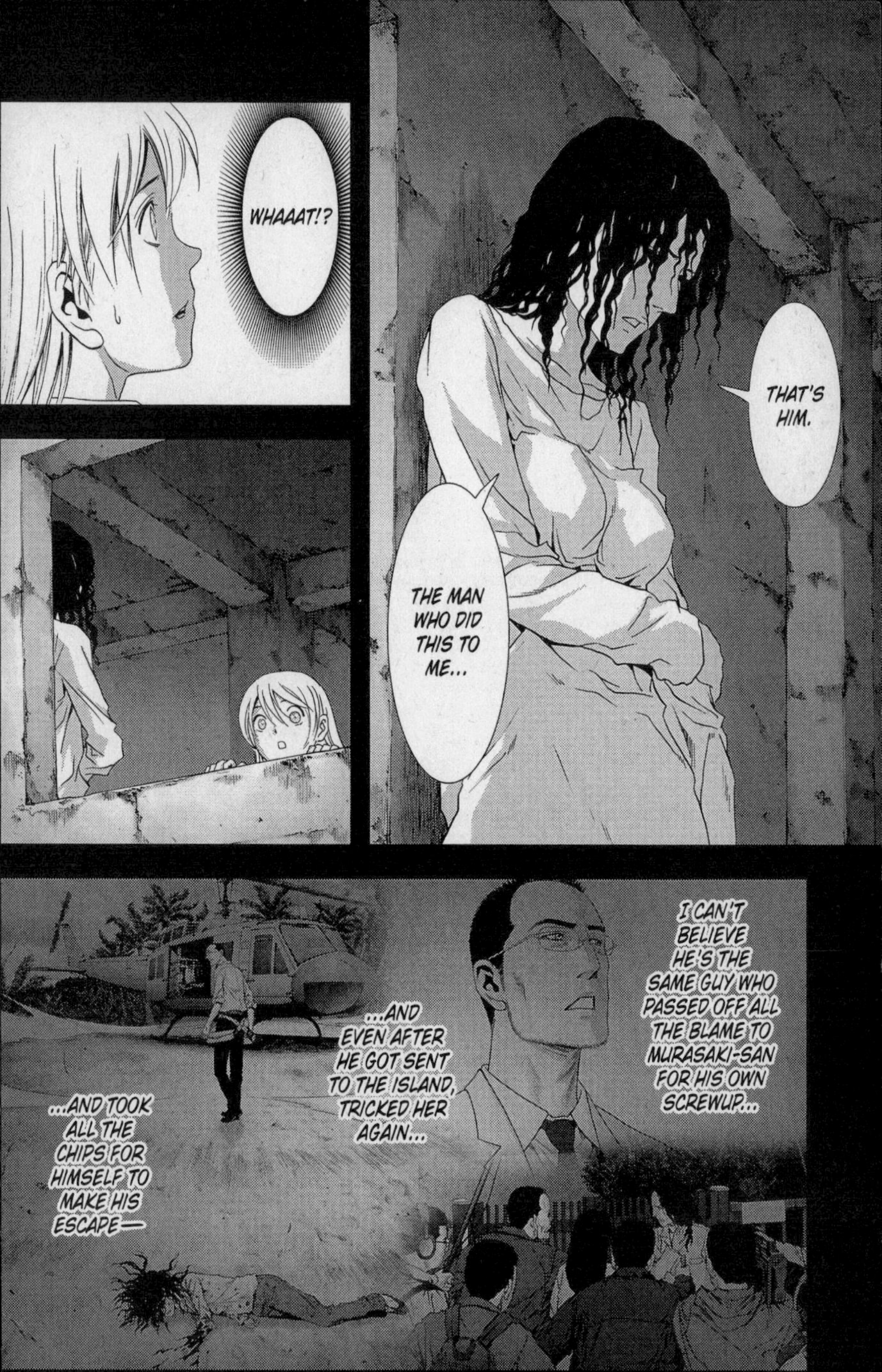
THAT'S HIM.
THE MAN WHO DID THIS TO ME...
WHAAAT!?
I CAN'T BELIEVE HE'S THE SAME GUY WHO PASSED OFF ALL THE BLAME TO MURASAKI-SAN FOR HIS OWN SCREWUP...
...AND EVEN AFTER HE GOT SENT TO THE ISLAND, TRICKED HER AGAIN...
...AND TOOK ALL THE CHIPS FOR HIMSELF TO MAKE HIS ESCAPE—

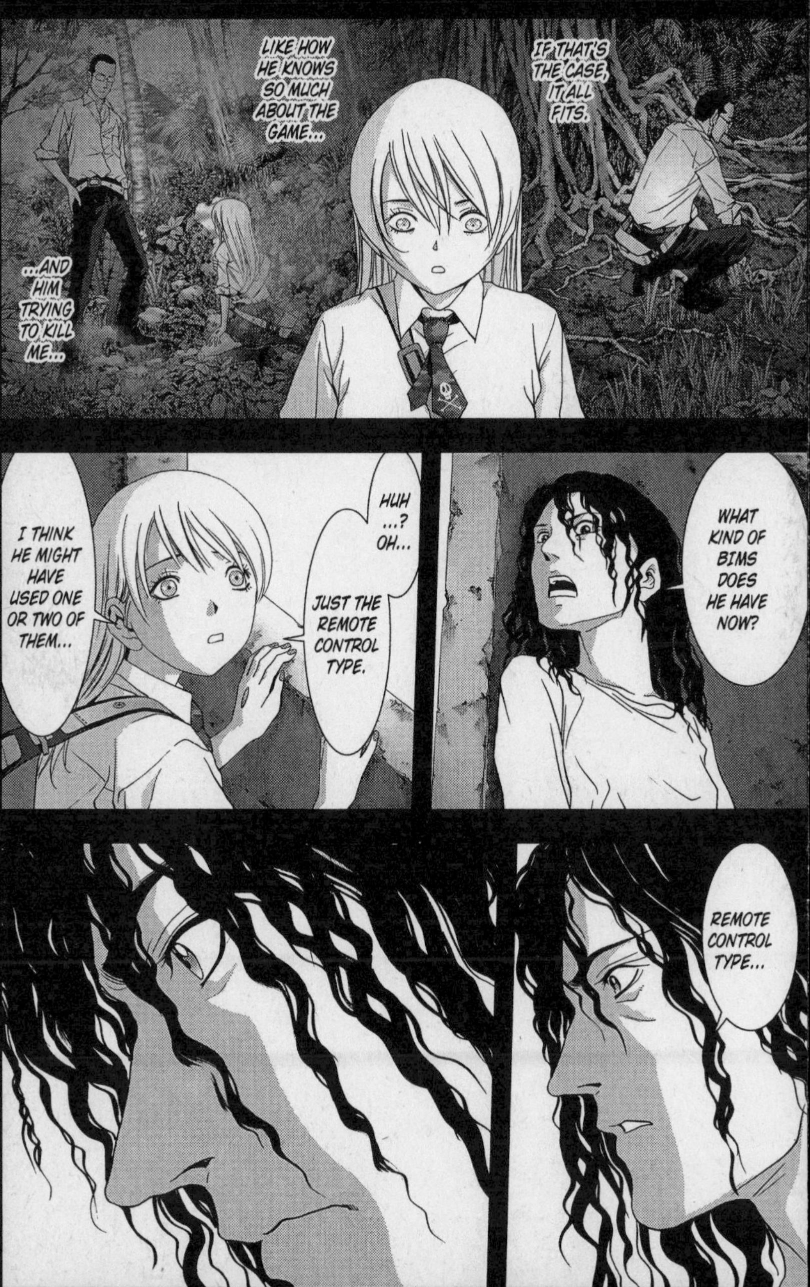
IF THAT'S THE CASE, IT ALL FITS.
LIKE HOW HE KNOWS SO MUCH ABOUT THE GAME...
...AND HIM TRYING TO KILL ME...
WHAT KIND OF BIMS DOES HE HAVE NOW?
HUH ...? OH...
JUST THE REMOTE CONTROL TYPE.
I THINK HE MIGHT HAVE USED ONE OR TWO OF THEM...
REMOTE CONTROL TYPE...

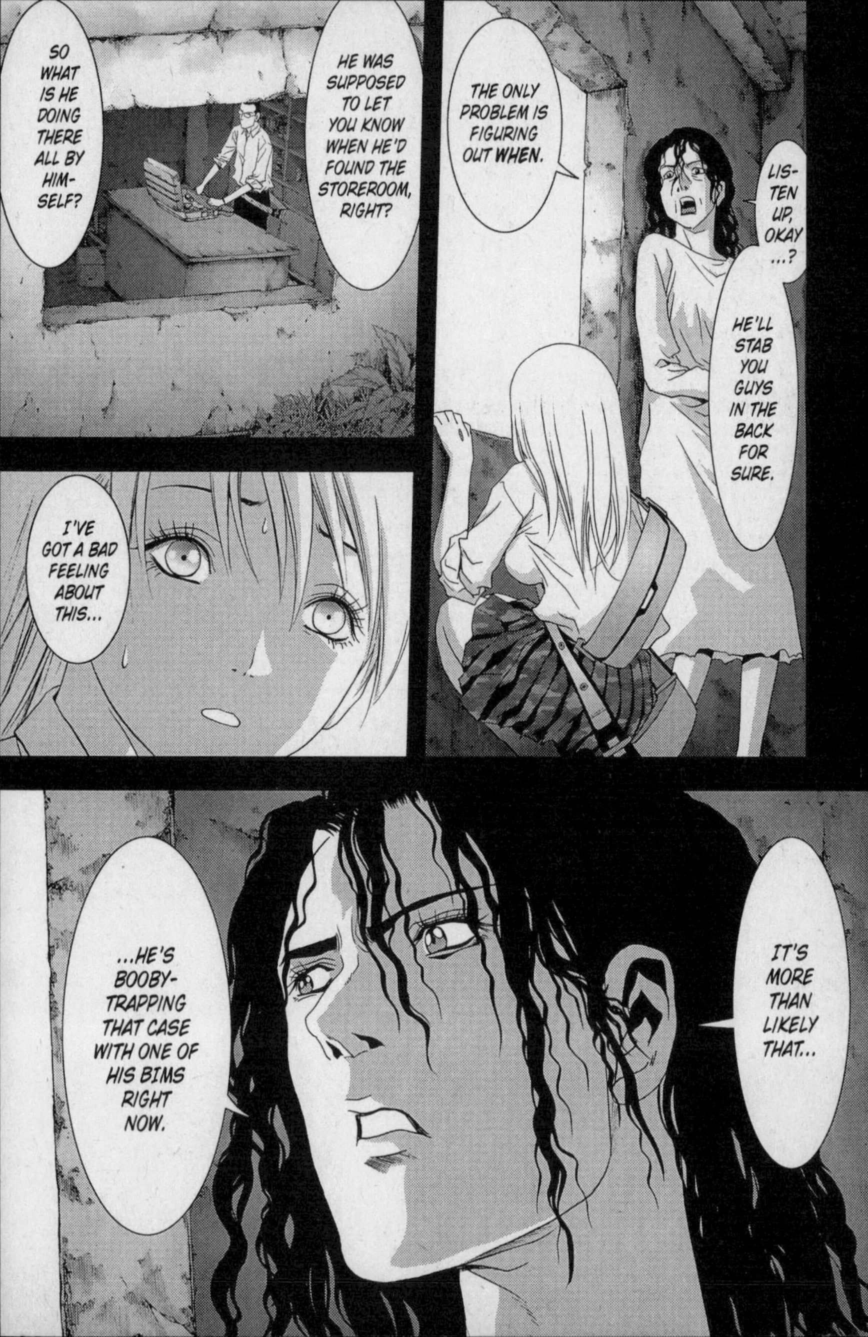
LISTEN UP, OKAY...?
HE'LL STAB YOU GUYS IN THE BACK FOR SURE.
THE ONLY PROBLEM IS FIGURING OUT **WHEN**.
HE WAS SUPPOSED TO LET YOU KNOW WHEN HE'D FOUND THE STOREROOM, RIGHT?
SO WHAT IS HE DOING THERE ALL BY HIMSELF?
I'VE GOT A BAD FEELING ABOUT THIS...
IT'S MORE THAN LIKELY THAT...
...HE'S BOOBY-TRAPPING THAT CASE WITH ONE OF HIS BIMS RIGHT NOW.

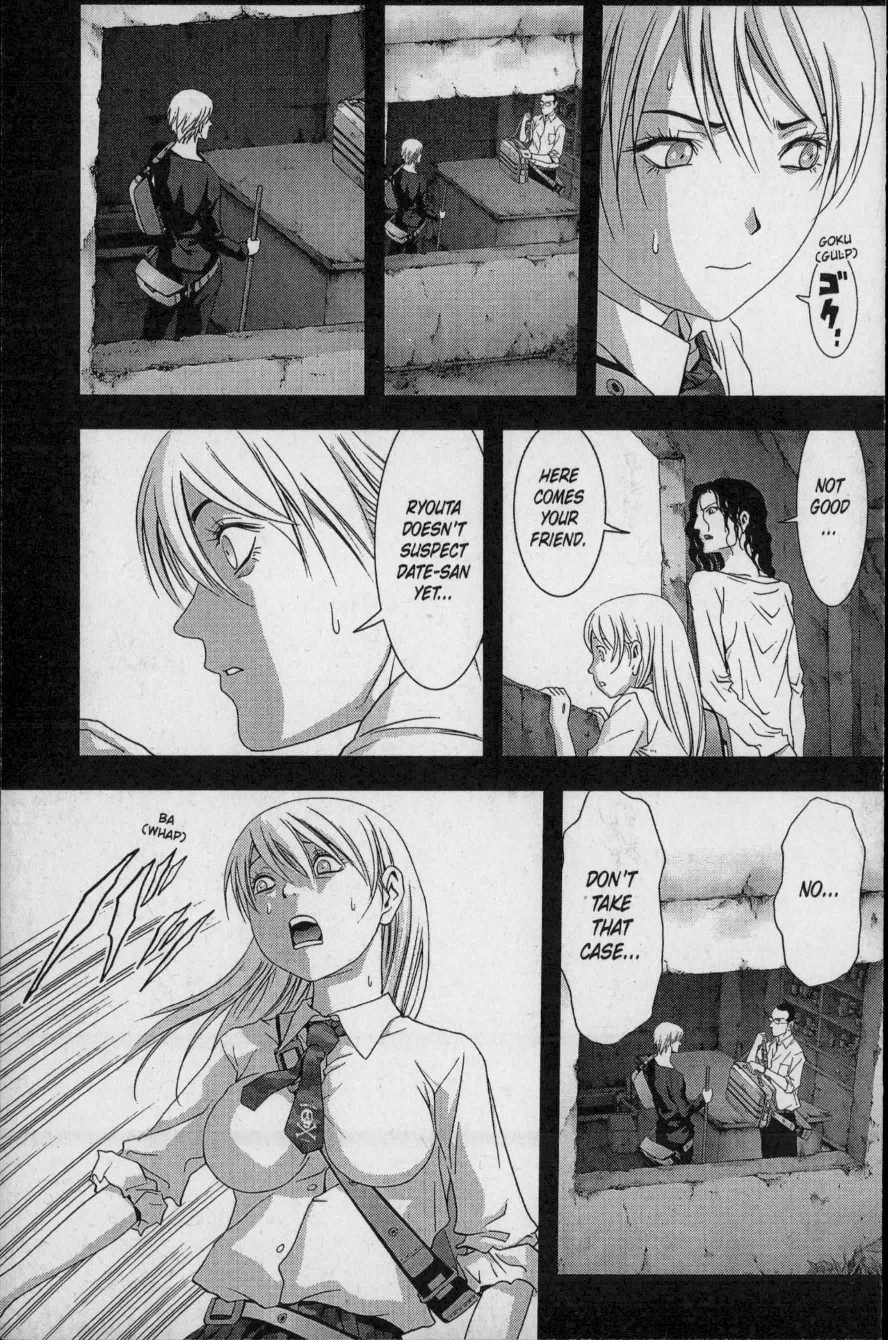
GOKU (GULP)
ゴクッ
NOT GOOD ...
HERE COMES YOUR FRIEND.
RYOUTA DOESN'T SUSPECT DATE-SAN YET...
NO...
DON'T TAKE THAT CASE...
BA (WHAP)
バッ

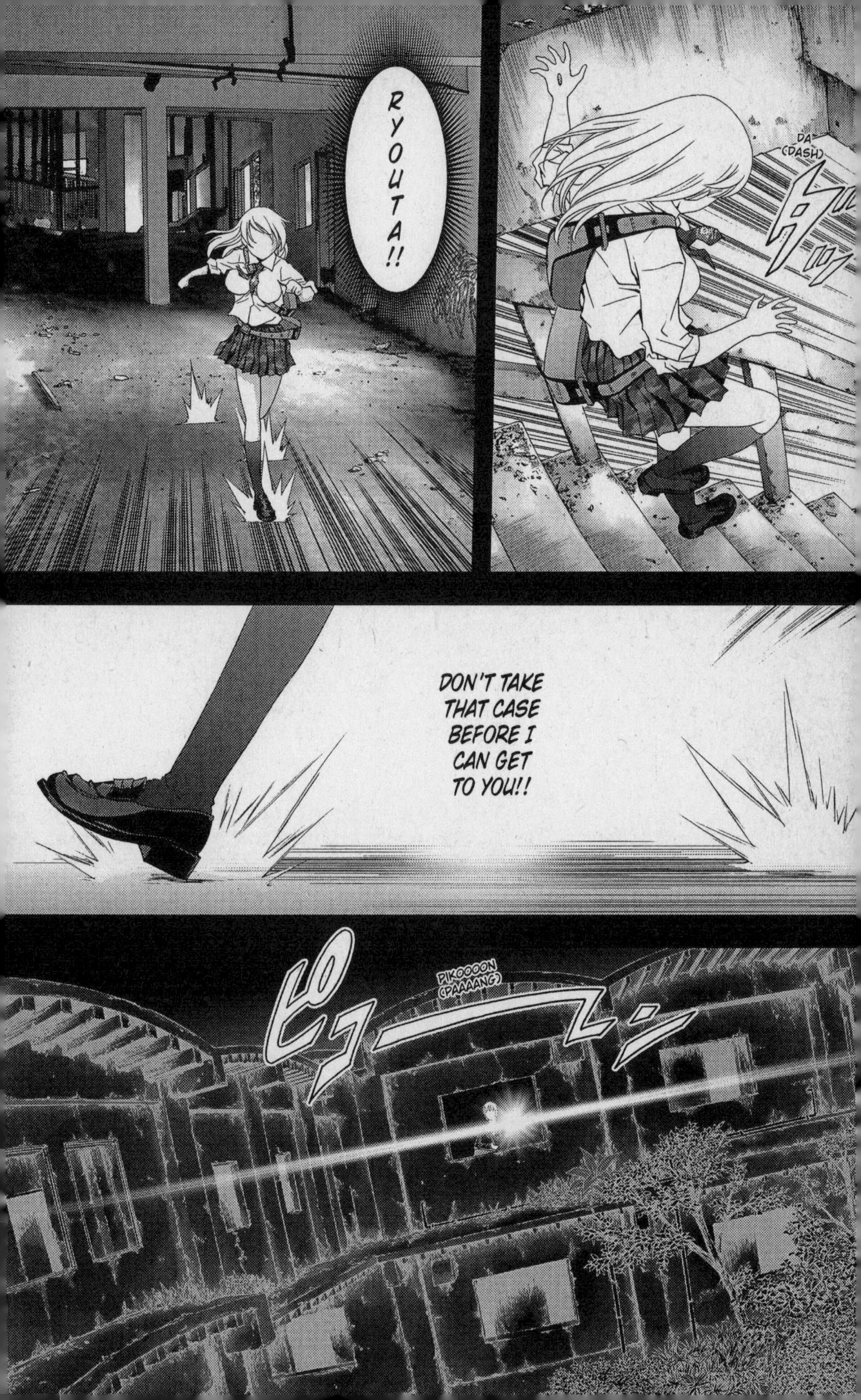
DA (DASH)
RYOUTA!!
DON'T TAKE THAT CASE BEFORE I CAN GET TO YOU!!
PIKOOOON (PAAAANG)

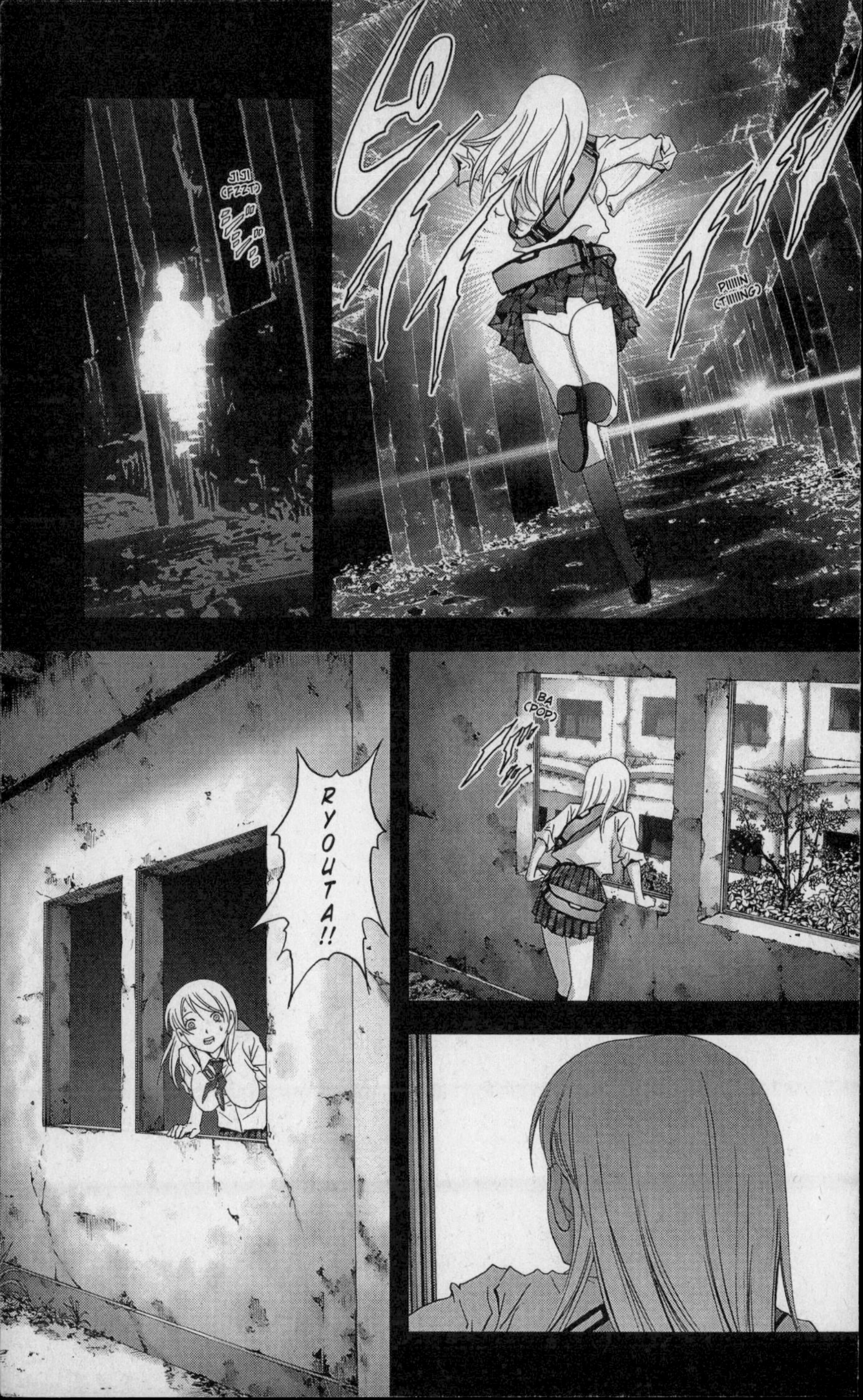
PIIIIN (TIIIING)
JIJI (FZZT)
BA (POP)
RYOUTA!!

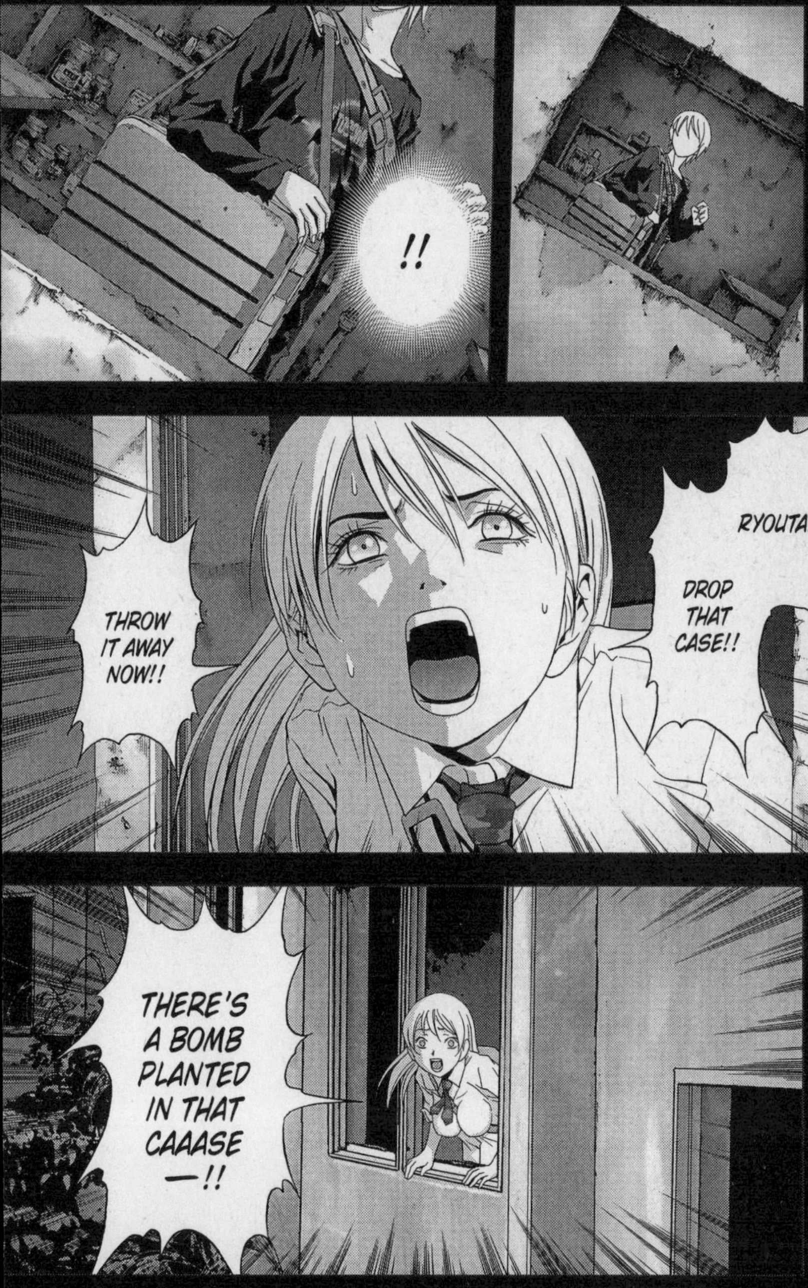
!!
RYOUTA!!
DROP THAT CASE!!
THROW IT AWAY NOW!!
THERE'S A BOMB PLANTED IN THAT CAAASE—!!

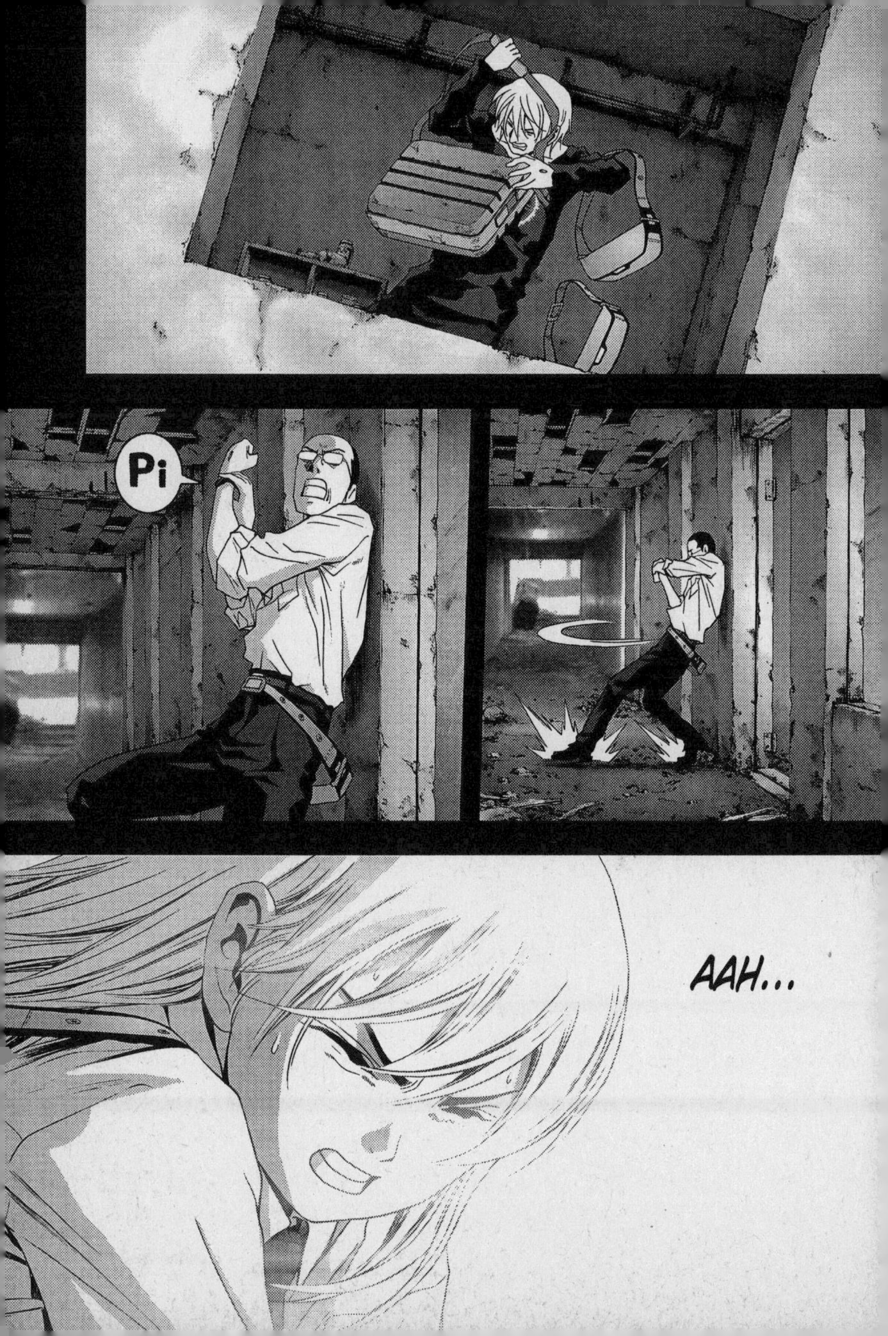
Pi
AAH...

RYOUTAAAAAAA!!

WE'RE RUNNING FOR IT!!

PULL YOURSELF TOGETHER!!

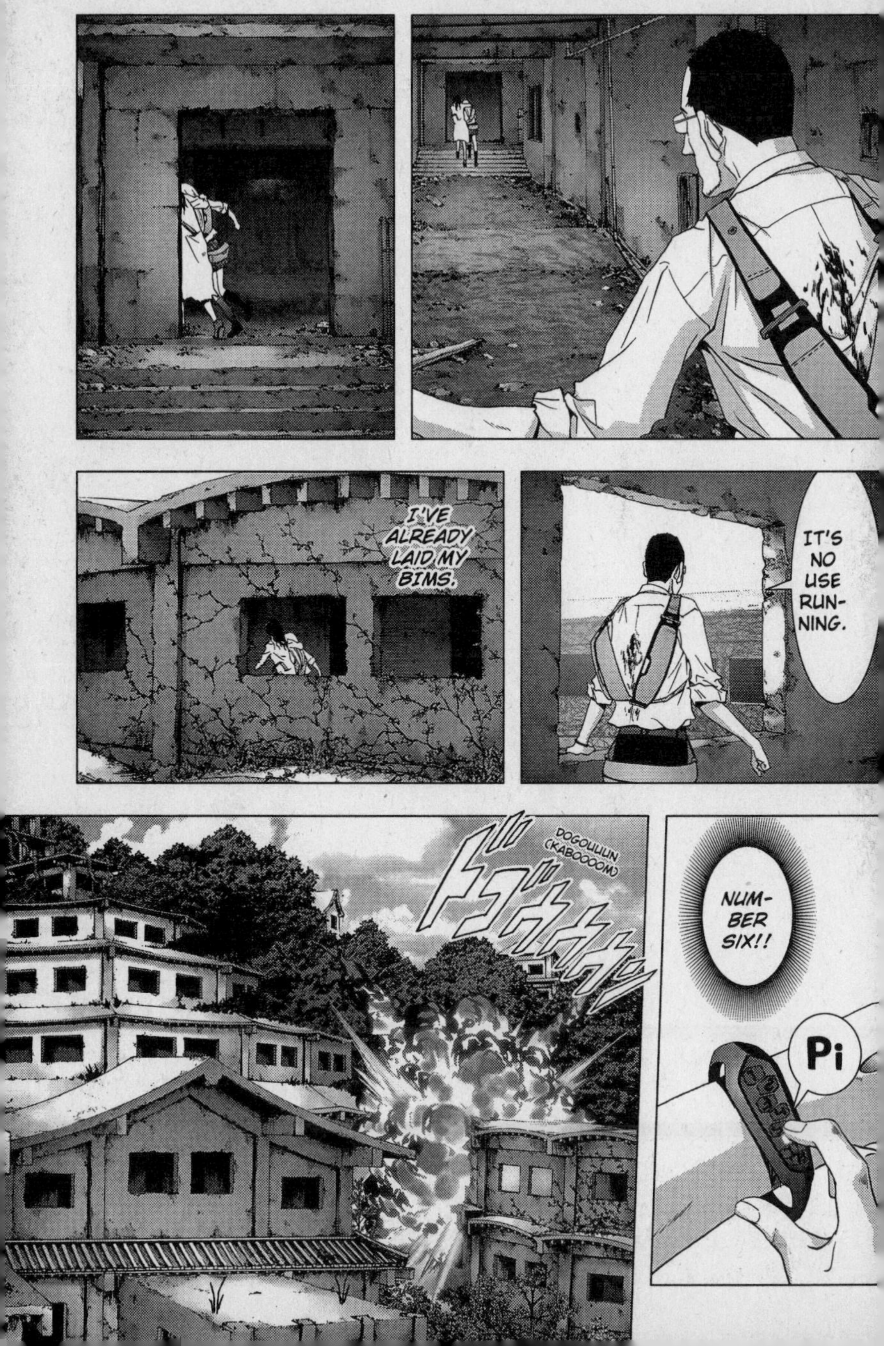
IT'S NO USE RUNNING.
I'VE ALREADY LAID MY BIMS.
NUMBER SIX!!
Pi
DOGOUUUN (KABOOOOM)

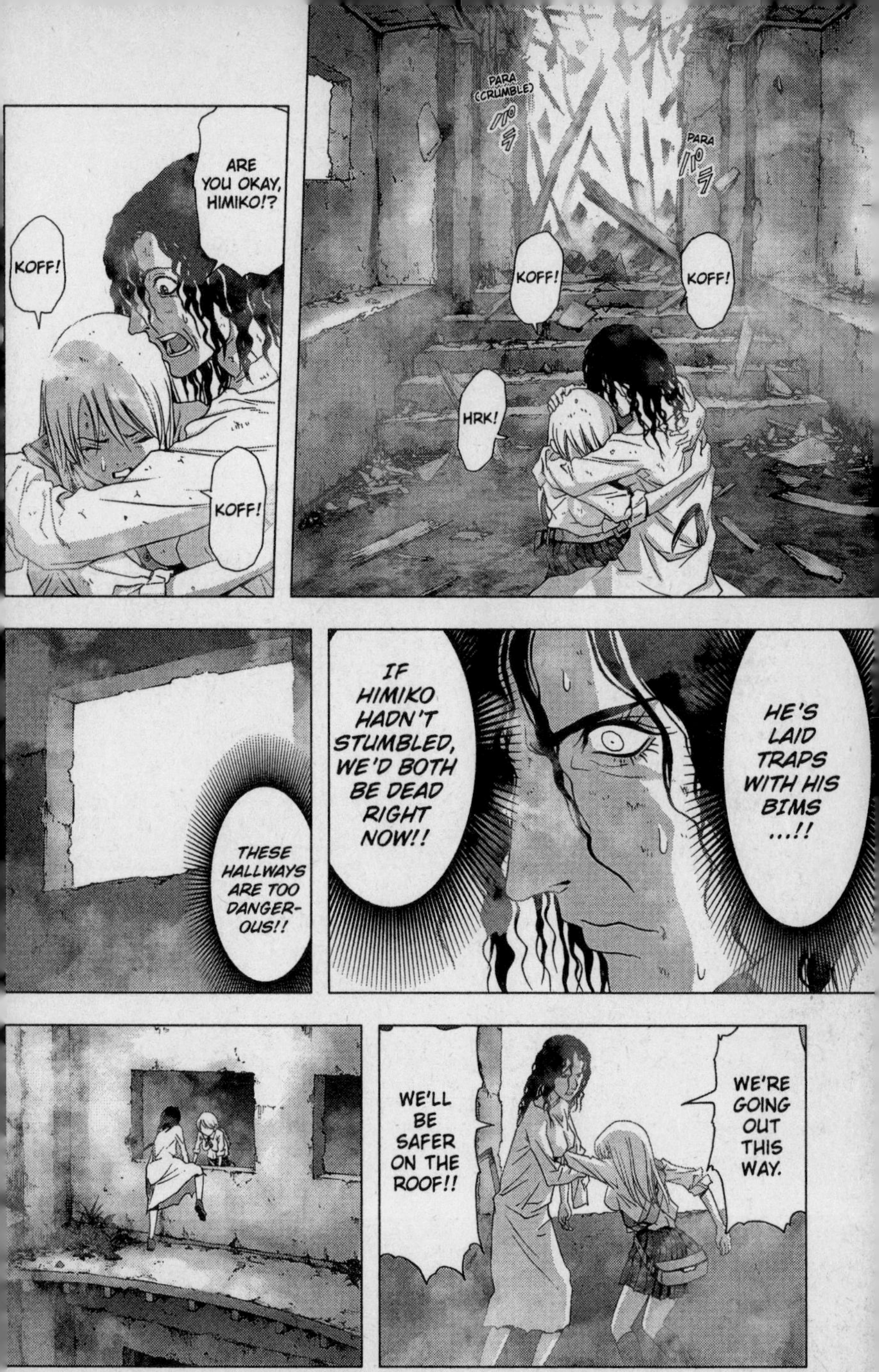
PARA
パラ
PARA (CRUMBLE)
パラ
KOFF!
KOFF!
HRK!
ARE YOU OKAY, HIMIKO!?
KOFF!
KOFF!
HE'S LAID TRAPS WITH HIS BIMS ...!!
IF HIMIKO HADN'T STUMBLED, WE'D BOTH BE DEAD RIGHT NOW!!
THESE HALLWAYS ARE TOO DANGER-OUS!!
WE'RE GOING OUT THIS WAY.
WE'LL BE SAFER ON THE ROOF!!

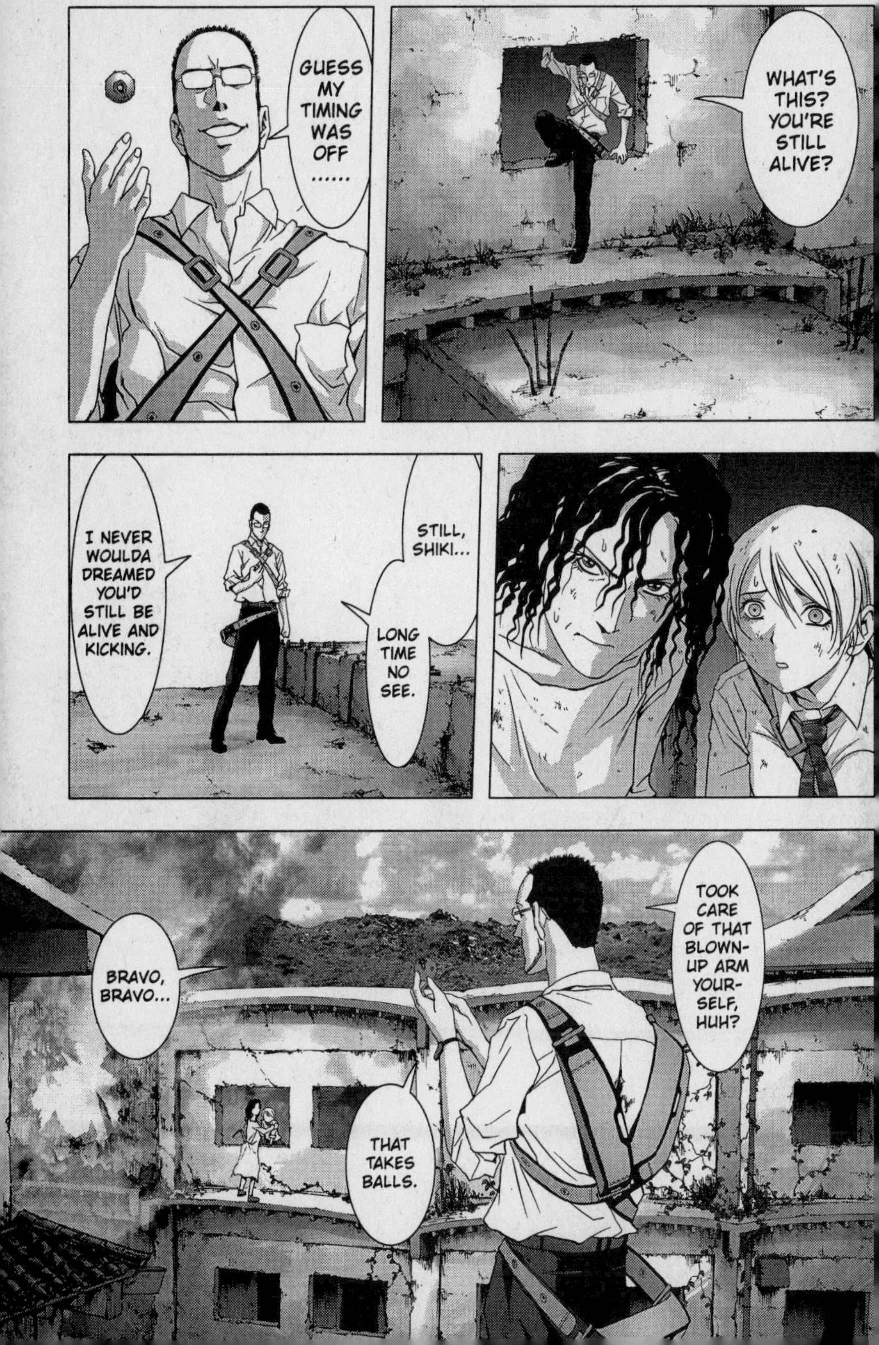
WHAT'S THIS? YOU'RE STILL ALIVE?
GUESS MY TIMING WAS OFF ......
STILL, SHIKI...
LONG TIME NO SEE.
I NEVER WOULDA DREAMED YOU'D STILL BE ALIVE AND KICKING.
TOOK CARE OF THAT BLOWN-UP ARM YOURSELF, HUH?
THAT TAKES BALLS.
BRAVO, BRAVO...

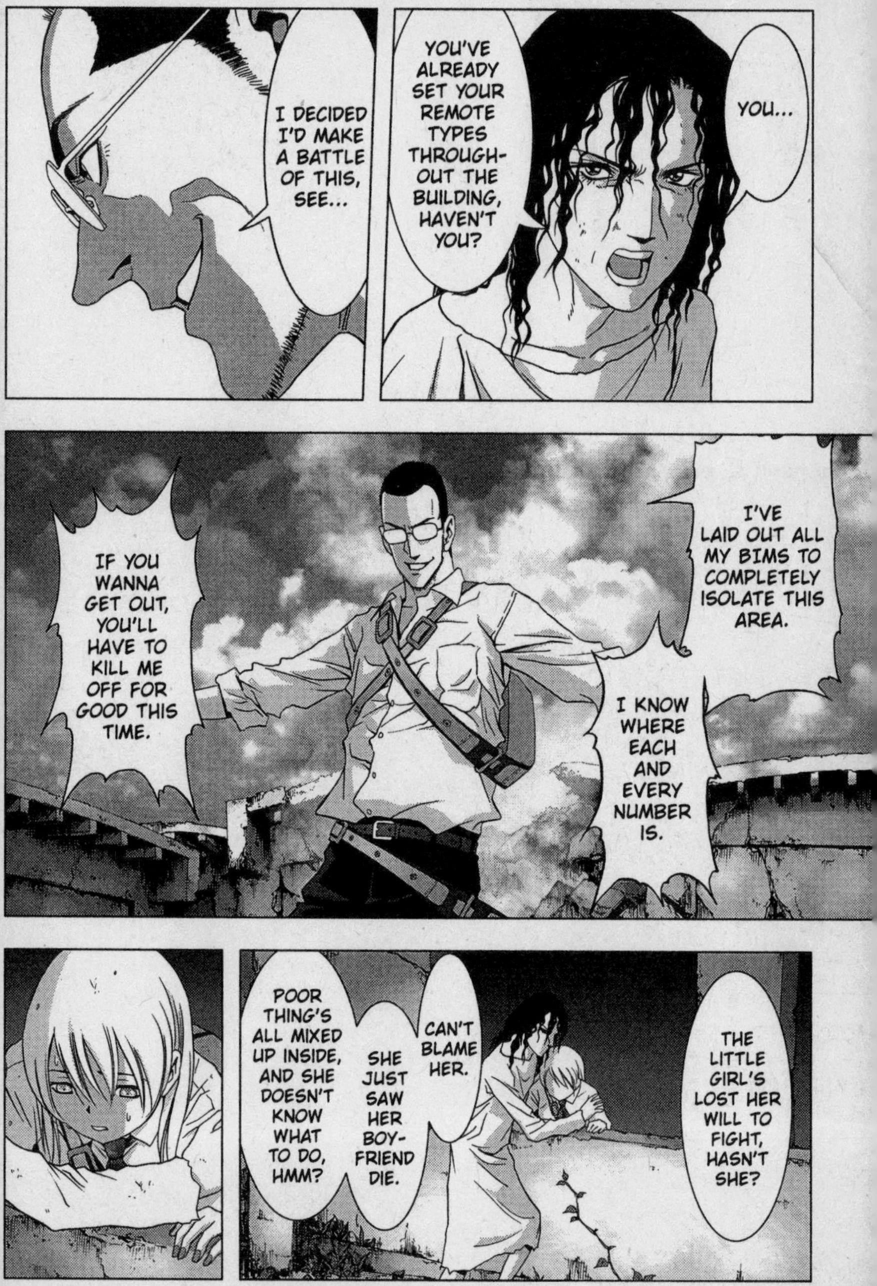
YOU...
YOU'VE ALREADY SET YOUR REMOTE TYPES THROUGHOUT THE BUILDING, HAVEN'T YOU?
I DECIDED I'D MAKE A BATTLE OF THIS, SEE...
I'VE LAID OUT ALL MY BIMS TO COMPLETELY ISOLATE THIS AREA.
I KNOW WHERE EACH AND EVERY NUMBER IS.
IF YOU WANNA GET OUT, YOU'LL HAVE TO KILL ME OFF FOR GOOD THIS TIME.
THE LITTLE GIRL'S LOST HER WILL TO FIGHT, HASN'T SHE?
CAN'T BLAME HER.
SHE JUST SAW HER BOYFRIEND DIE.
POOR THING'S ALL MIXED UP INSIDE, AND SHE DOESN'T KNOW WHAT TO DO, HMM?

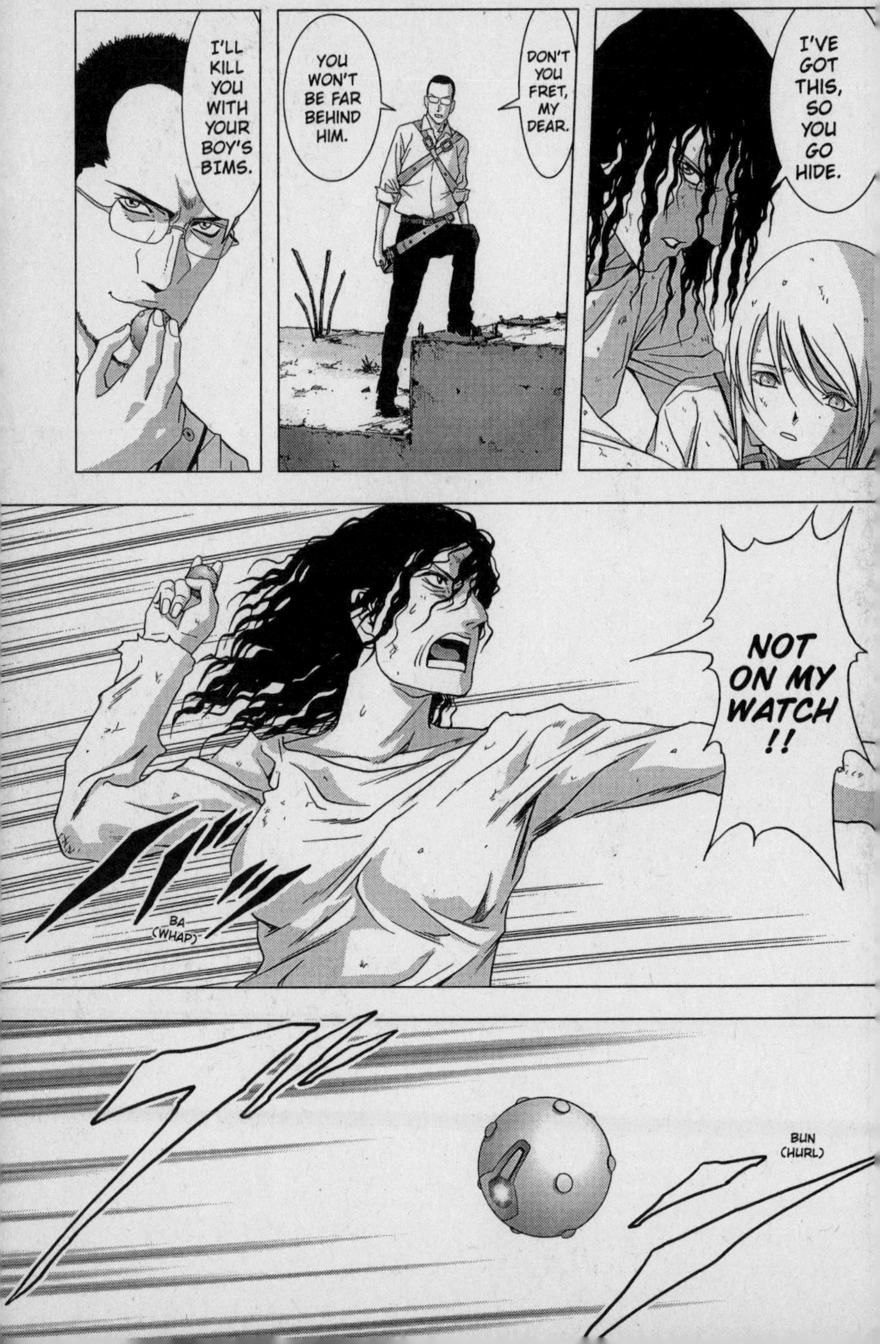
I'VE GOT THIS, SO YOU GO HIDE.
DON'T YOU FRET, MY DEAR.
YOU WON'T BE FAR BEHIND HIM.
I'LL KILL YOU WITH YOUR BOY'S BIMS.
NOT ON MY WATCH !!
BA (WHAP)
BUN (HURL)

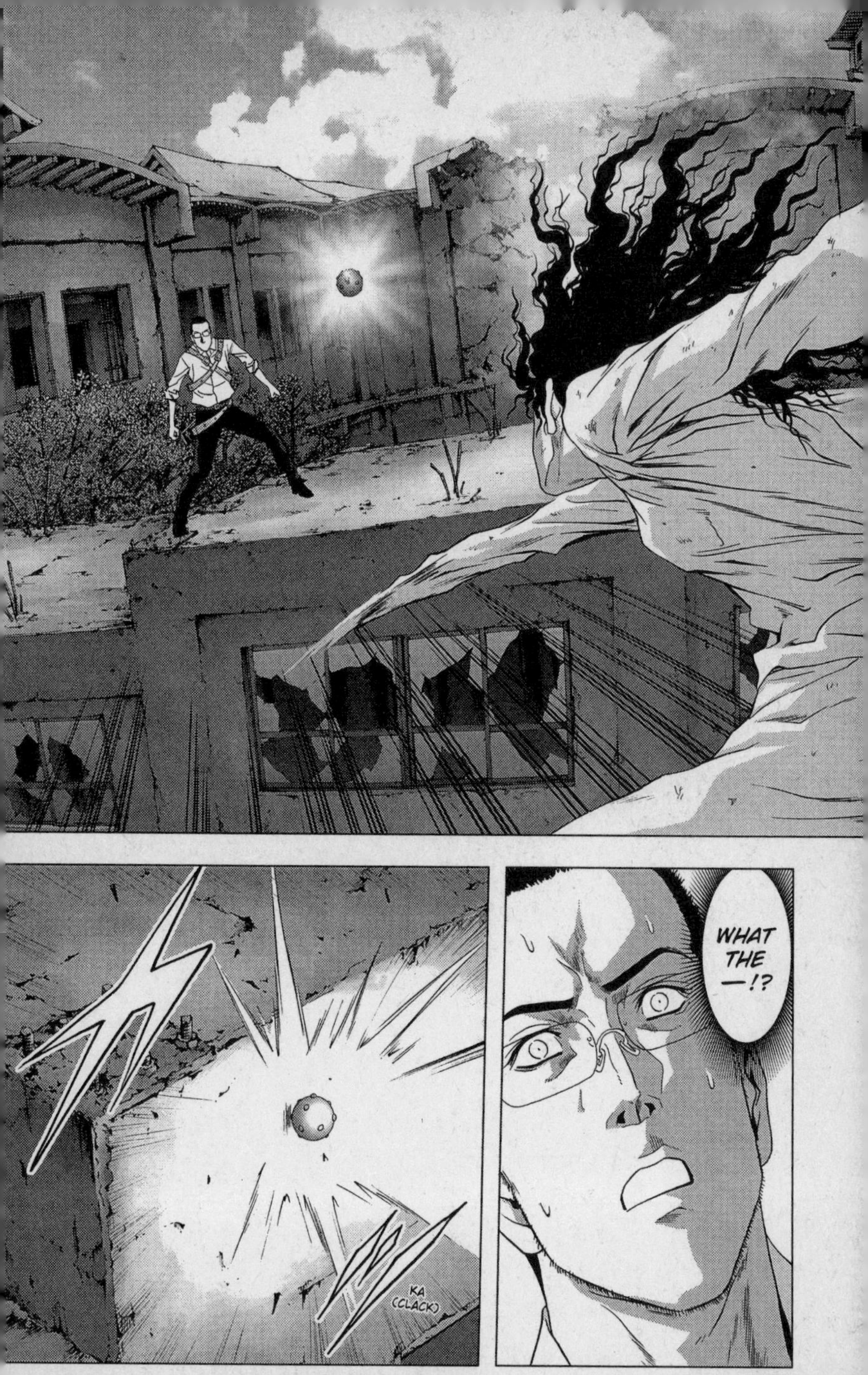
WHAT THE —!?
KA (CLACK)

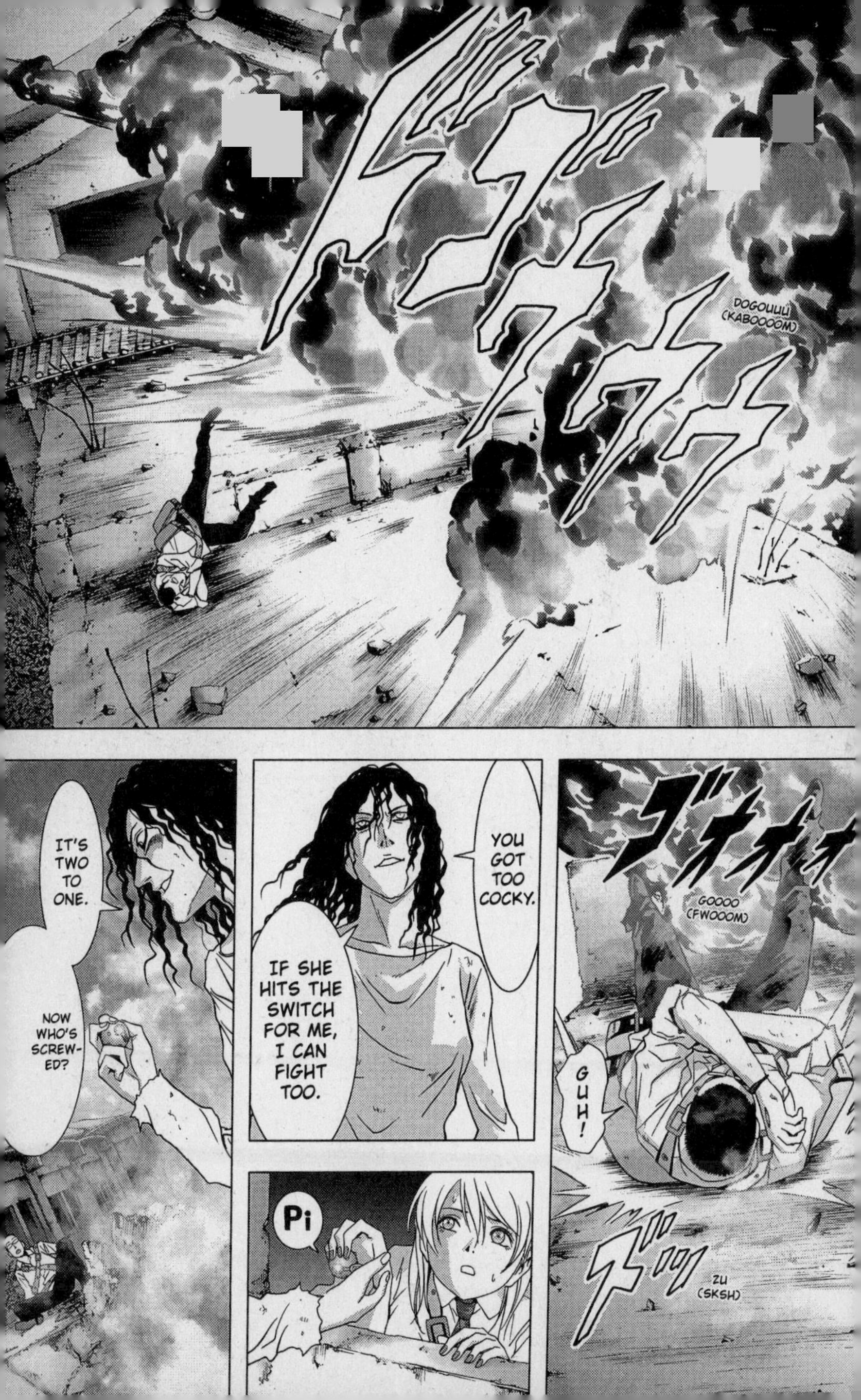
DOGOUUU
(KABOOOOM)
GOOOO
(FWOOOM)
GUH!
ZU
(SKSH)
YOU GOT TOO COCKY.
IF SHE HITS THE SWITCH FOR ME, I CAN FIGHT TOO.
Pi
IT'S TWO TO ONE.
NOW WHO'S SCREWED?

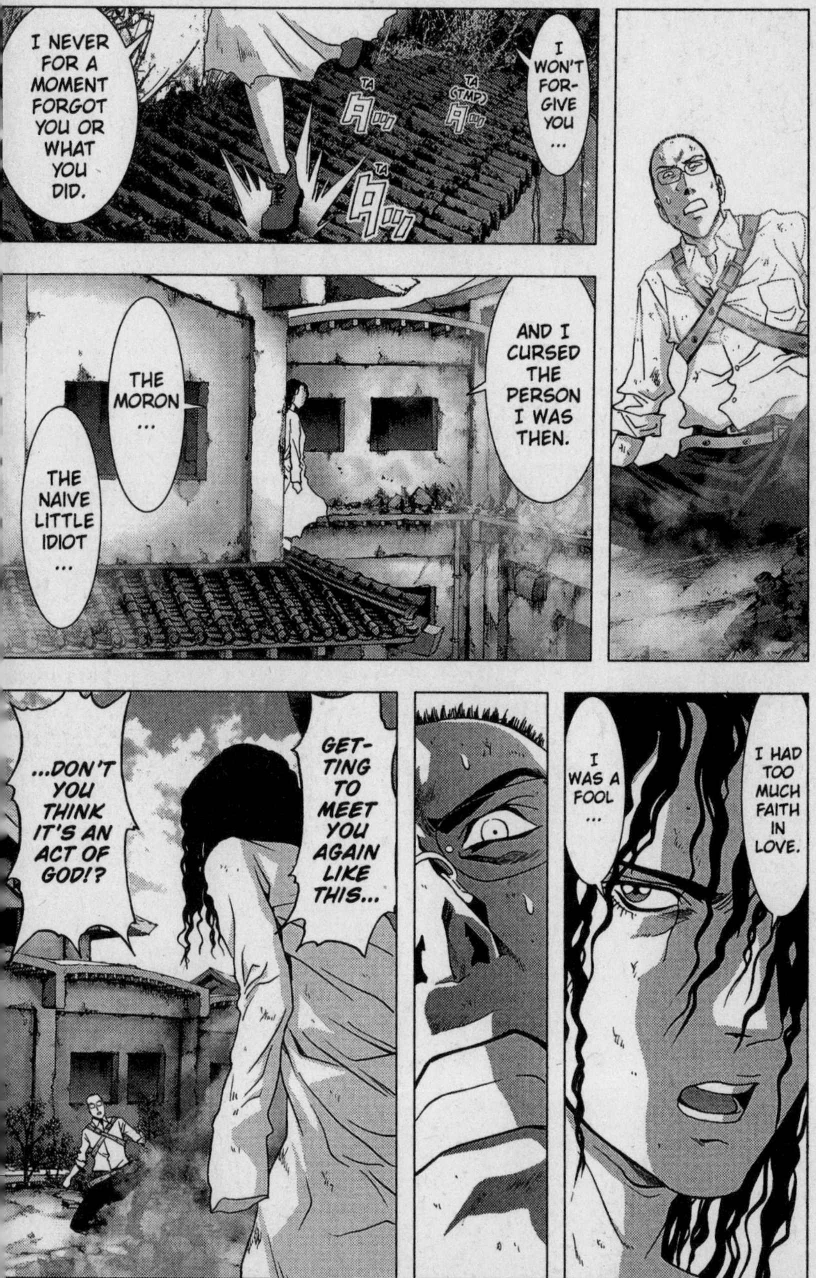
I WON'T FORGIVE YOU ...
TA (TMP)
TA
TA
I NEVER FOR A MOMENT FORGOT YOU OR WHAT YOU DID.
AND I CURSED THE PERSON I WAS THEN.
THE MORON ...
THE NAIVE LITTLE IDIOT ...
I HAD TOO MUCH FAITH IN LOVE.
I WAS A FOOL ...
GETTING TO MEET YOU AGAIN LIKE THIS...
...DON'T YOU THINK IT'S AN ACT OF GOD!?

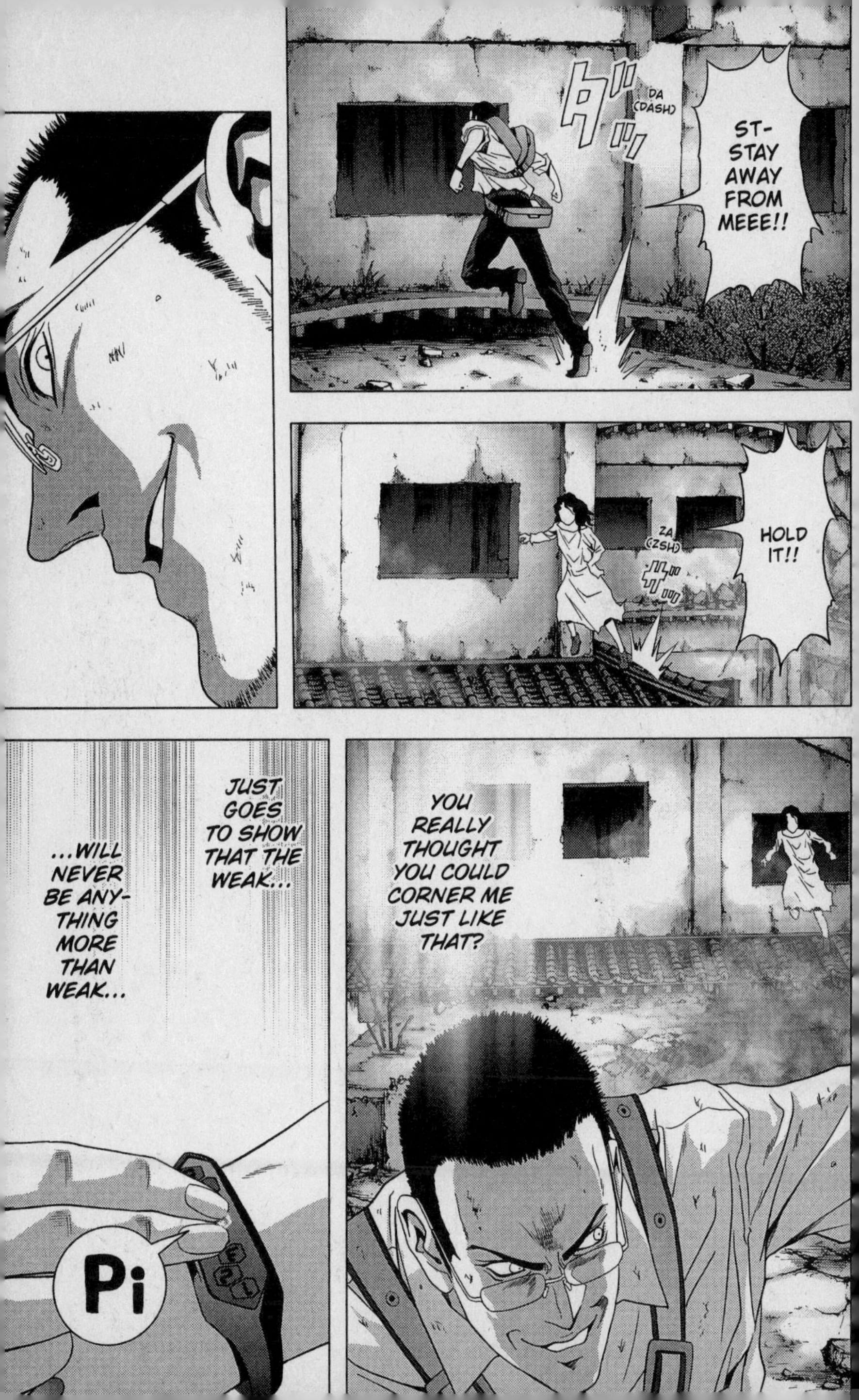
ST-STAY AWAY FROM MEEE!!
DA (DASH)
HOLD IT!!
ZA (ZSH)
YOU REALLY THOUGHT YOU COULD CORNER ME JUST LIKE THAT?
JUST GOES TO SHOW THAT THE WEAK...
...WILL NEVER BE ANYTHING MORE THAN WEAK...
Pi

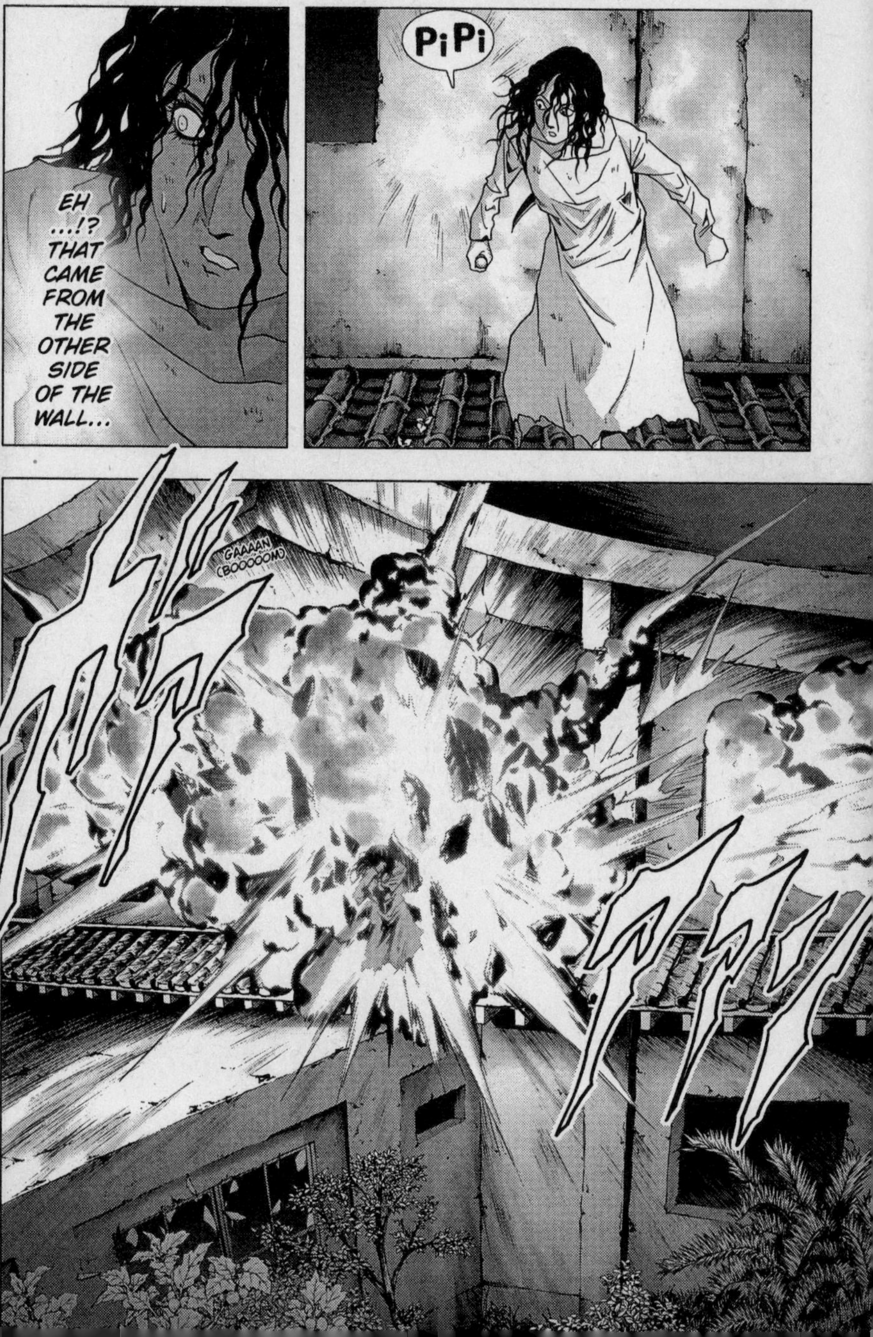
PiPi
EH ...!? THAT CAME FROM THE OTHER SIDE OF THE WALL...
GAAAAN (BOOOOOM)

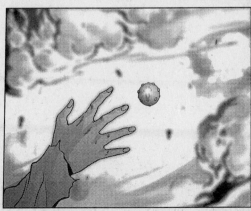

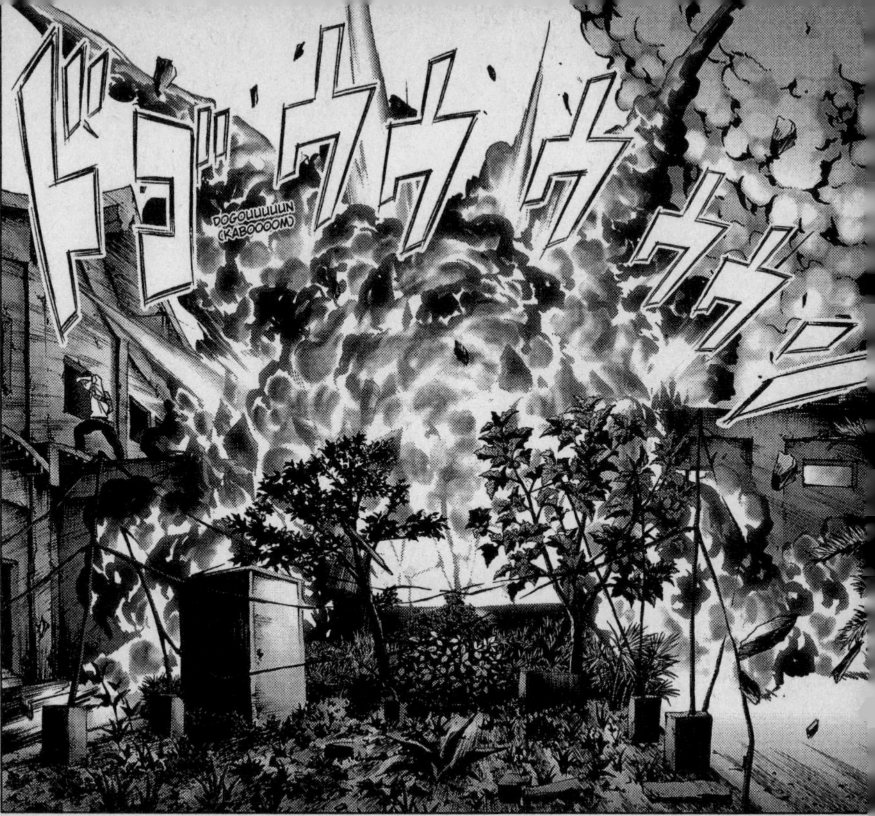
DOGOUUUUUN
(KABOOOOM)

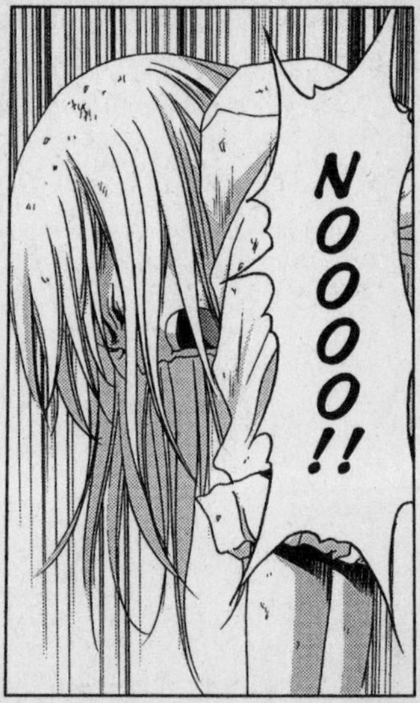
NOOOOOO!!

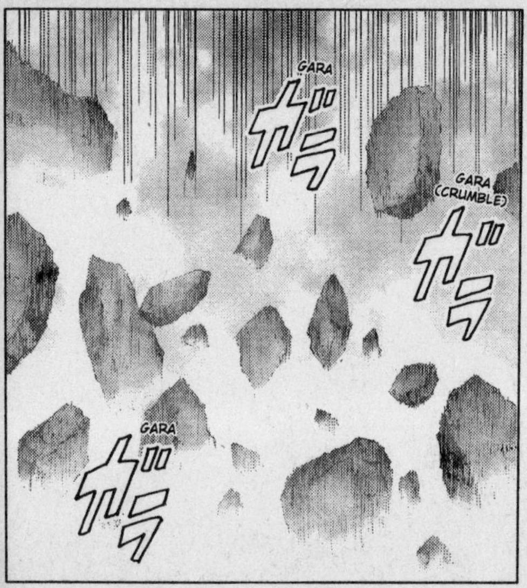
GARA
GARA
(CRUMBLE)
GARA

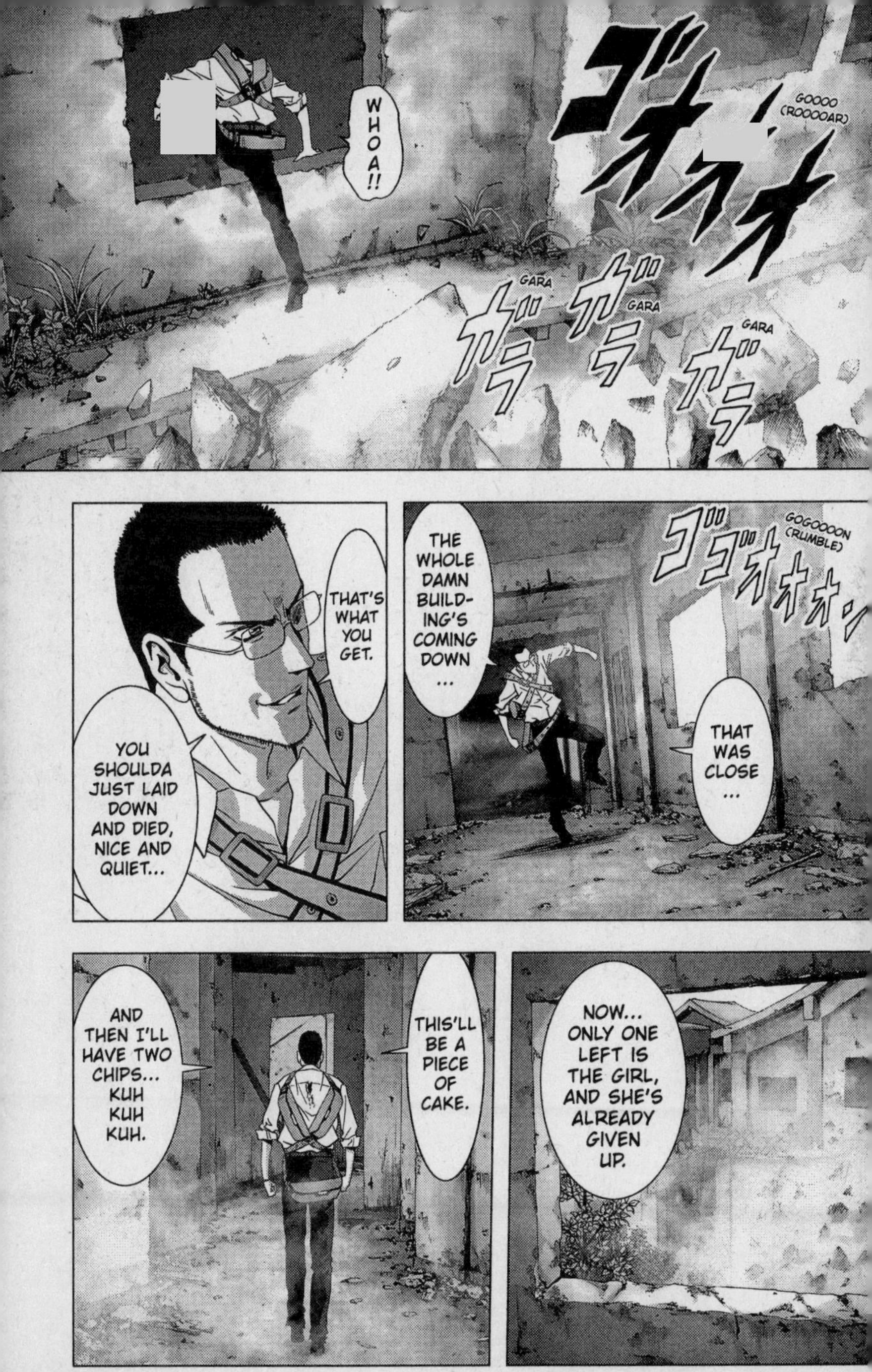
GOOOO (ROOOOAR)
WHOA!!
GARA
GARA
GARA
GOGOOOON (RUMBLE)
THE WHOLE DAMN BUILDING'S COMING DOWN...
THAT WAS CLOSE...
THAT'S WHAT YOU GET.
YOU SHOULDA JUST LAID DOWN AND DIED, NICE AND QUIET...
NOW... ONLY ONE LEFT IS THE GIRL, AND SHE'S ALREADY GIVEN UP.
THIS'LL BE A PIECE OF CAKE.
AND THEN I'LL HAVE TWO CHIPS... KUH KUH KUH.

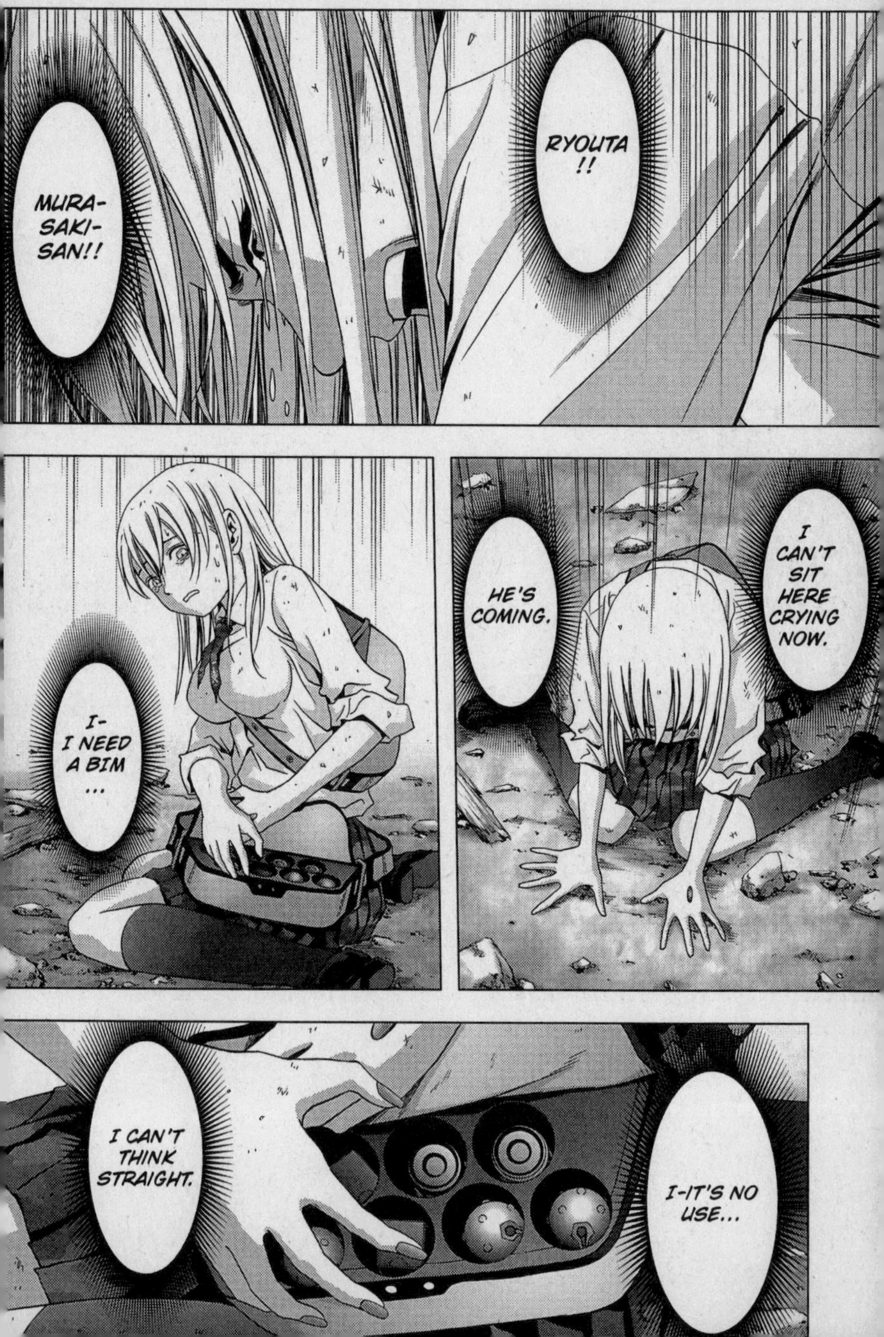
RYOUTA !!
MURA-SAKI-SAN!!
I CAN'T SIT HERE CRYING NOW.
HE'S COMING.
I- I NEED A BIM ...
I-IT'S NO USE...
I CAN'T THINK STRAIGHT.

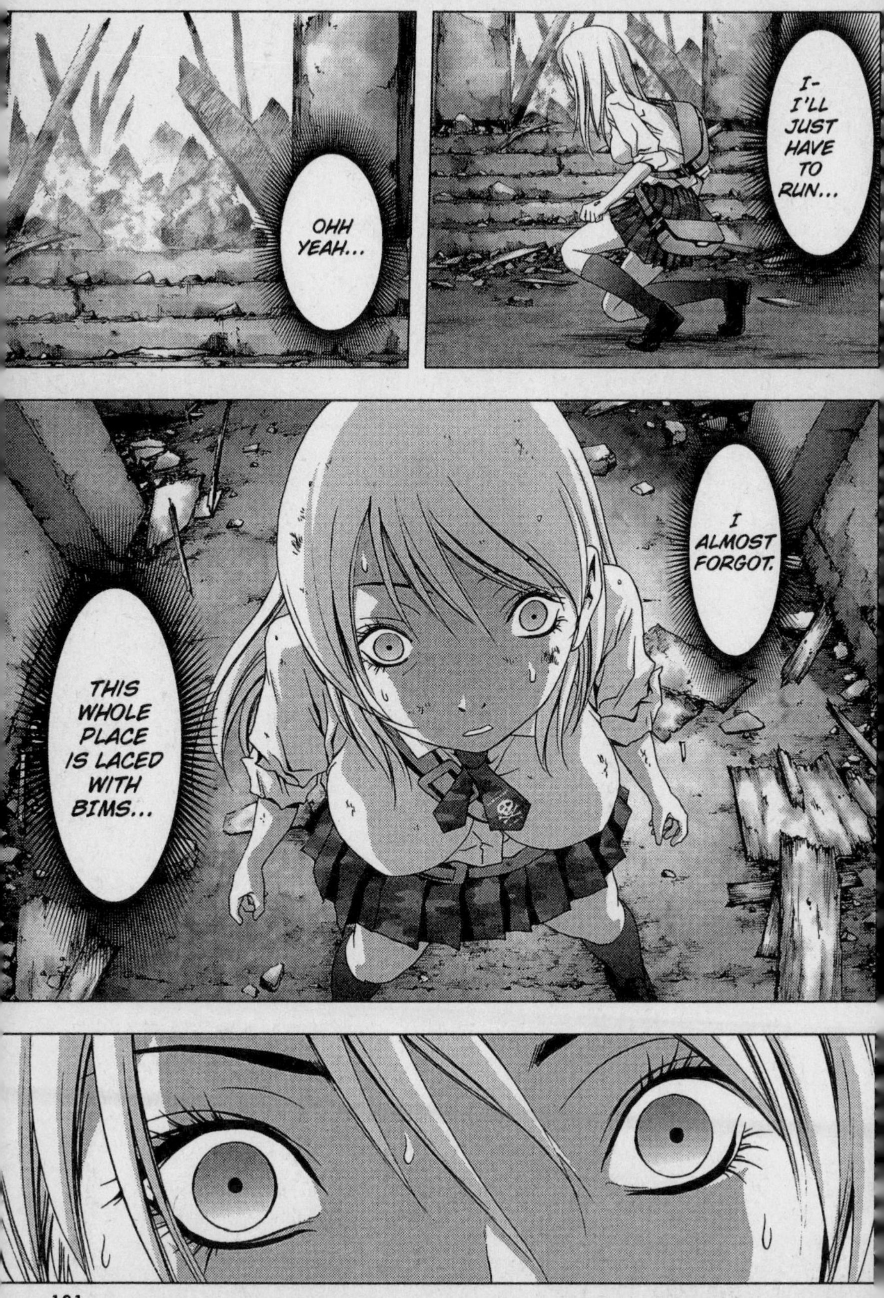
I- I'LL JUST HAVE TO RUN...
OHH YEAH...
I ALMOST FORGOT.
THIS WHOLE PLACE IS LACED WITH BIMS...

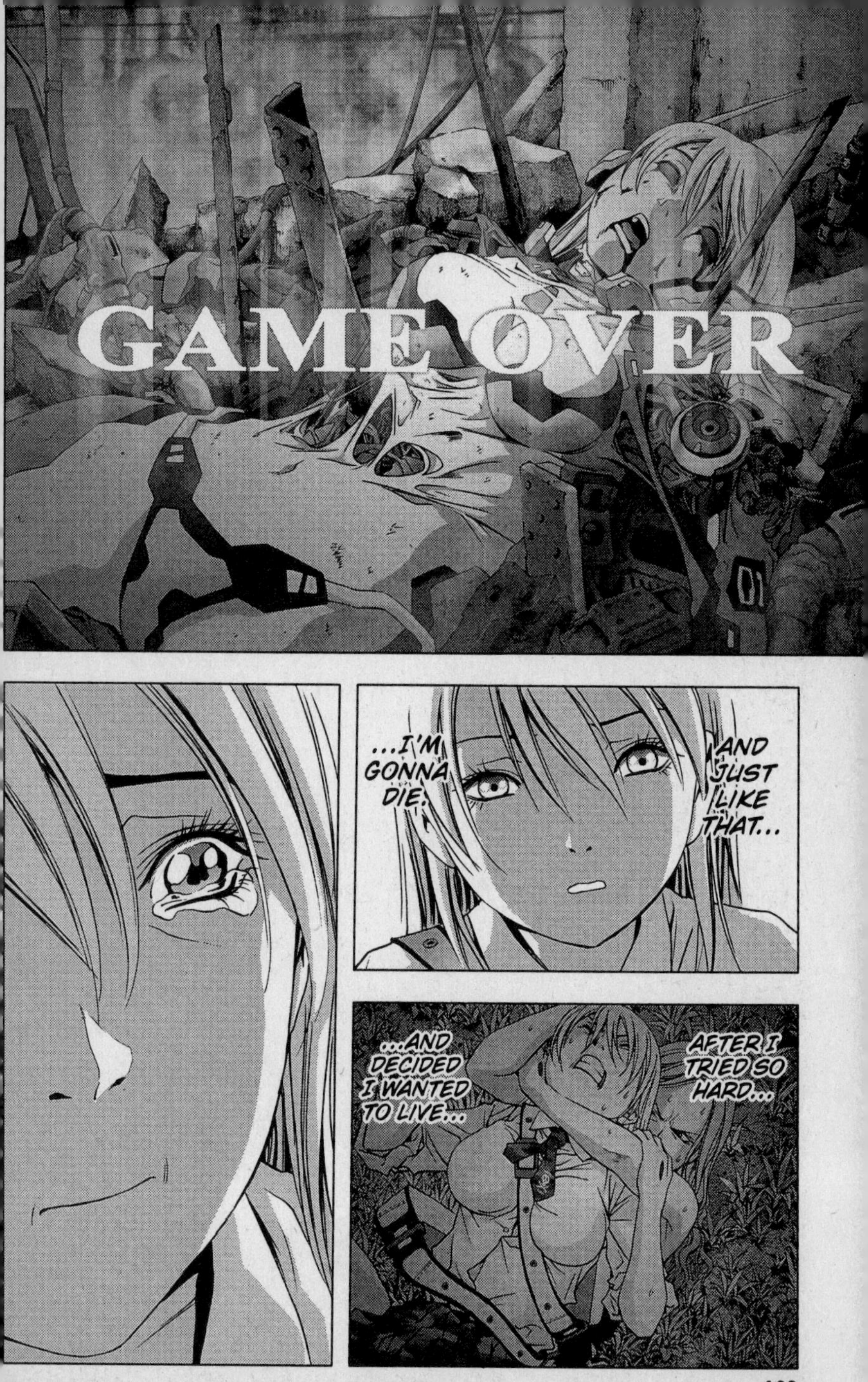
GAME OVER
AND JUST LIKE THAT...
...I'M GONNA DIE.
AFTER I TRIED SO HARD...
...AND DECIDED I WANTED TO LIVE...

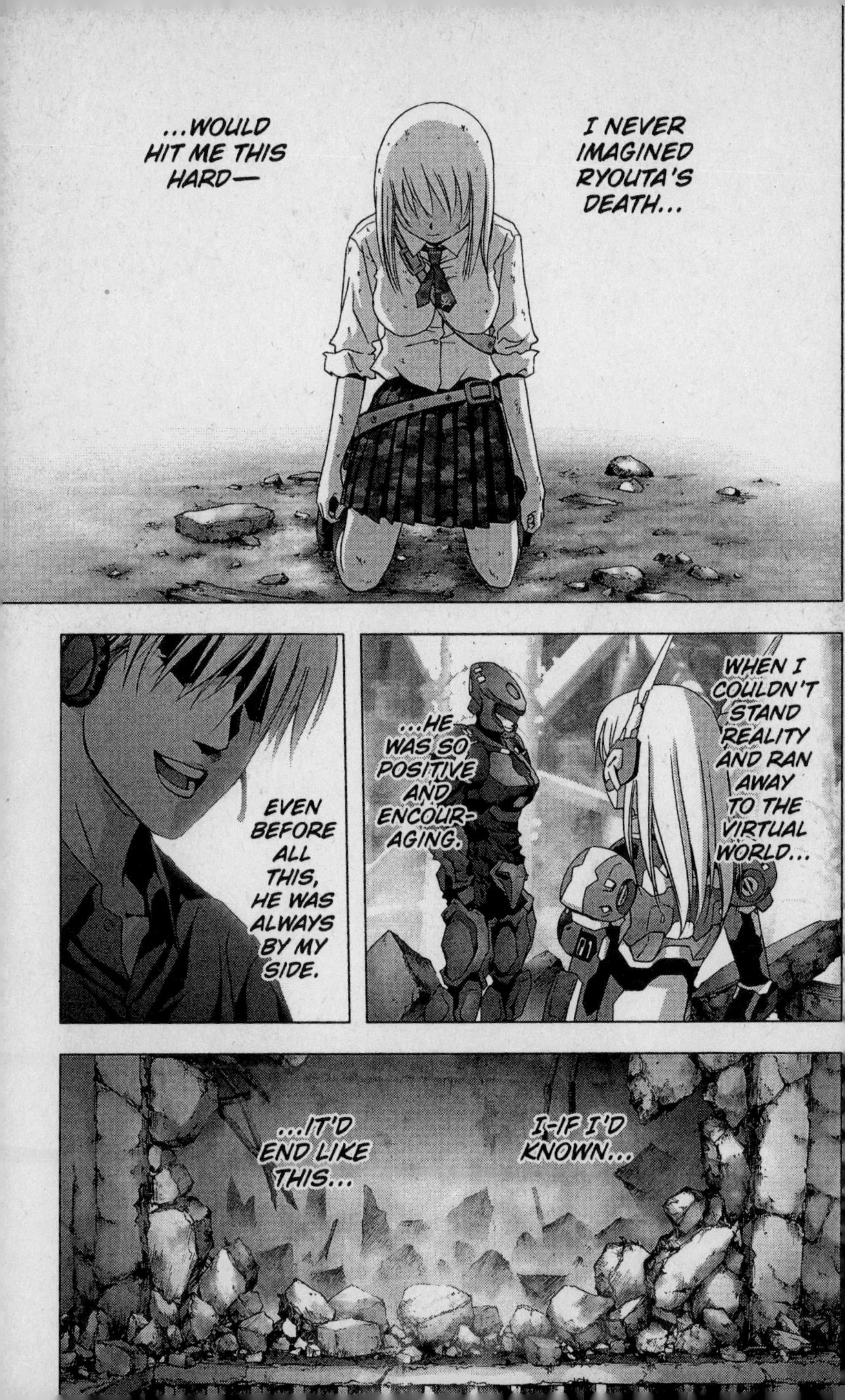
I NEVER IMAGINED RYOUTA'S DEATH...
...WOULD HIT ME THIS HARD—
WHEN I COULDN'T STAND REALITY AND RAN AWAY TO THE VIRTUAL WORLD...
...HE WAS SO POSITIVE AND ENCOUR-AGING.
EVEN BEFORE ALL THIS, HE WAS ALWAYS BY MY SIDE.
I-IF I'D KNOWN...
...IT'D END LIKE THIS...

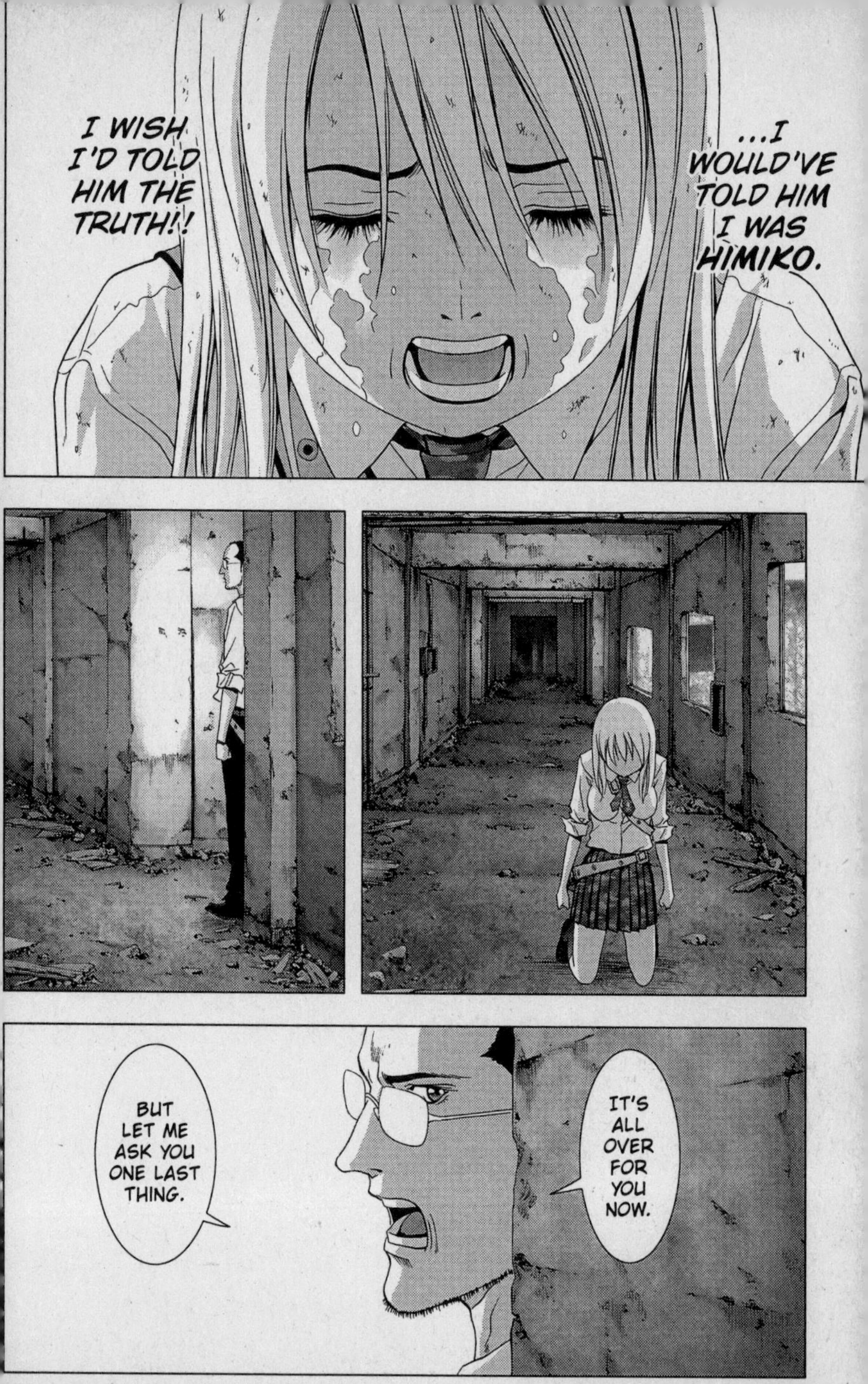
...I WOULD'VE TOLD HIM I WAS HIMIKO.
I WISH I'D TOLD HIM THE TRUTH!!
IT'S ALL OVER FOR YOU NOW.
BUT LET ME ASK YOU ONE LAST THING.

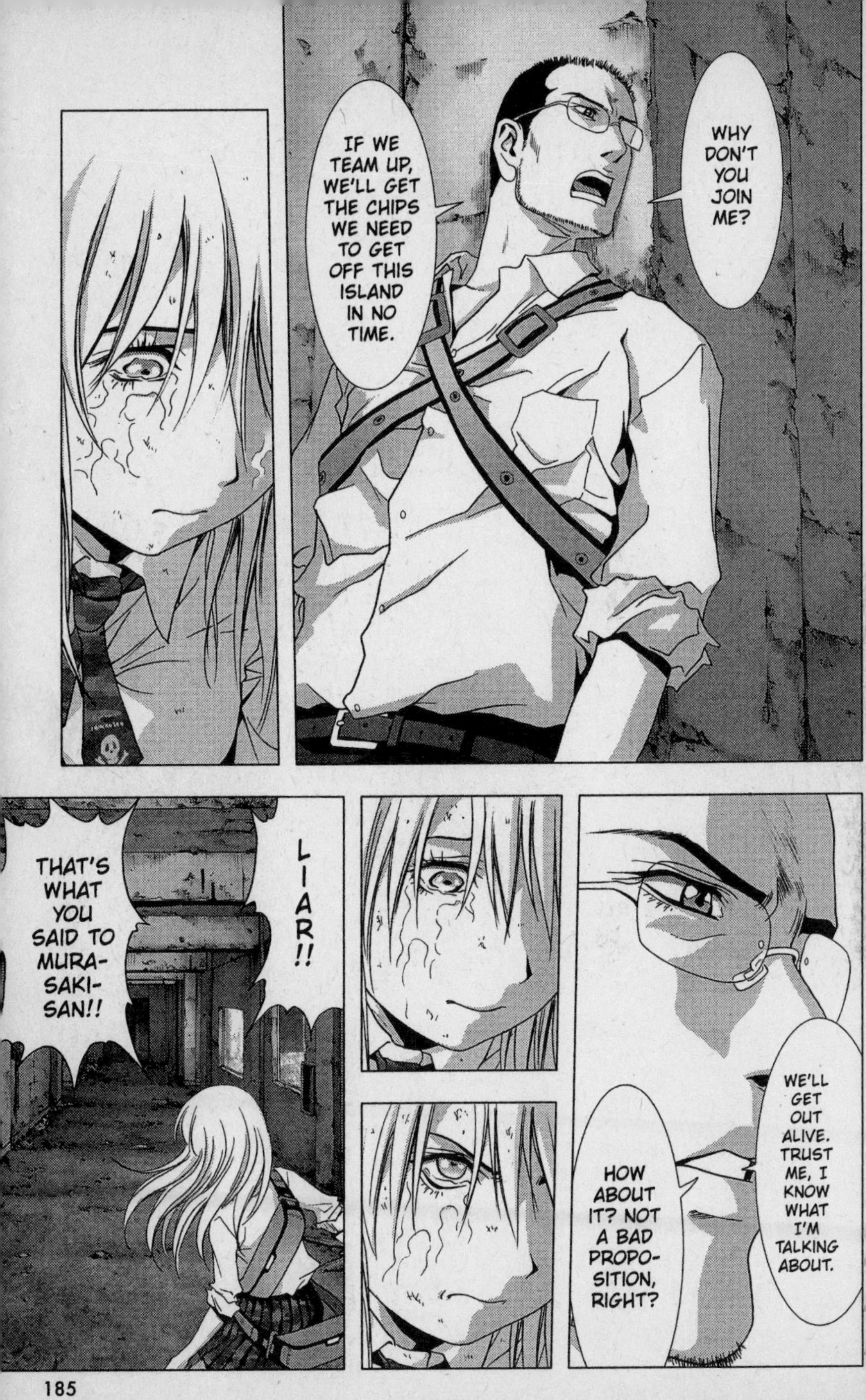
WHY DON'T YOU JOIN ME?
IF WE TEAM UP, WE'LL GET THE CHIPS WE NEED TO GET OFF THIS ISLAND IN NO TIME.
WE'LL GET OUT ALIVE. TRUST ME, I KNOW WHAT I'M TALKING ABOUT.
HOW ABOUT IT? NOT A BAD PROPO-SITION, RIGHT?
LIAR!!
THAT'S WHAT YOU SAID TO MURA-SAKI-SAN!!

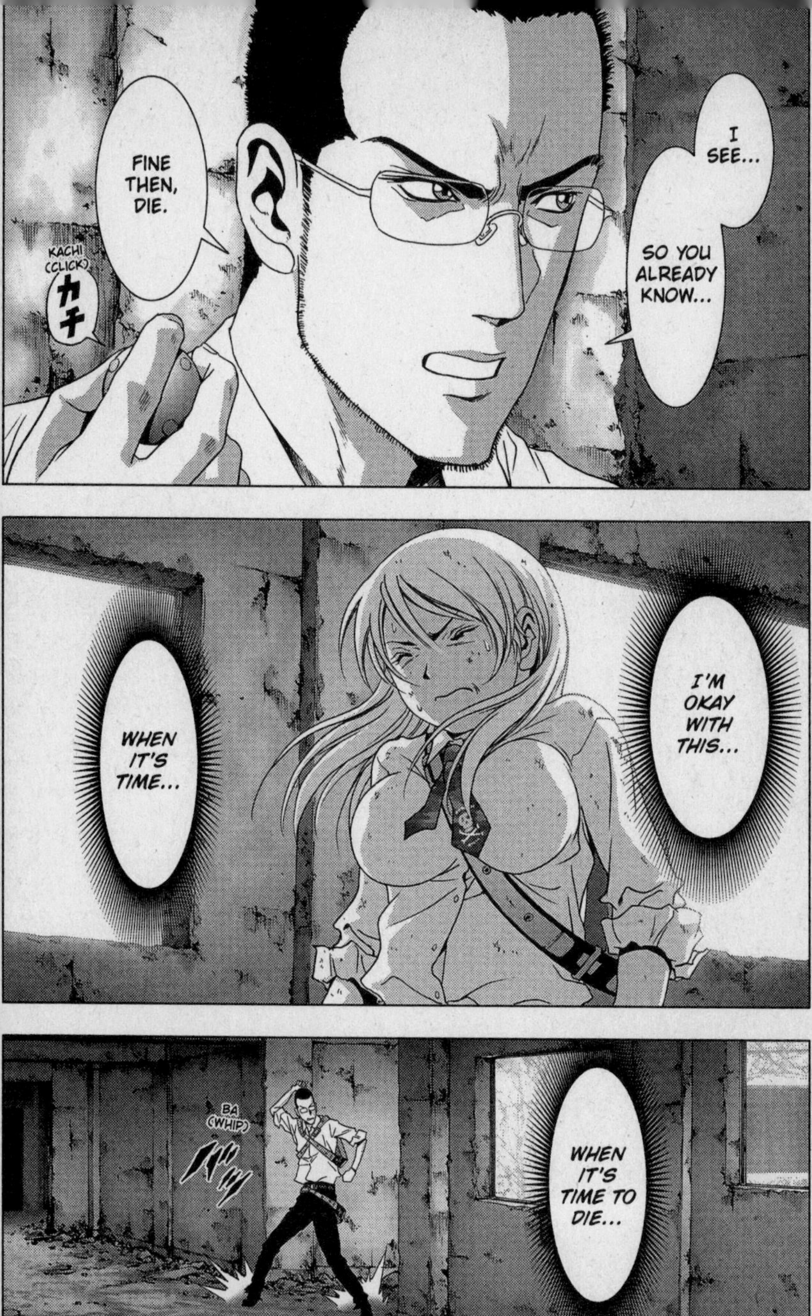
I SEE...
SO YOU ALREADY KNOW...
FINE THEN, DIE.
KACHI (CLICK)
カチ
I'M OKAY WITH THIS...
WHEN IT'S TIME...
WHEN IT'S TIME TO DIE...
BA (WHIP)

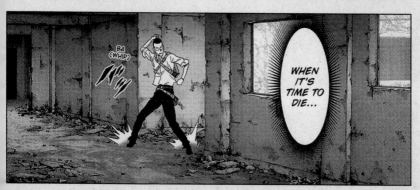

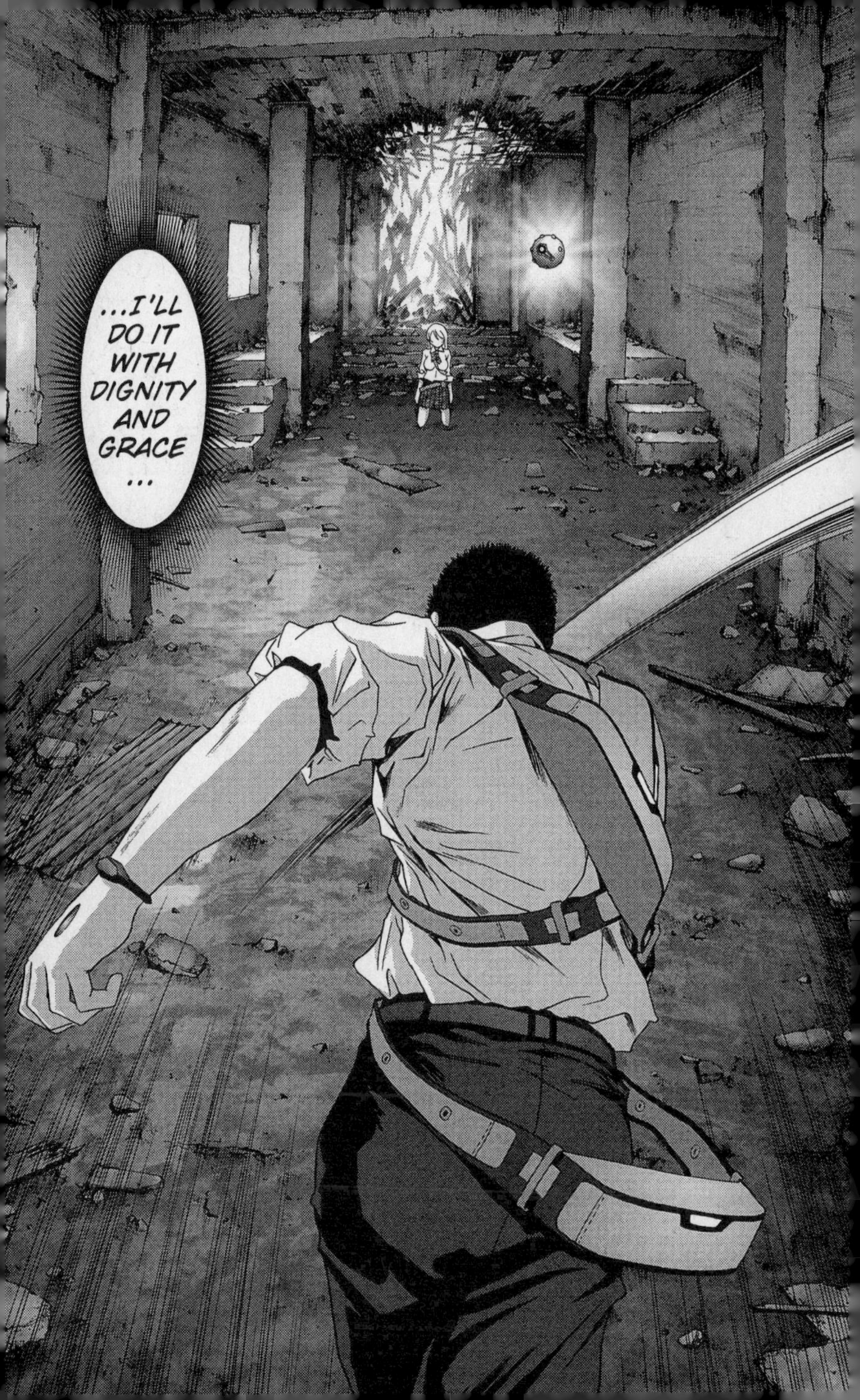
...I'LL DO IT WITH DIGNITY AND GRACE ...

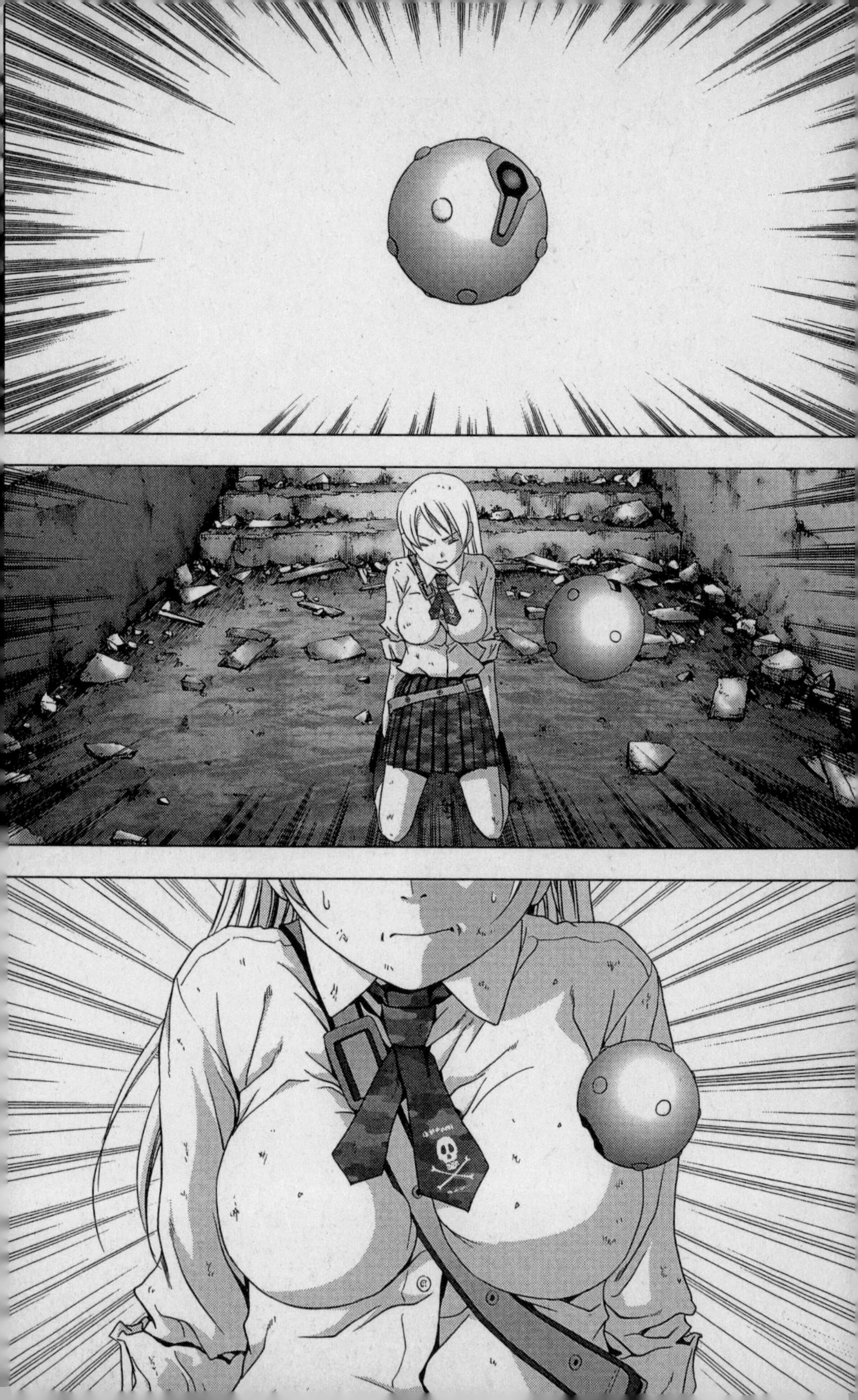

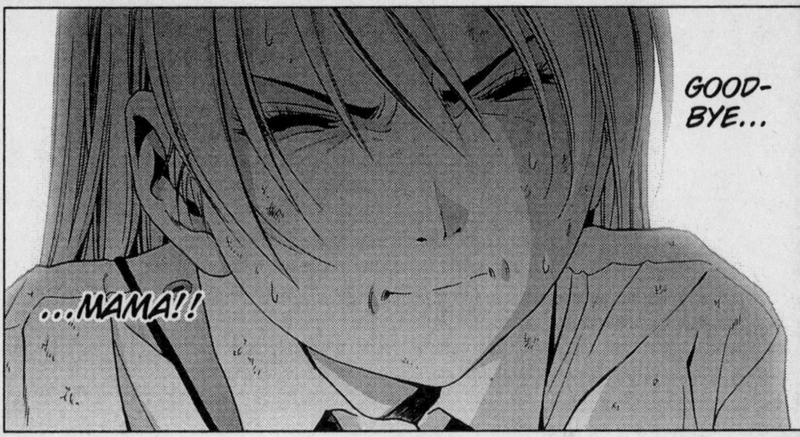
GOOD-BYE...
...MAMA!!

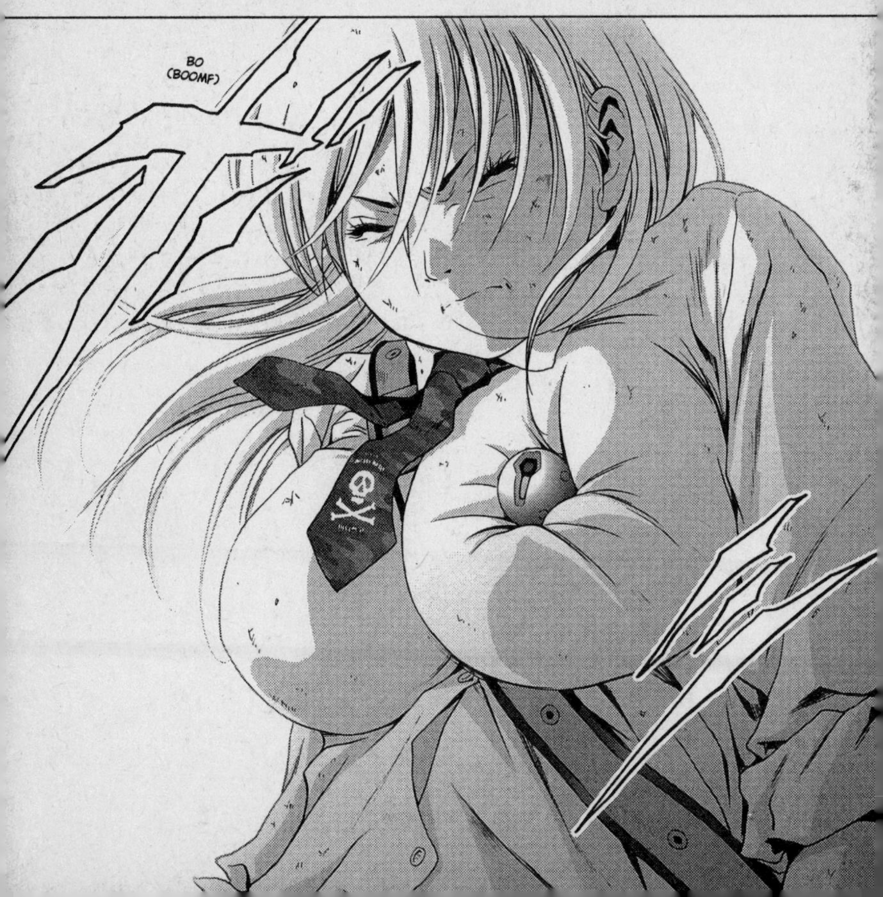
BO
(BOOMF)

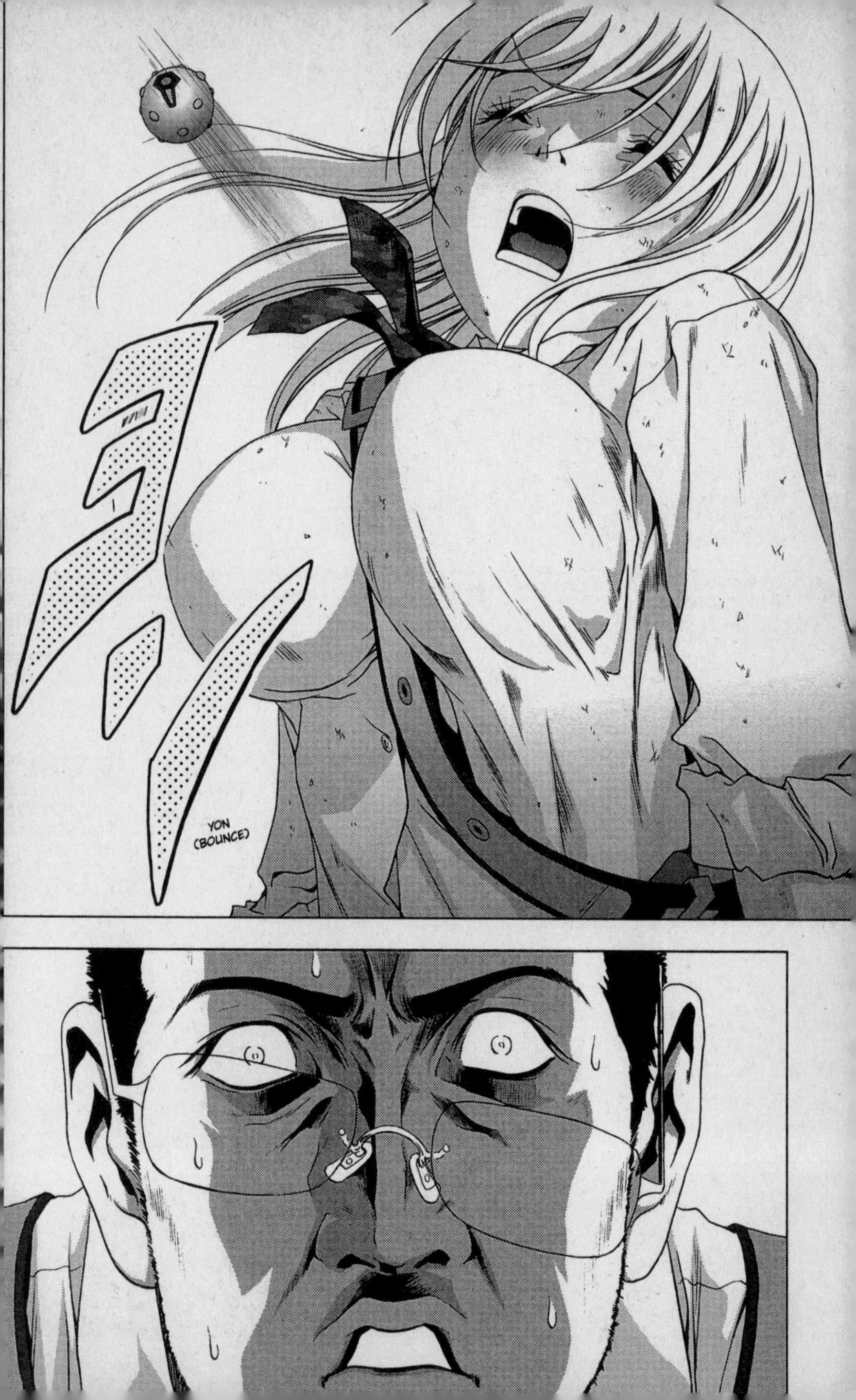
YON
(BOUNCE)

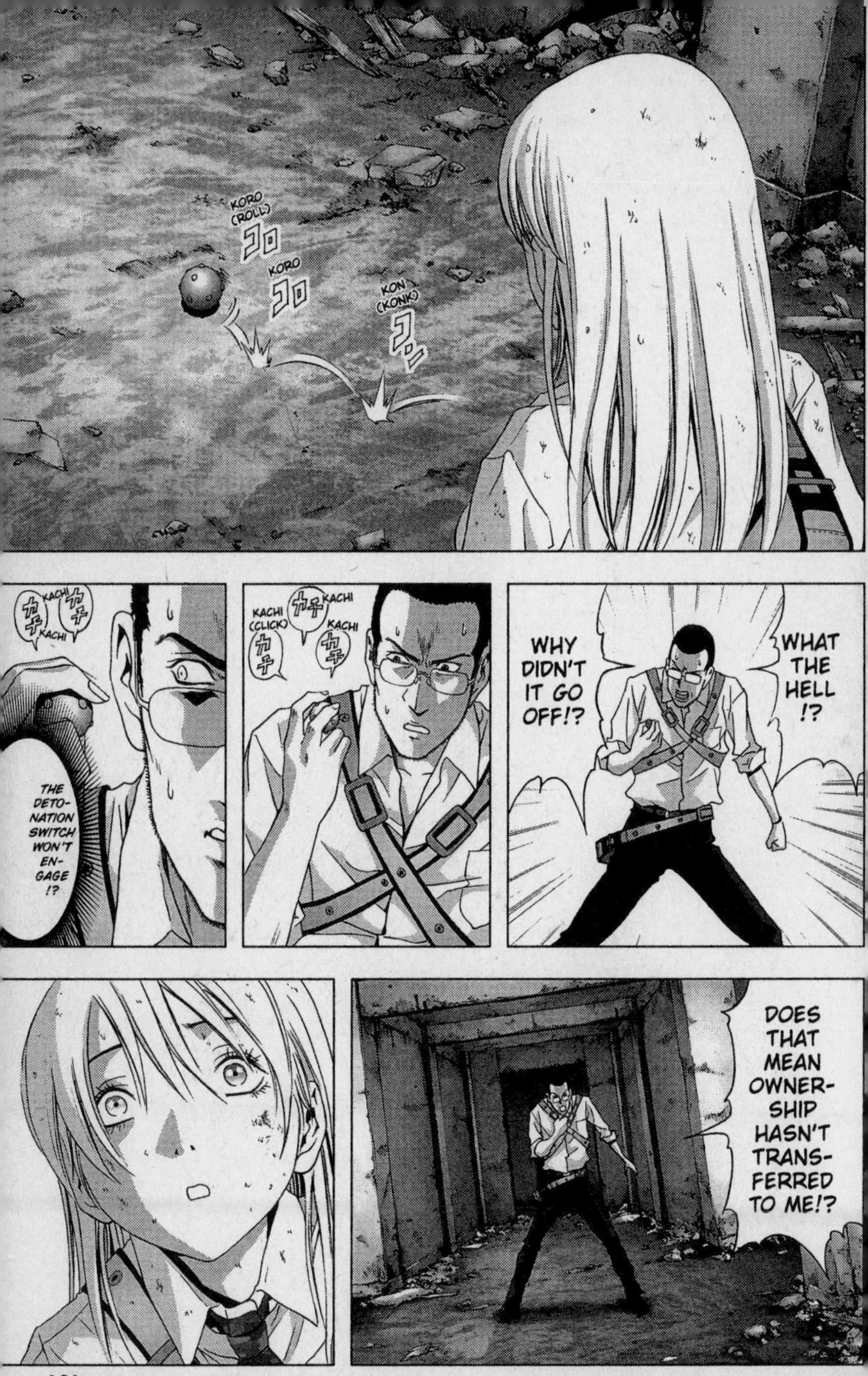
KORO (ROLL)
KORO
KON (KONK)
WHAT THE HELL!?
WHY DIDN'T IT GO OFF!?
KACHI
KACHI (CLICK)
KACHI
KACHI
KACHI
THE DETONATION SWITCH WON'T ENGAGE!?
DOES THAT MEAN OWNERSHIP HASN'T TRANSFERRED TO ME!?

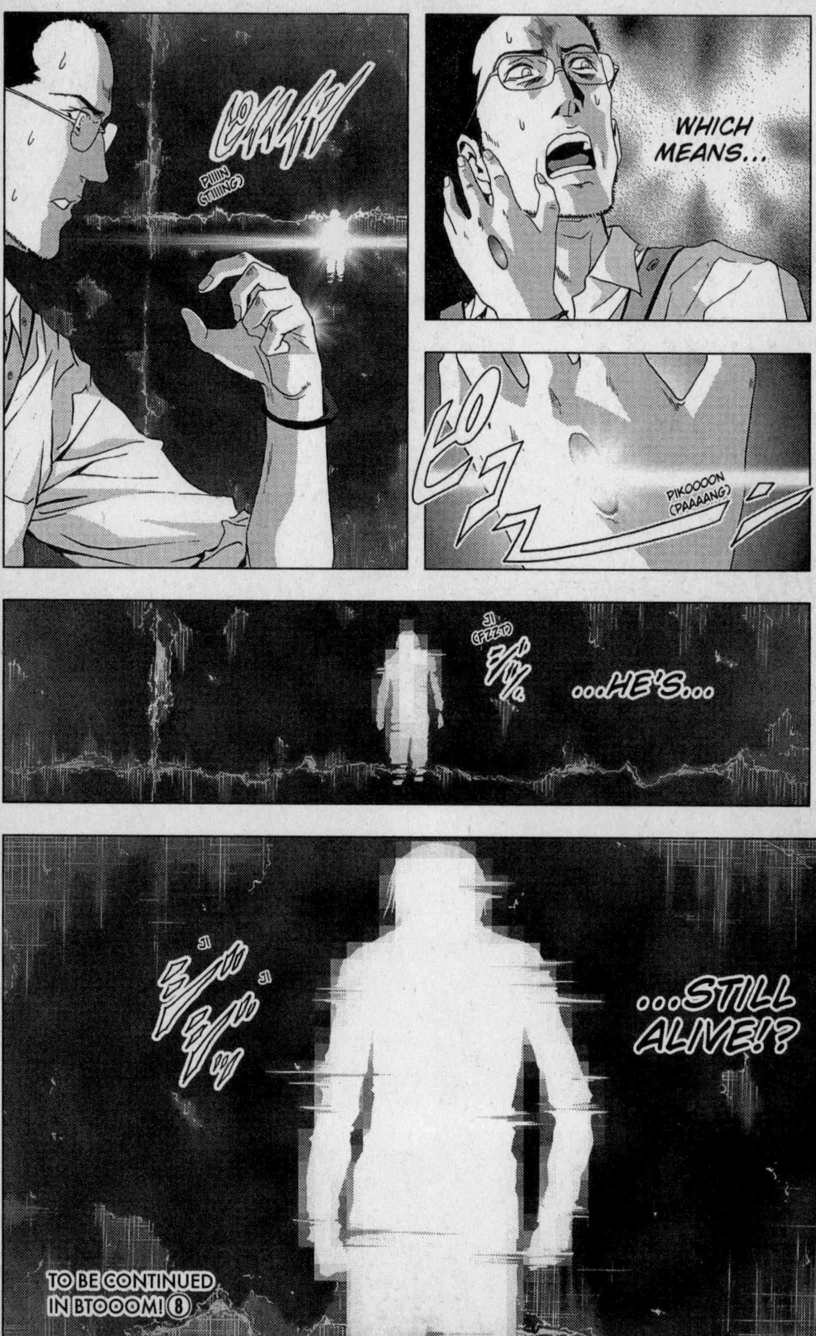
WHICH MEANS...
PIKOOOON (PAAAANG)
PIIIN (TIIIING)
JI (FZZT)
...HE'S...
JI
JI
...STILL ALIVE!?
TO BE CONTINUED IN BTOOOM! 8

BTOOOM! [7]

JUNYA INOUE

Translation: Christine Dashiell • Lettering: Terri Delgado

BTOOOM! © Junya INOUE 2009. All rights reserved. English translation rights arranged with SHINCHOSHA PUBLISHING CO. through Tuttle-Mori Agency, Inc., Tokyo.

English translation © 2014 by Hachette Book Group, Inc.

Yen Press
Hachette Book Group
237 Park Avenue, New York, NY 10017

www.HachetteBookGroup.com
www.YenPress.com

Yen Press is an imprint of Hachette Book Group, Inc. The Yen Press name and logo are trademarks of Hachette Book Group, Inc.

First Yen Press Edition: August 2014

ISBN: 978-0-316-24544-9

10 9 8 7 6 5 4 3 2 1

BVG

Printed in the United States of America

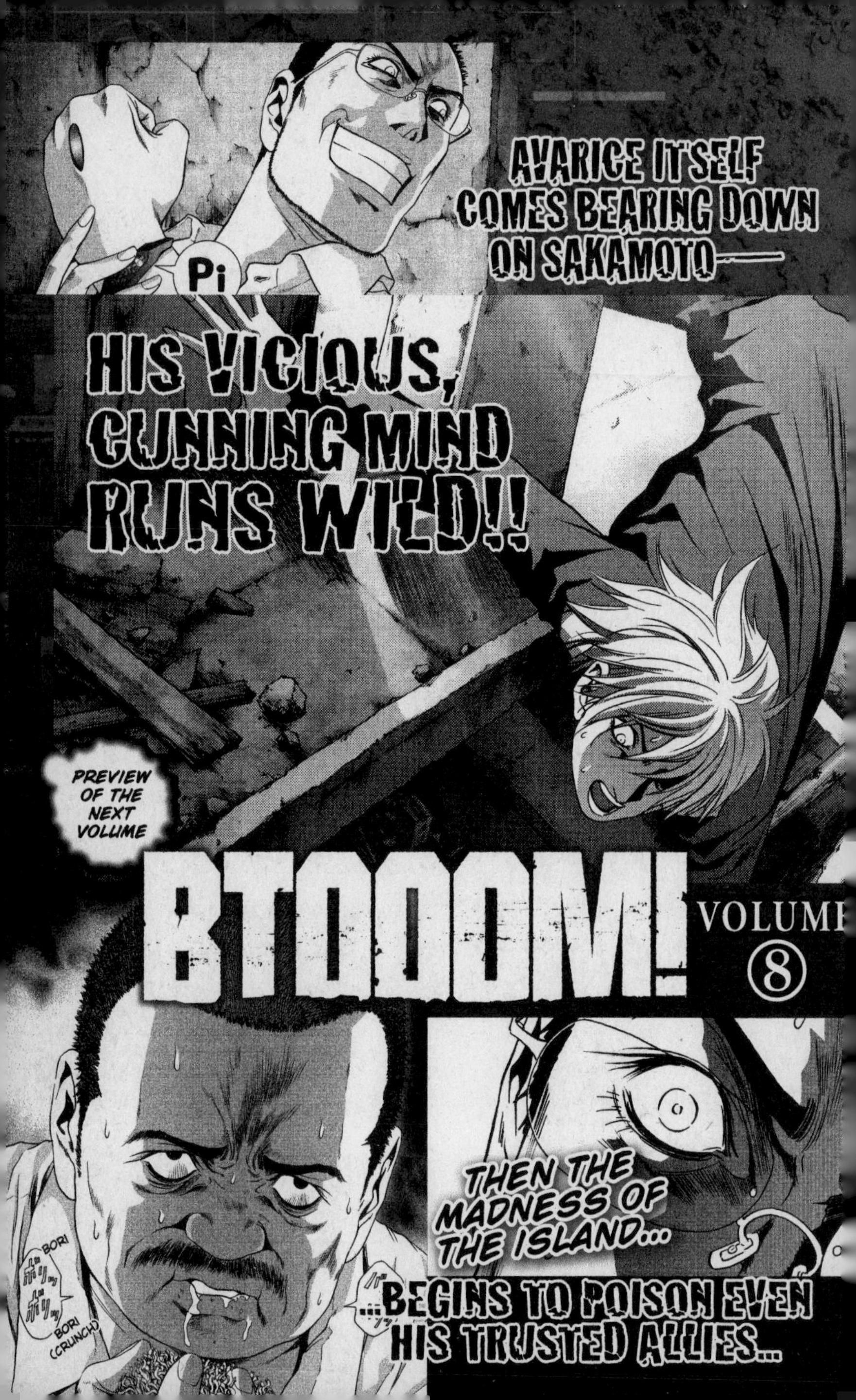
AVARICE ITSELF COMES BEARING DOWN ON SAKAMOTO—
Pi
HIS VICIOUS, CUNNING MIND RUNS WILD!!
PREVIEW OF THE NEXT VOLUME
BTOOOM!
VOLUM
8
THEN THE MADNESS OF THE ISLAND...
...BEGINS TO POISON EVEN HIS TRUSTED ALLIES...
BORI
BORI (CRUNCH)